The Survival
of
Charles Darwin

The Survival
of
Charles Darwin

*A Biography of a Man
and an Idea*

RONALD W. CLARK

Random House *New York*

Library of Congress Cataloging in Publication Data
Clark, Ronald William.
The survival of Charles Darwin.
Bibliography: p.
Includes index.
1. Darwin, Charles, 1809–1882. 2. Evolution—
History. 3. Naturalists—England—Biography. I. Title.
QH31.D2C57 1985   575'.0092'4   84-42507
ISBN 0-394-52134-X

Acknowledgments

My main thanks are due to Mr. George Pember Darwin for his permission to quote from the unpublished material by Charles Darwin at Cambridge University Library, Cambridge, England, and at the Royal Botanic Gardens Library, Kew, England; The Syndics of Cambridge University Library for permission to use the facilities of the Library; Mr. Peter J. Gautrey, Under-Librarian, Department of Manuscripts, Cambridge University Library, for his unstinting help and advice in the use of the Darwin Papers for which he is responsible, and for reading a portion of the manuscript; and Mr. Philip Titheradge, Curator of the Down House Museum, which is owned by The Royal College of Surgeons of England, for his help and advice.

I also wish to thank Christ's College, Cambridge, for permission to use Darwin's letters to William Darwin Fox, which are quoted from a set of Xerox copies held in the Darwin Papers at Cambridge University Library; the Librarian, Royal Botanic Gardens, Kew, for permission to consult the Darwin-Henslow letters; The Syndics of Cambridge University Library for permission to consult the Bateson Papers and the Hurst Papers; Mrs. Jean Pingree, Archivist, Imperial College of Science and Technology, London, for her help in consulting the Huxley Papers; The Linnean Society of London for permission to consult the Alfred Russel Wallace Papers and Notebooks; Mrs. Virginia Murray, Archivist, John Murray (Publishers) Ltd., London, for permission to consult the John Murray Archives; Mrs. J. G. Links, London, for permission to quote the letter from the Reverend Whitwell Elwin to John Murray; The Royal Society, London, for permission to consult their archives relating to letters from Darwin to Colonel Edward Sabine and to Sir John Herschel; The National Library of Scotland, Edinburgh, for a photostat of Darwin's letter to Thomas Francis Jamieson; and Dr. Richard Wrangham for help regarding the poem by Bishop Wilberforce.

While the opinions in the book and responsibility for facts given are entirely my own unless the reverse is made clear, I thank the following for their help and advice and for reading parts of the manuscript: Professor R. J. Berry, Department of Zoology, University College, London; Dr. L. Beverly Halstead, Department of Geology and Zoology, University of Reading, Reading, England; Professor John Maynard Smith, Dean of the Biology Department, University of Sussex, Falmer, England; and Mr. Stan Weinberg, Coordinator of The Iowa Academy of Science Panel on Controversial Issues, Ottumwa, Iowa.

I am grateful to Professor V. Orel, Director of the Gregor Mendel Department of Genetics, Moravské Museum, Brno, Czechoslovakia, for the photograph of Nicolai Ivanovitch Vavilov and William Bateson.

I also thank the staffs of the libraries of the British Museum (Natural History), South Kensington, and the Science Museum, London, for their unfailing help.

R. W. C.

Contents

CONTENTS

SURVIVAL OF THE FITTEST

List of Illustrations

THE PREPOSTEROUS THEORY

1

A Young
Country Gentleman

THE survival of Charles Darwin's reputation, and of his theory explaining how life evolved over countless aeons, was due not only to genius, that quality which one of his predecessors, the Comte de Buffon, has described as "nothing but a great aptitude for patience," but also to good management aided by good luck.

At first glance Darwin appears an unlikely survivor in the immortality stakes, having most of the decent qualities that deter a man from fighting with tooth and claw. The knowledge that his life was being spent in sapping the religious beliefs so dear to family and friends more than once restrained him from pushing home an attack—a caution that only in retrospect was seen to have tactical advantages. As member of a family near the top of the affluent pre-Victorian middle class, he had no need to struggle for success. Indeed, if any man born into the comfy provincial existence of early-nineteenth-century England was fitted to the role of country parson, it was Charles Darwin. For a while it was thought that this was to be his destiny, and only a quirk of fate prevented his life from being cocooned in an annual round of homely sermons and quiet good works, a life whose excitements would have gone little further than hunting and shooting, and whose environment would have been bounded by Tennyson's "moan of doves in immemorial elms / And murmuring of innumerable bees" that had no link with the vulgarities of science.

These possibilities faded once chance took Darwin on his five-year voyage in HMS *Beagle*, a voyage that awakened his innate scientific instincts and aroused that much-debated factor in his make-up: ambition. "As far as I can judge of myself," he was later to write, "I worked to the utmost during the voyage from the mere pleasure of investigation, & from my strong desire to add a few facts to the great mass of facts in natural science. But I was also ambitious to take a fair place among scientific men—whether more ambitious or less so than most of my fellow-workers I can form no opinion."

The urge, which was to lie dormant for almost a quarter of a century after the return of the *Beagle* to England in 1836, surfaced when Alfred Russel Wallace appeared with his own theory of evolution, extraordinarily like Darwin's but unsupported by anything comparable to Darwin's massive accumulation of evidence. Ambition then helped keep Darwin's intellect on the trot long after the initial furor over his most famous book, *On the Origin of Species by Means of Natural Selection, or the Preservation of Favoured Races in the Struggle for Life*—usually called *The Origin of Species* or just *The Origin* —had died away.* And despite his almost obsessional need for peace and quiet, ambition helped to keep him at the center of the scientific scene. Aided by T. H. Huxley—"Darwin's bulldog," who was prepared to bite when his master disliked even barking—he survived the attacks of both Church and fellow scientists until evidence of evolution, accumulating throughout the nineteenth century and into the twentieth, carried him across the watershed into the land of the immortals.

Great changes have been made to the ideas outlined in *The Origin of Species* in 1859. This is hardly surprising. The Copernican revolution, which transformed the earth from the static center of the universe to a planet circling an insignificant star, has been considerably refined throughout the centuries. Newton's synthesis of the physical world had to be qualified when Einstein showed that neither time nor space were quite the simple entities that scientists had believed. Freud's ground plan of the subconscious mind has required numerous amendments, while Rutherford's revolutionary but simple concept of the nuclear atom has been developed by the last quarter-century's discoveries in particle physics. Yet

---

*Many titles of books published in the nineteenth century and earlier were printed with lower-case letters for words in the body of the title—for example, Darwin's title appears as *On the Origin of Species by means of natural selection, or the preservation of favoured races in the struggle for life.* In *The Survival of Charles Darwin*, capitalization and punctuation have been introduced, in text and back matter, to bring titles into line with current practice.

Copernicus, Newton, Einstein, Freud and Rutherford are still acknowledged as intellects whose cerebrations changed the world. So with Charles Darwin, the unlikely survivor.

Today it is impossible to appreciate the changes Darwin wrought in man's view of the universe, and of his own place in it, without understanding the basically different outlook of the 1830s. The belief on which all rested was that the biblical story of the Creation was history rather than symbolic mythology. The science of geology, it is true, was beginning to pose awkward questions, but few men or women could bring themselves to consider the huge vistas of the past that the science appeared to be opening up. As for living things, surely there could be little doubt that they were, as Genesis maintained, a pyramid of immutable species at the top of which there stood Man himself. These beliefs affected even the political battles that raged in Britain for and against reform, as well as around many other parliamentary disputes and on the very development of the country, since many felt that God blessed conventional transport by coach and was against such innovations as the iron horse and the railways. Then came Darwin. Many years later, proof of Einstein's general theory of relativity had, as the *Times* put it, dealt with the fabric of the universe. Darwin was cartooned as the man tearing apart the fabric of belief.

The naturalist who appeared to be doing this was by no means the prototype revolutionary. Indeed, he was quite the opposite— a shy, kindly Englishman of liberal ideas and insular habits who, except for his five-year voyage in the *Beagle,* left the shores of Britain only once and then merely for a brief holiday in Paris. Ill health reinforced a natural devotion to home, which, during one period of middle age, he did not leave for a whole year. Journeys beyond London, only some twenty miles away from his Kentish home, tended to be great expeditions, while London itself was visited on an almost rationed basis. Professional friends came to Darwin's home, but they did not come very frequently, and for the greater part of his life, "recluse" was to some extent an honest description of the naturalist whose upbringing had, by contrast, been as conventional as his work was to be iconoclastic.

Thus any story of Darwin's life has to describe the interaction of private character and public influence, to explain how he not only survived the dangerous process of changing the world's beliefs but also left a legacy that carried his ideas through the reactions that such events almost inevitably provoke.

Today, when only the near-lunatic fringe tries to deny the broad facts of evolution, however much the experts may argue about its details or its mechanics, it is easy to underestimate the strength of the views Darwin and his followers had to change. It is true that men such as John Ray in the seventeenth century, and the Comte de Buffon, Darwin's grandfather Erasmus and Lamarck in the eighteenth, were among those who had begun to question accepted ideas. Yet these were isolated examples of odd men out, and if it were true that by Darwin's day the climate was becoming ripe for evolution, it was a climate that did not affect the great mass of informed opinion throughout the world. The weight and influence of the Christian Church combined with the opinion of the overwhelming mass of mankind to buttress a world view in which there was no place for evolution. The situation was to be radically changed, not for a year or a decade, but for the foreseeable future, by Charles Robert Darwin.

Born in the Shropshire town of Shrewsbury on February 12, 1809, Darwin had a youth unmarked by the slightest trace of genius. Indeed, his father, Robert Waring Darwin II, the town's most prosperous doctor, was to remark: "You care for nothing but shooting, dogs, & rat-catching, & you will be a disgrace to yourself & all your family." Over half a century later, Einstein's headmaster, asked what profession the young Einstein should adopt, replied: "It doesn't matter; he'll never make a success of anything." Similar remarks spatter more than one childhood of the famous, and if a rational explanation can be found for them, it is probably rooted in a child's built-in reluctance to conform and a disregard for what others think.

Charles's grandfather was Erasmus Darwin, a notable physician of the late eighteenth century whose two-volume 1,400-page *Zoonomia, or the Laws of Organic Life* attempted "to reduce the facts belonging to ANIMAL LIFE into classes, orders, genera, and species, and by comparing them with each other, to unravel the theory of disease." His mother, Susannah Wedgwood, was daughter of the Josiah Wedgwood whose pottery works at Etruria, a village he had built for his workmen, became world-famous. With these exceptions there was nothing in his ancestry to suggest future distinction; neither did his early years do anything to alter the prospect of a happy, mediocre life. His mother died when he was eight, and her place was partly taken by Caroline Sarah, one of his three older sisters, the others being Marianne and Susan Elizabeth. There was an elder brother Erasmus Alvey, named after grandfather Erasmus, and a younger sister, Emily Catherine, born the year after Charles.

When Darwin tried at the age of twenty-nine to remember his early years, the recollections were no less fuzzy than most men's. His first memory was of sitting, aged between three and four, on his sister Caroline's knee while she peeled an orange for him; a cow ran past the window and made him jump, so that he received a cut on the hand whose scar still showed nearly three decades later. The same year there was a visit to Abergele, on the Welsh coast, of which he remembered only the maidservants in the house the family was occupying. He dimly recalled the Waterloo celebrations of 1815, but of his mother's death two years afterward little more remained in his memory than the fact that his father wept. "I recollect my mother's gown," he wrote, "& scarcely anything of her appearance; except one or two walks with her I have no distinct remembrance of any conversations & then only of very trivial nature."

He collected pebbles and minerals and later remembered that he was very fond of gardening. About this, he honestly admitted, "I . . . invented some great falsehoods about being able to colour crocuses as I liked." The year after his mother's death he went with his brother to Liverpool, but the trip left little impression on his mind "except most trifling ones—fear of the coach upsetting—a good dinner—& an extremely vague memory of ships." Two months after his return he caught scarlet fever, but appears to have recovered without difficulty or complications.

The record is unremarkable, and even at Shrewsbury School, where he followed his brother after a year at Mr. Case's local preparatory school, he made as little impact as the school made on him. Although his short autobiography, written at the age of sixty-seven, is distinctly unreliable as evidence, it is clear that, as he recorded there, Shrewsbury "as a means of education to me was simply a blank." The lessons that mattered were self-taught. Gilbert White's *The Natural History of Selborne,* an account of wildlife in and around an eighteenth-century Hampshire village, which became a classic, set him on the path of nature study, and a second cousin, William Darwin Fox, led him to specialize in beetles. Fox was at Christ's College, Cambridge, with Darwin, and the two men kept up a correspondence containing more than 150 letters from Darwin until Fox's death in 1880. The Vicar of Delamere in Cheshire for thirty-five years, Fox followed his cousin's career with interest, enjoyed his books, and in 1868 helped Darwin's work by sending him a return of sheep and cattle.

Collecting beetles became first a hobby and then a near-obsession with Darwin. "I am dying by inches, from not having any body to talk to about insects," he wrote to Fox from Shrewsbury in June 1828. In his fifties he admitted to his cousin, "I really hardly know anything in this life that I have more enjoyed than our beetle-hunting expeditions." And he remembered for years the pleasure with which he had read in one journal of how he had "captured" an unidentified insect in the Fens. "That was the proudest moment in my life," he told a visitor to his home. "Talk of Societies, talk of medals, it was nothing to that. There was something about the very word 'captured' that seemed to give importance to what I had done."

One trait of Darwin's life was the all-consuming determination with which he would concentrate on the job in hand, a determination that tied him to species work for two decades before *The Origin* emerged. There are two examples of this from his youthful days of beetlemania. On holiday at Barmouth, in North Wales, he discovered what a schoolboy colleague called the two largest vipers he had ever seen. Darwin killed them and buried them, knowing that beetles would have collected around the corpses when he came back in a week's time. And he himself has given striking proof of his zeal: "one day, on tearing off some old bark, I saw two rare beetles & seized one in each hand; then I saw a third & new kind, which I could not bear to lose, so that I popped the one which I held in my right hand into my mouth. Alas it ejected some intensely acrid fluid, which burnt my tongue so that I was forced to spit the beetle out, which was lost, as well as the third one."

Darwin's proficiency with a gun—the sign both of the English country gentleman and of the naturalist, whose equipment in the 1820s was the gun, not the camera—led him to a closer investigation of the lives and habits of the countryside's birds and beasts. But he eventually gave up shooting. "I discovered, though unconsciously & insensibly, that the pleasure of observing & reasoning was a much higher one than that of skill & sport. The primeval instincts of the barbarian slowly yielded to the acquired tastes of the civilized man." From his earliest days he delighted in open-air life. At the age of eleven he went on a riding tour to Pistyll

Rhayader in central Wales with brother Erasmus. Two years later there was a similar tour with sister Caroline, and he noted in a small personal journal under "1822 June": "My first recollections of having some pleasure in scenery dates as far back as this." In an essentially outdoor family, female as well as male, Darwin was a tough walker and, as a young man, accompanied by two friends, made a knapsack tour of North Wales, climbing Snowdon and walking thirty miles most days through country less seamed with mountain paths than it is today.

His sisters exercised a good deal of influence over him, and he later attributed his humane feelings and behavior largely to them. He was, during these early years, much among women, what with his sisters and the Wedgwood girls at Maer, the Wedgwood estate only an easy ride away. There were also Sarah and Fanny [Frances] Owen, the two daughters of William Owen, a friend of his father's who lived at Woodhouse, West Felton, on the outskirts of Oswestry some fifteen miles from the Darwins in Shrewsbury. Darwin had been taught the rudiments of shooting by Owen and he became a frequent visitor to Woodhouse. "My father," Darwin's daughter Henrietta Emma was to write years later, "kept to the end of his life a warm friendship for Sarah . . . and many were the stories we heard about his visits to Woodhouse." However, it was Fanny who drew much of Darwin's attention, although his comment to William Darwin Fox that she was, "as all the world knows . . . the prettiest, plumpest, charming personage that Shropshire possesses, ay & Birmingham too," was qualified by his addition, "always excepting the blooming Bessy [not identified but possibly Sarah Elizabeth Wedgwood II] . . ." "He was very fond of all the Owens," Henrietta recalled, "and he had evidently been greatly attracted by Fanny Owen. I can remember, as a child, the expression of his face, and the very place where he stood in Stonyfield [a field so called by the Darwins because of the flints brought to the surface by recent ploughing] at Down as he told me once how charming she looked when she insisted on firing off one of their guns, and though the kick made her shoulder black and blue, gave no sign."

Darwin and Fanny kept up a playful correspondence. But there is little indication that this was more than semiyouthful banter, and in 1833 Darwin, deep in South America, learned that the charming Fanny was to marry a wealthy twenty-six-year-old member of Parliament.

On leaving Shrewsbury School he traveled north to Edinburgh, its university then unrivaled in Britain for the training of surgeons and physicians. But the experience of operations without anesthetics dissuaded him from following his father into a medical career. His squeamishness, which in later years comes to the surface as a faint but visible line through much of his work, could not be overcome. One of his daughters was to write that the children "used to dread going in [to his study] for sticking-plaster, because he disliked to see that we had cut ourselves, both for our sakes and on account of his acute sensitiveness to the sight of blood."

At Edinburgh, where Darwin quickly realized at the university that a doctor's life was not for him, he correctly guessed that lack of a profession would be no great inconvenience. "I became convinced [at Edinburgh] from various small circumstances," he wrote years later, "that my Father would leave me property enough to subsist on with some comfort, though I never imagined that I should be so rich a man as I am; but my belief was sufficient to check any strenuous effort to learn medicine."

If Darwin's months in Edinburgh ended any chance of his starting on a medical career, they also consolidated his interest in natural history. The Firth of Forth was a fine place on which to study marine creatures, as his diary—"The Edinburgh Ladies' & Gentlemen's Pocket Souvenir for 1826"—makes clear. "Caught a sea mouse," he reports for February 9, "Aphrodita Aculeata of Linnaeus; length about three or four inches; when its mouth was touched it tried to coil itself in a ball but was very inert; Turton states it has only two feelers. does not Linnaeus say 4? I thought I perceived them. found also 3 Palleta Vulgaris & Solen Siliquor." On February 15: "Caught an orange coloured (Zooptuti?); was fixed to a rock and when kept in a bason would turn itself inside out & when touched retracted itself in again; much in the same way as a Glove is turned inside out; put it in Spirits."

On March 2, he found the shore "was literally covered with Cuttle fish, when touched they emitted a dark coloured fluid & I think even on seeing any body coming; their process of swimming is extremely curious. they first inflate themselves with water & then fixing their tentacles on the sand, at this same slightly bending their bodies send forth the water to distance of three or four feet with considerable noise & it seems by the reaction that they first put themselves in motion. they thus proceed with considerable rapidity, their tail being the only part exposed. — they swim tail foremost." And nine days later he finds "A great many Seamice on the shore. When thrown on to the sea, rolled themselves up like hedgehogs."

Darwin was not content merely with walking on the shores of the firth and frequently went out with the dredging vessels from nearby Newhaven. It was on these that he made the observations reported in the minute book of the Plinian Society for March 27, 1827. "Mr. Darwin communicated to the Society two discoveries which he had made," this says. "1. That the ova of the Flustra [the sea mat, a genus of the *Polyzoa*] possess organs of motion. 2. That the small black globular body hitherto mistaken for the young Fucus lorius is in reality the ovum of the Pontobdella muricata."

In his notebook, crammed as it was with details of marine creatures, he proudly recorded the first of these two discoveries. "Having procured some specimens of the Flustra Carbacea from the dredge boats at Newhaven; I soon perceived without the aid of a microscope small yellow bodies studded in different directions on it. They were of an oval shape & of the colour of the yolk of an egg, each occupying one cell. Whilst in their cells I could perceive no motion; but when left at rest in a watch Glass or shaken they glided to and for with so rapid a motion as at some distance to be distinctly visible to the naked eye. When highly magnified, the cilia, which were chiefly distributed on the broader end, were seen in rapid motion; the central ones being the longest. I may mention that I have also observed ova [which Darwin notes in his autobiography were in fact larvae] of the Flustra Foliacea & Truncata in motion. That such ova had organs of motion does not appear to have been hitherto observed either by Lamarck, Cuvier, Lamouroux, or any other author. . . ."

Robert Darwin was only mildly dismayed at this interest in natural history rather than medicine. A satisfactory country parsonage could no doubt be found for the boy. He therefore proposed that his son should enter the Church. "I asked for some time to consider," Darwin wrote in his autobiography, "as from what little I had heard & thought on the subject I had scruples about declaring my belief in all the dogmas of the Church of England; though otherwise I liked the thought of being a country clergyman. Accordingly I read with care Pearson on the Creed & a few other books on divinity; as I did not then in the least doubt the strict & literal truth of every word in the Bible, I soon persuaded myself that our Creed must be fully accepted." He then added a sentence which was censored out by his family when the autobiography was first published in 1887 and was revealed only in 1959 when his granddaughter, Nora Barlow, published the unexpurgated text as *The Autobiography of Charles Darwin, 1809–1882*. "It never struck me," he wrote, "how illogical it was to say that I believed in what I could not understand & what is in fact unintelligible. I might have said with entire truth that I had no wish to dispute any dogma; but I never was such a fool as to feel & say 'credo quia incredible' [I believe the impossible]."

So in the autumn of 1827 Charles Darwin went up to Christ's College, Cambridge, his immediate aim a B.A., his ultimate destiny presumably a living from which he could expound the tenets of a religion that maintained that the earth had been created at 9:00 A.M. on October 23, 4004 B.C.; that all its species of living creatures had been produced in the following six days; and that all those species had remained unchanged. The date had been worked out by James Ussher, Archbishop of Armagh, and John Lightfoot, the most learned Hebraist of his day, on the basis of medieval historical guesswork and published at the end of the seventeenth century. From 1701 onward the date began to be printed in the Authorised Version of the Bible, a practice that continued well into the nineteenth century. But this presented no problem to the orthodox young Darwin.

At Cambridge, where he graduated tenth in 1831 after three-and-a-bit comparatively uneventful years, he "became slightly acquainted with several of the learned men [there] which much quickened the little zeal which dinner parties & hunting had not destroyed." Nevertheless, he was hardly an assiduous student, noting in his personal journal that he spent the Christmas vacation of 1830 at Cambridge and adding: "Continued to collect insects; to hunt, shoot & be *quite* idle." During his university life he was subjected to two opposed influences epitomizing the forces that were to beat round his head once his theory of evolution had been published. One was that of William Paley, the eminent divine and former Fellow of Christ's. Paley's writings had provided a main argument for those who saw the evidence of heavenly design in nature and for whom Darwin's natural selection was to be quite unacceptable, even if it was not blasphemy, which it probably was. Thus the lens of a fish's eye was more spherical than the lens in the eye of land vertebrates because each was adapted to the refractive index of the medium, water or air. "The marks of *design* are too strong to be gotten over," Paley declared. "Design must have had a designer. That designer must have been a person. That person is God." Paley's *View of the Evidences of Christianity* was compulsory reading for undergraduates, and Darwin not only read it but could write: "The logic of this book & as I may add of [Paley's] 'Natural Theology' gave me as much delight as did Euclid." And half a century later he remembered that "getting up Paley's Evidences and Moral Phil. thoroughly well as I did, I felt was an admirable training, and everything else bosh."

But there was also the influence of the geologist Charles Lyell, whose researches had increasingly supported the principle of uniformitarianism put forward by James Hutton at the end of the eighteenth century. Until the publication of Hutton's *Theory of the Earth* in 1785 the visible geological record was conventionally accounted for by a series of catastrophic changes, an explanation that did not offend the biblical conception of an earth that had existed for only some 6,000 years. Typical "catastrophists" were Jean Louis Rodolphe Agassiz, the Swiss American who was to be Darwin's main opponent in the United States and for whom the glaciers were "God's great plough"; and, in his later stages of belief, Captain Robert FitzRoy, R.N.,* commander of HMS *Beagle*. For FitzRoy, the disappearance of species found in the geological record was easily explicable: they were the animals that had failed to get into the Ark during the great flood. By contrast with the catastrophists, Hutton's uniformitarianism maintained that the forces changing the earth's surface—the deposition of sediment, the eruption of volcanoes and erosion by wind and water—had been uniformly at work over countless aeons: an explanation that made nonsense of the biblical story.

The radical change in the possible estimates of the earth's age, supported by Lyell's *Principles of Geology*, published between 1830 and 1833, was increasingly strengthened during Darwin's postgraduate years. This change would make credible the almost unimaginably long series of millennia that were required if evolution was to replace creation as the explanation of organic life on earth. It was, moreover, a geological explanation for which evidence could easily be found in Britain during the early nineteenth century. Construction of the canals that kept the products of the

---

*The captain's name is spelled variously in the records as FitzRoy, Fitzroy, Fitz-Roy and Fitz Roy, two versions sometimes appearing in the same document.

industrial revolution on the move—and later the construction of the railways—laid bare in homely detail the stratigraphical record on which uniformitarianism was based. William Smith, the geologist and engineer known as "Strata" Smith, not only recorded the strata, which resembled, "on a large scale, the ordinary appearance of superposed slices of bread and butter," but also noted that they could be identified by the fossils they held.

The hugely augmented age of the earth that Lyell and the excavators showed to be likely gave a new plausibility to the various schemes of biological evolution that had already been suggested. Yet to Lyell, at least, this great opening up of the vistas of time had little significance to the story of organic life. He continued to believe in the immutability of species. He believed that while domestic breeders could create new kinds of dog or cattle, they could do no more than that. And man's morality and powers of reason, he was confident, cut off the human race from any link with its predecessors.

In addition to the two influences of Lyell and Paley, which helped mold Darwin's thought while at Cambridge, there was also that of Alexander von Humboldt, one of the greatest naturalists and travelers of the early nineteenth century. Born in Berlin in 1769, Humboldt traveled extensively throughout Europe, North and South America, and Asia as far as the Ural and Altai mountains. Wherever he went, he collected scientific information—botanical, geological and meteorological—frequently putting on a foundation of observation what had previously rested on superstition and gossip. He recorded his travels in many books, and in *Cosmos* outlined the connections between the known facts of the physical sciences. Years after Darwin had come down from Cambridge, Sir Joseph Dalton Hooker, the botanist who became his most important confidant, asked him whether it would be right to call Humboldt the greatest scientific traveler who had ever lived. Darwin thought this was so, and added: "I have lately read 2 or 3 [of his books] again. His Geology is funny stuff; but that merely means that he was not in advance of his age. I shd say he was wonderful, more for his near approach to omniscience than for originality." Without Humboldt, the young Darwin's eagerness to take ship in the *Beagle* might have been successfully damped down and the history of evolution have been very different.

In the late summer of 1831, he had no particular plans for the future and, apparently, few qualifications. His main distinction was one of character, and most of his colleagues remembered him as being, in the words of one of them, "of the most placid, unpretending & amiable nature," a description that could with equal accuracy be applied to him throughout the rest of his life. The only hint of things to come was from John Henslow, professor of botany, who was quoted by one of Darwin's fellow graduates as frequently commenting: "What a fellow that Darwin is for asking questions." Darwin himself seems to have thought that he had frittered away his opportunities at a university. While planning what to read on the *Beagle*, he wrote that he hoped to have "the same opportunity of drilling my mind that I threw away whilst at Cambridge." This was obviously something of an exaggeration, although his preoccupation with sport is shown by his early notes on guns and shooting, included in which are the two following quotations from the game laws: "No common person or gamekeeper can demand your certificate without producing his own," and "An unqualified person can only be convicted once in a day."

His regime at Cambridge appears to have been similar to that of most of his fellow undergraduates. Half a century later he wrote in a characteristically modest self-analysis: "Special talents, none, except for business, as evinced by keeping accounts, being regular in correspondence, and investing money very well; very methodical in my habits. Steadiness; great curiosity about facts, and their meaning; some love of the new and marvellous. Somewhat nervous temperament, energy of body shown by much activity, and whilst I had health, power of resisting fatigue. An early riser in the morning. Energy of mind shown by vigorous and long-continued work on the same subject. . . . Memory bad for dates or learning by rote; but good in retaining a general or vague recollection of many facts. Very studious, but not large acquirements. I think fairly independently, but I can give no instances."

This was a very fair account of the virtues Darwin displayed throughout a long life. They were not particularly remarkable and certainly did not suggest that he might rise to the top in any of the professions. By the time he left Cambridge, his interest in natural history had increased, but Paley appeared to have been more influential than Lyell, and Darwin's future still seemed to lie within the Church. Certainly some scientific areas were barred to him, since he was unable, as he put it, to understand any of the great leading principles of mathematics. In 1828, writing to William Darwin Fox about receiving no letters from him, he added: "I hope it arises from your being 10 fathoms deep in *the Mathematics* and if you are God help you, for so am I, only with this difference, I stick fast in the mud at the bottom & there I shall remain in static quo." Later he was to regret his deficiencies in mathematics, observing of those who could master the subject, "men thus endowed seem to have an extra sense." Geology was, less surprisingly than it might seem, a considerable interest. But just as some clergymen were later to find it possible to reconcile their faith with natural selection, so did some find it possible to accept both the geological and the biblical record. Among them were Adam Sedgwick, Darwin's professor of geology at Cambridge, and William Whewell, his professor of mineralogy. Both, like John Henslow, had become Darwin's friends, and it was as a potential cleric with scientific leanings that in the summer of 1831 he set off on a geological walking tour in North Wales with Sedgwick. Darwin remembered years later: "after a day or two he sent me across the country in a line parallel to his course, telling me to collect specimens of the rocks, and to note the stratification. . . . In the evening he discussed what I had seen; and this of course encouraged me greatly, and made me exceedingly proud; but I now suspect that it was done merely for the sake of teaching me, and not for anything of value which I could have told him. . . ." At Capel Curig the two men parted, and Darwin made in a straight line for Barmouth, thirty miles away on the Welsh coast, traveling by compass and map and never following any track unless it coincided with his course. This took him into some of the roughest areas of Snowdonia and, as he later wrote, he "came on some strange wild places & enjoyed much this manner of travelling."

It was later on this tour that Darwin received a brusque lesson after telling his companion that a shell of the tropical mollusk *Voluta* had been found in a gravel pit in Shrewsbury. Far from being excited at the news, Sedgwick said that if this were so, "it would be the greatest misfortune to geology, as it would overthrow all that we know about the superficial deposits of the midland counties." At an early stage Darwin thus learned that innovations can be as unpopular in science as innovations elsewhere.

In August, back in Shrewsbury, he contemplated his future. He was now aged twenty-two, a university man with a financially sound family background and no pressing demands on his time. But at Cambridge he had been excited not only by Humboldt's *Personal Narrative* but also by Sir John Herschel's *Preliminary Discourses on the*

Study of Natural Philosophy, which influenced such thinkers as Whewell and Mill; together, they had left him with "a burning zeal to add even the most humble contribution to the noble structure of Natural Science." If this contribution involved a touch of adventurous travel, then so much the better. The chance for making it was offered in a letter he found waiting for him in Shrewsbury.

It came from Henslow and discussed a voyage to Tierra del Fuego and then home by the East Indies—a voyage around the world and to the edge of it, it must have seemed, an offer that was enough to send any young man's blood racing, quite apart from the opportunities it presented to investigate natural science. The proposal came at the end of a long chain that had started when the government had in 1828 commissioned HMS *Beagle* for a hydrographic survey of South America. After one voyage, the *Beagle* was now refitting in England in preparation for the next. Her commander, Captain Robert FitzRoy, R.N., had on his return written: "There may be metal in many of the Fuegian mountains, and I much regret that no person in the vessel was skilled in mineralogy, or at all acquainted with geology. . . . I could not avoid . . . inwardly resolving that if ever I left England again on a similar expedition, I would endeavour to carry out a person qualified to examine the land; while the officers and myself would attend to hydrography."

But in London, FitzRoy asked Captain Francis Beaufort, R.N., hydrographer to the navy, not for a geologist but for a naturalist to sail with him on his second voyage. Beaufort passed on the request to his friend the Reverend George Peacock, later Lowndean Professor of Astronomy at Cambridge. Peacock first asked his naturalist friend Leonard Jenyns, an Anglican clergyman, if he would take the post. But Jenyns (who later changed his name to Blomefield), a close friend of Darwin's, held a living in Cambridgeshire and felt that he could not abandon it for a voyage round the world. Peacock then passed on the request to Henslow. A number of other young men appear to have been approached and to have turned down the offer. One reason may have been finance, for if a young man was to make the most of the opportunities offered, he would have to bear the expense of overland exploration when the ship was in dock or when he was not needed at sea. Darwin's regular admissions in letters home to his sisters that he was cashing another bill for £80 or £100—usually with desperate assurances that the expected scientific results would be good value—support the estimate that the five-year voyage round the world cost him between £1,500 and £2,000, a considerable sum in those days. Susannah Wedgwood had brought a dowry of £25,000 when she married Robert Darwin in 1798 and it is ironic that the fortune of the devoutly Christian Wedgwoods played its part in the Darwin family's prosperity—and thus had a hand in providing Charles with the key to evolution.

Henslow's letter to Darwin stated bluntly that "Capt. F. wants a man (I understand) more as a companion than a mere collector & would not take any one however good a Naturalist who was not recommended to him likewise as a *gentleman*." The requirement was perhaps not unnatural for a naval officer whose direct line of descent went back to the first Duke of Grafton, a bastard son of Charles II by Barbara Villiers. FitzRoy was only four years older than Darwin, and later events confirmed that his main requirement was not so much a naturalist as a man of his own generation and class who would share the rigors of a five-year isolation in a ninety-foot vessel. It had initially been planned that Robert McCormick, later to serve as zoologist and surgeon to Joseph Dalton Hooker when he sailed to the Antarctic in HMS *Erebus* in 1839, should double as the *Beagle*'s naturalist. McCormick did in fact sail in the ship from England as the ship's surgeon. But it quickly became clear that he was by no means the ideal man for the Captain's table, and in April 1832 he came home from Rio de Janeiro, technically because of ill health, at what was the first practicable opportunity. Thus the Darwinian earthquake that shook the second half of the nineteenth century may have been largely the result of Captain FitzRoy's unwillingness to face another years-long voyage with an unsuitable companion.

Darwin jumped at the offer passed on by Henslow. His father counseled rejection. The rejection was countermanded on the advice of his uncle Josiah Wedgwood II, from the Wedgwoods' family home at Maer Hall, Maer, Staffordshire, who advised Dr. Darwin that "the pursuit of Natural History, though certainly not professional, is very suitable to a Clergyman," which it was then hoped Charles would become. Early in September, Charles Darwin met Captain FitzRoy in London. At first there seemed likely to be a hitch, since FitzRoy disliked the shape of Darwin's nose, and William Darwin Fox was told of "a discouraging letter from my Captain" and informed that the trip might still fall through.

Then the Captain took his naturalist-designate by sea down to Plymouth, where he could inspect the ship in which he would sail.

"I like what I see of him much," FitzRoy wrote to Captain Beaufort, "and I now request that you will apply for him to accompany me as Naturalist." Darwin had been equally impressed. "[He] says the stormy sea is exaggerated," he wrote to his sister Susan; "that if I do not chuse to remain with them, I can at any time get home to England, so many vessels sail that way, & that during bad weather (probably two months), if I like, I shall be left in some healthy, safe and nice country; that I shall always have assistance; that he has many books, all instruments, guns, at my serivce.
. . . There is indeed a tide in the affairs of man, and I have experienced it." The two men had hit it off, an augury of the message FitzRoy was to send to Beaufort when the *Beagle* had been at sea for a few weeks: "Darwin is a very sensible, hard-working man and a very pleasant messmate. I never saw a 'shore-going fellow' come into the ways of a ship so soon and so thoroughly. . . ."

Thus Darwin had become set on a course previously followed by Antonio Pigafetta, the naturalist who had sailed with Magellan on his first circumnavigation of the world; by Sir Joseph Banks, later president of the Royal Society, who had accompanied Captain Cook on his first voyage to the South Seas; by François Péron, who had gone with Jean-François de Galaup, Comte de La Pérouse, on his Far Eastern voyages; and by the naturalist Robert Brown, librarian to the Linnean Society of London, who had been naturalist to Captain Matthew Flinders's Australian expedition. Darwin's greatest supporters in the evolution controversy, Joseph Dalton Hooker and Thomas Henry Huxley, were similarly to win their naturalists' spurs on lengthy adventurous voyages.

Relations between Darwin and FitzRoy throughout the five-year voyage of the *Beagle* were occasionally to be stormy, Darwin's innate liberalism clashing with FitzRoy's extreme conservatism. There was also the wide disparity between their religious views. Darwin's were loosely held and open to change. FitzRoy's, initially held with inflexible rigidity, were made even more so by the very experiences of the voyage that inexorably pushed Darwin toward a belief in the mutability of species and a disbelief in Genesis. Indeed, FitzRoy's *Narrative* of the voyage ended with a twenty-five-page affirmation of the biblical version of the Noachian Flood and a warning "against assenting hastily to new theories." This was of course the forerunner of the Admiral FitzRoy of thirty years later, by then ex-governor of New Zealand, brandishing a Bible above his head at the famous meeting in Oxford of the British Association for the Advancement of Science and declaring that that volume alone was the source of all truth. "It is a pity," Darwin was to tell Lyell, "he did not add his theory of the extinction of *Mastodon* etc., from the door of the Ark being made too small."

Captain FitzRoy, joined by Darwin in Plymouth during the last weeks of 1831, commanded the Royal Navy's third HMS *Beagle*, a 10-gun, 235-ton, sloop-brig 90 feet long and of 24-foot, eight-inch beam that had been launched in May 1820. In preparation for her five-year voyage, she had been undergoing a major refit, which was to cost almost as much as her original construction. If the admiralty had taken care almost to rebuild the ship, equal trouble had been taken to provide her with a first-class crew, its members being largely specially selected West Country "men of war's men," considered the best in the Royal Navy. With Darwin went the tools of the nineteenth-century naturalist: simple microscope and hand lens, compass, magnet and mountain barometer, as well as equipment for chemical analysis, all chosen with the help of William Yarrell, the zoologist. Darwin also took a small library that included an edition of Humboldt's travels inscribed: "J. S. Henslow to his friend C. Darwin on his departure from England upon a voyage round the World, 21 Sept. 1831." With him there also went the first volume of Lyell's *Principles of Geology*, a book Henslow had advised him to carry but on no account to believe. At Plymouth, there were unexpected delays due to weather and to refitting the *Beagle*.

"I was also troubled with palpitations and pain about the heart," Darwin wrote later, "and like many a young ignorant man, especially one with a smattering of medical knowledge, was convinced that I had heart-disease. I did not consult any doctor, as I fully expected to hear the verdict that I was not fit for the voyage, & I was resolved to go at all hazards." Perhaps he was suffering from no more than a simple case of nerves.

2

The Voyage of Discovery

DARWIN started his momentous voyage in HMS *Beagle* with biblical faith undimmed and no warning that his observations of nature would be the pebbles that loosed the avalanche. Even during the second year of the voyage he could write to one of his sisters: "Although I like this knocking about, I find I steadily have a distant prospect of a very quiet Parsonage, and I can see it even through a grove of Palms." It is by no means exactly clear when the significance of what he was noting first began to trouble him; exegesis of his papers, ranging in date and reliability from his notes of the voyage to his autobiography written forty-four years later, can be used to provide a distracting spread of dates. Their range is only partly the result of difficulty in deciding when vague suspicion hardens into tentative idea and when idea changes into credible theory. Yet as the *Beagle* chopped down the English Channel toward the open sea on December 27, 1831, Darwin would have known that over almost any investigation of nature there loomed one intractable problem: the riddle of species.

For those who believed in divine creation, few problems existed. For them, each species had been created in its still-existing form, and it was unnecessary to know on which of the six days of creation each had come into existence. Six days might seem a short time for the work, but this little difficulty was already being removed by the more daring who tentatively suggested that "day" might be purely a figurative word and that the period involved might be as long as the latest geological argument demanded. By Darwin's time, the date of 4004 B.C. for the start of everything was already becoming less of a hurdle to be overcome.

To those who took a more sophisticated view and believed that species might not be immutable but had evolved from one form into its successor, there were other problems. Not the least was presented by the lack of any clear definition of what a species actually was. As Darwin put it to Hooker, "to define a species is to wish to define the indefinable," but today it is estimated that there have been nearly two billion different species since the start of the Cambrian period nearly six hundred million years ago. In theory, all members of a species were descended from the same original pair; in theory, members of the same species could produce fully fertile offspring, while matings between different species could produce only infertile offspring or none. Common sense ordained that all members of the same species looked alike, behaved similarly and shared a multitude of easily identifiable characteristics. But within a species there are subspecies, and within subspecies there are varieties, each showing differences from their neighbors. How important, it was asked, do these differences have to be before the distinction of a separate species can be claimed? How small a difference can separate one variety from another? One answer in the mid-nineteenth century was that if domestic animals reverted to the type of their supposed wild ancestors, this showed them to be a variety rather than a distinct species.

These questions baffled naturalists in the nineteenth century just as, at a different level, they still baffle today. Darwin was frank about the predicament. "I look at the term species, as one arbitrarily given for the sake of convenience to a set of individuals closely resembling each other," he wrote in *The Origin of Species*, "and that it does not essentially differ from the term variety, which is given to less distinct and more fluctuating forms. The term variety, again, in comparison with mere individual differences, is also applied arbitrarily, and for mere convenience sake." Forty years later, William Bateson, laying the foundations of genetics, the science that was to reveal the machinery of evolution, stated: "We see all living nature—animals and plants—divided into the groups which we call *species*, groups often so sharply marked off that there can be no doubt where they begin and end; groups often, on the other hand, so irregularly characterised that no two people would divide them alike."

In Bateson's day, Liberty Hyde Bailey, the American biologist, described the situation with brutal honesty, writing: "It would be profitless at this time to enter into a disquisition as to what a species is. The many discussions of this subject are so many admissions that no one knows. . . . Our formal nomenclature in practice recognizes only two grades—'species' and 'variety,' with no two persons agreeing which is one or the other." And Thomas Hunt Morgan, whose work on fruit flies in the famous fly room at Columbia University during the second decade of the twentieth century began to lay bare the machinery of inheritance, was as blunt, declaring: "We should always keep in mind the fact that the individual is the only reality with which we have to deal, and that the arrangement of these into species, genera, families, etc. is only a scheme invented by man for purposes of classification. Thus there is no such thing in nature as a species, except as a concept of a group of forms more or less alike."

Today the problem is even more complicated, and as Thomas J. M. Schopf, the American geophysicist, pointed out in 1979, "the general pattern of the systematic literature seems to be that a group is subdivided into more and more species with the advent of each new method of analysis." Citing only one major group, the small aquatic creatures called *Bryozoa*, he notes that new characters were revealed by thin sections in 1964, by scanning electron microscopy in 1973, by chromosomal analysis in 1977 and by gel electrophoresis in 1978, before pointing out that "the 'Truth' of any given biological species should not be dependent upon the technological accident of what instrument is brought to bear on the taxon [a group of organisms based on similarity of structure or origin]."

The perennial discussion about what makes up an independent species, or does not make it up, has never concealed the fact that there are great visible differences between some living organisms and apparent links between others. From the earliest times this has led to speculation that one kind of creature has over the years developed into another. Darwin, like all educated men of his time, was aware of these speculations even though he regarded them with a skeptical Christian mind. Even among the Christians, however, there had originally been uncertainty. Emanuel Rádl, the historian of biology, has pointed out in *The History of Biological Theories* that the early Christian Fathers had propounded many theories of how the world began. "While St. Clement, St. Origen, and St. Athanasius tried to prove that all forms of organisms were produced simultaneously by one creative act," Rádl states, "the school of Cappadocia, with St. Basil at its head, taught that God originally created only 'elements,' which reached their final purpose by a process of development. St. Gregory of Nyssa and St. Augustine expressed this same idea even more clearly. The very dreams of the early Christians themselves—their pictures of a lost or of a future Paradise, of the Millennium, of the end of the world —are but expressions of the view that things today are not as they once were, nor as they will yet be."

Before the Christian Era, there had been an even greater diversity of opinions. In the sixth century B.C. the theory was put forward that there had been a gradual evolution from chaos to order and that aquatic animals had evolved into terrestrial ones by adaptation. Two hundred years later, Empedocles proposed that imperfect forms of animals were replaced by better forms through a process of adaptation, while those unable to adapt died off. Marcus Aurelius wrote in the second century A.D.: "Nature which governs the whole will soon change all things which thou seest, and out of their substance will make other things, and again other things from the substance of them, in order that the world may be ever new."

These philosophical speculations were largely ignored during the Dark Ages as the Christian view of a divine creation based on the Bible became predominant. Only with the rise of science in the middle of the seventeenth century did men again begin to ask how living organisms had developed over the millennia. Among the first was John Ray, who has been called the father of natural history in Britain. "Nature, as the saying goes," he wrote in 1682, "makes no jumps and passes from extreme to extreme only through a mean linking one type with another and having something in common with both—as for example the so-called zoophytes between plants and animals."

Belief in the development of organisms from simple to more complicated was expressed on numerous occasions in the eighteenth century, but usually with scant evidence, or none, to support it. Georges Louis Leclerc, Comte de Buffon, gave the earth what was then a revolutionary age of some 75,000 years, believed that man might have existed for some 40,000 years, and saw development as using imperceptible differences, not only as differences of size and form, but also as differences in movements and between succeeding generations of all species. The writer Oliver Goldsmith maintained in 1774: "Nature is varied by imperceptible gradations, so that no line can be drawn between any two classes of its productions, and no definition made to comprehend them all.''

A change was soon evident in the nineteenth century, its first sign being *The Temple of Nature,* written by Charles Darwin's grandfather Erasmus and published in 1803, the year after his death. The poem—long, didactic and, like many of his others, scientific rather than poetic—traced evolution from primitive life in the oceans.

> Organic Life beneath the shoreless waves
> Was born, and nurs'd in Ocean's pearly caves;
> First forms minute, unseen by spheric glass,
> Move on the mud, or pierce the watery mass;
> These, as successive generations bloom,
> New powers acquire, and larger limbs assume;
> Whence countless groups of vegetation spring,
> And breathing realms of fin, and feet, and wing.

Almost contemporary with Erasmus Darwin, there came a number of naturalists whose theories, limited as they were by lack of experimental evidence, yet included ideas which were to reverberate through the rest of the century. Jean-Baptiste-Pierre-Antoine de Monet, Chevalier de Lamarck (1744–1829), claimed both that characteristics acquired by an animal in its lifetime could be passed on to its descendants and that a change of environment could cause some organs to perish and new ones to develop. "At the end of many successive generations," he was to claim, "those individuals which belonged originally to another species, find themselves in the end transformed into a new *species* distinct from the other."

Etienne Geoffroy Saint-Hilaire of Paris had meanwhile suggested a method of evolution that contained two seminal ideas. One was that evolution was caused by the direct action of the environment, which produced important changes in the egg, an idea elaborated later in the century by August Weismann. In addition, Geoffroy Saint-Hilaire believed that a new species might be produced by a number of large variations in one generation, the "jumps" which were to be postulated by Hugo De Vries in the form of mutations in the early 1900s. It was, in fact, becoming so easy to think about the unthinkable that as early as 1834 the University of Munich offered a prize for the best thesis on the causes of the mutability of species.

By the time that Darwin began his voyage in the *Beagle,* there was thus already in existence a background of discussion not only about the mutability of species but also about the question that was to divide evolutionists from the publication of *The Origin of Species* to the present day: did change take place by the slow accumulation of many minor differences or more quickly but more jerkily as the result of a smaller number of major differences, which biologists call saltations?

But if evolution was an idea that had flickered in and out of naturalists' minds throughout the centuries, it was one for which no naturalist had yet collected any substantial body of supporting evidence. Isolated examples could be cited, but they were flimsy stuff even to naturalists, let alone to the established body of lay opinion, which believed that the birds of the air and the beasts of the field—as well as all other living organisms—had come into existence, once and for all, during the six periods of creation. Darwin's voyage in the *Beagle*, one of the best-recorded voyages in modern history, was, with its repercussions, to change all that.

Captain FitzRoy's task, as Darwin described it on the first page of his *Journal of Researches* (1845),* was "to complete the survey of Patagonia and Tierra del Fuego, commenced under Captain King in 1826 to 1830: to survey the shores of Chile, Peru, and of some islands in the Pacific—and to carry a chain of chronometrical measurements round the World." But FitzRoy was first to survey the coasts of Brazil and the Argentine. The *Beagle* would then round Cape Horn, survey the coast of Chile, sail north to the Galápagos Islands, then westward across the Pacific. After visiting Tahiti, and calling at New Zealand and Australia, she would make for home across the Indian Ocean, rounding the Cape of Good Hope, and after crossing the southern Atlantic for a last look at Brazil, would turn north for England.

This peripatetic schedule gave Darwin considerable freedom for weeks-long excursions, particularly in South America. FitzRoy was agreeable to putting him ashore and picking him up hundreds of miles away, as long as survey work was not affected, and the result was that the young Darwin had unrivaled opportunities for geological and botanical exploration in areas little known to science.

His journeys were something of a relief from the lack of space on board, even though he made the best of his circumstances with

*See the Bibliography for details of different editions and titles of this *Journal.*

fortitude and goodwill. Although he ate at the Captain's table, he was confined for much of the five years that the voyage lasted to the cramped quarters of a nineteenth-century Royal Navy officer. "I have just room to turn round & that is all," he reported to Henslow, while Lieutenant (later Admiral) Sir James Sulivan, who served on the *Beagle*, has stressed the pokiness of Darwin's quarters. "The narrow space at the end of the chart-table was his only accommodation for working, dressing and sleeping," Sulivan wrote; "the hammock being left hanging over his head by day, when the sea was at all rough, that he might lie on it with a book in his hand when he could not any longer sit at the table. His only stowage for clothes being several small drawers in the corner, reaching from deck to deck; the top one being taken out when the hammock was hung up, without which there was not length for it, so then the foot-clews took the place of the top drawer. For specimens he had a very small cabin under the forecastle."

To make matters worse, Darwin suffered from seasickness to the end of the voyage. "We worked together for several years at the same table in the poop cabin," wrote Admiral John Lort Stokes, who served on the *Beagle* as mate and assistant surveyor during the voyage, and was to command the vessel in the 1840s, ". . . he with his microscope and myself at the charts. It was often a very lively end of the little craft, and distressingly so to my old friend, who suffered greatly from sea-sickness. After, perhaps, an hour's work he would say to me, 'Old fellow, I must take the horizontal for it,' that being the best relief position from ship motion; a stretch out on one side of the table for some time would enable him to resume his labours for a while, when he had again to lie down." It is significant of Darwin's character that, although a landlubber, he seems to have earned the sympathy of the crew, Alexander Burns Usborne, the master's assistant, later writing: "at times, when I have been officer of the watch, and reduced the sails, making the ship more easy, and thus relieving him, I have been pronounced by him to be 'a good officer,' and he would resume his microscopic observations in the poop cabin."

In addition to fighting debilitating seasickness, Darwin had to keep on good terms with the Captain. The task was made easier than it might have been by his solid respect for the man despite disagreements on moral, ethical and, later, religious grounds. "As far as I can judge," he wrote to his sister Caroline from Botafogo Bay on April 25, 1832, "he is a very extraordinary person. I never before came across a man whom I could fancy being a Napoleon or a Nelson. I should not call him clever, yet I feel convinced nothing is too great or too high for him. His ascendancy over everybody is quite curious—the extent to which every Officer and Man feels the slightest rebuke or praise would have been before seeing him incomprehensible. It is very amusing to see all hands hauling at a rope, they not supposing him on deck, and then observe the effect when he utters a syllable; it is like a string of dray horses, when the Waggoner gives one of his awful smacks. His candour and sincerity are to me unparalleled; and using his own words his 'vanity and petulancy' are nearly so. I have felt the effects of the latter. . . . His greatest fault as a companion is his austere silence produced from excessive thinking; his many good qualities are great & numerous; altogether he is the strongest marked character I ever fell in with."*

There appears to have been one major row between the two men. This broke out after FitzRoy had defended the practice of slavery, which Darwin abhorred. But peace was quickly made, and the two men were still on friendly terms when the *Beagle* docked at Falmouth some five years after leaving Plymouth. Yet another ten years on, Darwin wrote him an affectionate note saying: "Fare-well, dear Fitzroy, I often think of your many acts of kindness to me, and not seldomest on the time, no doubt quite forgotten by you, when before making Madeira, you came and arranged my hammock with your own hands, and which, as I afterwards heard, brought tears into my father's eyes."

The ability to mix with all manner of men was one characteristic of value to Darwin throughout a long life. It certainly helped when he went ashore with members of the ship's company on expeditions that sometimes lasted a number of weeks. "I am become quite a Gaucho," he wrote to Caroline, "drink my Mattee & smoke my cigar & then lie down & sleep as comfortably with the Heavens for Canopy as on a feather bed. It is such a fine healthy life on horse-back all day, eating nothing but meat—& sleeping in a bracing air, one awakes as fresh as a lark." This was the man who, corresponding years later with pigeon breeders and horticulturalists, would be treated as an inquirer to be helped rather than an academic from a different world.

---

*Some slight alterations have been made in the capitalization and punctuation in quotations from Darwin's manuscript letters to conform with current practice.

His companions on the *Beagle* soon ceased to wonder at the young man who caught sixty-eight species of beetle in a single day and shot eighty species of birds in a morning's walk. He chased ostriches with the rest of them, practiced using the lasso and the three-balled bola, and climbed to the summit of the Sierra de la Ventana.

Throughout the voyage he regularly sent back parcels of specimens to Henslow in Cambridge, aided after the first few months by a personal servant, Syms Covington, who had begun the voyage as "Fidler and Boy to Poop Cabin," and who was, in the spring of 1832, upgraded to help Darwin. "I do not think it just thus to take a seaman out of the ship," Darwin wrote to his sister Catherine in a message to be relayed to his father, "and 2nd. when at sea I am rather badly off for any one to wait on me. The man is willing to be my servant, & all the expences [*sic*] would be under sixty £ per annum. I have taught him to shoot & skin birds, so that in my main object he is very useful." And he added that he would "now make a fine collection in birds & quadrupeds which before took up far too much time." Covington, in fact, did far more than this. Some of Darwin's notes and records while at sea appear in Covington's hand, and among his ornithological lists Darwin has one headed: "Birds from Galapagos Archipelago collected by Syms Covington." After the *Beagle* had returned to England, Covington became a personal assistant, and Darwin maintained a friendly correspondence with him long after he had finally emigrated to Australia.

As for the officers, Darwin told Henslow after he joined the ship, they "are a fine set of fellows, but rather rough, & their conversation is oftentimes so full of slang & sea phrases that it is as unintelligible as Hebrew to me," but there is every indication that he and the more sophisticated naval officers rubbed along together pretty well. Darwin had no knowledge of the sea or of seamanship, but he was eager to learn and quickly won the confidence of a company that tended to be suspicious of landsmen and particularly of academics.

His energy, in such contrast to the lassitude of later years, is suggested by a letter to Henslow that accompanied two boxes and a cask. "One of the former," he said, "is lined with tin-plate & contains nearly 200 skins of birds & animals—amongst others a fine collection of the mice of S. America. The other box contains spirit bottles, & will only require just looking at to see how the Spirit stands. But the Bird-skins, if you will take the trouble will be much better for a little airing. The Cask is divided into Compartments, the upper contains a few skins, the other a jar of fish, & *I am very anxious to hear how the Spirit withstands evaporation,* an insect case, which would require airing, a small box of stones, which may be left in statu quo, a bundle of seeds, which I send as a most humble apology for my idleness in Botany. . . . Also a bag of the sweepings of a Granary; it will be a Botanical problem to find out to what country the weeds belong: . . . I also send to the care of Dr. Armstrong in Plymouth, an immense box of Bones & Geological specimens. . . ." His enthusiasm is evident in another letter to Henslow in which he apologized for some of the geological specimens not being numerous enough. "But I maintain that no person has a right to accuse me," he went on, "till he has tried carrying rocks under a Tropical sun ["all" deleted]. I have endeavoured to get specimens of every variety of rock, & have written notes upon all."

Darwin's preoccupation with geological specimens was considerable. Geology had been one of his specialties when he left Britain; now it not only continued to hold his attention but was eventually to lead him on to the question of questions. "But Geology carries the day," he wrote to William Darwin Fox; "it is like the pleasure of gambling. Speculating on first arriving what the rocks may be; I often mentally cry out 3 to one tertiary against primitive; but the latter have hitherto won all the bets." And to Henslow he confessed: "I am quite charmed with Geology, but like the wise animal between two bundles of hay, I do not know which to like the best, the old crystalline group of rocks or the softer & fossiliferous beds. When puzzling about stratification, &c., I feel inclined to cry a fig for your big oysters and your bigger Megatheriums. But then when digging out some fine bones, I wonder how any man can tire his arms with hammering granite." With geology his main interest, he said that he was anxious to write a book on the subject; in fact, he was to write three—*The Structure and Distribution of Coral Reefs* (1842), *Geological Observations on the Volcanic Islands, Visited during the Voyage of H.M.S. Beagle* (1844), and *Geological Observations on South America* (1846).

News of Darwin's collections quickly spread, and, from Cambridge, Adam Sedgwick commented to Dr. Butler, headmaster at Shrewsbury: "His [Dr. Darwin's] son is doing admirable work in South America, and has already sent home a collection above all price. It was the best thing in the world for him that he went out on the voyage of discovery. There was some risk of his turning out an idle man, but his character will be now fixed, and if God spares his life he will have a great name among the Naturalists of Europe."

Enthusiasm for collecting in almost all fields is clear in Darwin's records of the voyage. His dedication to the task in hand comes through in everything that he wrote during the five seminal years of the voyage—and he wrote a great deal. There were first some eighteen small field notebooks that he carried one after another on shore and on ship and in which he recorded the details of what he saw and what he collected. In addition, he made natural history observations in another six little pocket books and kept separate geological, zoological and ornithological notes on larger sheets of paper. The details in the notebooks were expanded whenever he had time and written up on board on foolscap or quarto sheets in entries that sometimes covered a week or more. These formed the "Journal" of his adventures, which, as opportunity offered, was sent back to his family in England; sometimes described as his "diary." In 1876 it was bound up into a "Manuscript Journal" totaling 189,000 words.

In 1891 his son Sir Horace Darwin had three copies of the journal typed, stating at the beginning: "The following is a copy of the original diary written by Charles Darwin during the voyage of H.M.S. 'Beagle.'" In 1933 Sir Horace's daughter Nora Barlow published extracts from the journal under the title *Charles Darwin's Diary of the Voyage of H.M.S. "Beagle,"* and in 1979 a facsimile of the journal was published.

All the separate writings made on the voyage of the *Beagle* were to be drawn upon when, after his return to England, he wrote his *Journal and Remarks, 1832–1836*, which was to be one volume of the three-volume official account of the *Beagle*'s achievements, and was later to be published as *Journal of Researches*.

Some of his entries made at sea, like an account of deer in South America, were brought up to date after he arrived back in England. "The most curious fact with respect to these animals is the over-poweringly strong and offensive odour which proceeds from the body of the buck," he wrote in the expansion of his field note-books. "It is quite indescribable. Several times while skinning the specimen [a later Darwin insertion adds: "which is now mounted at the Zoological Museum"], I was almost overcome by nausea. I tied up the skin in a silk pocket handkerchief & so carried it home.

This handkerchief, after being well washed, I continually used and it was of course as repeatedly washed. Yet, every time when unfolding it for a space of one year and seven months, I distinctly perceived the odour. — Is not this an astonishing instance of the permanence of some matter, which nevertheless in its nature must be most subtle and volatile.''

A fortnight after leaving Plymouth he was testing the utility of a contrivance that, he recorded, "will afford me many hours of amusement & work, — it is a bag four feet deep. Made of bunting, & attached to [a] semicircular bow: this by lines is kept upright & dragged behind the vessel." The following day he was sorting his catch—and already responding to the sights of a new world. "Many of these creatures, so low in the scale of nature," he wrote, "are most exquisite in their forms & rich colours. — It creates a feeling of wonder that so much beauty should be apparently created for such little purpose."

The unremitting work aroused mixed feelings in FitzRoy, judging by his remarks when Darwin and Covington later began gathering massive fossils from a cliff on the Argentine coast. Here, "notwithstanding our smiles at the cargoes of apparent rubbish which he frequently brought on board," FitzRoy put on record, "he and his servant used their pick-axes in earnest, and brought away what have since proved to be most interesting and valuable remains of extinct animals."

Mammals, birds and insects, in addition to the geology of the country, were all described and, if possible, fitted into gaps in the biological record. Thus after collecting outside Rio de Janeiro, first one, then a second *Planaria*, a genus of turbellarian worm, Darwin writes: "This like the last . . . was caught in the forest crawling on soft decayed wood. It is quite a different species. Back snow white, edged each side by very fine lines of reddish-brown. — also within are two other approximate ones of same colour. — sides on foot white nearer to the exterior red lines thickly clouded by 'pale blackish purple'; animal beautifully coloured. — foot beneath with white specks — but [a] few black dots on edge and more on head. — length of body one inch, not so narrow in proportion as other species; anterior extremity not nearly so much lengthened — the body in consequence of more uniform breadth. . . . Having found two species is fortunate as it more firmly establishes this new subdivision of the genus Planaria."

Darwin is adept at recording first impressions and not above admitting later that he may be wrong. Thus through most of a long account of the geology of Quail Island in the Cape Verde group, he subsequently drew a line with the appended comment: "I have drawn my pen through those parts which appear absurd."

If an air of scientific devotion still rises from his pages after a century and a half, so does that of a high-spirited youth stepping out to meet new experiences wherever he can. He recalls that the "greatest event of the day has been catching a fine young shark with my own hook." When the *Beagle* first entered the harbor at Rio de Janeiro, FitzRoy decided to make a display of smartness in shortening sail before the ships of all nationalities anchored there. Darwin, although not a member of the crew, was conscripted as the ship sailed in, bearing every foot of canvas that could be spread upon her yards. A fellow officer has recalled that Darwin was ordered to hold a main-royal sheet in each hand and a topmost studding tack in his teeth. At the command "Shorten sail" he was to let go and clap on to any rope he saw was shorthanded. For long afterward he was to boast that "the feat could not have been performed without him," said Midshipman Philip Gidley King.

During a 300-mile journey down the river Paraná he heard that he was near two volcanoes and noted that he would "run the risk of being eat up alive to see two real good burning Volcanoes." More than one revolution was fomenting or in progress, and in Argentina he found it necessary to get a laissez-passer from the commanding general—made out to "El Naturalista Don Carlos Darwin." "The Minute I landed, I was almost a prisoner," he reports, "for the city is closely blockaded by a furious cut throat set of rebels. By riding about (at a ruinous expense) amongst the different generals I at last obtained leave to go on foot without passport into the City. I was thus obliged to leave my Peon & luggage behind; but I may thank kind Providence I am here with an entire throat." In Montevideo, where there had been a mutiny and the *Beagle*'s crew occupied the main fort to protect the inhabitants, he reports with evident satisfaction: "It was something new to me to walk with Pistols & Cutlass through the streets of a Town."

He enjoys the unexpected, such as the ceremony of crossing the Equator, when he is ducked by King Neptune, and even the occasion when the mate cries down to him, "Darwin, did you ever see a Grampus" and he arrives on deck in a rush to find himself greeted with cries of "April Fool."

Beneath this boyish enjoyment there is a wonder at the richness of the tropics. He writes of "the unspeakable pleasure of walking under a tropical sun, on a wild & desert island" and in Brazil says that not even Humboldt was able to describe the scene adequately. "The delight one experiences in such times bewilders the mind," he records; "if the eye attempts to follow the flight of a gaudy butter-fly, it is arrested by some strange tree or fruit; if watching an insect one forgets it in the strange flower it is crawling over, — if turning to admire the splendour of the scenery, the individual character of the foreground fixes the attention: The mind is a chaos of delight, out of which a world of future & more quiet pleasure will arise. I am at present fit only to read Humboldt, he like another sun illumines everything I behold."

On another occasion he writes: "The day has passed delight-fully: delight is however a weak term for such transports of pleas-ure: I have been wandering by myself in a Brazilian forest: amongst the multitude it is hard to say what set of objects is most striking; the general luxuriance of the vegetation bears the victory, the elegance of the grasses, the novelty of the parasitical plants, the beauty of the flowers, — the glossy green of the foliage, all tend to this end. — A most paradoxical mixture of sound & silence pervades the shady parts of the wood: — the noise from the insects is so loud that in the evening it can be heard even in a vessel anchored several hundred yards from the shore; yet within the recesses of the forest when in the midst of it a universal stillness appears to reign. — To a person fond of natural history such a day as this brings with it pleasure, more acute than he ever may again experience."

But there was more to it than pleasure. From an early stage in the five-year voyage there are indications in Darwin's notebook and journal, brief and tenuous at first, that his observations were raising doubts about the immutability of species. To start with, he appears to have been only vaguely, and slightly, worried. Certainly he did not quickly abandon the prospect of a clerical future, a way of life that would have been hard to reconcile with the revolution-ary ideas that eventually seized him. "I am sorry to see in your last letter," wrote his brother Erasmus in August 1832, "that you still look forward to the horrid little parsonage in the desert. I was beginning to hope I should have you set up in London in lodgings somewhere near the British Museum or some other learned place. My only chance is the Established Church being abolished, & in some places they are beginning to demand pledges to that effect." In November 1832, Robert Hamond, one of the *Beagle*'s mates, later recalled, Darwin had joined with him in "a request to the Chaplain of Buenos Ayres, where we were then staying, to have the Sacrament of the Lord's Supper administered to us, previous to going to Tierra del Fuego. We were both then young," he continued, "and looked on that Ordinance as many young did, and do, as I suppose they do now, as a sort of vow to lead a better life." And as late as 1834, almost three years into the voyage, Darwin appears to have kept his orthodox views, writing in his journal: "I have already found beds of recent shells, yet retaining their colors at an elevation of 1300 feet, & beneath this level the country is strewed with them. It seems not a very improbable conjecture that the want of animals may be owing to none having been created since this country was raised from the sea."

Yet however much Darwin clung to the ideas with which he had been brought up, doubts continued to intrude. They were encouraged, almost alarmingly, by the huge changes that he realized the South American landscape must have undergone and the length of the geological epochs that they must have required. "This grand range," he wrote of the Cordilleras, the mountains stretching down the length of South America, "has suffered both the most violent dislocations, and slow, though grand, upward and downward movements in mass: I know not whether the spectacle of its immense valleys, with mountain masses of once-liquified and intrusive rocks, now bared and intersected, or whether the view of those plains, composed of shingle and sediment hence derived, which stretch to the borders of the Atlantic Ocean, is best adapted to excite our astonishment at the amount of wear and tear which these mountains have undergone."

And on the Portillo Pass in Chile he could think: "But, on the other hand, when listening to the rattling noise of these torrents, and calling to mind that whole races of animals have passed away from the surface of the globe, during the period throughout which, night and day, these stones have gone rattling onwards in their course, I have thought to myself, can any mountains, any continent, withstand such waste?"

On various shore excursions he noted facts that suggested that certain species might have developed almost beyond recognition over the millennia. The giant quadrupeds whose fossils he sketched were now extinct; but there were points of resemblance between them and their modern counterparts. There were three birds whose wings had clearly once been used for flight but now had other functions: the penguin, which used them as fins for swimming; the "steamer" duck, which used them for paddling; and the ostrich, which used them as sails. Could these conceivably be examples of species in transition? If that were so, it would destroy the whole concept of immutable species. And what else might it not destroy?

By the late summer of 1833, one possible solution of a problem eventually to be solved by natural selection appears to have arisen in his mind, since his *Journal of Researches* records: "Every animal in a state of nature regularly breeds; yet in a species long established, any *great* increase in numbers is obviously impossible, and must be checked by some means. We are, nevertheless, seldom able with certainty to tell in any given species, at what period of life, or at what period of the year, or whether only at long intervals, the check falls; or, again, what is the precise nature of the check." And in the spring of 1835, having crossed the Cordilleras by two passes, he could write: "At an elevation from 10–12,000 ft. there is a transparency in the air & a confusion of distances & a sort of stillness which gives the sensation of being in another world; & when to this is joined, the picture so plainly drawn of the great epochs of violence, it causes in the mind a most strange assemblage of ideas."

These examples, like others scattered through Darwin's notebooks and journal, are no more than evidence that he was tentatively beginning to question the creation of species as laid down in Genesis. More doubts were to follow. It is sometimes claimed that it was Darwin's study of the Galápagos flora and fauna that carried him into a belief in the inevitability of evolution, but it does not appear to have been as simple or as straightforward as that. Darwin's convictions strengthened gradually over the years with the steady accumulation of detail; among those details, the life of the Galápagos was to be crucial, although not as directly as is usually assumed.

The *Beagle* anchored off Chatham Island, the easternmost of the Galápagos group, on the morning of September 17, 1835. Including thirteen large and numerous smaller islands, 650 miles off the coast of Ecuador, which had acquired them from Spain in 1832, the group had first been visited by Fray Tomás de Berlanga, bishop of Panama, in 1535. "It looked," he wrote, "as though God had caused it to rain stones." Woodes Rogers, a buccaneer who many years later landed there with Alexander Selkirk, the real Robinson Crusoe, gave no better account of the islands, describing them as "nothing but loose Rocks, like Cynders, very rotten and heavy and the Earth so parch'd, that it will not bear a Man, but breaks into Holes under his Feet, which makes me suppose there has been a Vulcano here; tho' there is much shrubby Wood and some Greens on it, yet there's not the least Sign of Water, nor is it possible, that any can be contain'd on such a Surface."

Darwin gave no more enticing an account in 1835. "Nothing could be less inviting than the first appearance," he wrote. "A broken field of black basaltic lava is every where covered by a stunted brushwood, which shows little signs of life. The dry and parched surface, having been heated by the noonday sun, gave the air a close and sultry feeling, like that from a stove: we fancied even the bushes smelt unpleasantly."

If the volcanic landscape suggested a prehistoric past, the reptilian fauna, including the giant land iguanas, the giant marine iguanas and the giant tortoises, had a nightmare quality. "I frequently got on their backs," Darwin wrote of the tortoises, "and then upon giving a few raps on the hinder part of the shell, they would rise up and walk away; — but I found it very difficult to keep my balance."

There was one peculiarity about these tortoises that was pointed out to Darwin by Nicholas O. Lawson, an Englishman who had been made vice-governor of the archipelago by the Ecuadorean authorities. Lawson told him, Darwin reported, that the tortoises "differed from the different islands, and that he could with certainty tell from which island any one was brought. I did not for some time pay sufficient attention to this statement, and I had already partially mingled together the collections from two of the islands. I never dreamed that islands, about fifty or sixty miles apart, and most of them in sight of each other, formed of precisely the same rocks, placed under a quite similar climate, rising to a nearly equal height, would have been differently tenanted . . . but I ought, perhaps to be thankful that I obtained sufficient materials to establish this most remarkable fact in the distribution of organic things."

There were also the different varieties of mockingbirds found on different islands. Darwin referred to them in his ornithological notes, written some nine months after he had left the Galápagos and while the *Beagle* was on the home run to England. "When I recollect the fact that from the form of the body, shape of scales & general size, the Spaniards can at once pronounce, from which Island any Tortoise may have been brought," he begins his discussion. "When I see these Islands in sight of each other, & ["but" deleted] possessed of but a scanty stock of animals, tenanted by these birds, but slightly differing in structure & filling the same place in Nature, I must suspect they are only varieties. The only fact of a similar kind of which I am aware, is the constant asserted difference — between the wolf-like Fox of East & West Falkland Islds. — If there is the slightest foundation for these remarks the zoology of Archipelagoes — will be well worth examining; for such facts would undermine the stability of Species."

Thus far, and with the Galápagos a long way astern, there was no significant mention of the famous finches, different varieties and species of which were found on the different islands and which are often recorded as the major determinant of Darwin's views on evolution. The truth, it has been indisputably shown by Frank Sulloway in a fifty-three-page paper in the *Journal of the History of Biology,* is less clear-cut. Darwin made only a single passing reference to the finches in the journal of his *Beagle* voyage, mentioned them briefly in the *Journal of Researches* which he wrote after his return to England, and only in a second edition, published in 1845, nearly a decade after he had left the Galápagos, did he add his famous sentence about the birds: "Seeing this gradation and diversity of structure in one small, intimately related group of birds, one might really fancy that from an original paucity of birds in this archipelago, one species had been taken and modified for different ends." Furthermore, he made no mention of them in *The Origin.*

The finches were certainly curious, since although all the thirteen varieties or species had apparently originated from one source, their beaks were very different—"small finch-like beaks, huge finch-like beaks, parrot-like beaks, straight wood-boring beaks, de-curved flower-probing beaks, slender warbler-like beaks," as a later ornithologist described them. The ease with which such differences could be described and understood possibly provided the main reason for the importance that they were subsequently to be given. Captain FitzRoy ignored such nice distinctions and merely commented: "All the birds that live on these lava-covered islands have short beaks, very thick at the base, like that of a bull-finch. This appears to be one of those admirable provisions of Infinite Wisdom by which each created thing is adapted to the place for which it was intended. In picking up insects or seeds which lie on hard iron-like lava, the superiority of such beaks over delicate onces, cannot, I think, be doubted. . . . "

While on the Galápagos, Darwin was barely interested in the riddle of the finches, "the focus," as Sulloway calls it, "for a considerable legend in the history of science, one that ranks alongside other famous stories that celebrate the great triumphs of modern science." Until his meeting with Lawson during the second week of his five-week visit to the islands, "most of the specimens of the finch tribe were mingled together," as Darwin put it. His collecting and labeling of the finches was on an almost casual basis, and Sulloway concludes, after a clinical assessment of Darwin's methods: "After he left Charles Island, his collecting procedures continued to reflect the typological and creationist assumptions he had brought with him to that archipelago. What localities he did record were noted as largely incidental information to remind himself later of scarce species or noteworthy habitats. He continued, moreover, to collect only a few specimens of each species; and he entirely failed to collect finches on the third island he visited—Albemarle—even though almost every finch within miles was gathered in front of him at a spring near Bank's Cove."

Darwin frankly believed that in some cases the separate islands possessed their own representatives of the different species, and this almost necessarily would cause a fine gradation in their characters. But he then continued: "Unfortunately I did not suspect this fact until it was too late to distinguish the specimens from the different islands of the group; but from the collection made for Captain FitzRoy, I have been able in some small measure to rectify this omission."

He worked hard in the Galápagos. "Amongst other things, I collected every plant, which I could see in flower, & as it was the flowering season I hope my collection may be of some interest to you," he wrote to Henslow. "I shall be very curious to know whether the Flora belongs to America, or is peculiar. I paid also much attention to the Birds, which I suspect are very curious. . . . "

They set out westward on October 20 and crossed the Pacific Ocean via Tahiti without incident. Darwin had mixed feelings. "I have always felt that I owe to the Voyage the first real training or education of my mind," he was later to write. "I was led to attend closely to several branches of natural history, and thus my powers of observation were improved, though they were already fairly developed. The investigation of the geology of all the places visited was far more important, as reasoning here comes into play."

Yet Darwin was, even in his twenties, showing that love of home which after his return was to help keep him not only in England for the rest of his life but psychologically rooted to his own house. "I never was intended for a traveller," he wrote to Henslow; "my thoughts are always rambling over past or future scenes; I cannot enjoy the present happenings, for anticipating the future; which is about as foolish as the dog who dropt the real bone for its shadow." He had been at sea only a few weeks when he followed a report of his work to his father with the comment: "There is only one sorrowful drawback, the enormous period of time before I shall be back in England—I am often quite frightened when I look forward." In September 1833 he wrote to Caroline from Buenos Aires saying that it was now spring in Argentina and everything was budding and fresh, and adding: "but how great a difference between this & the beautiful scenes of England. I often think of the Garden at home as a Paradise." A long while before he returned he was to confess: "I never see a Merchant vessel start for England, without a most dangerous inclination to bolt. . . . There never was a ship so full of homesick heroes as the 'Beagle.' " In March 1834 he significantly confided to Henslow that "if nothing unforeseen happens I will stick to the voyage; although, for what I can see, this may last till we return a fine set of white-headed old gentlemen." In July 1834 he told Catherine that a friend's handwriting on a note she had enclosed was "enough alone to make me long for this voyage to come to some end," and four months later he was telling her that he had "long been grieved & most sorry at the interminable length of the voyage (although I never would have quitted it) but the minute it was all over I could not make up my mind to return. I could not give up all the geological castles in the air which I had been building for the last two years." And in March 1835, when future plans at last appear to have been settled and the crew hoped to be back in England by September 1836, he told Henslow: "I am heartily glad of it, nothing should induce me to stay out any longer. As it is, it will be nearly as long as a seven years transportation. But now that I do clearly see England in the distance, I care for nothing, not even sea sickness. . . ." Little wonder that in mid-1836 he should write to Susan: "I loathe, I abhor the sea & all ships which sail on it."

But there was still half the world to be crossed. From the southern Pacific they made New Zealand and then Australia, crossed the Indian Ocean to turn the Cape of Good Hope and to sail for home. At Cape Town he dined with Sir John Herschel, who was halfway through a four-year study of the Southern Hemisphere's sky. Darwin recorded the occasion in his journal as "the most memorable event which, for a long period, I have had the good fortune to enjoy." And more than forty years later he remembered that Herschel "never talked much, but every word which he uttered was worth listening to."

Herschel had gained his fame, as his father had done, in helping to reveal that the solar system was merely a comparatively tiny speck in a vast universe. But like many great men of his day, he could not avoid the other great arguments of his times. Only four months before his dinner with Darwin he had written to Lyell, and it would seem almost inconceivable that he did not discuss with Darwin a main subject of that letter. "I allude," wrote Sir John, "to that mystery of mysteries the replacement of extinct species by others. Many will doubtless think your speculations too bold—but it is as well to face the difficulty at once. For my own part—I cannot but think it an inadequate conception of the Creator, to assume it as granted that his combinations are exhausted upon any one of the theatres of their former exercise—though in this, as in all his other works we are led by all analogy to suppose that he operates through a series of intermediate causes & that in consequence, the origination of fresh species, could it ever come under our cognizance would be found to be a natural in contradistinction to a miraculous process—although we perceive no indications of any process actually in progress which is likely to issue in such a result."

Were such thoughts among the words that Darwin thought "worth listening to"? One cannot be certain; but it seems likely that the species question was worrying him increasingly as HMS *Beagle* crossed the southern Atlantic to Brazil and then sailed north for England.

It was Sunday, October 2, 1836, before the ship docked at Falmouth, a flourishing port on England's southwest coast. Darwin without delay took the coach to Shrewsbury, 250 miles away, which he reached on the fifth. "I arrived here yesterday morning at breakfast-time," he wrote to Captain FitzRoy, "and, thank God, found all my dear good sisters and father quite well. My father appears more cheerful and very little older than when I left. My sisters assure me I do not look the least different, and I am able to return the compliment. Indeed, all England appears changed excepting the good old town of Shrewsbury and its inhabitants, which, for all I can see to the contrary, may go on as they now are to Doomsday."

FitzRoy, for his part, was already going the social rounds in London, taking tea with the diarist Caroline Fox and explaining to her the work on board his ship of young Charles Darwin, the "flycatcher" and "stone-pounder," as he described him.

3

Evolution of an Idea

IF any thoughts of a clerical future lingered in the "flycatcher's" mind during his first days back in England, they quickly evaporated. As he collected his specimens from the ship after she had sailed round the coast and up the Thames to London, where he successfully lobbied for a £1,000 government grant to assure publication of *The Zoology of H.M.S. "Beagle,"* the twenty-seven-year-old Darwin was still an avowed Christian. But the country vicarage had disappeared from his plans. In its place there crystallized a picture of the bustling argumentative community whose world was that of the Geological, the Linnean and the Royal societies.

For the almost casual letters he had sent back to Professor Henslow during the voyage had opened a door onto the scientific world in a way that he had never anticipated. Henslow had read the letters to the Cambridge Philosophical Society, in whose *Proceedings* they had been printed. He had, moreover, passed them to Sedgwick, who read parts of them to the Geological Society of London. It would be a gross exaggeration to say that Darwin had arrived back home to find himself famous. Yet his first original scientific observations had been welcomed by the experts; the impact on his contemporaries of the fossil, botanic and other specimens he collected from the *Beagle* could at least be imagined. And there were to be his journal and other scientific accounts of the voyage that were eventually to be published. A humble contribution to the noble structure of science, no doubt, but one that held out the prospect of something a good deal more substantial.

Lyell lost no time in seeking him out and invited him to dine and meet Richard Owen, later to become the foremost zoologist of his day and Darwin's implacable enemy. "The idea of the Pampas going up, at the rate of an inch in a century, while the Western Coast and Andes rise many feet and unequally, has long been a dream of mine," Lyell wrote to Darwin a few weeks later when speculating on earth movements. "What a splendid field you have to write upon!" The Geological Society had, at the moment, no vacancies for new members but, Darwin was assured, "you stand the first of those who are knocking at the door for admission."

He did not have long to wait, and by April 21, 1837, Lyell was writing to Sedgwick, "Darwin is a glorious addition to any society of geologists, and is working hard and making way, both in his book and in our discussions. I really never saw that bore [Dr. James Mitchell] so successfully silenced, or such a bucket of cold water so dexterously poured down his back, as when Darwin answered some impertinent and irrelevant questions about S. America." Less than a year later he was voted on to the Council and shortly afterward had taken on the burdens of one of the two secretary-ships—reluctantly, since he was already being warned by his doctor of overwork but was unwilling to refuse an appointment that took him to the heart of things. He was a controversial speaker, and after he had addressed the Geological Society in March 1838, in a lecture entitled "On the Connexion of Certain Volcanic Phenomena and on the Formation of Mountain-Chains and the Effects of Continental Elevations," Lyell wrote to his father-in-law, Leonard Horner: "in support of my heretical doctrines [Darwin] opened upon De la Beche [Sir Henry Thomas De la Beche, appointed in 1832 by the British government to carry out a geological survey of Britain], [John] Phillips [geologist and later Keeper of the Ashmolean Museum, Oxford], and others (for [George Bellas] Greenough was absent) his whole battery of the earthquakes and volcanos of the Andes, and argued that spaces at least a thousand miles long were simultaneously subject to earthquakes and volcanic eruptions. . . ."

It was also to the Geological Society that Darwin gave the results of what became a famous investigation on worms. While visiting Maer, Josiah Wedgwood II had pointed out the curious way in which layers of cinders, burnt marl or lime, spread on the surface of pasture lands, eventually disappeared under the grass. Earthworms, Darwin suggested, were not only responsible for the disappearance, but also brought up the finer particles of earth and left them on the surface. Intrigued by a subject of combined geological and biological interest, he made a series of diggings and decided that worms, after swallowing and digesting the finer portions of the soil, carried them to the surface and voided them in their castings. "The author," says the report of his paper in the Society's *Proceedings*, "concluded by remarking that it is probable that every particle of earth in old pasture land has passed through the intestines of worms, and hence, that in some senses, the term 'animal mould' would be more appropriate than 'vegetable mould.' "

He spoke frequently to the Society, but although he would read over papers carefully before the meeting, continued to feel nervous, as he remembered years later. "I could somehow see nothing all around me but the paper," he admitted to his son William, "and I felt as if my body was gone, and only my head left." Yet he still retained some of the vivacity that was missing from his later years. At the somewhat hilarious gatherings of the Society's Dining Club, it has been written, "the hardy wielders of the hammer not only drank port—and plenty of it—but wound up their meal with a mixture of Scotch ale and soda water, a drink which, as reminiscent of the 'field,' was regarded as especially appropriate to geologists. Even after the meetings, which followed the dinners, they reassembled for suppers, at which geological dainties, like 'pterodactyle pie' figured in the bill of fare, and fines of bumpers were inflicted on those who talked the 'ologies' "—the penalty for talking shop.

Oddly enough, it was on a geological question that Darwin made one of his rare scientific errors. In June 1837, he visited the "parallel roads" of Glen Roy in the Scottish Highlands. These are three shelves that indent both sides of the narrow glen, everywhere horizontal and parallel to each other, each shelf on one side of the glen exactly corresponding in height to its partner on the other side. Darwin spent a week in the glen and on September 6 noted in his personal journal: "Finished paper on Glen Roy — one of the most difficult & instructive tasks I was ever employed on." His answer to the mystery of the "roads," given in his paper published in 1839, was that they were beaches formed when Glen Roy had been filled with a branch of the sea. He propounded his theory in no uncertain terms, and a decade later, after Leonard Horner had suggested that he should write something further for the Geological Committee of the Royal Society, replied that he was puzzled as to how he should do it. "If Agassiz [Louis Agassiz, who was later his opponent in the debate over *The Origin of Species*] or Buckland [William Buckland, former president of the Geological Society] are on the Committee they will sneer at the whole thing and declare the beaches are those of a glacier lake, than which I am sure I could convince you that there never was a more futile theory."

Darwin clung to his view until 1861, when, at his suggestion, Thomas Francis Jamieson visited Glen Roy to investigate. Jamieson showed that the "roads" were, in fact, the former shorelines of a glacier lake. "Your arguments seem to me conclusive," Darwin admitted to him. "I give up the ghost. My paper is one long gigantic blunder. . . . I have been for years anxious to know what was the truth, & now I shall rest contented, though ashamed of myself. How rash it is in science to argue because any case is not one thing, it must be some second thing which happens to be known to the writer."

Darwin almost compensated for his mistake on Glen Roy by being one of the first to maintain that glaciers had once covered large areas of Britain. In his day, this was still a fact for which science was hardly prepared. In 1831, when he and Sedgwick had traversed North Wales, they had visited Cwm Idwal in the Nant Ffrancon Pass, one of the most dramatic geological areas in the country. But, he later wrote, "neither of us saw a trace of the wonderful glacial phenomena all around us: we did not notice the plainly scored rocks, the perched boulders, the lateral and terminal moraines. Yet these phenomena are so conspicuous that, as I declared in a paper published many years afterwards in the Philosophical Magazine, a house burned down by fire did not tell its story more plainly than did this valley. If it had still been filled by a glacier, the phenomena would have been less distinct than they are now."

But the unthinkable had slowly become credible. A British Ice Age in the geologically recent past was revealed as worthy of investigation, and in 1841 William Buckland had read a paper to the Geological Society "On Diluvio-glacial Phenomena in Snowdonia and in Adjacent Parts of North Wales." Darwin had little time for Buckland, describing him in his autobiography in uncharacteristically caustic terms as "though very good humoured & good-natured [he] seemed to me a vulgar & almost coarse man. He was incited more by a craving for notoriety, which sometimes made him act like a buffoon, than by a love of science." But Darwin had studied in South America the erratic blocks that provided Buckland with much of his evidence in Wales and now took an early opportunity of following in Buckland's footsteps. His subsequent paper stands, as Sir Archibald Geikie was later to say, "almost at the top of the long list of English contributions to the history of the Ice Age."

One of Darwin's most urgent tasks after his return to England was to make certain that the specimens he had collected on the *Beagle* would find a suitable home. Since he had traveled on a Royal Navy vessel, he felt that they should remain in Britain. Otherwise he might have sent at least some of them to the Paris Museum of Natural History, where he believed they would have been better cared for—although in that case, as he wrote to Richard Owen, he would "feel like a knight who had lost his armorial bearings." Some specimens eventually went direct to the British Museum. Others went to the Zoological Society of London's Museum, and the fossil mammals to the Royal College of Surgeons, although all these were later sent either to the British Museum or to what was to become the Natural History Museum—formally, the British Museum (Natural History).

In March 1837 Darwin met John Gould, the Zoological Society's taxidermist, and a leading British ornithologist who was to produce forty-one magnificent folio volumes of birds, illustrated by no less than 2,999 plates. Gould's report astounded Darwin. There were, he was told, three species of mockingbird from the Galápagos among his specimens—the very possibility of which, he had already admitted, would undermine the stability of species—while the finches belonged to thirteen different species. If ever there was one moment when Darwin was pushed across the border dividing creationism from evolution, this may well have been that moment.

By this time he had moved into bachelor apartments in Great Marlborough Street, off Regent Street, a few doors from his brother, Erasmus. A countryman at heart, he disliked London, writing to William Darwin Fox, "It is a sorrowful, but I fear too certain truth, that no place is at all equal, for aiding one in Natural History pursuits, to this odious dirty smoky town, where one can never get a glimpse, at all, that is best worth seeing in nature." And to Leonard Jenyns he wrote: "I miss a walk in the country very much; this London is a vile smoky place, where a man loses a great part of the best enjoyments in life. But I see no chance of escaping, even for a week, from this prison for a long time to come." Indeed, he now settled down in London and, with the help of Syms Covington, began writing up the *Beagle* material, a task he estimated would take him two years. "Now the scheme [is]," he wrote on March 28, 1837, "that the Captain makes a plum pudding out of his own journal and that of Capt. King's kept during the last [i.e., the previous] voyage, which together will make two volumes and the third I am to have to myself. I intend making it in a journal form, but following the order of places rather than that of time, giving results of my geology and habits of animals where interesting."

In Great Marlborough Street he also began serious work on the species problem, the obsession that was to become the intellectual core of his life. After returning to England, he was later to write, it occurred to him "that by following the example of Lyell in Geology, & by collecting all facts which bore in any way on the variation of animals & plants under domestication & nature, some light might perhaps be thrown on the whole subject." These facts were recorded in four notebooks, which, particularly during recent years, have been the subject of an enormous amount of analysis and exegesis. The first notebook was started in July 1837, but before this, Darwin stated in his autobiography, he had "long reflected" on the subject of the origin of species. The second notebook was begun in February 1838, the third in July of the same year and the fourth in October. Two more had been used between 1839 and 1842. From these, from the extended material written up from the notes taken on the *Beagle*, and from his reading lists that have survived, it is possible to build up a picture of how his ideas developed—or, more accurately, a number of pictures, since many of the entries can be interpreted in more than one way, and Darwin's thoughts were themselves in a constant state of flux as he discarded parts of his developing theory, added fresh ideas, and then again dropped the result into the melting pot.

"During the voyage of the 'Beagle,'" he was later to write, "I had been deeply impressed by discovering in the Pampean formation great fossil animals covered with armour like that on the existing armadillos; secondly by the manner in which closely allied animals replace one another in proceeding southwards over the Continent; & thirdly by the South American character of most of the productions of the Galapagos archipelago, & more especially by the manner in which they differ slightly on each island of the group."

His observations gradually began to erode his belief in the immutability of species. But it was a slow process. The new theory did not arise fully formed from the waves, a creation as self-contained as Archbishop Ussher's inspiration of what had happened on an October morning in 4004 B.C. In July 1837 Darwin noted in his personal journal that he had that month opened his first notebook on "Transmutation of Species," and continued: "— Had been greatly struck from about Month of previous March on character of S. American fossils — & species on Galapagos Archipelago. — These facts origin (especially latter) of all my views."

The views were expanded and built up with the help of the material that he now began to accumulate. He had earlier "determined to collect blindly every sort of fact, which cd bear any way on what are species." They came from breeders of domestic animals, from papers in scientific journals, and in the answers of scientific friends and acquaintances to specific questions that Darwin asked them over many years. In January 1841 he wrote to William Darwin Fox, saying: "I continue to collect all kinds of facts, about 'Varieties & Species,' for my some-day work—[to] be so entitled;—the smallest contributions thankfully accepted;—descriptions of offspring of all crosses between all domestic birds & animals, dogs, cats, &c., &c., very valuable. Don't forget, if your half-bred African cat should die, that I should be very much obliged for its carcase sent up in [a] little hamper for skeleton— it or any cross-bred pigeons, fowl, duck, &c., &c., will be more acceptable than the finest haunch of Venison, or the finest turtle." Some fifteen years later, his work still continuing, he noted to Fox: "I shd . . . be very glad for a 7 days duckling and for one of the old birds should one ever die a natural death," and a few weeks afterward suggested his unexpressed feelings when he wrote to Fox again, saying: "I have done the black deed & *murdered* an angelic little Fan-tail, & Pouter at 10 days old." In 1856 he asks Laurence Edmondston, the Scottish naturalist: "Is the Rabbit wild in the Shetlands? . . . A Shetland specimen put in a jar with lots of salt wd be a treasure to me." And in 1858 he asks the entomologist Henry Tibbats Stainton seven questions on insects that he wanted answered for his work on sexual selection before adding: "Now you will think me, I fear, the most unreasonable & troublesome man in Gr[ea]t Britain; & I can hardly expect you to go *seriatim* through my queries. But I shd be truly obliged for any hints, with permission to quote you."

One of his most valuable correspondents throughout the 1840s and 1850s was William Bernhard Tegetmeier, a well-known writer on poultry whom he continually bombarded with questions about "breeds of fowls, Turkish fowls, Indian jungle fowls, rumpless fowls, eggs with chicks just hatching, down in young birds, owls' eggs, laughing pigeons, runts, carriers, skanderoons, rabbits, length of cats' teeth, bees, sex-ratios at birth, race-horse records, and what not besides."

The main stream of information, however, came in replies to the questionnaires Darwin circulated to anyone who might be able to help. One that has survived was an eight-page pamphlet. Its twenty-one numbered paragraphs contained forty-four queries, of which the first was: "If the cross offspring of any two races of birds or animals, be interbred, will the progeny keep as constant, as that of any established breed; or will it tend to return in appearance to either parent?" Other questions asked: "Do you know instances of any peculiarities in structure, present for the first time in an animal of any breed, being inherited by the grand-children and *not by the children*?" and "Where any animal whatever (even man) has been trained to some particular way of life, which has given peculiarity of form to its body by stunting some parts and developing others, can you give any instances of the offspring inheriting it?"

Darwin continued these questionings long after he had ceased to believe in the immutability of species. Indeed, they went on even after publication of *The Origin of Species*, and a letter from him that the *Gardeners' Chronicle* published on January 21, 1860, is an illuminating example of the range of the queries he had been putting for more than two decades. "I hope," he began, "that some of your readers will respond to Mr. Westwood's wish, and give any information which they may possess on the permanence of cross-bred plants and animals. Will Mr. Westwood be so good as to give a reference to any account of the variability of the Swedish Turnip? I did not even know that it was reputed to be a cross-bred production. I am aware that this is supposed to be the case with some Turnips; but I have searched in vain for authentic history of their origin. No one, I believe, doubts that cross-bred productions tend to revert in various degrees to either parent for many generations; some say for a dozen, others for a score or even more generations. But cannot breeders adduce some cases of crossed breeds of sheep and pigs (such as the Shropshire or Oxford sheep, or Lord Harborough's pigs) which are now true? With respect to the Cottagers' Kale, I was so much surprised at the accounts of its trueness that

I procured seed from the raisers; but in my soil the plants were far from presenting a uniform appearance."

By the time that he opened his second notebook in February 1838, Darwin had, in the words of Gavin de Beer, who published and annotated the notebooks, become satisfied that transmutation "had occurred when populations were isolated and no longer able to prevent the variation that resulted from sexual reproduction and is normally kept in check by breeding throughout the population. In this way varieties become split off from species and eventually become species themselves, while old species become extinct, thereby increasing the separation between the surviving species, many of which after being split into daughter species become genera." This was what Darwin meant (in the first editions of *The Origin*), De Beer continues, "by 'my theory,' and it was already distinctively his even before he thought of natural selection because nobody before him had combined genetic variation, isolation, divergence, and extinction into a coherent theory of transmutation of species."

Yet Darwin was only at the first stage of his work. His open-mindedness, which played such a large part in delaying the writing and publication of *The Origin of Species*, was not the result of scientific caution alone. Flickering through much that he wrote over these years there is the implied belief that convincing evidence might, after all, be lacking for a theory that would distress so many relatives and friends. Willing to wait until he believed his case to be irrefutable, he ensured that his chances of survival were greater than those of his predecessors. "I worked on true Baconian principles," he later claimed of his work from the summer of 1837 on, "and without any theory collected facts on a whole-sale scale, more especially with respect to domesticated productions, by printed enquiries, by conversation with skilful breeders & gardeners, & by extensive reading." The "without any theory" should not be taken too literally. By 1837 he was doubting the immutability of species, and at one point gave the book he would one day write the title of "Transmutation of Species." He was beginning to believe that, if his doubts were confirmed, what was true at one level of life might be true at others. To this extent he was collecting facts in the hope of confirming or denying that new species had slowly come into existence as life had moved on through the long corridors of time, which geologists had shown stretched back into an inconceivably remote past. In fact, it can be argued that by this time he believed in evolution, tentatively if not yet firmly, and was questioning merely the mechanism by which it operated.

Throughout 1837 and 1838 he also continued with the *Beagle* work. It was tough going. "We have seen Darwin several times; not so often as we could have wished, but he is working so hard that he does not go out," Leonard Horner wrote in the summer of 1837 to his daughter, who had married Charles Lyell. "He had not when I saw him received any part of his MSS in type. During the week that Dr. Forchhammer was in town lately, we saw him four or five times, and were much pleased with him. I have not seen any one for a long time with a greater store of accurate knowledge." At times Darwin was surprised at his own literary adventurousness, writing in November 1837 to Henslow: "If I live till I am eighty years old I shall not cease to marvel at finding myself an author: in the summer, before I started, if anyone had told me I should have been an angel by this time, I should have thought it an equal improbability. This marvellous transformation is all owing to you."

Meanwhile he continued working on the material obtained from pigeon, horse and dog breeders whose deliberate crosses produced observable results, and began to add that of horticulturists. From all of them it seemed clear that by careful selection a breeder could, over a number of generations, produce animals and plants in which certain characteristics were emphasized; so much so, in fact, that the characteristics eventually indicated a new variety. At this point two questions arose. If the process of artificial selection were continued long enough, would not the changes produced cross that shadowy borderline that separated different varieties from different species? Although Darwin's mind was well tuned to appreciate the geological immensities of time that were as familiar to Lyell as the passing seasons, he could foresee little hope of finding an answer to this question. In the 1830s too little was known to start experimenting with the fruit flies, whose generations followed each other in days, let alone with the bacteria of twentieth-century biochemists, where the process is reduced to minutes. Common sense suggested that if careful breeding could produce the bulldog or the pouter pigeon, then production of new species was merely a matter of time. But, as Darwin's critics were to point out, that was a matter of faith.

More important was the fact that the faster horses, swifter pigeons and better-adapted dogs of the professional breeders were the end products of a plan specifically designed to create them. For nature in the raw there appeared to be only Paley's God, a designer in whom Darwin no longer had unqualified faith. As he was to ask years later, "Did He cause the frame and mental qualities of the dog to vary in order that a breed might be formed of indomitable ferocity, with jaws fitted to pin down the bull for man's brutal sport?"

But if God's directing influence was not involved, what was the machinery that over the millennia had been pushing life onward from one specification to the next? Darwin's answer was natural selection, a process that enabled the fittest to survive. Its application to evolution as a whole is linked with his reading of one particular sentence in the Reverend Thomas Malthus's *Essay on the Principle of Population; or, a View of its Past and Present Effects on Human Happiness; with an Inquiry into our Prospects Respecting the Future Removal or Mitigation of the Evils Which it Occasions*, and Malthus has been given an importance, sometimes greatly inflated, in Darwin's development of the theory. Chronology, which, as Winston Churchill once said, is the substance of history, tells a more cautious tale.

In the first of Darwin's transmutation notebooks, which was closed in February 1838, he stated that while the southern rhea, not being well adapted to its environment, might perish, the mockingbird, being well adapted, would increase and flourish. And he went on: ". . . death of a species is a consequence (contrary to what would appear from America) of non-adaptation of circumstances." So by February 1838 he was already seeing failure to adapt as a key to the transmutation of species. To Alfred Russel Wallace, the first man to plan an expedition in search of material related to the species question, he wrote years later: "I came to the conclusion that selection was the principle of change from the study of domesticated productions; and then, reading Malthus, I saw at once how to apply this principle." The reading began in September 1838 according to his contemporary notebooks, and took place in October according to his autobiography, written many years later. These later recollections note that it was "for amusement" that he turned to Malthus's famous book. Darwin's own copy of Malthus was the sixth edition of 1826, on which he himself had written the date "1841"—three years after it had made such an impression on him. It therefore seems possible, if not likely, that he had read the fifth edition (1817) of Malthus in the fine library at Maer. If so, the

Wedgwoods will have made a significant contribution not only to the Darwin finances but to Charles Darwin's intellectual history.

The sentence that struck him read as follows: "It may safely be pronounced, therefore, that population, when unchecked, goes on doubling itself every twenty-five years, or increases in a geometrical ratio." Details of Darwin's Malthus reading remained unknown for some time after his death because of his practice, when writing *The Origin of Species* some two decades after the notebooks were filled, of cutting out from the notebooks the pages containing the material he most needed. These pages, more than 300 in all, contained those with the Malthus entry, and for some years students of Darwin had to be content with the less specific reference in the autobiography. Some 230 pages were eventually recovered from material that his great grandson, Sir Robin Darwin, had deposited with the Science Museum and that were then transferred to the British Museum (Natural History). Other pages were found in the Cambridge University Library, and by comparing the scissor marks on the pages with those on the stumps left in the notebooks, many gaps in the pre-*Origin* record were eventually filled. Among them was Darwin's first reaction to Malthus.

On page 134 of the third "D" notebook, under the date of September 28, he wrote:

> We ought to be far from wondering of changes in number of species, from small changes in nature of locality. Even the energetic language of Decandolle [Alphonse Louis Pierre Pyrame de Candolle] does not convey the warring of the species as inference from Malthus — increase of brutes must be prevented solely by positive checks, excepting that famine may stop desire—in nature production does not increase, while no check prevail, but the positive check of famine & consequently death. . . .
>
> Population is increase[d] at geometrical ratio in FAR SHORTER time than 25 years—yet until the one sentence of Malthus no one clearly perceived the great check amongst men. — there is spring, like food used for other purposes as wheat for making brandy. — Even a *few* years plenty, makes population in man increase & an *ordinary* crop causes a dearth. Take Europe on an average every species must have same number killed year with year by hawks, by cold &c. — even one species of hawk decreasing in number must affect instantaneously all the rest. —The final cause of all this wedging, must be to sort out proper structure & adapt it to changes. — to do that for form, which

Malthus shows is the final effect (by means however of volition) of this populousness on the energy of man. . . . One may say there is a force like a hundred thousand wedges trying force every kind of adapted structure into the gaps in the oeconomy of nature, or rather forming gaps by thrusting out weaker ones.

Thus did Darwin see every organism fitting into a suitable niche.

But how—discarding the "for amusement" of his latter-day recollections—did Darwin come to Malthus? Silvan S. Schweber in "The Origin of the 'Origin' Revisited" has used Darwin's notebooks, as well as a mass of ancillary evidence, to suggest a line that began with a reading in the *Athenaeum* of David Brewster's *Edinburgh Review* account of Auguste Comte's *Cours de Philosophie Positive.* This led on to Dugald Stewart's life of Adam Smith, and this in turn led to a review of Adolphe Quetelet, the Belgian statistician. Here Darwin found a reiteration of Malthus's claim that, while population would grow geometrically, food supplies would do so only arithmetically. And so back to the original Malthus.

In his autobiography Darwin noted that "being well prepared to appreciate the struggle for existence which everywhere goes on from long-continued observation of the habits of animals and plants, it at once struck me that under these circumstances favourable variations would tend to be preserved & unfavourable ones to be destroyed. The result of this would be the formation of new species. Here then I had at last got a theory by which to work, but I was so anxious to avoid prejudice, that I determined not for some time to write down the briefest sketch of it." But the explanation he gave to Wallace very much nearer the event appears to have been more accurate. He had a theory, only half formed, by the time he read Malthus; then it became evident how the theory worked in practice. Malthus's illustration that while an unchecked population increased in a geometrical ratio of 1–2–4–8, subsistence increased in the arithmetical ration of 1–2–3–4, pointed the way to Darwin's uncomfortable solution: survival of the fittest, or, more accurately, nonsurvival of the less fit. Although somewhat allergic to mathematics, he had no difficulty in adapting Malthus's human statistics to the prodigalities of nature. A single salmon can produce more than 28 million eggs in its lifetime. A single rotifer's 30 eggs would multiply after 65 generations, if all descendants lived, into a sphere larger than the confines of the known universe.

A century and a half ago, Darwin lacked such facts and figures.

What he did know was that, of the prodigal populations that nature produced, there survived only a small percentage. He knew, also, that members of a species were, to an extent that varied from small to minute, different from each other. Even kittens from the same litter sired by the same tomcat showed differences as, for that matter, did human twins. From these two facts of life—the pressure on population and the variability within species—Darwin drew his main conclusion. If some variations were useful in the battle for survival, he wrote, "can we doubt (remembering that many more individuals are born than can possibly survive) that individuals having any advantage, however slight, over others, would have the best chance of surviving and of procreating their kind? On the other hand, we may feel sure that any variation in the least degree injurious would be rigidly destroyed. This preservation of favourable variations and the rejection of injurious variations, I call Natural Selection."

Whether Malthus was of primary importance or was merely "a little nudge that pushed Darwin across a threshold at which he was already standing" is likely to remain a subject for controversy. But Darwin's "D" notebook, begun on July 15, 1838, and apparently ending on October 2 of the same year, carries a later penciled note: "Towards close I first thought of selection owing to struggle." The important point is that in 1838 the idea of natural selection was no more than a belief and that much hard work was still required before Darwin launched it on the world. In particular, it was necessary to show that successions of minute variations were sufficient, even when taking place over the lengthy periods that geologists were now discussing, for the production of animals different enough from their predecessors to be classed as new species. From the start of his observations, Darwin appears to have taken it for granted that if species were not immutable, that fact would apply throughout the whole of the organic world. What was true of the birds and the plants he had collected on the *Beagle*'s voyage would be true of insects and true of mammals. If fishes had developed by a minute succession of variations from one species to another, then the same would be true of the primates. This brought Darwin to the delicate question of man himself. "As soon as I had become in the year 1837 or 1838, convinced that species were mutable productions," he later wrote, "I could not avoid the belief that man must come under the same law." However, discretion was better than publication, and at a late stage in his researches he wrote: "I think I shall avoid the whole subject [of man], as so surrounded with prejudices; though I fully admit it is the highest and most interesting problem for the naturalist."

In *The Origin* he merely remarked about the differences between the races of man that "some little light can apparently be thrown on the origin of these differences, chiefly through sexual selection of a particular kind, but without here entering on copious details my reasoning would appear frivolous." Years later, he said in his autobiography that although he did not discuss the origin of any particular species, he "thought it best, in order that no honourable man should accuse me of concealing my views, to add that by the work in question 'light would be thrown on the origin of man & his history.'" This was, as Darwin himself virtually admitted, a careful piece of side-stepping. But he went no further. "It would," he explained in his autobiography, "have been useless & injurious to the success of the book to have paraded without giving any evidence my conviction with respect to his origin."

Darwin appears to have learned this lesson in the art of survival from Lyell, who in June 1838 had told him: "In regard to the origination of new species I am very glad to find that you think it probable that it may be carried on through the intervention of intermediate causes. I left this rather to be inferred [in his *Principles of Geology*], not thinking it worthwhile to offend a certain class of person by embodying in words what would only be a speculation. . . ." It was, moreover, possible with but little difficulty to have the best of both worlds. When the intervention of intermediate causes had first occurred to him, Lyell continued, "the idea struck me as the grandest which I had ever conceived so far as regards the attributes of the Presiding Mind. . . ." The belief was to have a long history among those who tried to square their religious feelings with the evidence for the mutability of species. God moved in a mysterious way his wonders to perform, and that way might even include evolution.

Darwin's reluctance to tackle man's history was not only due to his wish to stir up religious opposition as little as possible, but the outcome of his innate desire for a quiet life and his hopes for the success of the book. There was also his genuine reluctance to offend relatives and friends. He himself had only slowly begun to give up his religious faith under pressure of the scientific evidence he was accumulating. It had been a gradual process, as he explained when he wrote his autobiography at the age of sixty-seven, explaining "disbelief crept over me at a very slow rate, but was at last complete. The rate was so slow that I felt no distress." He then continued, in words that his wife censored out of his account for more than half a century, "& have never since doubted even for a single second that my conclusion was correct. I can indeed hardly see how anyone ought to wish Christianity to be true; for if so, the plain language of the text seems to show that the men who do not believe, and this would include my Father, Brother & almost all my best friends, will be everlastingly punished.

"And this is a damnable doctrine."

Darwin was a kindly man. In public he dodged the issue as long as he could and felt it possible to claim of *The Origin* with almost Jesuitical casuistry that it need not offend religious feelings. And it is significant that while the first edition of *The Origin* ended with the words: "There is grandeur in this view of life, with its several powers, having been originally breathed into a few forms or into one . . ." he made an addition in the second edition that was very soon required. After "breathed" there now came the words "by the Creator." If politics is the art of the possible, Darwin knew that the art of survival consisted of not offending more readers than was absolutely necessary.

From 1838 on, his material on the species problem began steadily to increase; so did his bouts of ill health. Both developments are reflected in the entries in his personal journal. On February 25, 1838, he "speculated much about Existence of Species & read more than usual." On September 14 he records: "Frittered these foregoing days days [*sic*] away in working on Transmutation theories & correcting Glen Roy. Began Crater of Elevation Theory. . . . *All September* read a good deal on many subjects; thought much upon religion." For December 24 of the following year he reports: "became unwell & with the exception of two or three days remained so till the 24th of February. In the interval read a little for Transmut. theory, but otherwise lost three whole months." Throughout this period there are regular entries such as "did very little on account of being unwell" and "wasted some time by being unwell," while he records of the autumn of 1840, "when well enough did a good deal of species work."

His troubles included headaches, stomach pains, fatigue and a general indisposition. Although worry and overwork suggest some explanation, the regular continuation of such bouts throughout a long life has led to Darwin's being stigmatized as a hypochondriac.

It is unlikely that this was so, although later he may occasionally have overstressed ill health as a reason for avoiding social duties he disliked. But as the anthropologist Sir Arthur Keith has emphasized, "His ailments were felt, not imagined." Moreover, the disabling effects were real enough. In 1841 he tried to attend an evening meeting of the Geological Society's Council but, as Leonard Horner wrote to Lyell, found it too much. It had, Darwin wrote, "been a bitter mortification for me to digest the conclusion that the 'race is for the strong,' and that I shall probably do little more, but be content to admire the strides others make in science." In his personal journal for 1848, he wrote: "From July to end of year, unusually unwell, with swimming of head, depression, trembling, many bad attacks of sickness." To Syms Covington, his secretarial handyman from the *Beagle,* he wrote in the following year, at the age of forty: "I thought all this winter that I should not recover. . . . Speaking of walks, I fear my day is done, & I could never tire you again. I have not been able to walk a mile for some years, but now with the water cure I am getting stronger again."

It was possibly the prospect of improvement that induced him for six years, beginning in 1849, to make a daily diary of health. Written out a page to a month, its entries varied from "night pretty good" to "poor" and "poorly," and its monthly comments gave such information as "best month since April 1850." A code of dashes and underlinings reinforced the entries, and it is clear from Darwin's occasional comments—"I think I am not so strict as I used to be"—that he tried to keep the record as subjective as possible.

Although he gave up the diary in 1854 he remained worried about his health, and that year, when invited to become president of the British Association's Natural History Section at their Liverpool meeting, he replied that he was not equal to it, adding, "Very little fatigue, or excitement or anxiety (of which I sh^d have plenty) almost invariably brings on so much swimming of the head, nausea, & other symptoms, that the effect of sitting 2 or 3 (or even less) [*sic*] in a public chair would be quite intolerable to me." In 1860, he wrote to Leonard Horner that he had "gone back latterly to my bad ways, and fear I shall never be decently well and strong." Three years later, spending a week in London, he was "so liable to illness that he could not venture to come to [the Horners] either in the evening, or to breakfast." In 1869, with another thirteen years' heavy work to go, he writes of a scientist: "I would ask him to Down [House], but the fatigue to me of receiving a stranger is something which to you would be utterly unintelligible." And the same year, spending a holiday in North Wales, he writes to Hooker, "I have hardly crawled half a mile from the house, & then been fearfully fatigued. — It is enough to make one wish oneself quiet in a comfortable tomb."

Darwin, requiring a rest on the sofa after half-an-hour's conversation with a visitor, deploring in his notes and letters the fact that he could work only a limited number of hours each day, was a gravely different man from the exuberant Darwin of the *Beagle*. As Sir Peter Medawar has written: "Ill people suspected of hypochondria or malingering have to pretend to be iller than they really are and may then get taken in by their own deception. They do this to convince others." However, Darwin's inconveniencing afflictions were genuine, and more than one theory has been put forward to explain the symptoms that encouraged him to act like a recluse—a role, it must not be forgotten, that did give him the quiet necessary to accumulate, and process, the material for what was to become *The Origin*.

After his death it was maintained for a while, with some plausibility, that the trouble had been Chagas's disease. It was known that the causative agent was *Trypanosoma cruzi*, often carried by Benacus, the great black bug of the pampas, and Darwin had recorded that he had been bitten by the bug at Luxan in the Argentine. The latest alternative is brucellosis, or undulant fever, an infection whose symptoms had not been diagnosed in Darwin's day. This possibility was suggested in Argentina by Dr. J. Luis Minoprio, of Mendoza, to the paleontologist George Gaylord Simpson, who visited Mendoza and was told that brucellosis was common in the area. "I am inclined to agree with [Dr.] Minoprio on this point," Simpson has written, "but no one else seems to, preferring such (as it seems to me) quite unlikely diagnoses as neurosis or poisoning."

Early in the present century the more fashionable psychoanalytic explanation began to counterbalance others. It was assumed, on the flimsiest of evidence, that Darwin had developed a father complex owing to Robert Darwin's alleged mental bludgeoning of his son and that this was the basis of his later troubles. Like many psychoanalytic explanations, it was a conclusion that relied on faith rather than the possibility of proof or disproof; however, the same, it must be admitted, is also true of what today seems the more straightforward and likely cause. Darwin had only slowly given up his religious faith. His wife, Emma, whom he married in 1839, less than two years after he began collecting his species material, was never to do so. He feared that what was developing into his life's work might destroy her belief and with it part of her life, and the mental strain could have expressed itself in physical symptoms. But in addition to his personal distress there was a wider emotion. Pulled one way by a dedication to following the truth wherever it led, Darwin was yet part of a confident world, which he sensed he was destroying. He was an unhappy dynamiter, and the unhappiness only reinforced the misery it was so difficult to keep from his mind. Thus it is possible to avoid the larger lunacies of psychoanalysis and yet believe that Darwin's physical illnesses may have been, at least in part, the result of a mental conflict created by his work.

Additional evidence for this is provided by the fact that after 1870, when the main battle for evolution had been won, his health appears to have improved. There was still opposition, of course, but it no longer presented the same threat as it had earlier. The change of emphasis is suggested in a letter to Wallace: "I have taken up old botanical work and have given up all theories."

Earlier there had been a constant predisposition to accept illness, which was almost a feature of life at Down House. Gwen Raverat, the daughter of Darwin's son George, has explained how this came about: "The trouble was that in my grandparents' house it was a distinctive and a mournful pleasure to be ill. This was partly because my grandfather was always ill . . . and partly because it was so delightful to be pitied and nursed by my grandmother. . . . I have sometimes thought that she must have been rather too sorry for her family when they were unwell . . . the attitude of the whole Darwin family to sickness was most unwholesome. At Down, ill health was considered normal."

As far as Charles was concerned, there was one compensation, emphasized by his friend John Tyndall after Tyndall had met Asa Gray, the American botanist who was to become Darwin's main supporter in the United States. He "endeavoured to make it clear to Mrs. Gray," Tyndall wrote to Darwin a day or so later, "that your ill health was a benefit to you inasmuch as it compelled you to *ponder* a great deal, and this accounted for the extraordinary proportion of thought which your works display."

From 1837 onward the work included collection from a disparate range of sources. There were his *Beagle* experiences, items from a multitude of specialist journals, and a vast gathering of facts that served to strengthen his belief not only that species were mutable, but also that the "fit" between existing species and their environmental needs was the result of natural selection rather than of Paley's "Design."

Before the later ill health began to limit his activity, work formed the background to the more conventional labors of the young scientist-about-town. He discoursed and corresponded with men whose opinions mattered, who saw in him a rising star, and who wondered only whether he might not be too reserved, too wrapped up in some private work of his own, to gain his rightful place in the vigorous world of Victorian science.

Darwin already enjoyed the friendship of Britain's leading geologist, Charles Lyell, and he was soon to gain that of a man who was later to be of equal value to him. This was Joseph Dalton Hooker, only twenty-two in 1839. Son of Sir William Jackson Hooker, professor of botany at Glasgow University, he had been promised by Sir James Clark Ross that if he passed his medical examinations, he would be appointed naturalist to the expedition of discovery that Sir James was about to lead to the Antarctic. It was natural, therefore, that in the summer of 1839 Hooker should be discussing the prospect with a former officer of the *Beagle*. Darwin met the two men by chance in Trafalgar Square. "I was introduced," Hooker later wrote. "The interview was of course brief, and the memory of him that I carried away and still retain was that of a rather tall and rather broad-shouldered man, with a slight stoop, an agreeable and animated expression when talking, beetle brows, and a hollow but mellow voice; and that his greeting of his old acquaintance was sailor-like—that is, delightfully frank and cordial."

Hooker knew of the work that Darwin had carried out on the *Beagle,*, since proof sheets of the *Journal* had already been sent to Charles Lyell, who had passed them to his father; father had, in turn, passed them to his old friend Sir William Hooker, who had passed them on to his own son, since the voyage on which he hoped to embark was in some ways comparable to that of the *Beagle*. "I used to sleep with the sheets of the 'Journal' under my pillow," Hooker recalled years later, "that I might read them between waking and rising. They impressed me profoundly, I might say despairingly, with the variety of acquirements, mental and physical, required in a naturalist who should follow in Darwin's footsteps, whilst they stimulated me to enthusiasm in the desire to travel and observe."

By the time that Darwin first met Hooker, with repercussions that neither man will have foreseen, he had already put his private life on a fresh footing. Two years earlier he had drawn up a balance sheet listing the points for and against marriage. Among the advantages, he noted: "Charms of music and female chit-chat. These things good for one's health.—Forced to visit and receive relations *but terrible loss of time*." The balance was in favor of marriage, and he concluded his assessment with the words: "Never mind, trust to chance—keep a sharp look out.—There is many a happy slave." Darwin needed a wife, and he found one in his cousin Emma Wedgwood, whose father, Josiah II, had helped remove Robert Darwin's objections to Charles's joining the *Beagle*.

In marrying Emma on January 29, 1839, Darwin had picked the prototype of the Victorian wife, who devoted her life to caring for her husband and producing children at the acceptable and regular intervals. "I marvel at my good fortune," he wrote in old age, "that she, so infinitely my superior in every single moral quality, consented to be my wife." She had, he said, "borne with the utmost patience my frequent complaints from ill-health & discomfort." An accomplished needlewoman, who also rode, danced and skated, Emma brought not only the household and social graces but also a share of the Wedgwood financial prosperity, which added to the Darwins' already considerable wealth. A devout Christian, she never accepted her husband's views on evolution but was nevertheless, as he stressed, his "cheerful comforter throughout life" and the one person whose solicitude ensured that he was able to carry on with his work.

The marriage, like that of Darwin's father, Robert, was given a good financial start by the Wedgwoods, Josiah writing to Dr. Darwin to say: "I propose to do for Emma what I did for Charlotte and for three of my sons, give a bond for £5,000, and to allow her £400 a year as long as my income will supply it, which I have no reason for thinking will not be as long as I live." Dr. Darwin chipped in with £500 a year.

Late in 1838 Charles Darwin rented 12 Upper Gower Street, Bloomsbury, and on New Year's Day, 1839, began to get the home ready for his marriage on the twenty-ninth of January. By the twentieth he had the house well enough furnished to invite Charles Lyell and his wife to tea. "I was quite ashamed of myself today," he wrote to Emma that evening, "for we talked for half-an-hour unsophisticated Geology, with poor Mrs. Lyell sitting by, a monument of patience. I want *practice* in ill-treating the female sex. I did not observe Lyell had any compunction: I hope to harden my conscience in time: few husbands seem to find it difficult to effect this."

The Darwins were married at St. Peter's, Maer, on January 29, 1839, and later the same day took the train to London and moved into their first home. Upper Gower Street was part of an elegant neighborhood, but not particularly elegant in itself, and Darwin's daughter Henrietta often said that her father "used to laugh over the ugliness of their house in Gower Street, and the furniture in the drawing-room which he said combined all the colours of the Macaw in hideous discord." The house had a basement; above there was a ground floor and three storeys, on the uppermost of which Darwin had his study, half-filled with material from the *Beagle* voyage. At the back was a long narrow garden leading to a mews (a yard or street lined by buildings originally used as stables). Servants consisted of cook, housemaid and a man-servant variously known as footman or butler. This, after two predecessors, was Joseph Parslow, who stayed with the Darwins until 1875 and who became a much-appreciated part of the family furniture. In London, Darwin later complained, he did less scientific work than during any other period of his life. But he produced two papers for the Geological Society, one on earthquakes and one on erratic boulders. He finished writing his *Journal of Researches*, his zoological account of the *Beagle*'s voyage, and *The Structure and Distribution of Coral Reefs*, a book he had also begun as a result of observations during his journey around the world.

These were all strictly objective accounts. Nevertheless, careful observers no doubt saw the way that Darwin's mind was moving. Certainly Captain FitzRoy, by now even more convinced that the salvation of species had rested on Noah and the Ark, began to show a dislike for Darwin that eventually developed into something like paranoia. While it is obvious that FitRoy's hardening religious feelings provided the mainspring to this change, it was later sharpened by the enthusiasm with which Darwin's account of the voyage was received and the comparative lack of it that greeted the Captain's. Even before the *Beagle*'s return to Britain, FitzRoy had proposed to Darwin that they should collaborate in the story of the voyage—"that is," as Darwin told his family, "for him to have the disposal & arranging of my journal, & to mingle it with his own. Of course," he went on, "I have said I am perfectly willing, if he wants materials; or thinks the chit-chat details of my journal are any ways worth publishing."

Luckily enough, nothing came of this scheme. Three years later, Darwin appears to have become a little unimpressed with the Captain's efforts, as he explained in a letter to Susan. "I went to the Captain's yesterday evening to drink tea," he wrote in April 1839. "It did one good to hear Mrs. FitzRoy talk about her baby; it was so beautiful, and its little voice was such charming music. The Captain is going on very well, that is for a man who has the most consummate skill in looking at everything and everybody in a perverted manner. He is working very hard at his book, which I suppose will really be out in June. I looked over a few pages of Captain King's *Journal*: I was absolutely forced against all love of truth to tell the Captain that I supposed it was very good, but in honest reality no pudding for little schoolboys was ever so heavy. It abounds with Natural History of a very trashy nature. I trust the Captain's own volume will be better."

FitzRoy was already getting touchy about his young naturalist's coming volume, and after receiving a draft of Darwin's introduction replied on behalf of the Admiralty's officers:

Most people (who know anything of the subject) are aware that your going in the Beagle was a consequence of my original idea and suggestion—and of my offer to give up part of my accommodations—small as they were—to a scientific gentleman who would do justice to the opportunities so afforded. Those persons also know how much the Officers furthered your views—and gave you the preference upon all occasions—(especially [Lieutenant Bartholomew James] Sulivan, [Master's Assistant Alexander Burns] Usborne, [Ship's Surgeon Benjamin] Bynoe and [Mate and Assistant Surveyor John Lort] Stokes)— and think with me that a plain acknowledgment—without a word of flattery or fulsome praise—is a slight return due from you to those who held the ladder by which you mounted to a position where your industry, enterprise, and talent could be thoroughly demonstrated and become useful to our countrymen, and—I may truly say—to the world.

The sentence by which I was specially struck in your letter of Monday last—and for noticing which to my astonishment I was almost derided by a person I had thought your friend—and to whom therefore I went in the hope that he would suggest some change which I could not so well do being personally concerned—was this—"By the wish of Captain FitzRoy, and through the kindness of the Hydrographer Captain Beaufort &c."

I was also astonished at the total omission of any notice of the officers, either particular or general. My memory is rather tenacious respecting a variety of transactions in which you were concerned with them; and others in the Beagle. Perhaps you are not aware that the ship which carried us safely was the first employed in exploring and surveying, whose Officers were not ordered to collect, and were therefore at liberty to keep the best of all, nay, all their specimens for themselves. To their honour—they gave you the preference.

Some time ago it occurred to me that you had consulted with some person, not aware of the whole state of the case, who looked at the subject in a peculiar point of view, and I was informed yesterday by a conversation with Mr. Lyell that my conjecture was well founded.

He does not seem to consider that the connection of your volume with mine—and mine with Captain King's—is one of feeling and fidelity, not of *expediency*.

Believe me Darwin—I esteem *you* far too highly to break off from you willingly. I shall always be glad to see you and if there is any question to be discussed let us *talk* it over here [31, Chester Street, London]—or in your rooms—before referring it to the partial views and perhaps selfish feelings of persons who neither know, nor feel for, you—or for me—as your Father would feel for either of us.

> Pray believe me,
> Very sincerely yours,
> ROBT. FITZROY.

A technical account of the work carried out on the *Beagle* came in five separate volumes describing the zoology, edited and superintended by Darwin, although written by specialists, and published between 1839 and 1841. More popular, and more important in spreading Darwin's name, was his volume—VOL. III: *Journal and Remarks, 1832–1836*—in the three-volume *Narrative of the Surveying Voyages of His Majesty's Ships* Adventure *and* Beagle, *between the Years 1826 and 1836, Describing Their Examination of the Southern Shores of South America, and the* Beagle's *Circumnavigation of the Globe.* The first of the three volumes, all published in 1839, dealt with the earlier voyage under Captain King; the second, written by FitzRoy, ended with a twenty-five-page claim that the voyage had produced evidence in support of Genesis, of the Flood and of the Ark; the third, Darwin's *Journal and Remarks, 1832–1836*, which used material from his manuscript journal made from his eighteen small notebooks and from his more technical scientific notes, attracted much praise and helped to establish both his scientific standing and his ability as an author. Darwin's volume was ready before the other two and was actually in print in 1838—Leonard Horner, apparently, in view of his letter of May 20, 1838, to his wife, having received one of these early copies—although the three volumes did not appear together until 1839. To make the story of the *Journal* more complicated, it was also issued separately about August 1839, a volume priced at 18s. compared with the £3.18.0 for the set of three. In this separate volume, the title was changed to *Journal of Researches into the Geology and Natural History of the Various Countries Visited by H.M.S. "Beagle," under the Command of Captain Fitzroy, R.N., from 1832 to 1836*; at the same time Darwin added to his name on the title page the F.R.S. he had acquired on becoming a Fellow of the Royal Society earlier in 1839. However, when the volume was printed by John Murray in 1845, Darwin not only changed the title once again—to *Journal of Researches into the Natural History and Geology of the Countries Visited during the Voyage of H.M.S. Beagle Round the World, under the Command of Capt. Fitz Roy, R.N.*—but also incorporated a number of additions and amendments.

Even the Duke of Argyll, a later opponent, could praise the *Journal of Researches*. Although Leonard Horner was hardly unbiased, his reaction does much to explain the hold Darwin was able to retain on nonspecialist readers over the years. Mrs. Horner was enjoined by her husband to tell Darwin "that his book has been a very great treat to me. Those only will fully enjoy the book who have the advantage of knowing him personally; I fancy him talking to me all the while. I never read a book in a more conversational style, and it is quite delightful to me on that account. He comes out now and then with some of those exclamations which are so natural in talking, and so seldom written, and there is every now and then a piece of quaint humour which is very amusing; for instance about the numbers of hen ostriches trying to persuade an old cock to sit upon their common deposit of eggs, and the little beast that foolishly bores holes in a wall, and is marvellously surprised when he comes at the daylight on the other side."

It was not only men of science who were captivated by Darwin's style. J. E. Davis, second master of HMS *Terror*, companion ship to HMS *Erebus* on Ross's voyage to the Antarctic, who had borrowed Darwin's *Journal of Researches* from Hooker, later said: "I like Darwin's Journal much; he has accomplished what old Johnson said of Goldsmith when he heard he was going to write a Natural History: 'he will make it as interesting as a Persian tale.'"

Quite apart from naturalists and the general public, the admiralty also appears to have thought much of Darwin's work, as Darwin revealed in a note to Hooker after meeting in 1845 the official hydrographer, Captain Beaufort, whose efforts had brought him onto the *Beagle.* Beaufort, he reported, "*charged* me to keep a book & enter anything which occurred to me, which deserved examination or collection in any part of the world, & he wd sooner or later get it in the instructions to some ships. If anything occurs to you let me hear, for in the course of a month or two, I must write out something: I mean to urge collections of all kinds on any isolated islands. . . ."

Important as the book was in consolidating Darwin's reputation, writing it had hampered the work that had seized him soon after his return to England. His "Transmutation Notebooks" were still growing, the ragbag collections of a genius into which went references to papers read, speculations that had arisen in conversation, anything that could conceivably cast light on that mystery of mysteries, the species question. But obsessed as he was with the question, Darwin was usually modest about his own contribution. Thus in notebook "D" he wrote: "Seeing what von Buch (Humboldt) G. St. Hilaire & Lamarck have written I pretend to no originality of idea — (though I arrived at them quite independently & have used them since) the line of proof & reducing facts to law only merit if merit there be in following work."

The summer of 1842 was long undisputed as the period when Darwin first drafted out from his hoard of notes the first outline of what was eventually to become *The Origin of Species.* There was good enough reason for this, since there exists in the Darwin Archive at Cambridge a bundle of papers on whose covering sheet there is written in ink in Darwin's hand: "First Pencil Sketch of Species Theory. Written at Maer & Shrewsbury during May & June 1842"; and in his personal journal there is written for June 15, after a visit the previous month to Maer and Shrewsbury, the entry: "during my stay at Maer & Shrewsbury (5 years after commencement) wrote pencil sketch of my species theory." This would all appear to be conclusive.

Yet doubt was thrown on this chronology in 1974 when Peter J. Vorzimmer, an American researcher, noted that the bundle of papers contained in fact not only a thirty-five-page outline written in pencil but also a thirteen-page outline written in ink. This had been written, he maintained, in 1839. In 1982 this theory was assailed by a trio of Darwin scholars, David Kohn, Sydney Smith and Robert C. Stauffer, who analyzed the pages in the Cambridge bundle with their complex annotations, overwritings and changes. They also noted that following his first four "Transmutation Notebooks" Darwin had between 1839 and 1842 written the two further notebooks but had later dismembered them and removed all the pages that he considered of interest. And from their lengthy exegesis they concluded that "the mysterious 13-page ink manuscript, incorrectly dated by Vorzimmer to 1839" was in fact a copy of a draft outline made by Darwin in 1842.

The detailed exposition in the 1982 paper of how Darwin's beliefs expanded between 1837 and 1844 is cogently argued. But the paper does not refer to other points Vorzimmer makes to support his thesis. He pointed out that when Darwin in 1858 sent Hooker a yet later outline, he wrote over the contents page: "This was sketched in 1839 & copied out in full as was written & read by you in 1844." In 1859 Darwin, writing to Alfred Wallace, who had by this time put forward his own evolution theory, said: "It puts my extracts (written in 1839, now just twenty years ago!), which I must say in apology were never for an instant intended for publication, into the shade." Furthermore, in his autobiography, admittedly written as long afterward as 1876, Darwin was to write: "I gained much by my delay in publishing from about 1839, when the theory was clearly conceived, to 1859." Perhaps even more significant was the statement by Hooker and Lyell when the parallel theories of Darwin and Wallace were announced before the meeting of the Linnean Society in 1858. Hooker and Lyell, who had helped to stage-manage the occasion, described Darwin's contributions as "Extracts from a MS. work on Species . . . which was sketched in 1839, and copied in 1844 . . ." and Darwin's letter to Asa Gray, in 1857, "in which he repeats his views, and which shows that these remained unaltered from 1839 to 1857. . . ."

Whatever the exact chronology and significance of Darwin's early outlines and drafts, it was the pencil sketch of 1842 that remained in his memory. The first part described the selection of variations used in domestic breeding and went on to examine how the same process could be observed, working at a far slower rate, in wild species. Part two elaborated the fossil record and the geographical distribution of species. For Darwin, there was already little doubt about what it all meant. His theory of natural selection was the only theory that fitted the facts, whatever the protests raised by those who believed in the divine creation of immutable species. "With equal probability," he wrote, "did old cosmologists say fossils were created, as we now see them with a false resemblance to living beings; what would the Astronomer say to the doctrine that the planets moved according to the law of gravitation, but in consequence, from the Creator having willed each separate planet to move in its particular orbit. — I believe such a proposition (if we remove all prejudices) would be as legitimate, as to admit the certain groups of living and extinct organisms in their distribution, in *their* structure and in their relations one to another and to external conditions, agreed with the theory and showed signs of common descent, and yet were created distinct."

If Darwin's collection of facts since 1837 was the rubble that formed the foundation of his theory, the sketch of 1842 provided the ground plan of the building he was to erect on it. But it was only the start, and another decade and a half was to be required before the job was completed.

That decade and a half was to be spent not in London but in what was for Darwin a genuinely ideal environment. Emma had always preferred the country to the town, even London, where she enjoyed the opportunities of attending concerts. As for Darwin, he liked attending the meetings of the learned societies but found that social duties tended to interfere with his work. The couple had, therefore, lived in Gower Street little more than a year when they started looking about for something else. They eventually found it in Downe, 16 miles from London, a village of between 400 and 500 people some 500 feet up on the chalk downs southeast of the capital. And in September 1842 the Darwins moved to Down House, Downe, with their son William Erasmus, born in 1839, and their daughter Anne Elizabeth, born in 1841.

4

The Influence of Down

DOWN HOUSE, in the Kentish village of Downe, was a rambling old building in eighteen acres of grounds and fields. Until 1842, the village name had been spelled Down, but the government, fearful during the recurrent Irish troubles that it might be confused with County Down, had formally added an "e." Darwin refused to bring the name of his home into line.

There was already one celebrity in the village, since Sir John Lubbock, vice-president of the Royal Society and father of the Lubbock who was to become the 1st Lord Avebury, lived a mile away from Down House in High Elms whose 3,000 acres compared with Darwin's 18 acres. "My father came home one evening in 1841, quite excited, and said he had a great piece of news for me," the son has recalled. "He made us guess what it was, and I suggested that he was going to give me a pony. 'Oh,' he said, 'it is much better than that. Mr. Darwin is coming to live at Down.' I confess I was much disappointed, though I came afterwards to see how right he was."

Darwin was, in fact, to encourage the young Lubbock, who as naturalist coined the words "Paleolithic" and "Neolithic," and who as an M.P. brought bank holidays to Britain, earning himself the title "Saint Lubbock" among many thousands of workers, and introduced bills supporting public libraries and the preservation of ancient monuments. If he can "resist his future career of great wealth, business, and rank," Darwin told James Dwight Dana of Lubbock "[he] may do good work in natural history."

The walls of Down House were two feet thick, the windows rather small. There was a capital study and there were plenty of bedrooms. "We could hold the Hensleighs [Hensleigh Wedgwood, Emma Darwin's brother, his wife and their family], and you, and Susan and Erasmus all together," Darwin wrote to his sister Catherine. "House in good repair. Mr. Cresy (architect and friend) a few years ago laid out for the owner £1,500 and made a new roof. Water-pipes over house [water from deep well]—two bathrooms —pretty good offices and good stable-yard, etc. and a cottage." But a good deal of work had to be done before the house suited Darwin. And this, it turned out, was to be only the first installment, since for the next thirty years he continued to add rooms, take down walls, improve corridors, change the grounds and generally mold Down House to his individual taste. Perhaps there was something in the comment of one of his bricklayers, which Darwin reported to Susan. "A most deceptious property to buy, sir," and one whose surrounding countryside, crisscrossed by narrow, high-hedged lanes that wound up and down the steep Kentish hills, appeared to have altered little over the centuries. At times, as Darwin was to discover, snowdrifts sometimes prevented the post from being delivered. "It is really surprising," he wrote, "to think London is only 16 miles off." Even today, the area is one where at times the twentieth century seems barely to have started.

Here he and his family settled down into an environment that was to contain him happily for the rest of his life. More children followed, many of them at the usual Victorian intervals: Mary Eleanor in 1842, Henrietta Emma in 1843, George Howard in 1845, Elizabeth in 1847, Francis in 1848, Leonard in 1850, Horace in 1851 and Charles Waring in 1856. Death took three of them in infancy, not abnormal winnowing for Victorian times; Mary Eleanor, who died in 1842, twenty-four days after her birth; Anne Elizabeth, who died of fever at the age of ten; and Charles Waring, who was mentally subnormal and never learned to walk or talk, who died at the age of eighteen months. Darwin enjoyed his children, made sure that they did not interfere with his work, and, with a steadily growing fortune from investments, had few financial worries about their upbringing or future. They were rarely out of his thoughts, and he had no inhibitions about asking friends to help satisfy their requests. Thus after a long technical letter to Asa Gray, he had no hesitation in adding: "Forgive me for one bit more trouble. I have a Boy with the collecting mania and it has taken the

poor form of collecting Postage stamps; he is terribly eager for
'Wells, Fargo & Co. Pony Express' 2 and 4 stamps and 'Blood's 1.
Penny Envelope 1, 3, and 10 cents.' If you will make him this
present you will give my dear little man as much pleasure as a new
and curious genus gives us old souls."

Life at Down was one of comparative isolation and of no more
than normal Victorian hardship, lessened as this was by the work
of loyal servants, who included Joseph Parslow, the butler who had
first been employed in Upper Gower Street and who was to serve
the Darwins for forty years. But all water had to be drawn by hand
from the 325-foot well. A dozen paraffin lamps had to be cleaned
and filled each day by the irreplaceable "Brodie," the Darwin's old
Scottish nurse from the Moray Firth in northern Scotland. She was,
Henrietta Darwin was to write, "an invaluable treasure to my
mother and a perfect nurse to the children. . . . My image of her
is always sitting knitting, with her needles stuck into a bunch of
cock's feathers, Scotch fashion, patiently and benevolently looking
on whilst we rushed about and messed our clothes as much as we
liked." The prelude to a visit to London, and its finale was the
journey in a phaeton driven by Darwin's gardener-coachman to or
from Sydenham or Croydon railway station, "a long hilly stage of
10 miles" as Darwin sometimes warned visitors. At Down House,
insulated from the buffets of the time, Darwin could concentrate
on the question of questions. He had, after all, no reason to worry
about the task of earning a living: the taxable part of his income
was more than £1,000 a year, twice that paid to Richard Owen, the
leading zoologist of his day. Neither had he to worry with the
problem that hampered the real work of some other scientists. As
R. J. Berry of University College, London, has said in his percep-
tive brief study of Darwin's life, "he spent most of his life doing
what he himself wanted to do, untrammeled by administrative or
teaching chores, and unworried by questions of tenure, redun-
dancy, or research grants."

Moreover, he now had three distinct benefits. He had ample
space to carry out any botanical or agricultural experiments that
might cast light on the species question. His comparative isolation
gave him seclusion from London life and from the visits of all
except the special friends who he persuaded himself were necessary for serious work. But he could still reach London when he
wished, and as he wrote to William Darwin Fox: "I hope by going
up to town for a night every fortnight or 3 weeks to keep up my

communication with scientific men and my own zeal, and so not to turn into a complete Kentish Hog." Specimens that he needed for his work were addressed to "The Nag's Head" in the Borough, Central London, headquarters of the Downe carrier, and brought without delay to Down House. If a rare plant in flower was to come from Kew, as was sometimes the case, Joseph Parslow would be sent to collect it personally.

For a man with as questioning a mind as Charles Darwin's there was no danger of mental vegetation. Indeed, it appears certain that the placid tenor of life at Down, and the extent to which Darwin allowed it to absorb so much of his life, time and thoughts, played a crucial part in the slow but successful development of his work and beliefs. Outwardly, he concentrated on extending the estate, on planning alterations and additions to the house and grounds; inwardly, his mind was sifting, sorting and assessing the information that arrived in the post from academics and breeders, geologists and botanists, and it is difficult not to believe that the working out of natural selection's implications was often being solved in the subconscious while he relaxed in more mundane work.

Within a few years of moving into Down House, he was becoming quite ambitious. "We are now undertaking some great earthworks," he wrote to Susan in 1845; "making a new walk in the kitchen garden; and removing the mound under the yews, on which the evergreens we found did badly, and which, as Erasmus has always insisted, was a great blemish in hiding part of the field and the old Scotch firs; and now that we have Sales's Corner, we do not want it for shelter. We are making a mound, which will be executed by all the family, viz., in front of the door out of the house, between two of the lime-trees. We find the winds from the N. intolerable, and we retain the view from the grass mound and in walking down to the orchard. It will make the place much snugger, though a great blemish till the evergreens grow on it. Erasmus [visiting from London] has been of the utmost service in scheming and in actually working; making creases in the turf, striking circles, driving stakes and such jobs; he has tired me out several times."

The air of leisurely family cooperation running through this letter, as through so much of Darwin's other family correspondence, creates an atmosphere strikingly different from that of intellectual battery and barricade which his work was to arouse. In the world beyond Down House, the very foundations of society might appear to be under attack. There, a long summer afternoon appeared to linger on indefinitely, undisturbed by scientific vilification or by wars or rumors of wars. Significantly enough, Bagshaw's *Directory* for 1847, listing Darwin as among the householders in Downe, described him simply as "farmer." Certainly he had an acute interest in how the estate was managed and sometimes played an active part in its running. On one occasion, he told Lyell, he had been able to read only about a dozen pages of Lyell's new book since he was "tired with haymaking."

He also had a keen interest in domestic routine and went so far as to write in his own hand in Emma's "Recipe Book" details of how to boil rice:

> To Boil Rice.
>
> Add salt to the water and when boiling hot stir in the rice. Keep it boiling for twelve minutes by the watch, then pour off the water and set the pot on live coals during ten minutes—the rice is then fit for the table.

After her father's death, Henrietta remembered the home in a paragraph that almost surrealistically summons up the atmosphere that enabled Darwin to work on year after year, insulated from many problems, concentrating on the one thing that mattered. "I think of a sound we always associated with summer days," she wrote, "the rattle of the fly-wheel of the well drawing water for the garden; the lawn burnt brown, the garden a blaze of colour, the six oblong beds in front of the drawing-room windows, with phloxes, lilies and larkspurs in the middle, and Portulacas, verbenas, Gazanias, and other low growing plants in front, looking brighter than flowers ever do now; the row of lime-trees humming with bees, my father lying under them; children trotting about, with probably a kitten and a dog, and my mother dressed in a lilac muslin, wondering why the blackcaps did not sing the same tune here as they did at Maer."

Cats and kittens, dogs and puppies, squirrels, horses and pigeons all formed part of the permanent scene. Darwin was particularly fond of dogs and once wrote to the local vicar, his friend John Brodie Innes: "Thanks for the very curious story about the dog & mutton chops. They are wonderful animals, & deserve to be loved with all one's heart, even when they do steal mutton chops." He himself owned a long line of dogs, ranging from Bob, the black-and-white half-bred retriever whose *"hot house face"* has been immortalized in his master's *The Expression of the Emotions in Man and Animals*, to Polly, the rough-haired fox terrier who always welcomed him with such affection when he returned home. Polly had once been accidentally burned on her back and here the hair had regrown red instead of white. Her father had been a red bullterrier and Darwin always commended the dog for the red mark, maintaining that this was in accordance with his theory of pangenesis, since the red hair showed the presence of latent red gemmules. "The two subjects which moved my Father perhaps more strongly than any others," one of Charles's sons was later to write, "were cruelty to animals & slavery. His detestation of both was intense, and his indignation was overpowering in case of any levity or want of feeling on these matters."

A regular donor to the Royal Society for the Prevention of Cruelty to Animals, Darwin was troubled throughout his life by the problems raised by vivisection. His views, those of a man who did not hesitate to kill in order to obtain specimens, are most succinctly expressed in a letter to Professor Ray Lankester. "You ask my opinion on vivisection," he wrote. "I quite agree that it is justifiable for real investigations on physiology; but not for mere damnable and detestable curiosity. It is a subject which makes me sick with horror, so I will not say another word about it, else I shall not sleep tonight." And in *The Descent of Man*, which twelve years after *The Origin* was to pin man onto the evolutionary tree, he noted that "every one has heard of the dog suffering under vivisection, who licked the hand of the operator; this man, unless he had a heart of stone, must have felt remorse to the last hour of his life." A hint of the foundation for his feelings is given in the second of his "Transmutation Notebooks," where he writes: "the soul by consent of all is superadded, animals not got it, not look forward. If we choose to let conjecture run wild then animals our fellow brethren in pain, disease, death, suffering and famine, our slaves in the most laborious works, our companions in our amusements, they may partake from our origin in one common ancestor, we may be all netted together." An echo of the same sentiment was to be raised by Asa Gray. "We are sharers not only of animal but of vegetable life, sharers with the higher brute animals in common instincts and feelings and affections," he told members of the theological school at Yale. "It seems to me that there is a sort of meanness in the wish to ignore the tie. I fancy that human beings may be more humane when they realize that, as their dependent associates live a life in which man has a share, so they have rights which man is bound to respect."

The new place that evolution gave to animals certainly played some part in Darwin's loss of religious faith, as he explained in a sentence censored out by his family when his autobiography was first published after his death. "A being so powerful & so full of knowledge as a God who could create the universe, is to our finite minds omnipotent & omniscient, & it revolts our understanding to suppose that his benevolence is not unbounded, for what advantage can there be in the sufferings of millions of the lower animals throughout almost endless time?" Darwin's personal feelings for animals is testified by numerous stories of how he prevented his coachman from pressing his horses too hard. And his eldest son, William, has recalled how his father, "hearing that a farmer in his neighborhood had starved some sheep . . . took the matter up, collected evidence, instituted a prosecution, and secured a conviction." He had a particularly deep dislike of killing without reason. After he had once killed a crossbeak by throwing a stone at it, he was so unhappy that he did not mention the incident for a year. He explained, his son Francis recalled, "that he should never have thrown at it if he had not felt sure that his old skill had gone from him." His attitude to animals, qualified as it was by his attitude to scientific research, was strongly echoed by that of his wife and his daughters, and when George Romanes was invited to meet Huxley at Down House he was warned not to discuss experiments on animals before the Darwin women "since it would horrify them."

One aspect of Darwin's life at Down well illustrates his character and makes it easier to understand how so much criticism of his beliefs not only failed to be effective, but tended to roll off him like the proverbial water off a duck's back. This was his friendly relationship with the Reverend John Brodie Innes, with whom the allegedly arch-Satanic Darwin maintained an intimate correspondence for thirty-six years.

Soon after Innes arrived at Downe in 1846, Darwin was sending his regular subscription to the local Sunday school and regretting that it could not be more since he was also contributing to four others. "We never thoroughly agreed on any subject but once and then we looked hard at each other and thought one of us must be very ill," Innes wrote after Darwin's death. Innes, indeed, was by no means numbered among the progressive churchmen who were able to tolerate evolution, if not welcome it. "I am not a convert to the theory you found on [the facts]," he wrote to Darwin after publication of *The Descent of Man.* "I hold to the old belief that a man was made a man though developed into niggers who must be made to work and better men able to make them, if those radicals did not interfere with the salutary chastisement needful, neglecting the lesson taught by the black ants slaves to the white. Also that a horse was made a horse though perhaps my old cart mare who is peacefully grazing before my windows and the Zephyr colt may have had a common ancestor in the dim distance."

With Innes, and later his successor, Darwin discussed parish affairs, and gave counsel and advice. In 1850 he founded the Down Friendly Club, served as its treasurer almost until his death more than thirty years later, and greeted its members as they paraded on his lawn every Whitmonday. When in 1877 they proposed dissolving the club on the grounds that the government intended uniting the country's clubs and dividing their funds, he printed a warning against the move. "I hope," it concluded, "that you will admit that I can have no bad motive in expressing my deliberate judgment; it is no pleasure to me to keep your accounts and to subscribe to your funds, except in the hope of doing some small good to my fellow Members, who have hitherto always treated me in a considerate and friendly manner." He also had a hand in other local good works and reported to Innes on one occasion: "We have just had a curious scene on our lawn, viz. 67 half-reformed criminals & vagabond boys who have come down here for a holiday, & to each of whom I gave six pence."

Darwin's relationship with Innes is only part of the evidence from Downe that suggests how he exercised his influence. His belief that evolution was the motive force behind organic life was of course to be proved right, always a useful factor in acceptance of an idea. But it would be naïve to suggest that the success of an idea can be totally dissociated from the personality of the man or woman who propounds it; some of the world's great religions would, without much doubt, have been received with more skepticism but for the persuasion of their founders. And at Down, as well as outside it, Darwin could be the understanding human being rather than the controversial scientist.

In more ways than one he remained all his life the typical country gentleman, on the best of terms with his devout vicar and sitting on the local magistrate's bench. The latter work appears to have fatigued him as much as professional overexertion, and on one occasion he lamented to Hooker: "I attended the Bench on Monday & was detained in adjudicating some troublesome cases 1 1/2 hours longer than usual & came home utterly knocked up & cannot rally. — I am not worth an old button." He continued to sit on the bench almost until his death and as late as 1881 was explaining to his friend George Romanes that because of swine disease it was his duty as a magistrate to give daily orders allowing pigs to cross a public road even when going from one field to another on the same farm. This homely picture of a reluctant revolutionary licensing pigs across the public road is reinforced by Hooker's memory of "long walks, romps with the children on hands and knees, music that haunts me still. Darwin's own hearty manner, hollow laugh, and thorough enjoyment of home life with friends." Later, after Darwin's health grew worse—interestingly enough, as the implications of his work grew less and less avoidable—it was, Hooker has written, "an established rule that he every day pumped me, as he called it, for half an hour or so after breakfast in his study, when he first brought out a heap of slips with questions botanical, geographical &c., for me to answer, and concluded by telling me of the progress he had made in his own work, asking my opinion on various points. I saw no more of him until about noon, when I heard his mellow ringing voice calling my name under my window —this was to join him in his daily forenoon walk round the sand-walk. On joining him I found him in a rough grey shooting-coat in summer, and thick cape over his shoulders in winter, and a stout staff in his hand; away we trudged through the garden, where there was always some experiment to visit, and on to the sand-walk, round which a fixed number of turns were taken, during which our conversation usually ran on foreign lands and seas, old friends, old books, and things far off to both mind and eye."

If the great adventure of biological research was one essential of life at Down House, another was Darwin's happy relationship with his children. Never forcing them toward science, he gave them every support when they moved in that direction of their own accord—perhaps one reason for the fact that three sons, Francis, Horace and George, ended up with both Fellowships of the Royal Society and knighthoods. Although he had reservations about sending the boys to public schools, telling William Darwin Fox, "I cannot endure to think of sending my Boys to waste 7 or 8 years in making miserable Latin verses," and telling the same cousin two years later: "I hate schools & the whole system of breaking through the affections of the family by separating the boys so early in life, but I see no help & dare not run the risk of a youth being exposed to the temptations of the world, without having undergone the milder ordeal of a great school."

At home he never lectured down to them and always encouraged them in unusual outdoor activities. He taught William and George how to make an Australian throwing stick and spear, and gave them an English boomerang. "I remember him throwing it once in a high wind," George recalled, "& it came back behind him & went through a cucumber frame, which as he said was the only thing which had ever made the gloomy gardener Brooks laugh outright."

In the hundreds of letters that went to his children while they were at school, there is a constant stream of advice, much of it helping to explain Darwin's own success in both work and human relationships. To William, he writes on one occasion: "I am sorry that you cannot 'grind' at present; progress in life mainly depends on the great art of grinding: there can be no doubt of that." If this was a pointer to the work that was to be needed for *The Origin*, another piece of advice to William helps explain how Darwin dealt so successfully with at least some of its opponents. "You will surely find," he wrote, "that one of the greatest pleasures in life is in being beloved; and this depends almost more on pleasant manners than on being kind with grave and gruff manners. You are almost always kind and only want the more easily acquired external appearance. Depend upon it, that the only way to acquire pleasant manners is to try to please *everybody* you come near, your school-fellows, servants and everyone."

Yet despite his apparent optimism, there remained an undertow of doubt, which he expressed frankly to Syms Covington, by now settled and prosperous in Australia. "A young man may here slave for years in any profession and not make a penny," he wrote in 1850. "Many people think that Californian gold will half ruin all those who live on the interest of accumulated gold or capital, and if that does happen I will certainly emigrate. Whenever you write again tell me how far you think a gentleman with capital would get on in New South Wales." And more than four years later he asked of Covington, "To what shall you bring up your boys? I wish to god I knew what to do with mine."

One thing that he did do was to bring them, whenever possible, into the nature-observation activities that he carried on in the grounds of Down House. A striking example was the way in which five or six children were brought into Darwin's bee-watching work between 1854 and 1861. This had begun in September 1854, after George Darwin, then aged nine, saw some humble-bees entering a hole at the base of a tall ash tree. "I looked into this hole hoping to find the entrance to a nest, but was unable to see one," Darwin wrote. "Whilst I was examining the hole, another humble bee entered it, and, after flying off, returned almost immediately and, flying upwards for about a yard, flew away through a crutch between two large branches of the ash." Like subsequent bees, it followed the course of a dry ditch, stopping regularly at what Darwin called "buzzing places." "I could only follow them along this ditch by making several of my children crawl in, and lie on their tummies, but in this way I was able to track the bees for about twenty-five yards," he noted. "They always came out of the ditch by the same opening, but from here there were three routes leading in different directions. . . . There were several buzzing places on each of these routes, always a few yards apart. One of these was very odd because the bees had to fly down several feet to a fallen leaf at the bottom of a very thick hedge, and then fly back again by the way that they had come."

Darwin followed the bees' routes in some detail, found that they flew at about ten miles an hour and noted that their buzzing places were fixed to within an inch. "I was able to prove this by stationing five or six of my children each close to a buzzing place, and telling the one farthest away to shout out 'here is a bee' as soon as one was buzzing around. The others followed this up, so that the same cry of 'here is a bee' was passed on from child to child without interruption until the bees reached the buzzing place where I myself was standing." With the help of his children, Darwin continued his observations every summer until 1861, although unable to answer the riddles their movements posed, including the question written on one page of field-notes: "How on earth do bees coming separately out of nest discover same place, is it like dogs at corner-stones?"

Darwin obviously enjoyed this light relief from his more serious work, partly because one of his joys was the contemplation of nature itself, as he made clear in a revealing letter to Emma, written while he was "taking the cure" at Moor Park. This was a hydropathic establishment in Surrey, where he was taking the water cure, which had become fashionable in the 1830s and which involved the drinking of water and the taking of numerous baths. "Yesterday, after writing to you," he said, "I strolled a little beyond the glade for an hour & a half, & enjoyed myself—the fresh yet dark green of the grand Scotch firs, the brown of the catkins of the old Birches, with their white stems, and a fringe of distant green from the larches, made an excessively pretty view. At last I fell fast asleep on the grass and awoke with a chorus of birds singing around me, & squirrels running up the trees, and some woodpeckers laughing, and it was as pleasant & rural a scene as ever I saw, & I did not care one penny how any of the beasts or birds had been formed."

Moor Park appeared to do him good, as did most of the similar establishments whose cures he took, and after his return from one of them he decided to continue the water cure at home. For this he conscripted the help of a Mr. Lewis, who was asked, according to his son John, "to make him a tank 13 feet deep with a stage in the middle. And then there was a big cistern above that held six hundred and forty gallons. I had to pump it full every day for two years," John Lewis remembered years later. "Mr. Darwin came out and had a little dressing place, and he'd get on the stage and go down, and pull the string, and all the water fell on him through a two-inch pipe." The douche, shaped like a very diminutive church, stood on the lawn near the Down House well. "About noon every day," George Darwin recalled of his father, "he used to take a douche even in the coldest weather. I remember well one bitter cold day, with the snow covering everything, waiting about outside until he had finished & that he came out almost blue with cold and we trotted back at a good brisk pace over the snow to the sandwalk."

Despite illness, varying in intensity but an ever-present background to life that could not be ignored, Darwin's work went on, methodically and to a timetable that was only rarely broken as he visited friends, attended a hydropathic establishment in the hope of curing his chronic ill health, or spent the occasional few days with his brother Erasmus in London. His routine at Down House, which appears to have varied only slightly with the seasons, began with a short brisk walk on the eighteen-acre grounds and was followed by breakfast at seven-thirty. Work started at eight and lasted until nine-thirty, an hour and a half that Darwin considered the best part of the day for getting things done. At nine-thirty he went from his study to the drawing room for his letters, "rejoicing if the post was a light one and being sometimes much worried if it was not." Any family correspondence would be read aloud. From about ten-thirty he would return to work, which lasted until midday, when after his medicinal shower he took a walk around the property, often beginning with a trip to the greenhouse and then on along the "Sandwalk," a gravel walk surrounding one and a half acres of ground. After luncheon he would retire to the drawing room and read the daily paper before starting on his correspondence. His letters would be roughed out on the backs of manuscripts or notes supported by a thick board that rested on the arms of his chair.

With letters finished by about three, he would rest in his bedroom, often while a novel was read to him. Punctually at four he would take another half-hour walk, then return for an hour's work. An interlude in the drawing room, then a further rest at six would be followed by a simple tea at seven-thirty. This was followed by two games of backgammon with Emma and then the reading of a scientific book until retirement for bed at ten-thirty. The backgammon results were carefully recorded, and as late as 1876, when they had been at Down House for more than a third of a century, Darwin could tell Asa Gray that he had won 2,795 games compared with Emma's 2,490.

The daily programme had a comfortable lack of stress, but this was very largely the result of Darwin's ill health. Just how much this limited his activities is almost brutally demonstrated in a note in 1865 to William Darwin Fox, close friend as well as cousin, whom he had not seen for some while. "I should like extremely to see you again for a few minutes," Fox was told, "more than that I fear I cd not stand." The way in which the lassitude of illness governed what to most people would have been very ordinary traveling is shown in his almost pathetic response to an invitation from Hooker in 1844 to visit Kew Gardens, where Hooker's father was director, and where the son was eventually to succeed his father. He asks the times of the steamboats from London to Kew, adding: "I should wish to get back here [Down House] at night if I could. If I can keep my steam and courage up for this great expedition, I will take advantage of your kindness sometime in the course of the next month." Wife and children compounded his immobility, and when James Dwight Dana asked whether he would ever visit the United States, Darwin assured him "that no tour whatever could be half so interesting to me, but with my large family I do not suppose that I shall ever leave home."

Darwin was perhaps lucky to be living in the string-and-sealing-wax age of biology, a fact brought out in the account of his life by his son Francis. "His dissecting table," he has written, "was a thick board, let into a window of the study; it was lower than an ordinary table, so that he could not have worked at it standing; but this, from wishing to save his strength, he would not have done in any case. He sat at his dissecting table on a curious low stool which had belonged to his father, with a seat revolving on a vertical spindle, and mounted on large castors, so that he could turn easily from side to side." There were other uses for such an unconventional piece of furniture, and his son George remembered how he or one of his brothers would sit in the chair and pull themselves around the study with the help of a long walking stick whose handle could be looped over fixtures. "The drawers [of the dissecting table] were labelled 'best tools,' 'rough tools,' 'specimens,' 'preparations for specimens,' &c.," Francis Darwin has written. "The most marked peculiarity of the contents of these drawers was the care with which little scraps and almost useless things were preserved; he held the well-known belief, that if you threw a thing away you were sure to want it directly—and so things accumulated." At his right hand there were shelves on which he kept a varying miscellany of glasses, saucers, biscuit tins for germinating seeds, labels and saucers full of sand. It was among this clutter of simple equipment that Darwin prepared to change the world.

From his letters and notebooks it is possible to see how his original ideas hardened up almost month by month. By early 1844 he had reached a point of no return. His confidant at this stage was Hooker, who had returned to England during the last days of 1843. Darwin had learned of the results obtained in Antarctica and now suggested that some of his *Beagle* collections should be used to correlate results between the two expeditions. By January 11, moreover, he was telling Hooker that he had never ceased collecting facts for "a very presumptuous work & which I know no one individual who not say a very foolish one." He then continued that at last "gleams of light have come, & I am almost convinced (quite contrary to opinion I started with) that species are not (it is like confessing a murder) immutable. . . . I think I have found out (here's presumption!) the simple way by which species become exquisitely adapted to various ends."

Darwin still felt it necessary to keep the "almost" before "convinced." His views, moreover, were only for Hooker, and the longest record of them was the thirty-five-page penciled summary he had written two years previously. Whether he would ever have been pushed into print without a succession of accidents is a moot point. In Darwin, the strong belief that it was part of his duty to reveal the nature of the world was forever battling with the preference for a quiet life. In 1857 a human concern that he might be overtaken by Alfred Russel Wallace prodded ambition awake and led to the writing and publication of *The Origin*. Presentation of his views to the world, let alone their survival, was more dependent on chance than most scientific revelations have been.

In 1844 there came Robert Chambers's notorious *Vestiges of the Natural History of Creation*, a book of pseudoscience. One major theme was the evolution of the solar system according to the nebular hypothesis put forward by Pierre Laplace in the 1820s. Another was the evolution of living organisms. Any reasonable suggestions as to how this had occurred—and some had a vague resemblance to Darwin's theory of natural selection—were more than counteracted by Chambers's claim in the book that a British chemist had actually created life by passing an electric current through solutions of potassium silicate and copper nitrate. It was soon shown that the life observed was the well-known mite *Acarus horridus*, which had slipped into the solution owing to lack of elementary experimental precautions.

Chambers also suggested that man was directly descended from a large frog. "It is no great boldness," he maintained, "to surmise that a super-adequacy in the measure of this under-adequacy (and the one thing seems as natural an occurrence as the other) would suffice in a goose to give its progeny the body of a rat, and produce the ornithorynchus [duckbilled platypus], or might give the progeny of an ornithorynchus the mouth and feet of a true rodent, and thus complete at two stages the passage from the aves to the mammalia."

There was much in the same vein, and Chambers was excoriated by scientific reviewers. Typical was Adam Sedgwick, writing to Lyell. "If the book be true," he said, "the labours of sober induction are in vain; religion is a lie; human law is a mass of folly, and a base injustice; morality is moonshine; our labours for the black people of Africa were works of madmen; and man and woman are only better beasts!"

For Darwin, who wrote of *Vestiges* to Hooker, "the writing and arrangement are certainly admirable, but his geology strikes me as bad and his zoology far worse," Sedgwick's review contained a warning. "Nevertheless, it is a grand piece of argument against mutability of species," Darwin told Lyell, "and I read it with fear and trembling, but was well pleased to find that I had not overlooked any of the arguments, though I had put them to myself as feebly as milk and water."

Vestiges was something more than just a commercial success, which ran through four editions before the end of the year and many more after that. Tucked away amid the nonsense there were ideas that, if barely credible, at least gave men cause to think. More important were two other points. *Vestiges* brought the subject of evolution into the realm of lay discussion. It revealed, moreover, the strength of opposition that would be aroused by any hint that the story in Genesis was a load of rubbish. Darwin was not the man to commit the scientific solecisms that made Chambers a laughingstock in scientific circles. But as early as 1838, he was to write, he had "gradually come . . . to see that the Old Testament, from its manifestly false history of the world, with the Tower of Babel, the rainbow as a sign, &c., &c., & from its attributing to God the feelings of a revengeful tyrant, was no more to be trusted than the sacred books of the Hindoos, or the beliefs of any barbarian." Such a standpoint was essential to his view of the development of species; but the reception of the *Vestiges* underlined the need for care in saying so.

Anxious to put down his own findings in some form that would be derided as little as possible, Darwin wrote out his theory in further detail in 1844. This version, running to 231 folio pages, followed much the same lines as the brief essay of 1842. Part I, called "On the Variation of Organic Beings under Domestication and in the Natural State," recapitulated the experiences of animal and plant breeders, discussed variation in nature, and explained natural selection. Part II, "On Evidence Favourable and Opposed to the View That Species Are Naturally Formed Races Descended from Common Stocks," concentrated on the fossil record, admitted its inevitable gaps in the evidence, but came down firmly in favor of an explanation very different from that in Genesis. However, the sketch concluded with a comforter, of sorts, for the faithful. "There is a simple grandeur in the view of life," it maintained, "with its powers of assimilation & of reproduction having been originally breathed into matter under a few forms; & that, whilst this planet has gone cycling onwards according to the fixed laws of society & land & water have gone on replacing each other, —

that from so simple an origin, through the selection of infinitesimal varieties endless forms most beautiful & most wonderful have been evolved."

The thrust of the paragraph seems clear; whatever the origin of species, God had been doing a marvelous job. The careful trimming, aimed at appeasing the creationists, was not unique to Darwin. Lyell as well, it has been seen, seems to have recognized it as a help to gaining recognition for new ideas. He spelled out his position when writing to George Poulett Scrope, the geologist, of the contradictions between his *Principles of Geology* and Genesis: "If I have said more than some will like," he said, "yet I give you my word that full *half* of my history and comments was cut out, and even many facts; because either I, or Charles Stokes, or [William John] Broderip, felt that it was anticipating twenty or thirty years of the march of honest feeling to declare it undisguisedly." Lyell, like Darwin after him, realized that compromise was sometimes the better part of survival.

The sketch of 1844, worked out in more detail than its predecessor of 1842, still lacked not only the chapter and verse of academic footnotes but most of the specific examples still tucked away in Darwin's notebooks. It was nowhere near ready for publication; but it was too good to be lost, as Darwin made clear in a letter to his wife on July 5.

> I have just finished my sketch of my species theory. If as I believe that my theory in time and if it be accepted even by one competent judge, it will be a considerable step in science.
>
> I therefore write this in case of my sudden death, as my most solemn and last request, which I am sure you will consider the same as if legally entered in my will, that you will devote 400£ to its publication and further will yourself, or through Hensleigh [Emma Darwin's brother], take trouble in promoting it—I wish that my sketch be given to some competent person, with this sum to induce him to take trouble in its improvement and enlargement. I give to him all my books on Natural History which are either scored or have references at end to the pages, begging him carefully to look over and consider such passages, as actually bearing or by possibility bearing on this subject. I wish you to make a list of all such books as some temptation to an editor. I also request that you will hand over [to] him all those scraps roughly divided in eight or ten brown paper port-folios. The scraps with copied quotations from various works are those which may aid my Editor.

I also request that you or some amanuensis will aid in deciphering any of the scraps which the Editor may think possibly of use. I leave to the Editor's judgment whether to interpolate these facts in the text, or as notes, or used as appendices. As the looking over the references and scraps will be a long labour and as the *correcting* [underlined three times in ms letter] and enlarging and altering my sketch will also take considerable time, I leave this sum of 400£ as some remuneration, and any profits from the work. I consider that for this the Editor is bound to get the sketch published either at a publisher's or his own risk. Many of the scraps in the portfolios contain mere rude suggestions and early views now useless, and many of the facts will probably turn out as having no bearing on my theory.

He suggested that Lyell would be the best man to do the job and after him, Professor Edward Forbes. Then, "the next best (& quite best in many respects) would be Professor *Henslow*?? Dr. Hooker would be VERY good. . . ."

However, even had the sketch of 1844 been published, its impact would have been far less than that of the *Origin.* While it certainly contained the rudiments of the theory that Darwin was to expound fifteen years later, it lacked the wealth of examples he was then able to provide, the detailed working out of his arguments and many of his answers to the objections that he knew would be raised against it. In a phrase that he as a shooting man would appreciate, it could well have gone off at half cock.

The summer of 1844, during which Darwin set down the outline of his theory, also witnessed the growth into friendship of his relationship with Hooker, to whom he sent his outline for comment. On one of his rare visits to London early in the year, he had invited Hooker to meet him for breakfast at his brother Erasmus's house on Park Street. There had followed the invitation to Kew, an invitation turned down on the ground of Darwin's ill health, but at the end of the year Hooker visited Down House. Many invitations to come for a week and bring his work with him were to follow. "On these visits," Hooker later told Darwin's son William, "your Mother did everything to make me feel at home. Often I worked in the dining room (latterly in the billiard room) through which your mother often passed on her way to the store closet in the end, when she would take a pear, or some good thing, and lay it by my side with a charming smile as she passed out. . . . Your father and I never discussed scientific questions except for the half hour after breakfast and even that always fatigued him. At other times we had long chats by which I profited enormously, especially during the forenoon and afternoon *sand walks*, for which he invariably summoned me."

Much appears to have been discussed during these conversations on the dry sandwalk Darwin had constructed around one of the coppices on the estate. Certainly when it came to launching *The Origin* a decade and a half later, it was obvious that Hooker had soaked up every detail of the argument over the years.

Once Darwin had made certain in 1844 that the results of his species work would not be lost to the world, it would have been natural for him to take it further. He had no financial incentive to finish and publish, since he never expected to make a profit from his research. Neither was it necessary for him to turn to any other form of work that might be profitable. In the mid-1840s his fortune was estimated to total between £30,000 and £40,000 which was to be increased, following the death of his father in 1848, by £45,000. His outgoings, throughout most of his adult life, were considerably less than his income. For most practical purposes, money did not enter into his calculations.

Yet instead of continuing to concentrate on the species work, Darwin now turned to a separate study that was to occupy him for eight years—although the period was to include two years when illness severely limited his work. This was the study of Cirrepedia, or barnacles. While on the *Beagle* he had collected one specimen "which differed so much from all other cirripedes that I had to form a new sub-order for its sole reception." Now he began a study of the entire subclass of Crustacea, collecting specimens from all over the world and buying a new compound microscope to help in his work of dissection.

At first glance, the barnacle project appears a strange diversion from the all-important species question. However, before the end of 1845 Darwin had at last made up his mind on the matter. "The general conclusions at which I have slowly been driven from a directly opposite conviction," he wrote to Jenyns in October, "is that species are mutable, and that allied species are co-descendants from common stocks. I know how much I open myself to reproach for such a conclusion." But it was a conclusion that he had now unequivocally reached; he knew that justifying it might show up gaps in his training, and he set about filling them.

According to Hooker, Darwin's choice of subject was almost

inevitable. "Your father had Barnacles on the brain from Chili onwards!" he told Francis Darwin. "He talked to me incessantly of beginning to work at his 'beloved Barnacles' (his favourite expression) long before he did so methodically. It is impossible to say at what stage of progress he realised the necessity of such a training as monographing the Order offered him; but that he did recognize it and act upon it as a training in systematic biological study, morphological, anatomical, geographical, taxonomic and descriptive, is very certain; he often alluded to it to me as a valued discipline and added that even the 'hateful' work of digging out synonyms and of describing, not only improved his methods, but opened his eyes to the difficulties and merits of the works of the dullest cataloguers." Darwin, he went on, identified in conversation with him "three stages in his career as biologist, the mere collector, in Cambridge &c.; the collector and observer, in the 'Beagle' and for some years after; and the trained naturalist after, and only after, the Cirripede work."

The same view was taken by another colleague who was soon to become almost as regular a visitor to Down House as Joseph Hooker. This was Thomas Henry Huxley, man of science, who with Lyell and Hooker made up the trio whose energies and enthusiasm forced Darwin to launch *The Origin*. Like Darwin himself and Hooker, Huxley had entered the world of science via a round-the-world voyage when between 1846 and 1850 he served as assistant surgeon on HMS *Rattlesnake*. Back in England, he had sent Darwin a technical report on a number of specimens. Darwin had responded the following year when asked to support Huxley's candidature for a post at the University of Toronto in Canada, and the friendship had quickened, Darwin turning to Huxley as his specialist adviser on zoology as he turned to Hooker on botany.

"I remember, in the course of my first interview with Mr. Darwin," Huxley was later to write, "expressing my belief in the sharpness of the lines of demarcation between natural groups and in the absence of transitional forms, with all the confidence of youth and imperfect knowledge. I was not aware, at that time, that he had then been many years brooding over the species question; and the humorous smile which accompanied his gentle answer, that such was not altogether his view, long haunted and puzzled me."

Years later, after he had become Darwin's most outspoken defender, Huxley was to see the point of the barnacle work, remarking that Darwin "never did a wiser thing" and continuing: "Like the rest of us, he had no proper training in biological science, and it has always struck me as a remarkable instance of his scientific insight, that he saw the necessity of giving himself such training, and of his courage, that he did not shirk the labour of obtaining it . . . it was a piece of critical self-discipline, the effect of which manifested itself in everything [he] wrote afterwards, and saved him from endless errors of detail."

However, if the work on barnacles was to help Darwin's exposition in *The Origin*, it was also work he enjoyed. He had been so long in writing up his geological observations, he told Hooker, that he delighted in using his eyes and fingers again. And his enjoyment is evident in a letter to FitzRoy in which he writes of being "for the last half-month daily hard at work in dissecting a little animal about the size of a pin's-head, from the Chonos archipelago, and I could spend another month, and daily see more beautiful structure." Ill health was the recurring handicap, and in 1849 he wrote to Richard Owen: "I have lost for the last 4 or 5 months at least 4–5 of my time, & I have resolved to go this early summer & spend two months at Malvern & see whether there is any truth in Gully & the water cure: regular doctors cannot check my incessant vomiting at all. It will cause a sad delay in my Barnacle work, but if once well I cd. do more in 6 months than I now do in two years."

The subclass on which Darwin was working was complicated, and by the time that he had seen through the press his four barnacle volumes of 1854 he was considerably better equipped than previously to carry on with his all-important study of species. There were also specific connections between barnacles and evolution, as he pointed out in a letter to Hooker toward the end of the work. "I have lately got a bisexual cirripede, the male being microscopically small & parasitic within the sack of the female," he wrote. "I tell you this to boast of my species theory, for the nearest & closely allied genus to it is, as usual, hermaphrodite, but I had observed some minute parasites adhering to it, & these parasites, I now can show, are supplemental males, the male organs in the hermaphrodite being unusually small, though perfect and containing zoosperms: so we have almost a polygamous animal, simple females alone being wanting. I never should have made this out, had not my species theory convinced me, that an hermaphrodite species must pass into a bisexual species by insensibly small stages; & here we have it, for the male organs in the hermaphrodite are beginning to fail, & independent males ready formed."

Darwin's barnacles were described in four large volumes—one of them illustrated by the young John Lubbock, whom he had by this time started on his scientific career—and brought him the Royal Medal of the Royal Society in 1853, "quite a nugget, for it weighs 40 sovereigns," as he described it to Syms Covington. By the autumn of 1854, he was returning the thousands of specimens that had been lent to him. To Hooker he called this frittering away his time, partly in idleness, partly in doing odds and ends. "But I shall now," he concluded, "in a day or two begin to look over my old notes on species."

He also began pigeon breeding. He had a wooden loft built beside the house and took up the work with an enthusiasm that went beyond its implications for his species investigations. "I am getting on splendidly with my pigeons," he wrote to his son William in the mid-1850s, "and the other day had a present of Trumpeters, Nuns and Turbits; and when last in London, I visited a jolly old Brewer, who keeps 300 or 400 most beautiful pigeons and he gave me a pair of pale brown, quite small German Pouters: I am building a new house for my Tumblers, so as to fly them in summer."

Even before Darwin had finished his work on barnacles and had returned to the species question, the subject was being jolted into public consciousness by Herbert Spencer, a young and self-educated philosopher whose work was to have an unexpected link with Darwin's. Spencer had, after spells as schoolmaster, railway engineer and worker for the Complete Suffrage Movement, become a convert to the cause of organic evolution and in 1852 had written a seminal article in the *Leader* on "The Development Hypothesis," as evolution was then frequently called. He wrote:

Those who cavalierly reject the theory of Lamarck and his followers, as not adequately supported by facts, seem quite to forget that their own theory is supported by no facts at all. Like the majority of men who are born to a given belief, they demand the most rigorous proof of any adverse doctrine, but assume that their own doctrine needs none. Here we find scattered over the globe vegetable and animal organisms numbering, of the one kind (according to Humboldt) some 320,000 species, and of the other, if we include insects, some *two millions* of species (see Carpenter); and if to these we add the numbers of animal and vegetable species that have become extinct, (bearing in mind how geological records prove that, from the earliest appearance

of life down to the present time, different species have been succes-
sively replacing each other, so that the world's Flora and Fauna have
completely changed many times over), we may safely estimate the
number of species that have existed, and are existing on the earth, at
not less than ten millions. Well, which is the most rational theory
about these ten millions of species? Is it most likely that there have
been ten millions of special creations? or is it most likely that by
continual modifications, due to change of circumstances, ten millions
of varieties may have been produced, as varieties are being produced
still? . . . Even could the supporters of the development hypothesis
merely show that the production of species by the process of modification is conceivable, they would be in a better position than their opponents. But they can do much more than this. . . .

It is significant that these views, expressed seven years before
the publication of *The Origin*, were not accepted by T. H. Huxley,
soon to become "Darwin's bulldog." "I took my stand upon two
grounds," he subsequently wrote: "firstly, that up to that time, the
evidence in favour of transmutation was wholly insufficient; and,
secondly, that no suggestion respecting the causes of the transmutation assumed, which had been made, was in any way adequate to
explain the phenomena. Looking back at the state of knowledge at
that time, I really do not see that any other conclusion was justifiable."

Five years after the *Leader* article, Spencer outlined the gist of his
philosophy of evolution in "Progress: Its Law and Cause" in the
Westminster Review, the second shot in the campaign he was to wage
for the incorporation of the evolutionary idea into all the sciences.
The proposal was best expressed in the second edition of his *First
Principles*, published in 1867. "While we think of evolution as divided into astronomic, geologic, biologic, psychologic, sociologic,
&c.," he wrote, "it may seem to a certain extent a coincidence that
the same law of metamorphosis holds throughout all its divisions.
But when we recognize these divisions as mere conventional
groupings, made to facilitate the arrangement and acquisition of
knowledge—when we regard the different existences with which
they severally deal as component parts of one Cosmos; we see at
once that there are not several kinds of Evolution having certain
traits in common, but one Evolution going on everywhere after the
same manner."

Darwin was later to feel that Spencer might eventually "be

looked at as by far the greatest living philosopher in England; perhaps equal to any that have lived," although he was to admit: "With the exception of special points I did not even understand [his] general doctrine; for his style is too hard for me." But in the fifth edition of *The Origin* (1869), he was to adopt the phrase "the Survival of the Fittest," which Spencer had used in his *Principles of Biology* a few years earlier.

In the early days, however, he appears not only to have understood but to have approved, acknowledging a gift of Spencer's essays in November 1858 with the comment: "Your remarks on the general argument of the so-called development theory seems to me admirable. I am at present preparing an Abstract of a larger work on the changes of species; but I treat the subject simply as a naturalist, and not from a general point of view, otherwise, in my opinion, your argument could not have been improved on, and might have been quoted by me with great advantage."

Subsequent generations have tended to qualify Darwin's enthusiasm; partly, no doubt, because of Spencer's later influence on what became known as "social Darwinism." Ernst Mayr in his magisterial volume of 1982, *The Growth of Biological Thought: Diversity, Evolution, and Inheritance*, has summed up contemporary judgment. "It would," he has written, "be quite justifiable to ignore Spencer totally in a history of biological ideas because his positive contributions were nil. However, since Spencer's ideas were much closer than Darwin's to various popular misconceptions, they had a decisive impact on anthropology, psychology, and the social sciences. For most authors in these areas, for more than a century after Darwin, the word 'evolution' meant a necessary progression toward a higher level and greater complexity, which is what it had meant to Spencer rather than to Darwin."

5

The Making of
The Origin

DARWIN'S "Abstract" of which he wrote to Spencer in November 1858 was the result of a series of traumatic events. In the spring of 1855 he had written to William Darwin Fox: "I am hard at work on my notes, collecting and comparing them, in order in some 2 or 3 years to write a book with all the facts & arguments, which I can collect, *for and versus* the immutability of species." The plan then was for something much longer and almost certainly less readable than *The Origin* turned out to be. At the worst, it could have been a book that would never be finished at all.

These prospects were dramatically changed by the appearance on the scene of Alfred Russel Wallace, then in the Far East, to whom "a sudden flash of insight," as he called it, had revealed a solution to the species problem identical in its main idea to Darwin's.

Such coincidences are not unknown in science. Newton and Leibniz independently developed the calculus. Physicists in the United States, Britain, Germany and Japan independently discovered methods of catching the radio waves bounced back by aircraft and from them originating radar in three continents almost simultaneously. The Wallace-Darwin situation to some extent reflected, in similar manner, the intellectual climate of the times, which, at least since publication of Chambers's *Vestiges*, had nourished speculation about the species question and the origin of life.

It is sometimes assumed that while Darwin had been assiduously accumulating information for two decades, Wallace's "flash of insight" came entirely out of the blue. This is not so. Wallace's investigations into the species question did not go back as far as Darwin's; but they probed further, and were deeper, than is generally realized. Trained as a surveyor, he had acquired an amateur interest in botany, become a master at the Collegiate School at Leicester in 1843, and had there struck up what was to be a lifelong friendship with the naturalist Henry Walter Bates.

Wallace had become intrigued by the species question through reading Chambers's *Vestiges*. "I well remember the excitement caused by [its] publication . . . and the eagerness and delight with which I read it," he later wrote. "Although I saw that it really offered no explanation of the process of change of species, yet the view that the change was effected, not through any unimaginable process, but through the known laws and processes of reproduction, commended itself to me as perfectly satisfactory, and as affording the first step towards a more complete and explanatory theory."

Three years later, in 1847, Wallace proposed that he and Bates should visit the tropics in order, as Bates later put it, to "gather facts . . . 'towards solving the problem of the origin of species,' a subject on which we had conversed and corresponded much together." They went to the Amazon, and Bates's subsequent letters to Wallace show that they continued to discuss the species problem before Wallace left for England in 1850. Wallace himself has written: "my early letters to Bates suffice to show that the great problem of the origin of species was already distinctly formulated in my mind; that I was not satisfied with the more or less vague solutions at that time offered; that I believed the conception of evolution through natural law so clearly formulated in the 'Vestiges' to be, so far as it went, a true one; and that I firmly believed that a full and careful study of the facts of nature would ultimately lead to a solution of the mystery."

On the voyage home, Wallace's collections were destroyed in a disastrous shipboard fire, and he himself was lucky to reach land alive. Undeterred, he set out once again, this time for the Malay Archipelago, where he was soon preparing a book with the tentative title "[On the] Organic Law of Change." Its plan shows both the influence of Lyell and the turn of Wallace's mind in the early 1850s. In it, he wrote:

> We must at the outset endeavour to ascertain if the present condition of the organic world is now undergoing any changes, of what

nature & to what amount, & we must in the first place assume that the regular course of nature from early Geological Epochs to the present time has produced the present state of things & still continues to act in still further changing it. While the inorganic world has been strictly shown to be the result of a series of changes from the earliest periods produced by causes still acting, it would be most unphilosophical to conclude without the strongest evidence that the organic world so intimately connected with it, had been subject to other laws which have now ceased to act, & that the extinctions & productions of species and genera had at some late period suddenly ceased. The change is so perfectly gradual from the latest Geological to the modern epoch that we cannot help believing the present condition of the earth & its inhabitants to be the natural result of its immediately preceding state modified by causes which have always been & still continue in action.

Wallace's book was never written. But in the September 1855 issue of the *Annals and Magazine of Natural History* there appeared his paper "On the Law Which Has Regulated the Introduction of New Species." A cautious argument for the evolution of species, the paper maintained: "The following law may be deduced from these facts:—*Every species has come into existence coincident both in space and time with a pre-existing closely allied species.*" And it concluded: "Granted the law, and many of the most important facts in Nature could not have been otherwise, but are almost as necessary deductions from it as are the elliptic orbits of the planets from the law of gravitation."

Wallace's paper fell short of the theory on which Darwin was working, but there were sufficient similarities in it to alarm Lyell, who wrote to Darwin urging that he should delay no longer in publishing his own findings. Moreover, only a few weeks after reading the *Annals* paper, Lyell opened his own "species notebook"; at the top of the first page he wrote the name of Wallace. And Wallace's paper was pertinent enough to prod Edward Blyth, a naturalist in India with whom Darwin was in regular correspondence, to ask Darwin: "What think you of Wallace's paper in the *Ann*[*als and*] *M*[*agazine of*] *N*[*atural*] *H*[*istory*]? Good! Upon the whole."

Darwin still dallied, and it was April 1856 before he revealed to Lyell the position that he had now reached. Sir Charles, who had been knighted in 1848, and his wife were spending four days at Down House and on each of them Lyell appears to have had long discussions with Darwin on matters of joint interest. Only on the morning of the day that the visitors were to leave did the question of questions arise. "With Darwin: On the Formation of Species by Natural Selection—(Origin Query?)," Lyell wrote on page 137 of his "Scientific Journal No. I." "Genera differ in the variability of the species," he went on, "but all extensive genera have species in them which have a tendency to vary. When the condit.s alter, those individuals, which vary so as to adapt them to the new circums.s, flourish & survive while the others are cut off." He mentioned the struggle for existence, added a précis of his talk with Darwin in a few further lines, and concluded: "The reason why Mr. Wallace['s] introduction of species, most allied to those immediately preceding in Time, or that new species was in each geol.l period akin to species of the period immediately antecedent, seems explained by the Natural Selection Theory."

Lyell urged Darwin to publish his theory, and his other scientific friends appear to have agreed. "When Huxley, Hooker and [Thomas Vernon] Wollaston were at Darwin's last week," Lyell told Charles Bunbury on April 30, "they (all four of them) ran a tilt against species farther I believe than they are deliberately prepared to go. Wollaston least unorthodox. I cannot easily see how they can go so far, and not embrace the whole Lamarckian doctrine."

Surely now was the time for Darwin to start writing. But he still hesitated. "I hardly know what to think," he wrote to Lyell on May 3, "but will reflect on it, but it [publication] goes against my prejudices. To give a fair sketch would be absolutely impossible, for every proposition requires such an array of facts. If I were to do anything, it could only refer to the main agency of change—selection—and perhaps point out a very few of the leading features, which countenance such a view, and some few of the main difficulties. But I do not know what to think; I rather hate the idea of writing for priority, yet I certainly should be vexed if any one were to publish my doctrines before me."

Six days later he wrote to Hooker, reporting that Lyell had been urging publication and adding: "I am fixed against any periodical or Journal, as I positively will *not* expose myself to an Editor or Council allowing a publication for which they might be abused. If I publish anything it must be a *very thin* & little volume, giving a sketch of my views & difficulties; but it is really dreadfully unphilosophical to give a résumé, without exact references, of an unpublished work."

He was still anxious that his theory should be presented to the world only when every detail was buttressed by evidence, when all the questions that he knew would be raised could be countered by satisfactory answers. But he was also worried about priority. His ideas were farther ahead, and far more detailed, than those of Wallace. But he was only human. And it is difficult not to believe that two letters he wrote to Asa Gray—the first in the summer of 1856; the second, including a tolerably full description of natural selection, in the autumn of 1857—were a staking out of his claim. The motive may have been unconscious. But Darwin had an unconscious that helped him more than once, urging him to placate his opponents, to remain in the rearguard rather than the front line of the fray. Gray was professor of botany at Harvard. He and Darwin had met in London. Both men respected each other, and it was, perhaps, natural enough that he should now tell Gray at length how he had been captivated by the species question and of the conclusion he had reached—"the heterodox conclusion that there are no such things as independently created species—that species are only strongly defined varieties."

On May 14, 1856, he noted in his personal journal: "Began by Lyell's advice writing species sketch," and on June 10 he told William Darwin Fox that Lyell was strongly urging him to write a preliminary essay. "This I have begun to do," he said, "but my work will be horribly imperfect & with many mistakes so that I groan & tremble when I think of it." Once he had begun, the prospects of a "little volume" quickly vanished. "Sometimes," he wrote to Fox, "I fear I shall break down, for my subject gets bigger and bigger with each month's work."

To Wallace, Darwin sent his congratulations on the *Annals* paper. But lest there be any doubt about their respective positions, he added: "This summer will make the 20th year (!) since I opened my first note-book, on the question how and in what way do species and varieties differ from each other. I am now preparing my work for publication, but I find the subject so very large, that though I have written many chapters, I do not suppose I shall go to press for two years." Even that, he must have felt, was being overoptimistic. For both men the study of evolution remained a leisurely affair. To Wallace, the method by which evolution took place was still a riddle; to Darwin, who had spent twenty years worrying away at the problem, a further year or two hardly mattered. But by mid-October 1856, he had finished his second chapter, and by mid-December the third.

He worked tidily on at Down House, a pleasant middle-aged

country gentleman who only rarely left his rural retreat for London and the British Museum, where he must almost have brushed shoulders with another man about to change the world, Karl Marx, working on his own personal blockbuster. It was a placid life, and if there was any disturbing event in 1857, it was the visit of Captain FitzRoy to Down House. When the *Beagle*'s commander had, fourteen years earlier, been made governor of New Zealand, Darwin had sent kindly congratulations. But over the years, as Darwin's theory on the species question had moved in one direction, so the Captain's religious convictions had hardened. The visit was not a success, and it was the last time the two men met.

A more relevant event of 1857 was the publication of Philip Gosse's *Omphalos: An Attempt to Untie the Geological Knot*, a book that dramatically failed to deal with evolution, which in retrospect is farcical but which had tragic overtones for its author. Gosse was a naturalist of some distinction and a Fellow of the Royal Society, at whose meetings he had met both Hooker and Darwin. He was also a member of the Plymouth Brethren, a sect that propagated the literal truth of the Bible. Unwilling to accept Lyell's geological chronology, Gosse embarked on what his son, the writer Edmund Gosse, was to call "a strange act of wilfulness." This was the writing of *Omphalos*, a book that, while specifically addressing itself to the geological record, also attempted to disperse the proevolutionary atmosphere, which had been thickening in scientific circles throughout the 1850s.

On the species question, Philip Gosse had no doubts. "I assume that each organism which the Creator educed was stamped with an indelible specific character, which made it what it was, and distinguished it from everything else, however near or like. I assume that such character has been, and is, indelible and immutable; that the characters which distinguish species from species *now*, were as definite at the first instant of their creation as now, and are as distinct now as they were then."

It was perhaps no more than a rather dogmatic statement of a belief still held, in good faith if with minimal thought, by a large number of Christians. But when it came to explaining the awkward record of the rocks, "the Geological Knot" that Gosse was so intent on untying, the explanation was too much even for most of his supporters to swallow. "I venture to suggest in the following pages," he wrote, "an element, hitherto overlooked, which disturbs the conclusions of geologists respecting the antiquity of the earth. Their calculations are sound on the recognised premises: *but they have not allowed for the Law of Prochronism in Creation.*" This appeal to prochronism, the referring of an event to an earlier date than the true one, maintained that scientists had set too much store on fossils, which Gosse claimed had been put in place by the Creator in 4004 B.C., or some such comparatively recent date, so as to suggest for the earth a greater age than it really had. "It may be objected," he admitted, "that, to assume the world to have been created with fossil skeletons in its crust—skeletons of animals that never really existed—is to charge the Creator with forming objects whose sole purpose was to deceive us. The reply is obvious. Were the concentric timber-rings of a created tree formed merely to deceive? Were the growth lines of a created shell intended to deceive? Was the navel of the created Man intended to deceive him into the persuasion that he had had a parent?"

To Gosse, the shakiness of the argument was invisible, and he unwisely asked: "Who will say that the suggestion, *that the strata of the surface of the earth, with their fossil floras and faunas, may possibly belong to a prochronic development of the mighty plan of the life-history of this world,*—who will dare to say that such a suggestion is a self-evident absurdity?"

Many did say, including Charles Kingsley, Christian Socialist and author of *Westward Ho!* who told Gosse in private that he could not "give up the painful and slow conclusion of five and twenty years' study of geology, and believe that God has written on the rocks one enormous and superfluous lie for all mankind." Publicly, Kingsley added a footnote to his *Glaucus; or, the Wonders of the Shore*, which asked, "what rational man, who knows even a little of geology, will not be tempted to say—If Scripture can only be vindicated by such an outrage to common sense and fact, then I will give up Scripture and stand by common sense?" Gosse earned only ridicule from either side in the great debate. Evolution remained, as Winston Churchill was to describe Russia, "a riddle wrapped in a mystery inside an enigma," and it seemed possible that the nineteenth century might roll on for a good many years before the situation was radically altered.

Darwin's continuing attempt to alter it suffered a severe shock in the summer of 1857 as he went on with writing "the big book." As part of his investigation of variation, he had tried to discover quantitative rules governing the appearance of variation in nature, a search that involved comparing plant genera containing a large number of species with those containing a small number. He had gone some way with this when on July 13, 1857, he discussed the subject with John Lubbock, the much younger man whom he had encouraged since settling in Downe a decade and a half earlier. Lubbock quickly convinced him that he had been wrong to consider merely the relative size of genera, an approach that produced misleading results. Darwin told Hooker: "he has pointed out to me the grossest blunder which I have made in principle, & which entails 2 or 3 weeks' lost work; & I am at a dead-lock till I have these Books to go over again, & see what the result of calculation on right principle is.—I am the most miserable, bemuddled, stupid Dog in all England, & am ready to cry with vexation at my blindness & presumption." To Lubbock he wrote with an outspoken contrition that exemplifies how Darwin's attitude contrasted so strongly with that of his later cocksure opponents. "You have done me the greatest possible service in helping me to clarify my brains," wrote the Darwin who always deplored his own ignorance of mathematics. "If I am as muzzy on all subjects as I am on proportion and chance—what a book I shall produce! . . . I am quite convinced yours is the right way: I had thought of it, but should never have done it had it not been for my most fortunate conversation with you." Then he added a P.S. "It is enough to make me tear up all my MS and give up in despair. It will take me several weeks to go over all my materials. But oh, if you knew how thankful I am to you!"

A few months later he wrote a 2,500-word letter to Asa Gray which was detailed enough to be read to the Linnean Society the following year to buttress the statement that his claim for natural selection as a main engine of evolution had priority over the same belief by then being put forward by Wallace. On an undated copy Darwin wrote: "This was sent to Asa Gray 8 or 9 months ago, I think October 1857." However, the letter itself is dated by Darwin "Sept. 5th," to which his son Francis added "[1857]" while editing his father's correspondence—editing it, moreover, while Hooker, at least partly responsible for the "October" in the Linnean Society's proceedings, was still alive.

Darwin, who enclosed for Gray an abstract of the book he was writing, explained:

> Why I think that species have really changed, depends on general facts in the affinities, embryology, rudimentary organs, geological history and geographical distribution of organic beings. . . .

I think it can be shown that there is such an unerring power at work, or *Natural Selection* (the title of my book), which selects exclusively for the good of each organic being. The elder De Candolle, W. Herbert, and Lyell, have written strongly on the struggle for life; but even they have not written strongly enough. Reflect that every being (even the elephant) breeds at such a rate that, in a few years, or at most a few centuries or thousands of years, the surface of the earth would not hold the progeny of any one species. I have found it hard constantly to bear in mind that the increase of every single species is checked during some part of its life, or during some shortly recurrent generation. Only a few of those annually born can live to propagate their kind. What a trifling difference must often determine which shall survive and which perish!

. . . Now take the case of a country undergoing some change; this will tend to cause some of its inhabitants to vary slightly; not but what I believe most beings vary at all times enough for selection to act on. Some of its inhabitants will be exterminated, and the remainder will be exposed to the mutual action of a different set of inhabitants, which I believe to be more important to the life of each being than mere climate. Considering the infinitely various ways beings have to obtain food by struggling with other beings, to escape danger at various times of life, to have their eggs or seeds disseminated, &c. &c., I cannot doubt that during millions of generations individuals of a species will be born with some slight variation profitable to some part of its economy; such will have a better chance of surviving, propagating this variation, which again will be slowly increased by the accumulative action of natural selection; and the variety thus formed will either coexist with, or more commonly will exterminate its parent form. An organic being like the woodpecker, or the mistletoe, may thus come to be adapted to a score of contingencies; natural selection, accumulating those slight variations in all parts of its structure which are in any way useful to it, during any part of its life.

In this letter to Gray, Darwin hinted at how some of the more obvious objections to the theory of natural selection might be overcome, but concluded: "This sketch is *most* imperfect; but in so short a space I cannot make it better. Your imagination must fill up many wide blanks. Without some reflection, it will appear all rubbish; perhaps it will appear so after reflection."

Meanwhile he worked on, throughout the rest of 1857 and through the first months of 1858. The labor seemed endless, and he wrote almost in despair in May 1858 to Syms Covington in

Australia. "I have for some years been preparing a work for publication which I commenced 20 years ago, and for which I sometimes find extracts in your hand-writing! This work will be my biggest; it treats on the origin of varieties of our domestic animals and plants, and on the origin of species in a state of nature. I have to discuss every branch of natural history, and the work is beyond my strength and tries me sorely."

He badly needed encouragement, and he got it the following month, after he had sent Hooker a part of the manuscript on which he was at work. Hooker was impressed, and Darwin replied to him on the eighth. "You would laugh if you could know how much your note pleased me," he said. "I had *firmest* conviction that you would say all my M.S. was bosh, & thank God you are one of the few men who dare speak truth. Though I shd not have much cared about throwing away what you have seen, yet I have been forced to confess to myself that all was much alike, & if you condemned that you wd condemn all my life's work—& that I confess made me a little low—but I could have borne it, for I have the conviction that I have honestly done my best."

So with Hooker's encouragement he was prepared to work on, but on a full-scale exposition of his views on the species problem that might well be completed only many years ahead. Within a month the situation was dramatically changed.

At the beginning of 1858, Wallace, living at Ternate, Moluccas, in what is now Indonesia, was considering the impact Darwin's work would have on his own. "He is now preparing for publication his great work on species and varieties, for which he has been collecting information twenty years," he wrote to Bates. "He may save me the trouble of writing the second part of my hypothesis by proving that there is no difference in nature between the origin of species and varieties, or he may give me trouble by arriving at another conclusion, but at all events his facts will be given for me to work upon." But it was not only facts that Wallace still needed. Confident that life had evolved rather than been created, he still did not know what engine it was that powered the operation.

Then, either late in January 1858, or early the following month, Wallace fell ill with a bout of malaria. For a few days he was half delirious. He worried away at the species problem, and as he did so recalled Malthus, whose book he had read a dozen years previously, and the theory of population it expounded. "Vaguely thinking over the enormous and constant destruction which this implied," he wrote of the book that had made its impact on Darwin two decades earlier, "it occurred to me to ask the question, Why do some die and some live?" The answer appeared obvious. "From the effects of disease the most healthy escaped; from enemies, the strongest, the swiftest, or the most cunning; from famine, the best hunters." Quite independently from Darwin, Wallace had arrived at natural selection.

Two days later he had recovered sufficiently from his malaria to set down his beliefs on the species question, now that what he called the "sudden flash of insight" had come to him. They ran to 4,000 words and were headed "On the Tendency of Varieties to Depart Indefinitely from the Original Type." The manuscript arrived at Down House on the morning of June 18.

At least, for more than a century it was taken for granted that it arrived on June 18. However, a long round of research and detective work by John Langdon Brooks, which began in 1967, eventually led to the proposal that it might have arrived not in June but in May. This suggestion is plausible to anyone who has studied the deletions and amendments to original Darwin documents that have in some cases produced printed versions different from the manuscript originals. These changes are rarely significant and in most cases go no farther than a "tidying up" of Darwin's English or punctuation, or an attempted elucidation of his quickly written notes.

On receipt of Wallace's manuscript, Darwin sent it to Lyell with a covering letter dated "Down, 18th" in his own hand. To this there was subsequently added, in pencil and in an unknown hand, "[June 1858]," and Francis Darwin says in the text of *Life and Letters* that his father's work was interrupted by the receipt of Wallace's manuscript in June. Brooks builds up, with the help of information on the Far East postal services, a viable but unproven case for Darwin's having received the manuscript in May.

This possibility adds a further complication to the relationship between the contributions of Darwin and of Wallace to the idea of natural selection as the engine powering evolution. Darwin's fame within his own lifetime, and his steadily growing posthumous influence, almost inevitably produced a school of thought that inferred, and sometimes claimed, that he swam into success with the help of Wallace's ideas; that his higher place in the pantheon of scientific success was at least partly due to social class and secure financial position. These no doubt helped, but it is unrealistic to claim that they were more than small weights in the balance, and it is by no means certain that they were even that. Nevertheless, Darwin's ideas and Wallace's were so similar in some respects that the two men's solutions to the problems that arose as the implications of natural selection became apparent could hardly help cross-fertilizing each other. During the summer of 1858 Darwin was still hard at work on what he still planned to be "the big book," and whether his work from mid-May to mid-June occurred after or before he had read Wallace's paper is therefore of some significance.

Wallace could have sent his paper to one of the learned societies, or to one of the journals. Instead, he sent it to Darwin, whose opinion he respected, and asked him to deal with it as he thought best. Poor Darwin. His feelings were revealed in the letter he wrote to Lyell. "Your words have come true with a vengeance—that I should be forestalled," he began. "You said this, when I explained to you here very briefly my views of 'Natural Selection' depending on the struggle for existence. I never saw a more striking coincidence; if Wallace had my MS sketch written out in 1842, he could not have made a better short abstract! Even his terms now stand as heads of my chapters. Please return me the MS., which he does not say he wishes me to publish, but I shall, of course, at once write and offer to send to any journal. So all my originality, whatever it may amount to, will be smashed, though my book, if it will ever have any value, will not be deteriorated; as all the labour consists in the application of the theory."

Darwin, as might have been expected, proposed to Lyell that Wallace's consent to publication of his paper should be obtained as soon as possible. Lyell conferred with Hooker, and both agreed with Darwin. But, they added, Darwin's paper of 1844 should be published at the same time—a judgment of Solomon that called for the production of two babies rather than the division of one.

But this proposal raised anguished moral doubts in Darwin's mind. Had it not been for Wallace's paper he would never have considered anything less than the full-scale book, on which he might be working for many more years. Was it right, he asked himself, that he should now be persuaded into publication by another man's work? "I would far rather burn my whole book," he told Lyell, "than that [Wallace] or any other man should think that I had behaved in a paltry spirit. Do you not think his having sent me this sketch ties my hands?" This was only the first of Darwin's struggles with his conscience. He hated losing his priority, but he hated even more the chance of being suspected of ungentlemanly or nonsporting conduct. He solved the matter in the way one would have expected of him, by writing "half a letter" to Wallace, saying that he would not publish anything before Wallace had published, and "[giving] up all priority to him." Then, before he could post the letter, he received an anguished note from Lyell and Hooker. It urged him, he later told Wallace, "to send some MS to them, and allow them to act as they thought fair and honourably to both of us. I did so."

Lyell and Hooker were more rugged than Darwin and were unwilling that moral arguments about priority should interfere with what they were to call "the interests of science." What is more, they saw their opportunity. Robert Brown, ex-president of the Linnean Society, had recently died, and the last meeting of the summer session, called for June 17, had been canceled. Vacancies on the Council had to be filled within three months, and a special meeting had been called for July 1. What better occasion could there be for announcing, simultaneously, the views on the origin of species of both Darwin and Wallace?

Three items were read at the meeting: an extract from Darwin's 1844 paper; part of the letter he had written to Asa Gray in the autumn of 1857; and Wallace's recently arrived paper. By coincidence, but almost symbolically, there was no time for a paper by George Bentham, the botanist nephew of Jeremy Bentham and vice-president of the Linnean Society; it dealt with the immutability of species. Almost three decades later, Bentham was to provide an ironic footnote to the occasion. "Most fortunately," he wrote to Francis Darwin after Charles Darwin's death, "my paper had to give way to Mr. Darwin's, and when once that was read, I felt bound to defer mine for reconsideration. I began to entertain doubts on the subject, and on the appearance of the Origin of Species, I was forced, however, reluctantly, to give up my long cherished convictions, the result of much labour and study, and I cancelled all that part of my paper which urged original fixity, and published only portions of the remainder in another form. . . ."

In 1858 Hooker and Lyell spared no effort in underlining Darwin's priority, and the Linnean Society's *Proceedings* reports them as describing his contribution as an "Extract from a MS. work on Species, by Charles Darwin Esq., FRS, F.L.S., &c., sketched in 1839, and copied in 1844."

Darwin appears to have been much in the dark about what actually went on during the famous meeting of July 1. He could not attend because of family and domestic troubles. His son Charles had died of scarlet fever on June 28, a daughter was seriously ill with diphtheria, other members of the family had scarlet fever, while one of the nurses had the same infection and another had quinsy.

Hooker gave Darwin a report of the meeting, and on July 5 Darwin thanked him. "But in truth it shames me that you should have lost time on a mere point of priority," Darwin added. "I shall be curious to see proofs. I do not in the least understand whether my letter to A. Gray is to be printed [in the Linnean Society's *Proceedings*]; I suppose not, only your note; but I am quite indifferent, & place myself absolutely in your and Lyell's hands. . . . Lastly you said you would write to Wallace; I certainly should much like this, as it would quite exonerate me: if you would send me your note, sealed up, I would forward it with my own, as I know address etc."

Darwin was, in fact, somewhat hazy about his letter to Gray, and three days after the Linnean meeting asked Gray when he had sent it. As "the only very brief thing which I had written out was a copy of my letters to you, I sent it and I believe it has just been read . . . before the Linnaean Society; and this is the reason, why I should be glad of the date. . . . I am sure it was written in September, October or November of last year." His vagueness about the meeting was underlined when he wrote to Hooker again on the thirteenth. "I am MUCH *more* than satisfied at what took place at Linn. Soc.—I had thought that your letter & mine to Asa Gray were to be only an appendix to Wallace's paper. . . . You cannot imagine how pleased I am that the notion of Natural Selection has acted as a purgative on your bowels of immutability. Whenever naturalists can look at species changing as certain, what a magnificent field will be open—on all the laws of variation, on the genealogy of all living beings, on their lines of migration, etc. etc. . . ."

Had Darwin come to London for the meeting, he might have been disappointed. Although the interest was intense, Hooker later wrote, "the subject [was] too novel and too ominous for the old School to enter the lists before armouring. It was talked over after the meeting 'with bated breath.' Lyell's approval, and perhaps in a small way mine, as his Lieutenant in the affair, rather overawed those Fellows who would otherwise have flown out against the doctrine, and this because we had the vantage ground of being familiar with the authors and their themes." If there was any doubt that Darwin had hardly made an impact, it was removed when Thomas Bell, the Society's president, made his annual report. "The year which has passed . . . ," he said, "has not . . . been marked by any of those striking discoveries which at once revolutionize, so to speak, the department of science on which they bear."

However, the accounts of Darwin and Wallace were noted in September by Richard Owen in his presidential address to the British Association. His first reaction was cautious. Mr. Wallace, he said, "assuming, as is probable, that varieties do arise in a wild species, he shows how such deviations from type may either tend to the destruction of a variety, or to adapt a variety to some changes in surrounding conditions, under which it is calculated to exist, than the type-form from which it deviated. . . . Mr. Charles Darwin had previously to Mr. Wallace illustrated this principle by ingenious suppositions. . . ."

What little notice there was tended to be critical. The Reverend Arthur Hussey asked in the *Zoologist* whether the papers were not "founded upon the imaginary probable, rather than obtained by induction from ascertained facts, . . . the only solid and satisfactory basis of a new opinion." The *Dublin Review*, reviewing Hugh Miller's *The Testimony of the Rocks* in 1858, gave an indication of what a few years later would be the attitude of the Catholic Church to *The Origin*. "The salvation of man," it affirmed, "is a far higher object than the progress of science and we have no hesitation in maintaining that if in the judgment of the Church the promulgation of any scientific truth was more likely to hinder men's salvation than to promote it, she would not only be justified in her efforts to suppress it, but it would be her bounden duty to do her utmost to suppress it. . . . The truth ultimately can do no harm, although, temporarily, injury may follow from an unreasonable application of it."

The Dublin scientists also had their skeptics, and the Reverend Samuel Haughton told the Geological Society of Dublin in February 1859 that the idea had been noticed only because of "the weight of authority of the names [Lyell and Hooker] under whose auspices it has been brought forward. If it means what it says, it is a truism; if it means anything more, it is contrary to fact."

There was one exception to this generally skeptical reaction. It came from the Reverend H. B. Tristram, who said in "On the

Ornithology of Northern Africa," which appeared in the first volume of *The IBIS:* "Writing with a series of about 100 Larks of various species from the Sahara before me, I cannot help feeling convinced of the truth of the views set forth by Messrs. Darwin and Wallace in their communications to the Linnean Society." Tristram was letting his reason momentarily triumph over his religion and later became an anti-evolutionist on theological grounds. For a short while, however, he was a convert before his time.

The joint presentation of the Darwin and Wallace papers has often been lauded in somewhat unrealistic terms. Julian Huxley, T. H. Huxley's grandson and himself a prominent biologist, has described the occasion as "a monument to the natural generosity of both the great biologists," and Loren C. Eiseley, the American naturalist, was impressed by the "mutual nobility" of Darwin and Wallace. However, Wallace had limited opportunity for nobility or generosity, since his paper was read without his knowledge or specific consent, and he did not hear of the Linnean Society meeting until three months after it had taken place. Then he was glad of what had happened, telling his mother, "This assures me the acquaintance and assistance of these eminent men on my return home." But when his paper was printed in the *Journal* of the Linnean Society, it was printed, as he somewhat tersely noted, "without [his] knowledge, and of course without any correction of proofs." As for Darwin, he seems hardly to have been a free agent in the face of Lyell's and Hooker's pressure for publication.

There are today virtually no gaps in the story of how Wallace's paper came into Darwin's hands or of the background to their work. Even were Darwin's character not now known in the most intimate detail, it would be difficult to make a case for his having plagiarized Wallace's work—or anyone else's, for that matter. In any case the enormous amount of his correspondence that has been scrutinized during the last decades makes clear beyond all doubt that he was not that sort of man. In the field of evolution, moreover, Darwin distinguished himself not so much by noting the problem to be solved as by the credibility of his solution, followed by confirmation through the accumulation of evidence.

The one vital outcome of Wallace's paper was that it did at last push Darwin into writing an account that could be published within the near future. Even before publication of Wallace's paper in the *Annals*, he had, it is true, taken Lyell's advice and started writing. But the projected work was to include not only his theories but also his extensive evidence, replete with references, and was to cite far more detail than eventually filled the pages of *The Origin*. It could easily have taken a decade or more to complete, and while Darwin was toiling away in the solitude of Down House, other men might have gone galloping by. The introduction of natural selection by someone other than Darwin could have had unexpected results, as has been pointed out by Gregory Bateson, son of the man who was to help found the science of genetics. Wallace, he has remarked, once commented to Darwin: "The action of [natural selection] is exactly like that of the centrifugal governor of the steam engine, which checks and corrects any irregularities almost before they become evident; and in like manner no unbalanced deficiency in the animal kingdom can ever reach any conspicuous magnitude because it would make itself felt at the very first step, by rendering existence difficult and extinction almost sure soon to follow." Thus if Wallace rather than Darwin had introduced natural selection, the whole cybernetics movement, Gregory Bateson hazards, "might have occurred 100 years earlier as a result of Wallace's comparison between the steam engine with a governor and the process of natural selection."

But in the summer of 1858, with the prospect of a Wallace book coming up over the horizon, Darwin set to work on something different. "July 20th to August 12th at Sandown," he wrote in his personal journal for 1858: "begun Abstract of Species book." He was still not entirely happy about it, writing to Hooker: "It seems a queer plan to give an abstract of an unpublished work; nevertheless I repeat I am extremely glad I have begun in earnest on it."

"Wallace's impetus," Thomas Huxley confided to Hooker, "seems to have set Darwin going in earnest, and I am rejoiced to hear we shall learn his views in full, at last. I look forward to a great revolution being effected. Depend upon it, in natural history, as in everything else, when the English mind fully determines to work a thing out, it will do it better than any other."

The main impediment, as both Huxley and Hooker knew, was now Darwin's health. To Hooker he wrote in November, "but without you lived with me you cannot form any conception how incapable I am of any exertion of mind or body. Daily after my work is done at 12 o'clock my head swims so that I can hardly walk. . . ." And then, referring to a recent paper he had written, "That confounded Leguminous paper in G[ardeners'] Chronicle was done in afternoon and the consequence was I had to go to Moor

Park for a week, and I am resolved I will not attempt mental work in afternoon: my head, I do assure you, will not stand it."

But at least he was now tackling a book on a scale very different from what he had been contemplating before Wallace's paper arrived. He was later to appreciate the advantages of this, and once wrote that one element in the success of *The Origin* "was its moderate size, & this I owe to the appearance of Wallace's essay; had I published on the scale in which I began to write in 1856, the book would have been four or five times as large as the Origin, & very few would have had the patience to read it." But he was still a reluctant author, and from the summer of 1858 to the summer of 1859, his correspondence is filled with expostulations about difficulties real and imagined.

He at first hoped that he could squeeze the material into a paper, or a series of papers, for the Linnean Society. "I will condense to utmost," he promised Hooker. If the result was too long, he added, he would help pay for the printing. By Christmas Eve, 1858, he had written 330 folio pages and estimated that he still required another 150 to 200. This would make a printed volume of about 400 pages, something too big to form part of any society's journal. "I think [this] will be better in many respects," he confided to Hooker. "The subject really seems to me too large for discussion at any Society, & I believe Religion would be brought in by men whom I know."

By the spring of 1859, the manuscript was nearing completion. Darwin knew little about the problems of general publishing and turned to Lyell for advice. John Murray—who fourteen years earlier had bought the copyright in Darwin's account of the *Beagle* voyage for £150 from Henry Colburn, the original publisher—was an obvious choice. On March 31, Darwin took Lyell's advice and wrote to Murray. "The book," he said, after having given a brief description, *"ought* to be popular with a large body of scientific and semi-scientific readers, as it bears on agriculture, the history of our domestic productions and on whole fields of Zoology, Botany and Geology. I have done my best, but whether it will succeed I cannot say. I have been quite surprised at finding how much interested strangers and acquaintances have been in the subject. Only some small portions are at all abstruse. I hope to be ready for press early in May, and then most earnestly wish to print at a rapid rate, for my health is much broken, and I want rest."

Murray replied by return. After thanking Darwin for the details he had sent, he went on, "On the strength of this information & my knowledge of your former publications, I can have no hesitation in swerving from my usual routine & in stating at once even without seeing the MS that I shall be most happy to publish it for you on the same terms as those on which I publish for Sir Charles Lyell—viz.—I will print an edition, fixing the number of copies with your concurrence, according to what shall appear to me (on perusal of a part, at least, of the work) to be advisable. . . ." Darwin was to get two-thirds of the net proceeds. He was grateful, but insisted that he would not hold Murray to his offer if he was offended by the manuscript, the first few chapters of which he sent to the publisher a few days later.

There is some confusion about Murray's initial reaction. On April 11, Darwin told Hooker that he had heard from the publisher, who had read the first three chapters of the manuscript and who stood by his offer to publish. However, Emily Morse Symonds —writing in 1932 under the pseudonym George Paston—who had access to the publisher's correspondence, casts a different light on the situation. She claims that Murray was skeptical of Darwin's theory, "declared that the Darwinian theory was as absurd as though one should contemplate a fruitful union between a poker and a rabbit," and felt that a printing of 500 copies would be sufficient.

What is certain is that Murray did turn for advice to two acquaintances. The first was a legal friend, George Pollock, who commented that the book was too profound but proposed a printing of 1,000 copies. The help of the Reverend Whitwell Elwin, editor of Murray's *Quarterly Review*, was then invoked. Elwin—a devout Christian who a quarter of a century later could tell Murray: "More than ever (if that were possible) I believe, upon sure, unanswerable evidence, that the Lord God Omnipotent reigneth, and that the Bible contains His revelation to man"—discussed the matter with Lyell. The upshot was a long letter that might, but for Murray's judgment, have held back *The Origin* for a considerable time or even prevented publication in its successful form. However, Elwin's view was less condemnatory than has sometimes been suggested and his long letter to John Murray, a precursor of much later criticism, is worth quoting in full:

After you had the kindness to allow me to read the MS, I made a point of seeing Sir Charles Lyell who I understood had in some degree advised the publication. I had myself formed a strong opinion the other way, & I stated to him fully my conviction & the grounds of it. When we had thoroughly talked the matter over Sir Charles Lyell considered that I ought through you to convey my [word unclear; possibly "impressions"] to Mr. Darwin himself. I should have thought this presumptuous and impertinent in me if I had not received from Sir Charles, the assurance that Mr. Darwin would not consider it either the one or the other. Nevertheless, I speak with diffidence, & I am sorry that Sir Charles, who was just starting for the Continent, could not, before his return, find leisure to correspond with Mr. Darwin on the question.

I must say at the outset that it is the very high opinion I have of Mr. Darwin, founded on his Journal of a Naturalist, & the conviction amounting to certainty, of the value of any researches of his, which made me eager to get both him & his friends to re-consider the propriety of sending forth his treatise in its present form. It seemed to me that to put forth the theory without the evidence would do grievous injustice to his views & to his twenty years of observation & experiments. At every page I was tantalised by the absence of the proofs. All kinds of objections and possibilities rose up in my mind, & it was pretty fretting to think that the author had a whole array of facts and inferences from facts absolutely *essential* to the decision of the question which were not before the reader. It is to ask the jury for a verdict without putting the witness into the box. One part of the public, I suspect, under these circumstances will reject the theory from recalling some obvious facts apparently at variance with it & to which Mr. Darwin may nevertheless have a complete answer, while another part of the public will feel how unsatisfactory it is to go into the theory when only a fragment of the subject is before them, & will postpone the consideration of it till they can study it with more advantage. The more original the view, the more elaborate the researches on which it rests, the more extensive the series of facts in Natural History which bear upon it, the more it is prejudiced by a partial survey of the field which keeps out of sight the larger part of the materials.

A second objection to the publication of the treatise in its present form, though of less weight than the first, is yet of some moment. The Journal of Mr. Darwin is, as you have often heard me say, one of the most charming books in the language. No person could detail observations in Natural History in a more attractive manner. The dissertation on species is on the contrary in a much harder and drier style. I impute this to the absence of details. It is those which give relief and interest to the scientific outline—so that the very omission which takes from the philosophic value of the work destroys in a great degree its popular value also. Whatever class of the public he wishes to win he weakens the effect by an imperfect and comparatively meagre exposition of his theory.

I am aware that many facts are given in the work as it stands, but they are so often wanting to do more than qualify my criticisms. I state my views broadly & roughly. Mr. Darwin will understand my meaning as well as if I had spoken with nice precision.

Upon the supposition that my description of the work is correct Sir Charles Lyell agrees in my conclusions & bid me say this when I wrote you a letter for Mr. Darwin to read. Sir Charles tells me that he feared that in his anxiety to make his work perfect Mr. Darwin would postpone indefinitely the putting his material into shape, & that thus the world might at last be deprived of his labours. He also told me that another gentleman had put forward a similar theory & that it was necessary that Mr. Darwin should promulgate his conclusions before he was anticipated. Influenced by these considerations Sir Charles urged the publication of Mr. D's observations upon pigeons, which he informs me are curious, ingenious & valuable in the highest degree, accompanied by a brief statement of his general principles. He might then remark that of these principles the phenomena respecting the pigeons were one illustration, & that a larger work would shortly appear in which the same conclusions would be demonstrated by examples drawn from the wide world of nature.

This appears to me to be an admirable suggestion. Even if the larger work were ready it would be the best mode of preparing the way for it. Everybody is interested in pigeons. The book would be reviewed in every journal in the kingdom, & would soon be on every table. The public at large can better understand a question when it is narrowed to a single case of this kind than when the whole varied kingdom of nature is brought under discussion at the outset. Interest in the larger work would be roused, & good-will would be conciliated to the subsequent development of the theory in all its bearings. It would be approached with impartiality—not to say favour & would appeal to the large public which had been interested by the previous book upon pigeons, which book would be complete in itself, & open to none of the objections that I have urged against the present outline. Indeed I should say of the latter that for an outline it is too much, & for a thorough discussion of the question, it is not near enough.

I write this with the intention that you should forward it to Mr.

Darwin. He must be good enough to excuse the crude manner in which I state my impressions. I am obliged to write as fast as my pen can move or I should not be able to write at all. My sole object & desire is to secure his theory before coming before the world in the way which will do justice to the extraordinary merit of his investigations & procure for him that fame which belongs to him. I am but a smatterer in these subjects. What I say has no sort of authority except so far as it may chance to commend itself to Mr. Darwin's own reason. The book on pigeons would be a delightful commencement & I am certain its reception would be the best stimulus to the prosecution of his subsequent book. I should hope if he inclines to this view that the preparatory volume could soon be got ready for the press.

Murray sent Darwin a copy of Elwin's letter, and Darwin replied by return. "It is my deliberate conviction that both Lyell's and Elwill's [*sic*] suggestions (which differ to a certain extent) are impracticable," he said. "I have done my best. Others might, I have no doubt, have done the job better, if they had my materials; but that is no help. Nothing on earth can have been kinder than both Mr. Elwyn [*sic*] and Sir C. Lyell have been."

It seems difficult to believe that Lyell, after all his advocacy, should really have supported such a watering down of the book that he himself had urged Darwin to write. But the alternatives are that Elwin was genuinely confused about Lyell's suggestion or that he felt it was his Christian duty to fudge the proposal. Luckily, Murray stood firm and decided to publish the manuscript uncut, objecting only to the first part of Darwin's proposed title, "An Abstract of an Essay." But he accepted the phrase "natural selection" after Darwin had amended the title to: *On the Origin of Species by Means of Natural Selection, or the Preservation of Favoured Races in the Struggle for Life.*

Darwin continued to work hard, still disturbed that he was unable to include the full notes and references that he felt the book demanded, and constantly surprised by the quantity of material he had accumulated since 1837. "There is no end to the necessary digressions," he told Asa Gray. "I have just finished a chapter on Instinct, and here I found grappling with such a subject as Bees' cells and comparing all my notes made during twenty years, took up a despairing length of time."

Soon he was getting tired of the book that was to change the world. "I can see daylight through my work," he told William

Darwin Fox, "and am now finally correcting my chapters for press; & I hope in month or six weeks to have proof-sheets. I am weary of my work. It is a very odd thing that I have no sensation that I overwork my brain; but facts compel me to conclude that my Brain was never formed for much thinking. . . . You do me injustice when you think that I work for fame; I value it to a certain extent; but, if I know myself, I work from a sort of instinct to try to make out truth." But by this time he had a fresh relaxation or diversion. The previous year a billiard table had been installed at Down and, as he proudly told his son William, he had "made some splendid strokes!" Now he concluded his letter to his cousin with the information that billiards "does me a deal of good, & drives the horrid species out of my head."

Parts of the manuscript were sent to Hooker. He appears to have been satisfied, but his wife found a number of obscurities, a worry for Darwin that was reinforced when, in the summer, he began to receive proofs. "I find the style incredibly bad, and most difficult to make clear and smooth," he admitted to Murray. "I am extremely sorry to say, on account of expense, and loss of time for me, that the corrections are very heavy, as heavy as possible. But from casual glances, I still hope that later chapters are not so badly written. How I could have written so badly is quite inconceivable, but I suppose it was owing to my whole attention being fixed on the general line of my argument, and not on details." And to Hooker he commented a few days later, "I have fairly to blacken [the proofs] and fasten slips of paper on, so miserable have I found the style." When he learned of the £72.8.0. bill for corrections, Darwin was appalled, offered to share the cost with Murray and added: "I had no business to send, though quite unintentionally, such badly composed MS. to the printers."

However, one encouraging event took place early in November 1859. This was the writing of Hooker's "Introductory Essay" in his *Flora Tasmaniae,* published in 1860. In *Flora Antarctica,* published in two volumes, in 1844 and 1847, the "Summary of the Voyage" had stated that remote islands furnish "the best materials for a rigid comparison of the effects of geographical position and the various meteorological phaenomena on vegetation, and for acquiring a knowledge of the great laws according to which plants are distributed over the face of the globe." In April 1852, Hooker's "Introductory Essay" to *Flora Novae-Zelandiae,* published in two volumes, in 1853 and 1855, had moved toward the Darwinian position, stating that evolution explained perplexing questions of botanical affinity and distribution better than did any preceding ideas. Now, in the work on Tasmanian plants, Hooker supported, with few qualifications, the revolutionary theory of the book that Darwin was now seeing through the press. Coming from Britain's leading botanist, it was support that could not easily be brushed away.

By this time, poor health was crippling Darwin's final work on the proofs, and despite what he described to Hooker as his "insanely strong wish to finish my accursed Book," it was almost mid-September before he could write: "I corrected last proof yesterday; and I have now my Revises, index, &c., which will take me near to the end of month. So that the neck of my work, thank God, is broken."

Lyell, in Aberdeen for the annual meeting of the British Association, was sent a set of the proofs, and it was to the members of the Association that the news of Darwin's coming book was first given. Lyell, president of the Geology Section, waited for the arrival of the Prince Consort, who had agreed to speak to the meeting, before opening his address. In it he said: "On this difficult and mysterious subject [the origin of species] a work will very shortly appear, by Mr. Charles Darwin, the result of twenty years of observation and experiments in Zoology, Botany and Geology, by which he has been led to the conclusion, that those powers of nature which give rise to races and permanent varieties in animals and plants, are the same as those which, in much longer periods, produce species, and, in a still longer series of ages, give rise to differences of generic rank. He appears to me to have succeeded, by his investigations and reasonings, in throwing a flood of light on many classes of phenomena connected with the affinities, geographical distribution, and geological succession of organic beings, for which no other hypothesis has been able, or has even attempted, to account."

This was a delayed-action bomb whose significance many of those present must have appreciated. Since Lyell was among those who visited Balmoral Castle on Deeside a few days later as guests of Queen Victoria, it is difficult to believe that this event was not the beginning of what Lyell later described as the Queen's interest in evolution.

Soon afterward, Lyell gave his verdict to Darwin. "I have just finished your volume, and right glad I am that I did my best with

Hooker to persuade you to publish it without waiting for a time which probably could never have arrived, though you lived to the age of hundred, when you had prepared all your facts on which you ground so many grand generalisations."

Darwin was not so confident. "God knows what the public will think," he wrote to Wallace. It was still only an abstract of "the big book" on which he had been at work when Wallace's 4,000 words appeared upon his desk some seventeen months previously. "Murray," Darwin told Lyell, "has printed 1250 copies, which seems to me rather too large an edition, but I hope he will not lose."

6

On the Mystery of Mysteries

The Origin of Species was published by John Murray on November 24, 1859, at fifteen shillings. Legend maintains that all the 1,250 copies were sold on the day of publication; in fact, they were all taken up by booksellers, an indication of the controversy the book was to arouse, but not quite the same thing.

In fourteen chapters totaling some 155,000 words, Darwin related how his observations on HMS *Beagle* had seemed to throw light on the origin of species. Following his return to England, he had spent twenty years collecting evidence. And he had finally decided that species gradually changed by the accumulation of variations that gave their possessors the best chance of surviving in the struggle for existence all living things had to fight. Basically, the theory was the same as he had outlined in 1842 and 1844. But it was now better ordered, with a multitude of examples, and with concluding chapters in which he admitted that objections to the theory would be raised, and attempted to deal with them. Darwin's sweet reason, his willingness to consider fresh information that might qualify his ideas, hampered the attacks he knew would come. So did his caution in limiting his comments on man to the single sentence: "Light will be thrown on the origin of man and his history." This was decidedly an understatement of what might be expected to follow *The Origin*, as Darwin well knew. His notebooks are full of hints. "When two races of men meet," he writes in notebook "E," "they act precisely like two species of animals— they fight, eat each other, bring diseases to each other, &c., but then comes the more deadly struggle, namely which have the best fitted organization, or instincts (i.e. intellect in man) to gain the day." And writing to Lyell a few weeks after publication of *The Origin*, he added a P.S., "*Our* ancestor was an animal which breathed water, had a swim bladder, a great swimming tail, an imperfect skull, and undoubtedly was an hermaphrodite! Here is a pleasant genealogy for mankind."

In *The Origin* he not only took care to slide over man's place in the evolutionary chain but tended to hedge his bets in other ways, quoting, opposite the title page, from Whewell's *Bridgewater Treatise*, "On Astronomy and General Physics"—Dr. William Whewell's entry in the 8th Earl of Bridgewater's competition for essays on "The power, wisdom and goodness of God, as manifested in the Creation"—"But with regard to the material world, we can at least go so far as this;—we can perceive that events are brought about, not by insulated interpositions of Divine power exerted in each particular case, but by the establishment of general laws." As Edward Reed has pointed out, "Darwin was publicly satisfied to hint that God may have designed natural selection by breathing life into the first organism. Yet, privately, Darwin was unsatisfied to let God even create that first creature." And when writing to Asa Gray he showed more than a trace of ambivalence, saying: "With respect to Design, I feel more inclined to show a white flag than to fire my usual long-range shot. . . . If anything is designed, certainly man must be: one's 'inner consciousness' (though a false guide) tells one so; yet I cannot admit that man's rudimentary mammae . . . were designed. If I was to say I believed this, I should believe it in the same incredible manner as the orthodox believe the Trinity in Unity. You say that you are in a haze; I am in thick mud; the orthodox would say in fetid, abominable mud; yet I cannot keep out of the question. My dear Gray, I have written a deal of nonsense."

Lyell was to make much the same point. His "Geological Evidences of the Antiquity of Man," published four years after *The Origin*, certainly paved the way for Darwin's *Descent of Man*. But as late as 1868, Lyell could write to the Duke of Argyll saying: "I objected in my 'Antiquity of Man' to what I there called the deification of natural selection, which I consider as a law or force quite subordinate to that variety-making or creative power to which all the wonders of the organic world must be referred. I cannot believe that Darwin or Wallace can mean to dispense with that mind of which you speak as directing the forces of nature. They in fact admit that we know nothing of the power which gives rise to variation in form, colour, structure, or instinct."

From the first, Darwin was confident about *The Origin*. A fortnight before publication he wrote to Gray: "I cannot possibly believe that a false theory would explain so many classes of facts, as I think it certainly does explain. On these grounds I drop my anchor, and believe that the difficulties will slowly disappear." Lyell had given at least a partial blessing to the theory, and a few days after publication, Darwin suggested how much he had helped, admitting: "I do not think I am brave enough to have stood being odious without support; now I feel as bold as a lion." Hooker had also stood up and been counted, and on November 23 Darwin could tell Lyell: "I rejoice profoundly; for, thinking of so many cases of men pursuing an illusion for years, often and often a cold shudder has run through me, and I have asked myself whether I may not have devoted my life to a phantasy. Now I look at it as morally impossible that investigators of truth, like you and Hooker, can be wholly wrong, and therefore I rest in peace."

The satisfaction at having outside support lasted for some while, and as late as June 1861, he was writing to William Benjamin Carpenter, one of the foremost naturalists of his day, "When I reflect, as I often do, that such men as Lyell, yourself, Hooker & Huxley go a certain way with me, nothing will persuade me that I am so wholly and egrigiously [sic] in error, as many of my reviewers think." But he was anxious to have critical opinions as long as they were informed, and to Jenyns, who except for the tie of his parochial duties might have sailed on the *Beagle* rather than Darwin, he wrote revealingly, "I shall be very grateful for any criticisms. But I know perfectly well that you will not at all agree with the lengths to which I go. It took long years to convert me. I may, of course, be egregiously wrong; but I cannot persuade myself that a theory which explains (as I certainly think it does) several large classes of facts, can be wholly wrong; notwithstanding the several difficulties which have to be surmounted somehow, and which stagger me even to this day."

The Origin made four major claims. The animate world was not static but dynamic; it was constantly changing, and thus species now in existence were different from those that had existed in the past. Second, the changes that were the substance of this process —for which Darwin used the words "descent with modification," "transmutation" or "descent theory," rather than "evolution"—could be small and numerous or large and rare, with no very clear line dividing the two. But Darwin maintained, and was to maintain all his life, that the major variations—those that produced "sports," or monstrosities—rarely played any part in evolution.

Third, whereas naturalists such as Lamarck had proposed separate sources for mammals, for birds and for reptiles, Darwin contended that all living organisms had evolved through the millennia from a single source. Finally, he produced the two-stage concept of natural selection as the machinery of evolution. The first stage was the production of innumerable variations, a process that was obvious when even the members of the same family were observed. The second stage was the survival of those individuals whose variations best equipped them to fight the battle for existence fought against members of their own species struggling for survival in an overcrowded environment.

There were two separate parts to the theory that, while offensive to the religious establishment in themselves, acquired their real danger—like the two halves of a nuclear weapon—when they were brought together. One was that species had not been created by God but had evolved over the years; the other was that evolution had not been directed by God but had been governed by the apparently fortuitous facts of natural selection. While Darwin was proud of his theory of natural selection, his most important single contribution to the evolutionary argument, he saw as one of its main virtues the fact that it provided a counterblow to the idea of creation. This is made clear in two of his letters to Asa Gray. "I rest on the fact that the theory of natural selection explains many lapses of facts, which, as far as we can see, repeated acts of Creation do not explain," he told Gray a few weeks after publication of *The Origin.* "On this latter view we can only say 'so it is' and not all 'why it is so.' Pray do not decide either way till you have read Ch. XIII and the Recapitulation Ch. XIV which will, I think, aid you in balancing facts." And writing in the spring of 1861 of change of species by descent, he said: "That seems to me the turning point. Personally, of course, I care much about Natural Selection; but that seems to me utterly unimportant compared with the question of Creation or Modification."

Although *The Origin* was amended in detail in successive editions, and although Darwin added and altered in order to answer queries raised by his critics, the general scheme of the book remained unchanged throughout his life. Its thoroughness, at least partly the result of its long gestation, was no doubt one reason for the importance it immediately assumed, and continued to assume, not only in biology but in the wider realms of intellectual thought.

The book began with an account of variation under domestication, the way in which "individuals of the same variety or subvariety of our older cultivated plants and animals . . . generally differ more from each other, than do the individuals of any one species or variety in a state of nature." The discussion of how selection by man had helped to bring about the different breeds of animals, birds and plants was followed by one chapter describing variation in nature and by two describing the struggle for existence and natural selection, whose power was compared with that of man's selection.

Darwin next turned to the laws governing variation and then devoted chapters to the difficulties of his theory and to the various objections he knew would be raised against it. He admitted the imperfection of the geological record, showed that current ideas on sterility and hybridism were oversimplified, and ended his book with what was to become a famous contemplation of "an entangled bank, clothed with many plants of many kinds, with birds singing on the bushes, with various insects flitting about, and with worms crawling through the damp earth, [and the reflection] that these elaborately constructed forms, so different from each other, and dependent on each other in so complex a manner, have all been produced by laws acting around us."

Divine creation was ignored rather than denied, while speculation on man was limited to the thought that in the future "Light will be thrown on the origin of man and his history."

Yet however cautious and conciliatory Darwin had been, *The Origin* threw down the gauntlet in a way that could not easily be ignored. The day after publication, he received his first indication of what the future was to hold. "This morning," he told Lyell, "I heard . . . from Murray that he sold the whole edition the first day to the trade. He wants a new edition instantly, and this utterly confounds me. Now, under water-cure, with all nervous power directed to the skin, I cannot possibly do head-work, and I must make only actually necessary corrections." Murray was soon putting in hand a new edition of 3,000 copies despite a cautionary note from Darwin, who wrote: "I am very glad of 3,000 copies, but you must not run risk for my sake."

Then there came a stroke of good fortune. *The Times* was the most important leader of public opinion in Britain, and at *The Times* the review copy of *The Origin* was handed to a Mr. Lucas, whose knowledge of science was minimal. Mr. Lucas complained to an acquaintance at having to review such a book, and the acquaintance suggested that Professor Huxley might help. Lucas wrote to Huxley, adding only that he would—apparently to keep the record straight—have to start the review with two or three paragraphs of his own. Huxley had, in fact, written to Darwin the day before publication, in effect offering his services as what was to be called "Darwin's bulldog." "And as to the curs which will bark and yelp," he wrote, "you must recollect that some of your friends, at any rate, are endowed with an amount of combativeness which (though you have often and justly rebuked it) may stand you in good stead. I am sharpening up my claws and beak in readiness."

Now, out of the blue, there came this splendid piece of luck. "I was too anxious," Huxley later wrote, "to seize upon the opportunity thus offered of giving the book a fair chance with the multitudinous readers of 'The Times,' to make any difficulty about conditions, and being then very full of the subject, I wrote the article faster, I think, than I ever wrote anything in my life, and sent it to Mr. Lucas, who duly prefixed his opening sentences."

In the *Times* Huxley skillfully praised *The Origin* in terms that he believed might appeal to the paper's readers. Most naturalists, he said, had since Lamarck's time left speculations on the origin of species "to such dreamers as the author of the 'Vestiges.' " Darwin, by contrast, was "as greedy of cases and precedents as any constitutional lawyer, and all the principles he lays down are capable of being brought to the test of observation and experiment. The path he bids us follow professes to be not a mere airy track, fabricated of ideal cobwebs, but a solid and broad bridge of facts." The 5,000-word review filled three and a half columns, and on reading it Darwin observed: "The old fogies will think the world will come to an end." And to Hooker he wrote: "It will do grand service, especially as so nobly soaring above religious prejudices. I shall grow as arrogant as Whewell, perhaps even as Owen!"

Huxley's instinctive reaction to the book had been that it "provided us with the working hypothesis we sought. . . . My reflection, when I first made myself master of the central idea . . . was, 'How extremely stupid not to have thought of that!' " Even so, his detailed and private support for *The Origin* was not as unqualified as is often imagined today. "You have," he had written to Darwin on November 23, 1859, "loaded yourself with an unnecessary difficulty in adopting *Natura non facit saltum* so unreservedly." For Huxley, the importance of "jumps" in evolution—sudden changes after long periods without any—was always a possibility, a view that says a good deal for his judgment. Darwin himself had not always been as opposed to the idea of "jumps" as he was when *The Origin* finally appeared. "As in first cases distinct species inosculate, so must we believe ancient ones," he had written during the early days of his post-*Beagle* researches: "[.'.] not *gradual* change or degeneration from circumstances: if one species does change into another it must be per saltum—or species may perish."

It was not only Darwin's ruling out of "jumps" that now worried Huxley. "From the first time that I wrote about Darwin's book in the 'Times' and in the 'Westminster' until now," he said in 1863 to Charles Kingsley, one of the clerics who believed that religion and evolution could be reconciled, "it has been obvious to me that this [the claim that selection produced specific sterility] is the weak point of Darwin's doctrine. He *has* shown that selective breeding is a *vera causa* for morphological species; he has not yet shown it a *vera causa* for physiological species." And as late as 1887 he was able to write: "In my earliest criticisms of the 'Origin,' I ventured to point out that its logical foundation was insecure so long as experiments in selective breeding had not produced varieties which were more or less infertile; and that insecurity remains up to the present time." It is true that Huxley confessed there was one chapter for which he would be prepared to go to the stake: but that was where Darwin honestly if ambivalently admitted: "Those who think the natural geological record in any degree perfect, and who do not attach much weight to the facts and arguments of other kinds given in this volume, will undoubtedly at once reject my theory. For my part, following out Lyell's metaphor, I look at the natural geological record, as a history of the world imperfectly kept, and written in a changing dialect; of this history we possess the last volume alone, relating only to two or three countries."

The geologists were in fact to be quickly won over, although, as Archibald Geikie was to say, they "were perhaps somewhat slow in appreciating the bearings of this remarkable treatise on their own branch of science. It taught them a new method of interpreting the crust of the earth and showed them that what they had presumed to be a fairly continuous and complete record, was full of gaps,

even when these could not be detected by any visible stratigraphical breaks. I well remember the deep impression made on my
mind by the reading of [Darwin's] two chapters on the 'Imperfection of the Geological Record' and the 'Geological Succession of
Organic Beings.' It was a new revelation of the manner in which
geological history must be studied."

Lyell, who had for long been cautious, accepted Darwin's views
in the new edition of his *Principles* published in the 1860s, and did
so with such little reservation that Wallace was moved to concede
that "the history of science hardly presents so striking an instance
of youthfulness of mind in advanced life as is shown by this aban-
donment of opinions [on species] so long held and so powerfully
advocated."

Conversion had not been easy, and Lyell told his friend Thomas
Spedding, "you may well believe that it cost me a struggle to
renounce my old creed. One of Darwin's reviewers put the alternative strongly by asking 'whether we are to believe that man is
modified mud or modified monkey.' The mud is a great come-
down from the 'archangel ruined.' " And years later, Geikie, who
had succeeded Lyell as the grand old man of geology, could say
of *The Origin*: "We may compare [it] to a great symphony in which
the chords from the various departments of biology are blended
into one vast harmony, but where the deep under-tones of geology
seldom fail to be audible."

In the immediate aftermath of publication, Huxley was Darwin's
most influential champion. His review in *The Times* was, to Darwin's
delight, republished by the *Gardeners' Chronicle*, which in a later
issue percipiently discussed how natural selection might be used
to improve colonial wheat, cotton and sugar crops. And from now
on Huxley's personal support was wholehearted. It was certainly
to be needed in the campaign against Darwin's theory, which
began vigorously in the first weeks of 1860 and which was only to
peter out as the fact of evolution was tacitly accepted and the
debate began to center on the method by which it was achieved.
From the first there were some who could stomach the idea of
evolution—usually claiming that that was the way in which God
operated—but who balked at accepting the blind chance method
of natural selection.

While *The Times* backed Darwin, the more popular *Daily News*
was against him. Of the influential journals, the *Athenaeum*, *Fraser's*,
the *Edinburgh Review* and the *Quarterly Review* were hostile, the

Cornhill and *Macmillan's* favorable. With the editors of literary and political journals tending to be scientifically illiterate, a lot depended on their choice of reviewer. In the *Edinburgh* it was Richard Owen, the zoologist, hardly an impartial assessor of Darwin. In the *Quarterly Review* it was "Soapy Sam" Wilberforce, bishop of Oxford and one of Darwin's most vociferous critics.

What could not be denied was that Darwin had with one book broken through the barrier that had for so long prevented evolution from being a subject of serious popular discussion. The *Saturday Review* noted that the controversy had "passed beyond the bounds of the study and lecture-room into the drawing-room and the public street." In the *Westminster Review*, Huxley, striking his second major blow for the cause, accurately summed up the furor of controversy that Darwin had unleashed, saying that the "species question" had caught the attention of general society. "Everybody has read Mr. Darwin's book, or, at least, has given an opinion upon its merits or demerits," he wrote; "pietists, whether lay or ecclesiastic, decry it with the mild railing which sounds so charitable; bigots denounce it with ignorant invective; old ladies, of both sexes, consider it a decidedly dangerous book, and even savans, who have no better mud to throw, quote antiquated writers to show that its author is no better than an ape himself; while every philosophical thinker hails it as a veritable Whitworth gun in the armoury of liberalism, and all competent naturalists and physiologists, whatever their opinions as to the ultimate fate of the doctrines put forth, acknowledge that the work . . . is a solid contribution to knowledge and inaugurates a new epoch in natural history."

Although the *Gardeners' Chronicle* had revealed its attitude by reprinting Huxley's review, it published a month later a letter from Patrick Matthew that incorporated a 2,500-word extract from his book of almost thirty years earlier outlining his own version of natural selection. "Trusting to your desire that every man should have his own, I hope you will give place to the following communication," he began.

In your Number of March 3d, I observe a long quotation from "The Times," stating that Mr. Darwin "professes to have discovered the existence and *modus operandi* of the natural law of selection," that is, "the power in nature which takes the place of man and performs a selection, and *suâ sponte*," in organic life. This discovery recently published as "the results of 20 years' investigation and reflection" by Mr. Darwin turns out to be what I published very fully and brought to apply practically to forestry in my work "Naval Timber and Arboriculture," published as far back as January 1, 1831, by Adam & Charles Black, Edinburgh, and Longman & Co., London, and reviewed in numerous periodicals so as to have full publicity in the "Metropolitan Magazine," the "Quarterly Review," the "Gardeners' Magazine" [*sic*] by Loudon, who spoke of it as *the* book, and repeatedly in the "United Service Magazine" for 1831 &c. The following is an extract from this volume which clearly proves a prior claim.

There followed a 2,500-word extract, which starts:

There is a law universal in nature, tending to render every reproductive being the best possibly suited to its condition that its kind, or that organised matter, is susceptible of, which appears intended to model the physical and mental or instinctive powers, to their highest perfection, and to continue them so. This law sustains the lion in his strength, the hare in her swiftness, and the fox in his wiles. As Nature, in all her modifications of life, has a power of increase far beyond what is needed to supply the place of what falls by Time's decay, those individuals who possess not the requisite strength, swiftness, hardihood, or cunning, fall prematurely without reproducing—either a prey to their natural devourers, or sinking under disease, generally induced by want of nourishment, their place being occupied by the more perfect of their own kind, who are pressing on the means of subsistence.

Darwin replied without delay, and on April 21 the *Gardeners' Chronicle* printed his letter: "I freely acknowledge that Mr. Matthew has anticipated by many years the explanation which I have offered of the origin of species, under the name of natural selection," he wrote. "I think that no one will feel surprised that neither I, nor apparently any other naturalist, had heard of Mr. Matthew's views, considering how briefly they are given, and that they appeared in the appendix to a work on Naval Timber and Arboriculture. I can do no more than offer my apologies to Mr. Matthew for my entire ignorance of his publication. If another edition of my work is called for, I will insert a notice to the foregoing effect."

Matthew replied as courteously as Darwin, adding, "To me the conception of this law of Nature came intuitively as a self-evident fact, almost without an effort of concentrated thought. Mr. Darwin here seems to have more merit in the discovery than I have had—to me it did not appear a discovery. He seems to have worked it out by inductive reason, slowly and with due caution to have made his way synthetically from fact to fact onwards; while with me it was by a general glance at the scheme of Nature that I estimated this select production of species as an *a priori* recognisable fact—an axiom, requiring only to be pointed out to be admitted by unprejudiced minds of sufficient grasp."

Having staked his claim, Matthew harbored no personal ill-will, although later in the year he did object that the *Saturday Analyst and Leader* had been "scarcely fair in alluding to Mr. Darwin as the parent of the origin of species; seeing that I published the whole that Mr. Darwin attempts to prove more than twenty-nine years ago."

Darwin's attitude throughout the whole Matthew episode is open to different interpretations. He was certainly quick to admit that Matthew had "anticipated by many years" his explanation of the origin of species. Indeed, he could do little less, even had he not been the honorable man that he was. Nevertheless, his statements did less than justice to Matthew's position and in at least one respect were misleading, even if unconsciously so. In June 1860 he wrote to the French naturalist Professor Jean Louis Armand de Quatrefages de Bréau, referring to Matthew as "an obscure writer on forest trees," a description which tended to exculpate him from the omission of having read the book. Matthew was, however, a commercial fruit grower and hybridizer who owned and managed a flourishing orchard of more than 10,000 apple and pear trees in the Carse of Gowrie, north of the River Tay in Scotland. Moreover, Darwin's claim that no other naturalist had apparently heard of Matthew's views was belied by Loudon's review cited by Matthew in the *Gardeners' Chronicle*. John Claudius Loudon, the father of horticultural journalism, as he has been called, a distinguished authority on arboriculture and the editor of the *Gardeners' Magazine*, had referred to Matthew's comments, given in an appendix to his book, saying, "One of the subjects discussed in the Appendix is the puzzling one, of the origin of species and varieties—and if the author has hereon originated no original views (and of this we are far from certain) he has certainly exhibited his own in an original manner."

Only the transparent honesty of Darwin's character, which shines out so brightly from the archives, makes it possible to believe that by the 1850s he had no recollection of Matthew's work. But memory plays curious tricks; much that had happened before the *Beagle* voyage was overlaid by that decisive experience, and all that seems certain is that if Darwin had any previous knowledge of *Arboriculture,* it had slipped down into the unconscious.

The situation is more complex with Edward Blyth, a "very clever, odd, wild fellow, who will never do what he could do, from not sticking to any one subject," as Darwin once wrote of him. Blyth was a contemporary naturalist who spent much of his working life in India and who regularly corresponded with Darwin. During the mid-1830s, he contributed three articles on species and varieties to the British *Magazine of Natural History,* in which he suggested that the work of domestic breeders might be paralleled in nature. "May not, then, a large proportion of what are considered species have descended from a common parentage?" he added.

Cyril Darlington, writing on *Darwin's Place in History,* has noted: "In the course of his argument Blyth closely examines each of the problems which was to occupy Darwin's mind during the following forty years: blending inheritance as against mutation, the inheritance of acquired characters, geographical isolation, geological successions, island faunas, the origin of instinct and so on. In all these relations Blyth quotes a wealth of examples from his own observations of nature. These afterwards appear repeated, or indeed copied, by Darwin in his preliminary essays of 1842 and 1844."

However, Blyth contended that natural selection would tend to conserve species, and this can be taken as a reason for Darwin's omitting any reference to him in the historical introduction he added to the third edition of *The Origin.* Loren C. Eiseley has given Blyth greater credit for contributing to Darwin's views than do most naturalists, commenting "It was Darwin's contribution, of course, that he altered the struggle for existence and made of it a creative mechanism," but adding "In doing so, however, he passed by way of the stepping stone of Edward Blyth."

In the months that followed publication of *The Origin,* interest centered not on the number of strands Darwin had woven into the book but on the viability of its central thesis. The strongest opposition naturally enough came from the Church, although there were exceptions in the reports of the ecclesiastical press. "No one," noted the *English Churchman,* "whatsoever may be his personal ideas on the subject, can hesitate to treat the writer's views with the greatest respect, or to give those views the fullest and best consideration possible." They hoped also that the bigger book would be published, and "that Mr. Darwin will yet be enabled to give us the full results of his labours—results which, from his great experience, must necessarily prove of the deepest interest to naturalists of all denominations." The Protestants tended to criticize more loudly than the Catholics, who depended less on the Bible; it was only after publication of *The Descent of Man* a decade later, that the Catholics opened their heavy fire. Although various doctrines of evolution had been suggested over many centuries, those proposals had been put forward in such tenuous form, and supported by so little evidence, that the Church could afford to dismiss them with a wave of the surpliced arm. With the advent of Darwin, it was now felt, on grounds of both instinct and reason, that more specific refutation was demanded. It came at all levels. At the top, the ecclesiastical argument was not entirely unconnected with politics. In 1856, the Oxford and Cambridge University Act had abolished the religious tests for all except divinity degrees, and there was a gut reaction against a theory that appeared to diminish still further the Church's power and influence. At the other end of the scale, there was a sense of loss—genuinely felt, if somewhat hysterically expressed—that had to be warded off, by those whose religious faith was a solace in a hard world, and who did their worst to counter Darwin for the most innocent of motives. "Only let our scientific friends show the people, who are quick to learn, that there was no Adam, no Christ, no covenant with God, no hereafter," warned the *Family Herald*, "that nothing certain is known, and then that chaos which set in during the lower Empire of Rome will set in here; we shall have no laws, no worship, and no property, since our human laws are based upon the Divine."

It was, after all, not only the chronology of Genesis and Archbishop Ussher that was involved. The Fall, Original Sin, Atonement and Redemption, all helped form the backbone of faith and were events securely tied into sacred history. If that history was shown to be but fiction, then faith would lose its props. Moreover, if evolution was fact and not fairy tale, "the argument from design" —which gave God credit for the end products of creation, however he had achieved them—looked increasingly doubtful. Here some scientists tended to nod approvingly; for how could a natural law, which Darwin claimed natural selection to be, rest on variations that occurred by chance?

Darwin himself was personally and emotionally involved in this aspect of the argument by the reaction of his wife, whose religious faith remained unshaken. "She once said to my sister," Darwin's daughter Henrietta wrote, "that when she married she had resolved to enter into my father's tastes and thought she should be able, but found it impossible. He used to tell how during some dull lecture at the British Association he said to her: 'I am afraid this is very wearisome to you,' to which she quietly answered, 'Not more than all the rest.' He often quoted this with delight." Curiously enough, Emma Darwin's reaction to evolution was comparable to Martha Freud's refusal to take her own husband's psychoanalysis seriously and to the inability of Elsa Einstein, Albert's second wife, to understand relativity. The three men who created the intellectual climate of the twentieth century all failed to convert their wives.

After publication of *The Origin*, the apparent widening of the gulf between science and religion gave rise to various plans for reconciling them. They were numerous, and the *British and Foreign Evangelical Review*, no backslider when it came to defending the faith, noted: "Half a dozen schemes of harmony are better than one." At times, the evidence that accumulated was rather spuriously wished away. Thus after the discovery of human fossils in preglacial strata, the *Morning Advertiser* noted: "The 'man' who is without the 'living soul,' spoken of in Genesis, is not the man of whom the Bible speaks; he is, or was, if indeed such a creature ever existed, a mere animal, of no more account than the bats and lizards of those long-past times."

Some attempts at reconciliation were more respectable. Asa Gray could aver, metaphorically hand on heart, that God himself had ordained the variations on which all seemed to rest. "We should advise Mr. Darwin to assume, in the philosophy of his hypothesis," he wrote, "that variation has been led along certain beneficial lines." A comparable way of squaring evolution with religion by assuming that natural selection was an example of the wondrous ways in which God carried out his work was put forward by William Benjamin Carpenter. After saying in *Nature and Man*, that there was no cause for the variations on which natural selection was claimed to operate, he continued: "Consequently we must look to *forces* acting either *within* or *without* the organism, as the real agents in producing whatever developmental variations it may take on. Of the action of such forces, we at present know scarcely anything; and Mr. Darwin has not given us much help towards the solution of the problem. But this much seems to me clear: that just as there is at the present time a determinate capacity for a certain fixed kind of development in each germ, in virtue of which one evolves itself into a zoophyte, and another (though not originally distinguishable from it) into a man, so must the primordial germs have been endowed each with its determinate capacity for a particular course of development; in virtue of which it has evolved the whole succession of forms that has ultimately proceeded from it."

At times, Darwin appeared to have no truck with such apologies. At others he reacted differently, and a decade after publication of *The Origin* he congratulated Wallace, who had outlined a similar method of reconciling faith and natural selection. Lyell also appears to have agreed with this method of keeping one's religious faith yet not offending science by doing so, and wrote to Darwin, who had told him of his reaction to Wallace. "I quite agree with you that Wallace's sketch of natural selection is admirable," Lyell said. "I wrote to tell him so after I had read the article, and in regard to the concluding theory, I reminded him that as to the origin of man's intellectual and moral nature I had allowed in my first edition that its introduction was a real innovation, interrupting the uniform course of the causation previously at work on the earth. I was therefore not opposed to his idea, that the Supreme Intelligence might possibly direct variation in a way analogous to that in which even the limited powers of man might guide it in selection, as in the case of the breeder and horticulturist. In other words, as I feel that progressive development or evolution cannot be entirely explained by natural selection, I rather hail Wallace's suggestion that there may be a Supreme Will and Power which may not abdicate its functions of interference, but may guide the forces and laws of Nature. This seems to me the more probable when I consider, not without wonder, that we should be permitted to give rise to a monstrosity like the pouter pigeon, and to cause it to breed true for an indefinite number of generations, certainly not to the advantage of the variety or species so created."

Wallace later provided a more extensive scheme for those who were unable to abandon either the emotion of religion or the logic of science. He believed that God had intervened three times in the history of life: first when he had created living matter, secondly when he had breathed consciousness into its higher levels, and finally when he had given man a soul. In later years Wallace became a spiritualist and, believing that space was full of spirits, found it possible to believe that one of them had entered a monkey that became transformed into a man.

By contrast, there was in 1860 the almost perverse view put forward by the *Dublin Review*. First it denounced any idea that evolution could apply to man. "Mr. Darwin's work has done the cause of religion admirable service . . ." it then continued. "It accounts for the extinction of so many races of animals and plants, and the rise of others in a way that is a positive relief after the assertion of some Christian geologists, that we are bound to believe in a fresh creation at the close of each Geologic period. It accounts for the dispersal of animals and plants without the necessity of recurrence to many—some have said at lease five-and-twenty—distinct 'centres of creation.' . . . it makes the universality of the Deluge of far easier credence, and diminishes the number of fellow-voyagers with the patriarch in the ark." Darwin was probably more amused than put out by his conscription into defense of the Deluge. Certainly he had no objection to normal criticism, writing to Leonard Horner, Lyell's father-in-law, who liked *The Origin*, "I am the more pleased as I would rather have been well attacked, than have been handled in the namby-pamby-old-woman style of the cautious Oxford professors."

One surprising opponent of the idea that *The Origin* should be condemned by bell, book and candle, was the Reverend F. J. A. Hort, the Victorian scholar and divine who was to help revise the New Testament. "In spite of difficulties," he wrote of *The Origin*, "I am inclined to think it unanswerable. In any case it is a treat to read such a book." And, to another clerical friend: "But *the* book which has most engaged me is Darwin. Whatever may be thought of it, it is a book that one is proud to be contemporary with. I must work out and examine the argument more in detail, but at present my feeling is strong that the theory is unanswerable. If so, it opens up a new period in—I know not what not."

The same kinder-than-expected response came from the Duke of Argyll, a follower of the cataclysmic school in geology and devotedly skeptical of evolution. Although he felt, he told Lyell, that Darwin had failed fundamentally in providing sufficient proof for his theory, he described *The Origin* as "a most delightful [book], suggesting endless subjects for discussion and inquiry."

But it was not only among a few ecclesiastical scholars and agreeable skeptics that *The Origin* was less damned than might have been expected. Lyell, staying at Queen Victoria's Osborne in the summer of 1863, soon after publication of his *Antiquity of Man*, told his wife: "She asked me a good deal about the Darwinian theory as well as antiquity of man. She has a clear understanding, and thinks quite fearlessly for herself, and yet very modestly." Two years later he reported to Darwin from Germany that he had had "an animated conversation on Darwinism with the Princess Royal," Victoria's eldest daughter, who had married the German Crown Prince Frederick. She was, he said, "a worthy daughter of her father [Prince Albert], in the reading of good books and thinking of what she reads. She was very much *au fait* at the 'Origin' and Huxley's book [*Man's Place in Nature*], the 'Antiquity,' &c., &c. . . . She said after twice reading you she could not see her way as to the origin of four things, namely the world, species, man, or the black and white races. Did one of the latter come from the other, or both from some common stock? And she asked me what I was doing, and I explained that in recasting the 'Principles' I had to give up the independent creation of each species. She said she fully understood my difficulty, for after your book 'the old opinions had received a shake from which they never would recover.' "

This would have been an admission of defeat by those who regularly attended the meetings of the Victoria Institute, founded "To investigate fully and impartially the most important questions of Philosophy and Science, but more especially those that bear upon the great truths revealed in Holy Scripture, with the view of defending these truths against the oppositions of Science, falsely so called." The organization was set up following a "Declaration of Students of the Natural and Physical Sciences," published in *The Times* and eventually signed by upward of 700 men who believed "that it is impossible for the Word of God, as written in the book of nature, and God's Word written in Holy Scripture, to contradict one another, however much they may appear to differ." Yet the Earl of Shaftesbury, the Institute's president, after listening to the inaugural address, noted that the members "were quite confident that the Word of God was quite consistent with the truths of science—that, in fact, the one would be strengthened by a knowledge of the other."

Despite such attempts to have one's cake and eat it, the Institute threw all its influence against the acceptance of Darwinism and roundly condemned as pseudoscience any doctrine that denied the literal truth of the Bible. Occasionally it gave the opposition a free hand, as when a George Warington addressed the members "On the Credibility of Darwinism," and concluded that it was "a good working hypothesis for investigators to keep in mind." But the honorary secretary, James Reddie, reflected the feelings of the members when he declared that he was not convinced. "On the contrary," he said to loud "Hear, Hear"'s, "after hearing [Mr Warington's] arguments, I feel if possible only the more persuaded that the theory of Mr. Darwin is *inharmonious*, *inadequate*, *inconsistent*, and utterly *incredible*."

That Darwin could secure a beachhead in such territory, as he had with Hort and others, was partly owing to the essentially moderate tone that he adopted toward the Church's difficulties and, more surprisingly, the similar tone shown by Huxley. "It is clear to me," Huxley wrote to Charles Kingsley, "that if that great and powerful instrument for good or evil, the Church of England, is to be saved from being shivered into fragments by the advancing tide of science—an event I should be very sorry to witness, but which will infallibly occur if men like Samuel of Oxford [Samuel Wilberforce, bishop of Oxford] are to have the guidance of her destinies; it must be by the efforts of men who, like yourself, see your way to the combination of the practice of the Church with the spirit of science. . . . I don't profess to understand the logic of yourself, Maurice [John Frederick Denison Maurice, divine and social reformer], and the rest of your school, but I have always said I would swear by your truthfulness and sincerity, and that good must come of your efforts."

Kingsley himself was impressed by Darwin and wrote to Sir John Lubbock after their first meeting. "I trembled before him like a boy, and longed to tell him all I felt for him, but dare not, lest he should think me a flatterer extravagant. But the modesty and simplicity of his genius was charming. Instead of teaching, he only wanted to learn, instead of talking, to listen, till I found him asking me to write papers which he could as yet hardly write himself—ignorant, in his grand simplicity, of my ignorance, and his own wisdom. And yet of that man Owen said to me—'Darwin is just as good a soul as his grandfather—and just as great a goose.' "

Darwin impressed others with his undisguised, and what many would have described as religious, wonder at the world, and his admission that his instinctive beliefs were at times in conflict with the conclusions to which he was unwillingly driven. "One cannot look at this Universe with all living productions & man without believing that all has been intelligently designed," he wrote to

Herschel in 1861; "yet when I look to each individual organism, I can see no evidence of this. For, I am not prepared to admit that God designed the feathers in the tail of the rock-pigeon to vary in a highly peculiar manner in order that man might select such variations & make a Fan-tail; & if this be not admitted (I know it would be admitted by many persons) then I cannot see design in the variations of structure in animals in a state of nature, those variations which were useful to the animal being preserved & those useless or injurious being destroyed." And he was sometimes as easily shocked as the most unworldly-wise cleric, writing on a proof of the paper by E. Vansittart Neale, "On Typical Selections, as a Means of Removing the Difficulties Attending the Doctrine of the Origin of Species, by Natural Selection": "In the plainest and *coarsest* Language the Author makes God a great breeder of animals & who selects & works like an Improver of Short Horns or a Pigeon Fancier."

Later, in *The Descent of Man*, he could write that "the brain of an ant is one of the most marvellous atoms of matter in the world," and elsewhere, of the "many other facts, which are so obscure that we stand in awe before the mystery of life." The same feeling comes through in his description of the larval cirripede. In the second stage, "they have six pairs of beautifully constructed natatory legs, a pair of magnificent compound eyes, and extremely complex antennae. . . ." His family, his son Francis has written, "used to laugh at him for this sentence, which we compared to an advertisement." An air of wonder permeated much of his writing, and a hundred years later one commentator could even maintain: "I propose . . . that the triumph of Darwinism is the triumph of a Christian way of picturing the world over the other ways available to scientists."

The battle line between believers and unbelievers did not, in fact, separate devout Christians from the rest with the simplicity that is sometimes assumed. At times, moreover, religious shock was strongly supported by scientific distrust. Adam Sedgwick, Darwin's companion on the Welsh geological jaunt in 1831, protested as both cleric and geologist. ". . . I have read your book with more pain than pleasure," he wrote. "Parts of it I admired greatly, parts I laughed at till my sides were almost sore; other parts I read with absolute sorrow, because I think them utterly false and grievously mischievous. You have *deserted*—after a start in that tram-road of all solid physical truth—the true method of induction, and started off in machinery as wild, I think, as Bishop Wilkins's locomotive that was to sail with us to the moon." (John Wilkins, bishop of Chester, first secretary of the Royal Society and the author, 1630, of *The Discovery of a World in the Moone*.)

Sedgwick was even more damning when he reviewed *The Origin* in the *Spectator*. "Each series of facts is laced together by a series of assumptions, and repetitions of the one false principle. You cannot make a good rope out of a string of air bubbles." Darwin was unrepentant. "I do not think my book will be mischievous," he told Sedgwick, "for there are so many workers that, if I be wrong I shall soon be annihilated; and surely you will agree that truth can be known only by rising victorious from every attack."

So typical was Sedgwick of the contemporary educated bigot that one of his letters is worth quoting. "I have read Darwin's book," he said. "It is clever, and calmly written; and therefore, the more mischievous, if its principles be false; and I believe them *utterly false*. It is the system of the author of the *Vestiges* stripped of his ignorant absurdities. It repudiates all reasoning from final causes; and seems to shut the door upon any view (however feeble) of the God of Nature as manifested in His Works. From first to last it is a dish of rank materialism cleverly cooked and served up. As a system of philosophy it is not like the Tower of Babel, so daring in its high aim as to seek a shelter against God's anger; but it is like a pyramid poised on its apex. It is a system embracing all living nature, vegetable and animal; yet contradicting—point blank—the vast treasury of facts that the Author of Nature has, during the past two or three thousand years, revealed to our senses. And why is this done? For no other solid reason, I am sure, except to make us independent of a Creator."

Sedgwick did more than write. In the next Cambridge examination papers he inserted questions that reflected on *The Origin*, a move that brought from Darwin the observation: "Sedgwick's [paper] was not very fair towards the students; but Murray, the Publisher, thought it splendid for selling copies to the unfortunate Students"—since Dr. Whewell had for a while apparently banned *The Origin* from Trinity Library. At Oxford, opposition was to surface in a different way. Professor John Obadiah Westwood, professor of zoology, seriously proposed to the Oxford University Commission the establishment of a permanent lectureship for the exposure of the fallacies of Darwinism.

The criticism that Darwin had not been inductive, that he had sought facts to fit his theory rather than trawling for facts and producing a theory, was made by more than one critic. Huxley was particularly scathing about such criticism, and wrote: "Critics exclusively trained in classics or in mathematics, who have never determined a scientific fact in their lives by induction from experiment or observation, prate learnedly about Mr. Darwin's method, which is not inductive enough, not Baconian enough, forsooth, for them. But even if practical acquaintance with the process of scientific investigation is denied them, they may learn, by the perusal of Mr. Mill's admirable chapter, 'On the Deductive Method,' that there are multitudes of scientific inquiries, in which the method of pure induction helps the investigator but a very little way."

Darwin himself had written years earlier in the third of his "Species" notebooks: "The line of argument often pursued throughout my theory is to establish a point as a probability by induction & to apply it as hypotheses to other points & see whether it will solve them." And after publication of *The Origin*, he commented: "How odd it is that anyone should not see that all observation must be for or against some view if it is to be of any service!" He felt strongly about the criticism, protesting to Henslow that the undulatory theory of light—the wave theory, in contrast to the corpuscular theory—utilized hypothetical undulations in a hypothetical substance, the ether, and continuing: "I shd. really much like to know why such an hypothesis as the undulations of the ether may be invented, & why I may not invent (not that I did *invent* it, for I was led to it by studying domestic varieties) any hypothesis, such as natural selection." Moreover, of his book on coral reefs, he could write: "No other work of mine was begun in so deductive a spirit as this; for the whole theory was thought out on the west coast of S. America before I had seen a true coral reef. I had therefore only to verify and extend my views by a careful examination of living reefs."

Another scientific criticism was that while Darwin had argued his case from artificial selection, no breeder had produced new breeds capable of forming fertile crosses with each other; in other words, artificial selection had never produced other species, and there was no reason to believe that natural selection could do so.

More important were the technical riddles that had to be overcome by scientific faith and that were not to be solved until the turn of the century. One was the question of how natural selection could work in practice, in the face of what was christened "blending." Unless the more favored individuals always bred with the more favored, variance could be halved at each generation and, for practical purposes, wiped out in ten, and the chances of any favorable variation being preserved over a series of generations were, it was suggested, practically nil. Much was to be made of this point in a long review of *The Origin* written by Fleeming Jenkin and published only in 1867.

Even if the problem of blending could be argued out of the way, there still remained one uncomfortable fact: in the 1860s, and in fact until the end of the century, there remained an almost total ignorance of the way in which individual characteristics of one generation were actually passed on to the next. However, in view of the theory's revolutionary status, the scientific objections were fewer than might have been expected. Darwin himself gave one reason for this in his autobiography: "I had . . . during many years followed a golden rule, namely that whenever a published fact, a new observation or thought came across me, which was opposed to my general results, to make a memorandum of it without fail & at once; for I had found by experience that such facts & thoughts were far more apt to escape from the memory, than favourable ones. Owing to this habit, very few objections were raised against my views which I had not at least noticed & attempted to answer."

Nevertheless, skepticism remained in the air when, in the summer of 1860, the British Association for the Advancement of Science met in Oxford for its annual meeting. Its members were to witness one of the set-piece spectaculars of nineteenth-century scientific history but one that may in some essential details be different from the usually accepted story. All rests on exactly what was said during one afternoon's debate by Samuel Wilberforce, bishop of Oxford, and by T. H. Huxley. Wilberforce, third son of William Wilberforce, the antislavery philanthropist, and himself an impassioned opponent of slavery, was by no means the opinionated backwoodsman he is sometimes held to have been. "Watchfulness and work, not pomp and ease, were his characteristics," it has been said, and his administrative ability combined with his gifts of charm and oratory to lead him into a succession of important posts in the Church. He was not without humor and replied to his soubriquet of "Soapy Sam" by agreeing that he had earned it, since he was always in hot water and always came out of it with clean hands. Like most churchmen of his day, he was scientifically illiterate. But before the Oxford meeting he had taken care to be fully briefed by Richard Owen, by now an opponent of Darwin.

Although the confrontation had been expected, and although the meeting room in the university museum was packed, no verbatim record of what Wilberforce and Huxley said appears to have been made. A reminiscence written by Huxley years later is the nearest approach, and the reminiscence does not quote Wilberforce's vital words.

The previous day, Huxley had met Robert Chambers by chance in Oxford. Both men knew that on the following afternoon Dr. John William Draper was to read a paper to the Association on "The Intellectual Development of Europe Considered with Reference to the Views of Mr. Darwin." Both knew that the redoubtable Bishop Wilberforce was planning to attend. Wilberforce had the reputation, Huxley later wrote, "of being a first-class controversialist, and I was quite aware that if he played his cards properly, we should have little chance, with such an audience, of making an efficient defence." He told Chambers he had decided not to attend the session at which Dr. Draper would speak, as he "did not see the good of giving up peace and quietness to be episcopally pounded." But on being accused by Chambers of deserting the cause, Huxley agreed to attend "and have [his] share of what is going on." So, by luck more than intent, the way was paved for giving Darwin a very convenient psychological boost at a very convenient time.

Dr. Draper droned on for an hour. Then Henslow, in the chair, threw open the discussion. The historian John Richard Green, at the time a young undergraduate, gave his version of what followed. Hooker gave his in a letter written to Darwin a few days later. Huxley outlined events in a letter to his old friend Dr. Frederick Dyster, as did the Reverend W. Tuckwell in a little-known book of reminiscences. But none of these, nor the *Athenaeum*, which reported the occasion, quoted the actual words of the Wilberforce-Huxley exchange.

After Dr. Draper had finished, Wilberforce rose to reply. Fluent and florid, he recapitulated the common ground between scientists and the Church, distinguished between "a working and a causal hypothesis," and threw a compliment to Huxley, who, he remarked, was about to demolish him. And he expressed the disquietude he would feel were an ape in the zoo to be shown to him as an ancestor. He then, according to Mrs. Isabella Sidgwick, turned toward Huxley and "begged to know was it through his grandfather or his grandmother that he claimed his descent from a monkey?" Another, less personalized version is that he asked: "If any one were to be willing to trace his descent through an ape as his *grandfather*, would he be willing to trace his descent similarly on the side of his *grandmother*?" Yet it has also been suggested that he merely referred back to the disquietude he had mentioned earlier in his speech and may, indeed, have speculated on the possibility of his own simian ancestry.

Any of the three possibilities would have been enough to justify Huxley turning to his neighbor, Sir Benjamin Brodie, sergeant-surgeon to the Queen, and exclaiming: "The Lord hath delivered him into mine hands." But if Wilberforce had referred to his own ancestry and not to Huxley's, then Huxley overreacted—although to memorable effect.

According to Hooker, Huxley was unable to throw his voice successfully over so large an assembly. An intuitive speaker, he may have realized that he was failing to carry his audience with him. The knowledge may have drawn him into the words as he described them to Dyster: "If, then, said I, the question is put to me 'would I rather have a miserable ape for a grandfather, or a man highly endowed by nature and possessed of great means and influence, and yet who employs these faculties and that influence for the mere purpose of introducing ridicule into a grave scientific discussion'—I unhesitantly affirm my preference for the ape." Another version, recalled after Darwin's death to his son Francis by G. Johnstone Stoney, who was present, claims emphatically that Huxley rose and opened with the words: "*I* would rather be the offspring of two apes than be a man and afraid to face the truth."

Whatever the exact words, Huxley struck back as forcefully as he knew how. Insulting a bishop was, a century and more ago, a very rare practice; insulting him in public, in his own diocese, was even more so. Lady Brewster fainted at the shock. Most of the audience applauded.

But this was not the end of the debate. John Lubbock supported Darwin. Robert FitzRoy, by now an admiral and ex-governor of New Zealand, rose from his seat in the audience, recalled his arguments with Darwin on the *Beagle* almost thirty years before, and, brandishing a Bible above his head, declaimed that that was the source of all truth.

Finally Hooker was called upon to speak. No one is certain what he said. But he must have been astringent. "I swore to myself that I would smite the Amalekite, Sam, hip and thigh if my heart jumped out of my mouth," he wrote to Darwin. ". . . I hit him in the wind at the first shot in ten words taken from his own ugly mouth; and then proceeded to demonstrate in as few more: (1) that he could never have read your book, and (2) that he was absolutely ignorant of the rudiments of Bot. Science."

Judging from one account, Hooker probably influenced the meeting not by rhetorical fireworks but by his alleged final sentences. "I knew of this theory fifteen years ago," he said. "I was then entirely opposed to it; I argued against it again and again; but since then I have devoted myself unremittingly to natural history; in its pursuit I have travelled round the world. Facts in this science which before were inexplicable to me became one by one explained by this theory, and conviction has been thus gradually forced upon an unwilling convert."

Huxley himself appears to have had reservations after the event. That evening he was told that a guest at Dr. [Charles Giles Bridle] Daubeney's wished he could watch the incident over again. "Mr. Huxley, with the look on his face of the victor who feels the cost of victory, put us aside," said another guest, "saying 'Once in a life-time is enough, if not too much.' "

Huxley's intervention was to have two results. First, and unfortunately, it tended to suggest that the battle begun with *The Origin* was a straight battle between science and the Church, whereas on both sides there were many who had qualifications, a number who saw a case for conciliation and compromise. The more important result was summed up in a letter Darwin wrote to Huxley the following month: "From all that I hear from several quarters, it seems that Oxford did the subject great good. It is of enormous importance to show the world that a few first-class men are not afraid of expressing their opinion. I see daily more and more plainly that my unaided Book would have done *absolutely* nothing." But they were more than first-class men in the scientific sense. Hooker and Huxley were gentlemen of complete political, financial and sexual respectability. To have such men fighting publicly —"(which I am sure I never could do)," Darwin told Hooker—for even the most scandalous of causes made it more likely that that cause would survive.

A few days after the Oxford debate, Wilberforce's review of *The Origin* appeared in the *Quarterly Review*, then at the height of its power as a molder of opinion. The Bishop had been better briefed by Owen for the review than he had been for the Oxford debate. Or, perhaps more accurately, he was more sure-footed in the review than in debate with Huxley. He was, moreover, slightly more cunning, ladling out considerable praise in a review that began by noting that Darwin's "scientific attainments, his insight and carefulness as an observer, blended with no scanty measure of imaginative sagacity, and his clear and lively style, make all his writings unusually attractive. . . . The essay is full of Mr. Darwin's characteristic excellences. It is a most readable book; full of facts in natural history, old and new, of his collecting and of his observing; and all of these are told in his own perspicuous language, and all thrown into picturesque combinations, and all sparkle with the colours of fancy and the lights of imagination."

There was a good deal along these lines, examples of Darwin's "really charming writing," and the Bishop's statement that "if Mr. Darwin can . . . demonstrate to us our fungular descent, we shall dismiss our pride, and avow, with the characteristic humility of philosophy, our unexpected cousinship with the mushrooms." In a 17,000-word review there was space for this before the knife was put in. This came with the claim that Darwin had included man in his theory, a point that Darwin had taken care, as he believed, to sidestep. Wilberforce saw through that attempt, writing:

> First, then, he [Darwin] not obscurely declares that he applies his scheme of the action of the principle of natural selection to MAN himself, as well as to the animals around him. Now, we must say at once, and openly, that such a notion is absolutely incompatible not only with single expressions in the word of God on that subject of natural science with which it is not immediately concerned, but, which in our judgment is of far more importance, with the whole representation of that moral and spiritual condition of man which is its proper subject-matter. Man's derived supremacy over the earth; man's power of articulate speech; man's gift of reason; man's freewill and responsibility; man's fall and man's redemption; the incarnation of the Eternal Son; the indwelling of the Eternal Spirit,—all are equally and utterly irreconcilable with the degrading notion of the brute origin of him who was created in the image of God, and redeemed by the Eternal Son assuming to himself his nature.

But as well as doing his duty as a bishop, Wilberforce had his fun, asking, "Is it credible that all favourable varieties of turnips are tending to become men, and yet that the closest microscopic observation has never detected the faintest tendency in the highest of the Algae to improve into the very lowest Zoophyte?" Yet Owen had done his briefing well. "It is uncommonly clever," Darwin admitted to Hooker of the review; "it picks out with skill all the most conjectural parts, and brings forward well all the difficulties." And to Lyell he wrote: "By the way the Bishop makes a very telling case against me, by accumulating several instances where I speak very doubtfully; but this is very unfair, as in [some] cases . . . the evidence is, and must be very doubtful." He told John Murray that he thought Wilberforce's review was "very clever and I am quizzed splendidly. I really believe I enjoyed it as much as if I had not been the unfortunate butt. There is hardly any malice in it, which is wonderful considering the source whence many of the suggestions came." And, perhaps even more revealing of Darwin's character, he remarked to Asa Gray of the review that it was "uncommonly clever, not worth anything scientifically, but quizzes me in splendid style. I chuckled with laughter at myself."

There was, in fact, qualified admiration on both sides. "Did you see the Quarterly Review," Darwin asked the vicar of Downe, "the B. of Oxford made really splendid fun of me and my grandfather." By chance, the Bishop was with the Vicar when he received Darwin's letter. "I am glad he takes it in this way" said Wilberforce on being told of Darwin's comment, "he is such a capital fellow."

Darwin, it is clear, would never himself have gone into battle with the unreserved enthusiasm of Huxley, whose dislike of the Bishop lasted until 1873, when Wilberforce was thrown from his horse and died as his head hit a stone. "For once," maintained Huxley, "reality and his brains came into contact and the result was fatal." Yet there was another side to the coin. "In justice to the Bishop," he wrote to Francis Darwin in 1891, "I am bound to say that he bore no malice, but was always courtesy itself when we occasionally met in after years."

Moreover, it now seems likely that at least part of Wilberforce's attitude was as much dutiful reaction to what he saw as an attack on the Church as a demonstration of personal conviction. A hundred and twenty years after the famous debate, an undated poem was found among his papers that implies an attitude to Darwin of something less than total rejection. The poem was headed: "Lines written on hearing that Professor Huxley had said that 'he did not care whether his grand-father was an Ape' ":

> Oft had I heard, but deemed the tale untrue,
> That man was cousin to the Kangaroo;
> That he before whose face all nature quailed,
> Was but the monkey's heir, though unentailed;
> And that the limber Ape, whose knavish ways
> And tricks fantastic oft our laughter raise,
> Was just what *we* were in some previous state,
> Ages ere Noah shipped his living freight.
> But now a learn'd Professor, grave and wise,
> Stoutly maintains what I supposed were lies;
> And, while each listening sage in wonder gapes,
> Claims a proud lineage of ancestral Apes.
> Alas! cried I, if such the sage's dreams,
> Save me, ye powers, from these unhallowed themes;
> From self-degrading science keep me free,
> And from the pride that apes humility!
> But O should fate bring back these dreams accursed,
> And shuddering Nature find her laws reversed;
> Should this, the age of wonders, see again
> Men sunk to monkeys, monkeys raised to men;
> Be mine the lot, on some far-distant shore,
> Where Science wearies not nor savants bore—
> Where no learn'd Apes our fallen race may scorn,
> Nor point the moral which our tails adorn—
> To shun the sight of metamorphosed friends,
> Till time again shall shape their altered ends,
> To soothe each fond regret, howe'er I can;
> And, at the least, to dream myself a Man!
>
> S. Wilberforce.

Whatever the niceties of Wilberforce's feelings, Huxley's oratorical victory in 1860 dramatized the conflict between the Church and science. It was a good story, and Darwin was aware of its importance. "My book has stirred up the mud with a vengeance; and it will be a blessing to me if all my friends do not get to hate me," he wrote to Asa Gray. "But I look at it as certain, if I had not stirred up the mud some one else would very soon; so that the sooner the battle is fought the sooner it will be settled; not that the subject will be settled in our lives' time. It will be an immense gain, if the question becomes a fairly open one; so that each man may try his new facts on it pro and contra."

But the argument did little if anything to quieten the doubts of the scientific skeptics. When the Copley Medal of the Royal Society was awarded to Darwin in 1864 for researches into geology, zoology and physiological botany, the president, Major-General Edward Sabine, commented of *The Origin* that "speaking generally and collectively we have not included it in our award." Only when Huxley forced the reading of the Council minutes was it shown that no such exclusion had been discussed, yet alone decided upon. As for the Linnean Society of London George Bentham, its president, emphasized that speculation on the origin of species was "beyond the province of our Society" and that agreement or disagreement on the matter was "scarcely within the legitimate scope of our Society, to enter." John Edward Gray, president of the Botanical and Entomological societies, went out of his way to maintain at a meeting of the Zoological Society of London that "during all my experience, and after most careful search (for the origin of species has always been a most interesting subject of my contemplation), I have never found the slightest evidence for the support of such a theory, or the least modification of any species leading to such an opinion."

Darwin's reaction to the reception of *The Origin* was a mixture of surprise that it had been accepted so readily by some people and distress that he might have disturbed the faith of others, notably his wife. But distress was widespread, as suggested by a recollection of the entomologist Roland Trimen, who was working in the Insect Room of the British Museum in December 1859. "One day," he has written, "I was at work in the next compartment to that in which Adam White [writer on natural history] sat, and heard someone come in and a cheery mellow voice say, 'Good-morning, Mr. White; —I'm afraid you won't speak to me any more!' While I was conjecturing who the visitor could be, I was electrified by hearing White reply, in the most solemn and earnest way, 'Ah, Sir! if you had only stopped with the Voyage of the Beagle!' There was a real lament in his voice, pathetic to any one who knew how to this kindly Scot, in his rigid orthodoxy and limited scientific view, the epoch-making Origin, then just published, was more than a stumbling-block—it was a grievous and painful lapse into error of the most pernicious kind."

Darwin never forgot his own long struggle from belief to disbelief. James Dwight Dana, the American geologist, had refused to support the theory and when he later objected to Darwin's arguments, Darwin responded with an ameliorative reply that Dana's objections were "perfectly valid . . . pray do not suppose that I think for one instant that, with your strong and slowly acquired convictions and immense knowledge, you could have been converted. The utmost that I could have hoped would have been that you might possibly have been here or there staggered. . . . I remember well how many years I fought against my present belief." Of a correspondent who "goes far with me but cannot swallow all," Darwin wrote almost two decades after publication of *The Origin*, "No one could, until he had enlarged his gullet by years of practice, as in my own case." And to the vicar of Downe, he confessed: "I never expected to convert people under 20 years, though fairly convinced now that I am in the main right. For a week hardly passes without my hearing of some good judge coming some little way with me. And those who go an inch will surely have to go a yard with me. By far the greater part of the opposition is just the same as that made when the sun was first said to stand still and the world to go round."

Some of Darwin's clearest reactions to the controversy that was beginning to boil up in the early 1860s are contained in a letter he wrote to an unknown correspondent on March 14, 1861. "I feel not a shade of surprise at your entirely rejecting my views," he began, "my surprise is that I have been successful in converting some few eminent Botanists, Zoologists and Geologists. In several cases the conversion has been very slow and that is the only sort of conversion which I respect. I *entirely* agree with you that there is no more direct proof of variation being *un*limited in amount than there is that it is strictly limited. In a new and corrected Edit. of the Origin, which will appear in about a week or two, I have printed this as emphatically as I could. I did not formerly explicitly say this (but indirectly in several places) because I thought it was obvious. The manner in which I wish to approach the whole subject, and in which it seems to me it may fairly be approached, I can best illustrate in the case of Light. The ether is hypothetical, as are its undulations; but as the undulatory hypothesis groups together and explains a multitude of phenomena, it is universally now admitted as the true theory. The undulations in the ether are considered in some degree probable, because sound is produced by undulations in air. So natural selection, I look at as in some degree probable, or possible, because we know what artificial selection can do. But I believe in nat. selection, not because, I can prove in any single case that it has changed one species into another, but because it groups and explains well (as it seems to me) a host of facts in classification, embryology, morphology, rudimentary organs, geological succession and Distribution. . . ."

The new edition of *The Origin* that Darwin was awaiting in March 1861 was to be the third. Another three were to be published before his death. No two of the six editions were to be identical, and his willingness to answer criticisms and incorporate fresh material was a factor in his survival.

His original text, tailored together with some speed from a huge mass of material after the arrival of Wallace's 4,000-word manuscript, had been adamant on two points: the mutability of species through evolution and the importance of natural selection as the main process by which evolution was achieved. But within these guidelines Darwin was singularly undogmatic. He appears to have guessed intuitively—since the knowledge of his day would not have allowed anything more certain—that the details of evolution as they emerged would be of remarkable complexity, that some might contradict his own interpretation of facts and observations, and that others might raise fresh problems of their own. He accepted this and in later editions added, deleted and revised, typically changing the first edition's "The laws governing inheritance are quite unknown" to: "The laws governing inheritance are for the most part unknown" in the sixth. The fifth edition incorporated the phrase "The Survival of the Fittest," which Herbert Spencer had used earlier, while the sixth dropped "On" from the title. Thus care is needed in describing exactly when Darwin made any particular claim. As he himself admitted in a note to the sixth edition, "The second edition was little more than a reprint of the first," but "The third edition was largely corrected and added to and the fourth and fifth still more largely."

The changes were more considerable than is usually appreciated. In the words of Morse Peckham, who produced a variorum text on the centenary of the first publication: "Of the 3,878 sentences in the first edition, nearly 3,000, about 75 per cent, were re-written from one to five times each. Over 1,500 sentences were added, and of the original sentences plus these, nearly 325 were dropped. Of the original and added sentences there are nearly 7,500 variants of all kinds. In terms of net added sentences, the sixth edition is nearly a third as long again as the first."

Some alterations were of a political nature. At the end of his manuscript Darwin had written: "There is grandeur in this view of life, with its several powers, having been originally breathed into a few forms or into one." But in preparing the second edition he discreetly added "by the Creator" after the word "breathed."

He removed the errors that inevitably creep into a factual work of this kind, decreasing the huge number of elephants that he had said would be produced in a specific time by a single pair, and lamenting to E. Ray Lankester, "I got some mathematician to make the calculation, and he blundered and caused me much shame." His misinterpretation by enemies, calculated or accidental, induced him to make more than one cut. In the first edition he had described a black bear swimming for hours "with widely open mouth, thus catching, like a whale, insects in the water," and had then added: "I can see no difficulty in a race of bears being rendered, by natural selection, more and more aquatic in their structure and habits, with larger and larger mouths, till a creature was produced as monstrous as a whale." This gave his opponents an opportunity to claim that Darwin maintained that a bear could turn into a whale. He deleted the example when he might, indeed, merely have changed the clumsily written paragraph. He also tried to refute the suggestion that he had asserted that natural selection was the sole mechanism of evolution. His statement that it was not the exclusive means of modification, he said, had "been of no avail. Great is the power of steady misrepresentation; but the history of science shows this power does not long endure."

Compared with his minor comments and alterations, whose amiable lack of dogmatism helped to keep the theory of natural selection alive during the critical years after publication of *The Origin*, there were two other changes Darwin made in successive editions. The first was the inclusion in the third edition of "An Historical Sketch of the Recent Progress of Opinion on the Origin of Species, Previously to the Publication of the First Edition of This Work." It paid tribute to many of his predecessors, although as a narrative of the centuries-long development that had led to "Darwinism," as it was by now being called, it had its weaknesses.

Another change was the progressive alteration of the words "my theory" to "the theory," and when the sixth edition was published in 1872, only one out of the original forty-five *my*'s still remained. Darwin's initial apparent reluctance to give credit to his predecessors can only be held against him if the picture of the man provided by his correspondence and the reminiscences of those who knew him is totally ignored. For more than twenty years the species problem had been the background to his life, and it was natural that he should write of "my theory." Strictly, the phrase applied only to natural selection, yet Samuel Butler was able to make his gibe that with the fifth edition of *The Origin*, "there was a stampede of my's throughout the whole work, no less than thirty out of the original forty-five being changed into 'the,' 'our', 'this' or some other word, which, though having all the effect of my, still did not say 'my' outright. These my's were, if I may say so, sneaked out; nothing was said to explain their removal to the reader or call attention to it."

The initial lack of a historical background was no doubt an error, but understandable enough in the circumstances. The book lacked references, footnotes and all the other academic scaffolding with which Darwin had intended to buttress "the big book" that he had started in 1856 and that had been superseded after Wallace's paper had arrived. What more natural than that he should omit a history of the events before 1837? Moreover, there was, for no discernible reason, a long tradition of nonacknowledgement among writers on evolution. Lamarck had referred neither to Buffon nor to Erasmus Darwin. And Patrick Matthew, with his view on the origin of species the same as Darwin's, made no reference to any of the same three predecessors. There was something in Samuel Butler's cryptic comment: "Buffon planted, Erasmus Darwin and Lamarck watered, but it was Mr. Darwin who said 'That fruit is ripe,' and shook it into his lap." Darwin would no doubt have agreed, but he might have added that it credited him with good observation. Moreover, there was one other significant point that could have been made. Some eighty years later, *The Times* was to say of Einstein's general relativity, "[His genius] consists in taking up the uninterpreted experiments and scattered suggestions of his predecessors, and welding them into a comprehensive scheme that wins universal admiration by its simplicity and beauty." Much the same could be said of Darwin and *The Origin*.

More important than the addition of a historical background was a change of emphasis incorporated by Darwin as further information accumulated over the years. This was a veering toward the ideas of Lamarck, who had maintained that characteristics acquired in the lifetime of an animal could be inherited by its off-spring. Darwin had initially been extremely critical of Lamarck, describing the arguments as "veritable rubbish," "absurd though clever work," and "extremely poor." Yet in the later editions of *The Origin*, these arguments were by no means excluded. From the first, Darwin had maintained that while natural selection was the main mechanism that transformed species, it was not the only one; there were gaps in the evidence, and he began to fill them with the assumption that in some circumstances acquired characteristics could be inherited. An unprotected flank was thereby offered to enemies like Butler, who, seizing on one resulting ambiguity, could write: "This comes of tinkering. We do not know whether we are on our heads or our heels. We catch ourselves repeating 'important,' 'unimportant,' 'unimportant' 'important' like the King when addressing the jury in 'Alice in Wonderland.' "

The modifications Darwin made following publication of *The Origin* did little to damp down the honest protestations of those who regarded him as having spat within the body of the kirk. They did little to quell the doubts of scientific men who would today have attacked him on the grounds of Popperian unverifiability.

Another line of attack was launched by those who believed that the age of the earth was not great enough to allow for the slow accumulation of variations that Darwin insisted was required by evolution. He himself had settled for some 300 million years, basing his figure on the erosion of the Weald in southern England, which he believed had been primarily due to the action of the sea. Professor William Thomson, later Lord Kelvin, was among the first to open fire, stating at the meeting of the British Association in 1861 that it was "on the whole most probable that the sun has not illuminated the earth for 100,000,000 years, and almost certain that he has not done so for 500,000,000 years." Thomson followed this up in April 1862 with a paper delivered to the Royal Society of Edinburgh that put the age of the earth as between 25 and 400 million years, with 98 million as the most likely figure. But it was not until 1869 that he fully spelled out the implications, telling the Geological Society of Glasgow: "The limitation of geological periods, imposed by physical science, cannot, of course, disprove the hypothesis of transmutation of species; but it does seem sufficient to disprove the doctrine that transmutation has taken place through 'descent with modification by natural selection.' "

Darwin himself was impressed by the argument, and wrote to Wallace: "I should rely much on pre-Silurian time; but then comes Sir W[illiam] Thomson like an odious spectre." He attempted to deal with Thomson's objection in the fifth edition of *The Origin*, and in the sixth described the objection as "probably one of the gravest as yet advanced." But this was before knowledge of radioactivity. Subsequent discoveries showed that disintegration of radioactive matter within the earth created heat, which upset Thomson's calculations. They were also to be affected by discoveries within Darwin's lifetime, some made by his son George concerning the internal heat of the earth. Darwin was delighted, and George was told: "How this will please the geologists and evolutionists." There was, after all, time for evolution.

Such technical objections as Thomson's helped to keep the subject of evolution in the news; Darwin's reaction helped to propagate his image as a man more reasonable than might have been expected. The monkey cartoons continued, and Disraeli, asking the Oxford Diocesan Conference "Is man an ape or an angel?" could affirm: "Now, I am on the side of the angels." But by the mid-1860s evolution by natural selection had become in Britain a subject for serious discussion rather than a joke of the lunatic fringe. Darwin had survived the first and most dangerous campaign against him.

The spin-off from his personal character had helped, typified by the attitude of Leslie Stephen. A man rarely overimpressed by the assertions of science and scientists, Stephen gave such a taunting description of scientist-mountaineers at an annual dinner of the Alpine Club that John Tyndall resigned from the club. But Stephen's attitude to Darwin verged on hero worship, as is evident in "An Attempted Philosophy of History," an essay in the *Fortnightly Review*. After recalling that the influence of Henry Buckle—whose first volume of the *History of Civilization in England* had appeared in 1857—had already faded, Stephen continued: "Darwinism, on the contrary, has acted like a leaven affecting the whole development of modern thought. Even its antagonists virtually admit its vast importance. We classify the ablest thinkers by the relation which their opinions bear to it, and, whatever its ultimate fate, no one can doubt that it will be the most conspicuous factor in the history of modern speculation. I could not discuss Mr. Darwin's book without plunging into the very thick of the warfare which is still raging. I can speak of Buckle's theories as I might record the history of a half-forgotten skirmish in the Crimean War."

The respect between littérateur and scientist was mutual, and on at least one occasion Darwin welcomed at Down House Stephen's "Sunday Tramps," that Victorian league of literary walkers who followed the footpaths of London's Home Counties on weekends. He himself called on Stephen in London. "I was proud to welcome him, for of all eminent men that I have ever seen he is beyond comparison the most attractive to me," Stephen told his friend Caroline Elizabeth Norton. "There is something almost pathetic in his simplicity and friendliness."

7

Darwinism Takes Root

DARWIN was as lucky in the years immediately after publication of
The Origin as he had been with the selection of Huxley as *The Times*
reviewer.

In 1861 there took place three events—one affecting the general
public, the other two of scientific significance—that gave the idea
of evolution an extra touch of plausibility in a still-questioning
world. The first was the arrival in England of Paul Belloni Du
Chaillu, a U.S.-naturalized French traveler who brought with him
the skulls and stuffed bodies of gorillas that he had killed on the
Ogooué River in Equatorial Africa. Du Chaillu's stories of his
exploits were overdramatized, and although their truth was subsequently verified, he was in 1861 described as a fraud by some
members of the scientific establishment. However, the existence of
the gorilla, which had sometimes been questioned, was now accepted by, among others, that devout anti-Darwinian Richard
Owen and by Sir Roderick Murchison, the Scottish geologist. Du
Chaillu lectured at the Royal Institution. And throughout Britain
the gorilla now appeared as an ominous figure that could perhaps
be connected with the ancestry of man. Even Owen admitted that
the gorilla was nearer to man than any other ape. The middle-of-
the-road public tended to agree with the *Daily Telegraph*'s protest
that "human dignity and human feeling both revolt against the
absurdities of the would-be scientific men. God made man in his
own image, says the Book of Books; and though this is ancient
testimony to the divinity of our origin, it has not yet been upset by

modern conjecture or modern assumption." Some readers began to mutter that there was no smoke without fire. Maybe there was at least some link between man and the creature Du Chaillu described as "a being of that hideous order, half-man half-beast, which we find pictured by old artists in some representations of the infernal regions."

Of the two scientific matters that buttressed the evolutionary campaign, the most publicized was the open battle that developed between Owen and Huxley as the latter justified a declaration he had made at Oxford the previous year. There, Owen had all but staked his reputation on the claim that certain features, notably the hippocampus major (a structure in the floor of the lateral ventricle of the brain), were absent from simians although present in humans. In the *Natural History Review* and the *Proceedings of the Zoological Society*, Huxley convincingly proved that Owen was wrong. And if a confirmed opponent of evolution could be wrong on such a point, might not the whole reasoning of the opposition be based on similarly slippery foundations? "I do not believe that in the whole history of science," Huxley wrote of Owen to Hooker, "there is a case of any man of reputation getting himself into such a contemptible position. He will be the laughing-stock of all the continental anatomists."

If not of the anatomists, then at least of the readers of *Punch*, who on May 18 were presented with what Huxley called "a poetical squib," which he later learned had been written by Sir Philip Egerton, the distinguished paleontologist. Signed "Gorilla" and printed under a picture of that animal bearing the words: "Am I a Man and a Brother?" it concluded: "Next HUXLEY replies, / That Owen he lies, / And garbles his Latin quotation; / That his facts are not new, / His mistakes not a few, / Detrimental to his reputation. / 'To twice slay the slain,' / By dint of the Brain, (Thus Huxley concludes his review) / Is but labour in vain, / Unproductive of gain, / And so I shall bid you 'Adieu!' " The fact that the author was Egerton, Huxley wrote to Hooker, "speaks volumes for Owen's perfect success in damning himself."

Meanwhile Huxley made use of the encounter in the current lectures to workingmen that he gave regularly in London. "My working men stick by me wonderfully," he wrote to his wife on March 22, "the house being fuller than ever last night. By next Friday evening they will all be convinced that they are monkeys."

The second event of 1861 significant to evolution was the discovery in Bavaria of the fossil remains of the archaeopteryx, the most ancient of all fossil birds. The fossil record had so far been of questionable use to Darwin. The creationists had claimed that the finding of fossil shells on mountain summits supported Genesis and the story of Noah's Ark and the Flood, while Darwin himself was worried to the end of his life by the lack of intermediate fossil species. "The case at present," he admitted in *The Origin*, "must remain inexplicable; and may be truly urged as a valid argument against the views here entertained."

However, the archaeopteryx was something rather special. Darwin's theory had maintained that birds had evolved from reptiles, an unlikely proposition to most laymen and one that had provided a convenient starting point for attack. But now, from the lithographic limestone beds of the Upper Jurassic, there came the fossil of a creature that had clearly boasted feathers but whose vertebrae and tail were reptilian. "The fossil bird with the long tail and fingers to its wings," Darwin told James Dwight Dana, ". . . is by far the greatest prodigy of recent times. This is a great case for me, as no group was so isolated as birds; and it shows how little we knew what lived during former times."

The archaeopteryx was the first of other fossil discoveries that during the following years made it increasingly difficult to criticize the idea of evolution as merely unsubstantiated theory. Many came from the United States, where the huge areas of the unopened western states presented great opportunities for searchers of the fossil record. Prominent among these paleontologists was Othniel Charles Marsh, who employed William ("Buffalo Bill") Cody as guide for his expeditions and competed for fossils with Edward Drinker Cope with a ferocity more personal than scientific.

Marsh's first success was with the toothed birds from the Cretaceous period whose reptilian characteristics affirmed the link between birds and reptiles that had been seen in the archaeopteryx. His fossils eventually showed how heavy bone had become light and strong; how the forelimb had lengthened; how the reptilian sternum, the breastbone, had become enlarged and deepened to anchor the wing muscles; and how scales had developed into feathers. In Huxley's words, this "completed the series of transitional forms between birds and reptiles, and removed Mr. Darwin's proposition that 'many animal forms of life have been utterly lost, through which the early progenitors of birds were formerly connected with the early progenitors of the other vertebrate classes,' from the region of hypothesis to that of demonstrable fact."

Quite as important was the discovery by Marsh of fossils that revealed, in almost laboratory fashion, the evolution of horses throughout the millennia. The first were found at Antelope Station, Nebraska, in 1868, and included skeletons of four species, the smallest that of an animal only thirty inches tall. Marsh continued to build up his collection, and by 1876, when Huxley visited America, could show specimens that demonstrated the gradual change from the multitoed horse of Eocene times to the horse of the nineteenth century. The collection, Huxley told his wife, "is the most wonderful thing I ever saw. I wish I could spare three weeks instead of one to study it." Marsh, briefing Huxley for an important New York lecture, showed that the horse had originated in the New World and not the Old. "He then informed me," Marsh wrote, "that all this was new to him, and that my facts demonstrated the evolution of the horse beyond question, and for the first time indicated the direct line of descent of an existing animal." So strong was the evidence of the descent, it was later to be claimed, "that were there no other evidences of evolution to be found among the fossils this would be quite sufficient of itself to establish its truth." And two years before he died, Darwin was to maintain that Marsh's work had "afforded the best support to the theory of Evolution which has appeared within the last twenty years."

Almost a century later, statistical study of the fossil record was to give numerical muscle to the development, and George Gaylord Simpson was able to calculate that the evolution from *Hyracotherium* to *Equus* took place over sixty million years, during which each of eight genera lasted for an average of seven and a half million years. There were thirty species during the sixty million years and fifteen million generations, each of which reached maturity in four years.

In the 1860s, Du Chaillu's gorillas aroused popular interest in evolution and Huxley's victory over Owen, combined with the discovery of the archaeopteryx, gave the theory additional scientific support. But Marsh's work in America was particularly important in a continent where devout religious belief was still strong but where a people faced with the exploration and exploitation of a vast area found themselves instinctively sympathetic to the idea of survival of the fittest. The result was a clash of opinions in some ways more bitter than that in Victorian England.

The transatlantic equivalent of Darwin's "bulldog" was Asa

Gray, who in 1860 wrote many thousands of words on *The Origin* in the *American Journal of Science and Arts*, the *Atlantic Monthly* and the *Proceedings of the American Academy*. At first Gray had been cautious in his acceptance of natural selection but soon decided that it was no impediment to his religious beliefs. One reason was that man could be considered as an exception to the general plan, and accounted for by a series of special creations that avoided the need for any blood relationship between blacks on one hand and white men on the other. Another point on which Gray and Darwin differed was the American's belief that although natural selection was responsible for evolution, it acted on teleologically directed variations. In that case, Darwin responded, the number and direction of a fantail pigeon's feathers were ordered to satisfy the wishes of a few pigeon fanciers. Despite these qualifications, Gray was not only a supporter but an able one. "Every single word," wrote Darwin enthusiastically of one paper, "seems weighed carefully, and tells like a 32-pound shot."

Gray was no doubt encouraged in his support of Darwin by the aggressive opposition of Jean Louis Rodolphe Agassiz, the Swiss-American naturalist, also a professor at Harvard, who maintained that he would "outlive this mania" of evolution. Darwin, who well knew Agassiz's views on evolution, had sent him a copy of *The Origin* when it was first published. "I hope you will at least give me credit," he said in a covering letter, "however erroneous you may think my conclusions, for having earnestly endeavoured to arrive at the truth." Agassiz's reaction can be judged by one comment he made in the margin: "This is truly monstrous!" His convictions grew firmer with time. Agassiz "growls over [Darwinism] like a well-cudgelled dog," Gray told Hooker, "—is very much annoyed by it—to our great delight—and I do not wonder at it." The characters of the two men were as different as their ideas, and if Gray spoke with the voice of restrained reason, almost echoing the *if*'s and *but*'s with which Darwin strengthened rather than weakened his case, Agassiz would have no truck with evolution of any sort. "Far from agreeing with [the view of Darwin] I have, on the contrary," he wrote in the *American Journal of Science and Arts*, "taken the ground that all the natural divisions in the animal kingdom are primarily distinct, founded upon different categories of characters, and that all exist in the same way, that is, as categories of thought embodied in individual living forms. . . . I shall therefore consider the transmutation theory as a scientific mistake, untrue in its facts, unscientific in its method, and mischievous in its tendency." His dogmatism sometimes brought down more criticism than it deserved, as with William James, who wrote to his brother Henry: "The more I think of Darwin's ideas the more weighty do they appear to me, though of course my opinion is worth very little— still, I *believe* that that scoundrel Agassiz is unworthy either intellectually or morally for him to wipe his shoes on, and I find a certain pleasure in yielding to the feeling."

Agassiz appears to have maintained his uncompromising stance to the end of his life. But in 1872, the year before his death, he visited the Galápagos; it has been speculated that he was drawn to the islands by the wish to see for himself the birds and beasts that had influenced Darwin almost forty years earlier. Certainly a letter he wrote to his British friend Benjamin Peirce, has curious overtones.

Our visit to the Galapagos has been full of geological and zoölogical interest. It is most impressive to see an extensive archipelago, of *most recent origin*, inhabited by creatures so different from any known in other parts of the world. Here we have a positive limit to the length of time that may have been granted for the transformation of these animals, if indeed they are in any way derived from others dwelling in different parts of the world. The Galapagos are so recent that some of the islands are barely covered with the most scanty vegetation, itself peculiar to these islands. Some parts of their surface are entirely bare, and a great many of the craters and lava streams are so fresh, that the atmospheric agents have not yet made an impression on them. Their age does not, therefore, go back to earlier geological periods; they belong to our times, geologically speaking. Whence, then, do their inhabitants (animals as well as plants) come? If descended from some other type, belonging to any neighboring land, then it does not require such unspeakably long periods for the transformation of species as the modern advocates of transmutation claim; and the mystery of change, with such marked and characteristic differences between existing species, is only increased, and brought to a level with that of creation. If they are autochthones [original inhabitants], from what germs did they start into existence? I think that careful observers, in view of these facts, will have to acknowledge that our science is not yet ripe for a fair discussion of the origin of organized beings. . . .

If the Darwinian controversy had started in the United States with as much fire and fury as in England, if not more, it was soon overshadowed by the effects of the American Civil War. The

American Association for the Advancement of Science did not meet while the war continued, and although the National Academy of Sciences was formed in 1863, it made a point of avoiding controversial issues. Meanwhile, conciliatory noises began to be heard on both sides, and James McCosh, president of Princeton University —then the College of New Jersey—could say in *Christianity and Positivism*, defending theism by the argument from design: "I am inclined to think that the theory [of evolution] contains a large body of important truths, which we see illustrated in every department of organic nature; but that it does not contain the whole truth, and that it overlooks more than it perceives. . . . That this principle [natural selection] is exhibited in nature and working to the advancement of the plants and animals from age to age, I have no doubt. . . . But it has not been proven that there is no other principle at work."

This was more than a halfway house to the acceptance that came little more than a decade later when Henry Ward Beecher, the most influential American preacher of the age, published his *Evolution and Religion.* Although the arguments went on, they no longer continued with the ferocity that had marked the Gray-Agassiz confrontation. In a lecture given in England in 1886 Beecher had flatly stated: "I regard evolution as being the discovery of the Divine method in creation," and had gone on to maintain: "I hold that Evolution, so far from being in antagonism with true religion, will develop it with more power than any other presentation of science that ever has occurred in this world. The day will come when men will render thanks for that which now they deprecate."

Whatever the doubts raised by religious believers or questioning scientists, it became clearer during the 1860s in both America and Europe that the general line of Darwin's theory was gaining a firmer hold on the public imagination. As Herbert Spencer pointed out, those who continued to condemn it on the ground that it was supported by little tangible evidence tended to ignore the fact that there was no hard evidence at all for the only other alternative, that of special creation. Yet acceptance of "Darwinism" during the decade that followed publication of *The Origin*, the vital period during which it had to win at least partial acceptance if it were to survive, depended to some degree on national chauvinism and past history. This was particularly the case in France, where a belief in spontaneous germination still lingered and where loyal Frenchmen were reluctant to admit that the names of Cuvier and Lamarck could be superseded by that of an Englishman.

Darwin was unlucky in France, where, in Huxley's words, there existed a "conspiracy of silence" in the Académie des Sciences. When he at last found a publisher for *The Origin*, the translator, Mlle. Clémence-Auguste Royer, turned out to be a damaging enthusiast. Even her title for the book was radically different from Darwin's—*De l'Origine des Espèces, ou Des Lois du Progrès chez les Êtres Organisés*. And while Darwin had taken the utmost care to offend religious susceptibilities as little as possible, Mlle. Royer wrote a 60-page preface that stated: "The doctrine of M. Darwin is the rational revelation of progress, pitting itself in its logical antagonism with the irrational revelation of the fall. These are two principles, two religions in struggle, a thesis and an antithesis of which I defy the German . . . to find a synthesis. It is a quite categorical yes and no between which it is necessary to choose, and whoever declares himself for the one is against the other. For myself, the choice is made. I believe in progress." Darwin's enemies could sit back and wait with confidence.

In what Darwin called "a little dull book against me," the French scientist Marie Jean Pierre Flourens praised Darwin but condemned his ideas. "At last Mr. Darwin's work has appeared," he wrote of the French edition of *The Origin*. "One cannot help being struck by the talent of the author. But what unclear ideas, what false ideas! What metaphysical jargon clumsily hurled into natural history! What pretentious and empty language! What childish and out-of-date personifications! O lucidity! O French stability of mind, where art thou?"

In other countries, chance was important in determining how quickly *The Origin* was noted, and how strongly it was welcomed or decried. In Russia, the *Journal of the Ministry of National Education* published, presumably as a matter of policy, Lyell's laudatory address to the British Association in Aberdeen in 1859. After the Russian edition appeared in 1864, Dmitri Pisarev, a young radical and popularizer of science, wrote a book-length review of *The Origin* that maintained: "The conclusion is that every species constantly operates only for its own sake, and the fullest egoism constitutes the fundamental law of life for the entire organic world" —an early statement of what was to become the controversial subject of social Darwinism. From the first, Darwin received a serious reception in Russia, where even criticism from the Church was on a thoughtful rather than a polemical basis. His *Descent of Man* was published in Russian in 1871, the same year as its publication in Britain, and most of his other books appeared in Russian translation without undue delay. Between 1907 and 1909 his complete works appeared in Moscow in eight volumes, edited by the plant physiologist K. A. Timiriazev. The adulation continued, and in 1912 it was said that in Moscow and St. Petersburg one hardly dared mention Darwin's name without doffing one's cap. "To express doubts as to Darwin's scientific competence on any of the questions investigated by him was to defy truth itself." This half-century of eulogy continued into the early years of the Revolution and ended only in the later 1930s with the rise of Trofim Lysenko.

In Germany, where Nietzsche's philosophy of the Superman was so widely applauded, the German edition of *The Origin* was published in 1860. It was translated by Professor Heinrich Georg Bronn, no Darwinian himself but one who believed that such an important book should be available to German readers. Nevertheless he omitted Darwin's brief hint that the theory was applicable to man and added an appendix strongly critical of the author. As in France, the first edition was quickly superseded by a second, differently translated. In Germany, Darwin's main support came from Ernst Haeckel, who maintained that psychology was a branch of physiology and that mind could therefore be fitted into the scheme of evolution. So strong was his defense that Darwin, ever thoughtful of his colleagues, could write to Haeckel: "I do not at all like that you, towards whom I feel so much friendship, should unnecessarily make enemies, and there is pain and vexation enough in the world without more being caused."

In Austria, Darwin's views quickly took root, and when Sir Archibald Geikie visited the country in 1869, he was told by a German friend: "You are still discussing in England whether or not the theory of Darwin can be true. We have got a long way beyond that here. His theory is now our common starting-point." And Geikie was reminded that three years previously, when the Austrian Parliament met after the disastrous end of the war with Prussia, Professor Baron Karl von Rokitansky began an important speech in the Upper Chamber with the words: "The question we have first to consider is, Is Charles Darwin right or no?"

Elsewhere in the world, *The Origin* was strongly condemned. Gregorio Chil y Naranjo, for instance, had referred in a three-volume history of the Canary Islands to Darwin having "opened the gates." This was enough to induce the archbishop of Las Palmas to read a pastoral letter from the city's pulpits prohibiting the reading of the history and ordering owners to hand over their copies to the authorities.

By contrast, Darwinism made its first Japanese appearance in a book that quoted it to support indigenous religions against Christianity. Nobuchika Aoikawa's *Hokky-dam*, published in 1874, not only claimed that Genesis was absurd but that genetic descriptions in Shintoist classics and Buddhistic scriptures were in tune with Darwinism, whose truth was taken for granted. Three years later Edward Sylvester Morse, an American zoologist at Tokyo University, gave a series of public lectures on Darwin and evolution, and in 1881 there was published a Japanese translation of *The Descent of Man* to which a part of *The Origin* was added. The first complete edition of *The Origin* in Japanese was not issued until 1896, but during the next sixty-seven years no less than eleven different versions were published in fifteen Japanese editions.

In the rest of the world Darwin faced continuing sniping from the religious sidelines and criticism from a number, if a decreasing number, of scientists. However, slow acceptance continued to be qualified in differing degrees by certain unanswered questions. First, nothing whatsoever was known about the actual mechanism of inheritance, the machinery that must produce the variations so essential for the working of natural selection. Furthermore, it seemed likely that on any reasonable hypothesis "blending" would tend to remove rather than perpetuate the variations that did occur. Third, there was the question mark hanging over man himself. Was he, if evolution were accepted, part of the process, a mammal standing on the topmost rung of the ladder that reached from the primeval slime? And if he were, how was it possible to avoid devastating implications?

Darwin well knew that such questions would continue to haunt evolution until they were settled. They had, it is true, been asked when other, pre-Darwinian versions of evolution had been discussed. But those versions had been so insubstantial that there had been little point in extended discussion, and it is a measure of *The Origin*'s success that the quantity and quality of the evidence now made it important for those arguments to be thrashed out. Darwin certainly appreciated this. For behind his appearance of the recluse, part natural, part cultivated, that he showed from early middle age onward, there lay a man of the world who knew that he had embarked on a fight that would engage him for the rest of his life. Thus for the major part of the two decades and more that followed publication of *The Origin*, he spent his time in underpinning the ideas in the book. He did not do this by public lectures or speeches —he had friends like Huxley on whom he could depend for that —and the part that he played in the politics of science was inconsiderable.

Instead, he produced at Down House a long list of books, pamphlets and papers that elaborated on various aspects of evolution. At the same time he produced for journals, technical and popular, a constant stream of letters and notes dealing with a huge variety of natural history subjects. Gathered together in the not very accurately described *Collected Papers*, they included 157 items covering matters as different as "Ancient Gardening," "Hedgehogs," "Perception in the Lower Animals," "Action of Ammonia on Chlorophyll" and "Vermin and Traps." Among the most important of the books were *The Descent of Man*, in which he placed man firmly on the evolutionary ladder, *The Expression of the Emotions in Man and Animals*, which followed it, and the earlier *Variation of Animals and Plants under Domestication*, which covered the material intended for the first two chapters of "the big book" he had abandoned when Wallace had appeared on the scene.

From the early 1860s, Darwin devoted himself more and more to botanical work, partly because it enabled him to expand on various points made only briefly in *The Origin*, partly because, as he said, he had always followed up a variation in animals by a search for its equivalent in plants. He repeatedly insisted that he was no botanist—by which he meant professional botanist—but the work on which he now embarked was to have important botanical results and led to, among other things, the discovery of plant hormones, chemical weed-killers and the outbreeding of maize.

The first of the major books on which he began following publication of *The Origin* was *The Variation of Animals and Plants under Domestication*. But although started early in 1860, it was not completed for seven years, being interrupted by a number of the other questions he found it impossible entirely to put aside.

One, and the earliest to be dealt with, was a study of the ways in which orchids are fertilized by insects, and both to his publisher, John Murray, and to Hooker he emphasized that the work was intended to buttress the conclusions of *The Origin*. "I think this little volume will do good to the 'Origin', as it will show that I have worked hard at details . . ." he wrote to Murray on September 24, 1861. "It will perhaps serve to illustrate how Natural History may be worked under the belief of the modification of species." And to Hooker he wrote the following May, "I have found the study of Orchids eminently useful in showing me how nearly all parts of the flower are co-adapted for fertilisation by insects, & therefore the results of n[atural] selection, — even most trifling details of structure." Later, apparently long after his book on orchids was published, and reinforcing the point to Asa Gray, he wrote, "When I think of my beloved Orchids with rudiments of five anthers, with one pistil converted into a rostellum, with all the cohesion of parts, it really seems to me incredibly monstrous to look at an Orchid as created as we now see it. Every part reveals modification on modification." Darwin was not, of course, referring, as could possibly be thought today, to the products of commercial growers, but to the evolutionary processes that had resulted in the wild orchids he studied.

He had first become attracted to the cross-fertilization of flowers by insects as far back as 1838 or 1839, after, as he was to write in his autobiography, he had come "to the conclusion in my speculations on the origin of species, that crossing played an important part in keeping specific forms constant." He kept up the interest, although it was nearly two decades later that he began to contribute a number of short papers on the subject to the *Gardeners' Chronicle*. He became particularly interested in orchids, mainly because of the large range of features with which they ensure pollination by insects, but also because the plants could be easily studied at Orchis Bank, a quarter of a mile from Down House, where the fly—and musk—orchis grew among the junipers. Pistils, stamens and petals, he found, were all formed so as to aid cross-fertilization by one particular form of insect. This was equally true, he discovered, of the orchids that he secured from Kew and from botanists abroad.

When he finished his paper on the subject in September 1861, it ran to 140 folio pages, far too long for publication by the Linnean Society, as he had hoped. As with *The Origin*, he turned to John Murray. And as with *The Origin*, he was almost apologetic in proposing publication. Murray was glad to oblige, and the book was published in 1862 under the portmanteau title *On the Various Contrivances by Which British and Foreign Orchids are Fertilized by Insects, and on the Good Effects of Intercrossing*. His judgment was vindicated, for the book, though only a moderate financial success, was much praised. It is "quite unique—there is nothing in the whole range of Botanical Literature to compare with it," maintained Hooker. However, the Duke of Argyll tried to turn its conclusions back against the author. In spite of his objections to teleological explanations, the Duke argued, Darwin had been looking for a purpose in nature, had seen one in every feature, and had explained each as that best fitted for a particular task.

A century later, another evolutionist was to view Darwin's orchid work in a totally different light. "Orchids manufacture their intricate devices [which ensure cross-pollination] from the common components of ordinary flowers, parts usually fitted for very different functions," wrote Stephen Jay Gould in *The Panda's Thumb.* "If God had designed a beautiful machine to reflect his wisdom and power, surely he would not have used a collection of parts generally fashioned for other purposes. Orchids were not made by an ideal engineer; they are jury-rigged from a limited set of available components. Thus, they must have evolved from ordinary flowers."

Before the end of 1862, Darwin was planning another addition to Down, possibly as a result of his work on orchids. "And now I am going to tell you a *most* important piece of news!!" he wrote to Hooker on Christmas Eve. "I have almost resolved to build a small hot-house; my neighbour's really first-rate gardener has suggested it, & offered to make me plans, & see that it is well-done, and he is a really clever fellow, who wins lots of prizes, & is very observant. He believes that we should succeed with a little patience; it will be a grand amusement for me to experiment with plants."

The "almost" must have been quickly removed, for by the first days of February 1863, the building had been completed against the wall of the kitchen garden. "Hot house is ready & I long to stock it, just like a school-boy," Hooker was informed. "Could you tell me pretty soon what plants you can give me; & then I shall know what to order. And do advise me how I had better get such plants as you can *spare.* Would it do to send my tax-cart early in the morning, on a day that was not frosty, lining the cart with mats; & arriving here before night. I have no idea whether this degree of exposure & of course the cart would be cold could injure stove plants; they would be about 5 hours (with bait [the short stop to feed a horse during travel]) on journey home."

Darwin now thanked Sir John Lubbock, the neighbor whose gardener, a Mr. Horwood, had suggested the hothouse, and added that without him he would never have had the spirit to do the job —"and if I had should probably have made a mess of it. It will not only be an amusement to me, but will enable me to try many little experiments which otherwise would have been impossible."

There were to be numbers of experiments, and not only for *The Variation of Animals and Plants under Domestication*, the notes for which, collected over the years, Darwin began collating once the orchid book was out of the way. But again he was diverted from his path, this time by recollection of Asa Gray's *Note on the Coiling of the Tendrils of Plants,* which Gray had sent him in 1858. Now, in the aftermath of *The Origin*, he began to wonder where this phenomenon might fit into the subject of evolution. In the summer of 1863 he began to examine the tendril movements of plants in his study, asked Hooker whether he knew of any other previous literature on the subject, and by July was reporting, "I am getting very much amused by my tendrils—it is just the sort of niggling work which suits me, & takes up no time & rather rests me whilst writing." He was ill during the autumn and the first months of 1864, but his preoccupation with tendril movement appears to have helped him, and in March he told Hooker, "The only approach to work which I can do is to look at tendrils and climbers, this does not distress my weakened brain."

Before the end of the year his paper was finished. It justified his suspicions that natural selection was involved, since after studying more than a hundred different plants he was able to show that climbing plants existed in the wild surrounded by thick vegetation, that their struggle for life depended on their being able to climb toward the light, and that their tendrils and general climbing "equipment" were developed from other organs. The evidence for natural selection and the modification of existing organs was so significant that he included it in the next—fourth—edition of *The Origin.*

"The Movements and Habits of Climbing Plants" first appeared in the ninth volume of the *Journal of the Linnean Society* in 1865, but was long enough to be reprinted as a separate volume by Murray ten years later. Meanwhile, Darwin had at last found time to continue with his book on variation. Once again he stressed the help he had received from others. "In treating the several subjects included in the present and succeeding works," he said, "I have continually been led to ask for information from many zoologists, botanists, geologists, breeders of animals, and horticulturists, and

I have invariably received from them the most generous assistance. Without such aid I could have effected little." This not only gave credit where Darwin knew it should be given but also tended to emphasize that his theories of variation, as of evolution itself, were not personal idiosyncrasies but were based on the hard evidence of a multitude of respectable sources. As usual, he wrote at greater length than he intended, warning Murray on January 3, 1867, "I cannot tell you how sorry I am to hear of the enormous size of my book." It was to fill two volumes, each larger than *The Origin*, and on the ninth he admitted to Hooker: "But I feel that the size is quite ludicrous in relation to the subject. I am ready to swear at myself & at every fool who writes a book." The first edition sold out within a week, and Murray was able to produce a second edition within fourteen days—a Victorian achievement that should make contemporary printers and publishers wince.

Compared with *The Origin*, *Variation* was an innocuous book— except for its final chapter. That *Variation* raised such comparatively little controversy was due to the fact that most of its contentious argument was concentrated in the virtually self-contained chapter 27. A tribute in the *Pall Mall Gazette* is a significant indication of how Darwin had been able to ride out the earlier storms so successfully. We must, it said, "call attention to the rare and noble calmness with which he expounds his own views, undisturbed by the heats of polemical agitation which those views have excited, and persistently refusing to retort on his antagonists by ridicule, by indignation, or by contempt. Considering the amount of vituperation and insinuation which has come from the other side, this forbearance is supremely dignified." It was also effective. As a fighter Darwin knew that it was better to keep his temper.

Moreover, the idea of pangenesis, which he put forward in chapter 27, was so extraordinary that few readers took it seriously. Darwin himself, asking Huxley's opinion of the idea in manuscript, called it "a very rash and crude hypothesis," described it to Hooker as "fearfully imperfect," and forecast to Asa Gray that it would be called "a mad dream." Yet the hypothesis did, as Darwin wrote to Wallace, who subscribed to it, provide a possible explanation of how heredity could work. And it was, as he went on, "a relief to have some feasible explanation of the various facts, which can be given up as soon as any better hypothesis is found. It has certainly been an immense relief to my mind; for I have been stumbling over the subject for years, dimly seeing that some relation existed be-

tween the various classes of facts," a clear indication that the ignorance of any mechanism by which variation could be passed on
from one generation to the next had been worrying him almost
since he had first begun thinking about the species problem.

Darwin's answer was pangenesis. "I assume," he wrote of it,
"that cells, before their conversion into completely passive or
'formed material' throw off minute granules or atoms, which circu-
late freely throughout the system, and when supplied with proper
nutriment multiply by self-division, subsequently becoming developed into cells like those from which they were derived. These
granules for the sake of distinctness may be called cell-gemmules,
or, as the cellular theory is not fully established, simply gemmules
. . . the gemmules in their dormant state have a mutual affinity for
each other, leading to their aggregation either into buds or into
the sexual elements. Hence, speaking strictly, it is not the reproductive elements, nor the buds, which generate new organisms,
but the cells themselves throughout the body."

The basic idea, developed by various biologists in their efforts
to answer the riddle of how heredity worked, was not entirely new.
Richard Owen had put forward a similar theory in 1849; so similar
that he was later to complain: "It may be a defect of power; but I
fail, after every endeavour, to appreciate the 'fundamental difference' between Mr. Darwin's cell-hypothesis of 1868 and mine of
1849. Both of them I now regard as fundamentally erroneous; in
so far as they are absolutely based on 'pre-existence'—or 'omnis
cellula.' " Closer to Darwin's pangenesis were Herbert Spencer's
"physiological units," although he did not claim that these assumed units necessarily passed on to future generations changes
that had taken place during an organism's life. Nevertheless, Cyril
Darlington was to call Darwin "the gamekeeper of natural selection and the poacher of pangenesis," a scarcely justifiable slur,
since the cell theory, starting with Schleiden and Schwann in 1839
and subsequently developed by Rudolf Virchow, had led to numerous speculations as to how it might help to explain heredity. What
can we believe, Fleeming Jenkin wrote at the end of his review of
The Origin, "but that Darwin's theory is an ingenious and plausible
speculation, to which future physiologists will look back with the
kind of admiration we bestow on the atoms of Lucretius, or the
crystal spheres of Eudoxus, containing like these some faint half-
truths, marking at once the ignorance of the age and the ability of
the philosopher. Surely the time is past when a theory unsup-

ported by evidence is received as probable, because in our ignorance we know not why it should be false, though we cannot show it to be true."

Yet Darwin's pangenesis did at least postulate a mechanism to explain how hereditary characteristics might be passed on; and just as *The Origin* was more acceptable than its predecessors because of the soundness of its rational argument, so was pangenesis, unacceptable though it might be, shown to have a plausibility rather different from the ideas that had previously been put forward. From the first, Darwin himself was of two minds, both hopeful and yet aware of the weaknesses in his proposals. As early as 1865, he had sent Huxley a thirty-page manuscript, "The Hypothesis of Pangenesis." Huxley's reply does not appear to have survived, but its nature can be judged from Darwin's response in July. "I do not doubt your judgement is perfectly just, and I will try to persuade myself not to publish. The whole affair is much too speculative."

Nevertheless, published it was, and with few significant changes from the scheme outlined to Huxley, a theory in complete contradiction to modern beliefs. In pangenesis the entire body issued instructions to the reproductive cells, whereas in modern genetic theory it is the fertilized ovum that directs the development of the whole body. To Darwin there was, however, one great advantage in the theory. For he believed that if some change took place during the life of an organism, then the gemmules continually being created would take note of the change and ensure that the change was transmitted to the next generation. "Towards the end of the work," he was later to write, "I give my well-abused hypothesis of Pangenesis. An unverified hypothesis is of little or no value; but if anyone should hereafter be led to make observations by which some such hypothesis could be established, I shall have done good service, as an astonishing number of isolated facts can thus be connected together & rendered intelligible."

And, as if he knew that further support was needed, he wrote in the chapter on "Provisional Hypothesis of Pangenesis" in *The Variation of Animals and Plants under Domestication*: "As Whewell, the historian of the inductive sciences, remarks:— 'Hypotheses may often be of service to science, when they involve a certain portion of incompleteness, and even of error.' Under this point of view I venture to advance the hypothesis of Pangenesis, which implies that the whole organisation, in the sense of every separate atom or unit, reproduces itself." Pangenesis also helped to meet the argument that "blending" would remove any chance of variations being passed on without dilution from one generation to the next. This objection had been revived in the long review of *The Origin* in the *North British Review* by Fleeming Jenkin.

However, Darwin himself had written to Huxley in 1858: "Approaching the subject [of evolution] from the side which attracts me most, viz. inheritance I have lately been inclined to speculate, very crudely and indistinctly, that propagation by true fertilisation will turn out to be a sort of mixture, and not true fusion, of two distinct individuals, as each parent has its parents and ancestors. I can understand on no other view the way in which crossed forms go back to so large an extent to ancestral forms."

Although, as Darwin put it to Wallace, pangenesis might serve as a useful stopgap until something better turned up, it still provided no firm evidence as to how heredity worked; and while its support for particulate inheritance could be considered a forerunner of genetics, it was attacked by the scientific community with more force than natural selection had been. But just as Darwin had clung onto natural selection when he had been right, so now he clung onto pangenesis when he was wrong. To Hooker he maintained that his idea was no allegory. "I fully believe," he wrote, "that each cell does *actually* throw off an atom or gemmule of its contents; but whether or not, this hypothesis serves as a useful connecting link for various grand classes of physiological facts, which at present stand absolutely isolated." And two years after publication of *Variation* he could write to Ray Lankester of his "much despised child, 'Pangenesis,' who I think will some day, under some better nurse, turn out a fine stripling."

He was hardly encouraged by his friends: "None of [them] will speak out [on pangenesis], except, to a certain extent, Sir H[enry] Holland, who found it very tough reading, but admits that some view 'closely akin to it' will have to be admitted," he wrote to Wallace. "Hooker, as far as I understand him, which I hardly do at present, seems to think that the hypothesis is little more than saying that organisms have such and such potentialities." Disagreement with the general dissent came from his cousin Francis Galton, the grandson of the first Erasmus Darwin through his second marriage. Traveler, founder of the modern technique of weather mapping and inventor of fingerprinting identification, Galton was one of the first converts to natural selection. His contribution to the discussion was an early attempt to consider heredity by statistical means and the conclusion that major differences of any kind—distinctions good or bad—were apt to run in families. These views were outlined in *Hereditary Genius: An Inquiry into Its Laws and Consequences*, published the year after Darwin's *Variation* and with a final chapter discussing pangenesis.

But Galton was no man merely to discuss what might be tested experimentally, and before the end of 1869 he was writing for Darwin's help. "I want to make some peculiar experiments that have occurred to me in breeding animals and want to procure a few couples of rabbits of marked and assured breeds," he said. In this first letter he gave no details of what he was up to. Within three months, however, and probably within a few weeks, he had described to Darwin what he had in mind. Reading Darwin's account of pangenesis in *Variation*, he had for some inexplicable reason taken it for granted that when his cousin had written of gemmules circulating freely, he had meant circulating within the blood. He had therefore decided to transfuse rabbits of one breed with blood taken from another breed, to see whether the offspring yielded evidence for the pangenesis theory. But Darwin had made no statement involving blood. "I have not said one word about the blood, or about any fluid proper to any circulating system," he later protested in a letter to *Nature*. "It is, indeed, obvious that the presence of gemmules in the blood can form no necessary part of my hypothesis; for I refer in illustration of it to the lowest animals, such as the Protozoa, which do not possess blood or any vessels; and I refer to plants in which the fluid, when present in the vessels, cannot be considered as true blood." Even more extraordinary than Galton's unjustified extrapolation from what Darwin had written was the fact that he had mentioned his interpretation in *Hereditary Genius*, and that Darwin had read the book but had nevertheless failed to raise the error with Galton.

But the rabbit experiments were carried out, first at Galton's house in Rutland Gate, London, later at Down House, where, Darwin told Galton, "my former groom (now commuted into a footman) . . . says he will do his utmost" to keep the rabbits in good health. "The experiments were thorough, and misfortunes very rare," Galton later wrote. "It was astonishing to see how quickly the rabbits recovered after the effect of the anaesthetic had passed away. It often happened that their spirits and sexual aptitudes were in no way dashed by an operation which only a few minutes before had changed nearly one half of the blood that was in their bodies.

Out of a stock of three silver grey bucks and four silver grey does, whose blood had been thus largely adulterated, and of three common bucks and four common does whose blood had been similarly altered, I bred eighty-eight rabbits in thirteen litters without any evidence of alteration of breed."

Throughout the first months of 1870 Darwin received a series of reports from Rutland Gate, varying from "No good news" to "Good rabbit news." The whole Darwin family appears to have been concerned with the work, and Emma Darwin, writing to her daughter Henrietta, noted: "F. Galton's experiments about rabbits (viz. injecting black rabbit's blood into grey and *vice versâ*) are failing, which is a dreadful disappointment to them both. F. Galton said he was quite sick with anxiety till the rabbits' *accouchements* were over, and now one naughty creature ate up her infants and the other has perfectly commonplace ones. He wishes this exper.t to be kept quite secret as he means to go on, and he thinks he shall be so laughed at, so don't mention."

The disappointments continued, and in November Darwin asked his cousin, "Do you want one more generation? If the next one is as true as all the others, it seems to me quite superfluous to go on trying." For the rabbits went on breeding true whatever their transfusions. The fact was underlined by Galton's suggestion to Darwin: "The experiments have, I quite agree, been carried on long enough. It would be a crowning point to them if your groom could get a prize at some show for those he has reared up so carefully, as it would attest their purity of breed. There is such a show, I believe, impending at the Crystal Palace." Although Darwin would not use the word "disaster" to his friends, he saw that his theory of pangenesis would not be accepted.

However, this did not deter him from going on with his plan to "write out," at book length, various subjects he had merely touched upon in *The Origin.* He could be, and often was, almost compromisingly polite, brushing aside the slings and arrows of ignorance as if they did not exist, and to those who saw him as an evil influence he was the mildest of anti-Christs. Yet beneath the somewhat hesitant polemicist, as homely and as gentle with his opponents as he was with his wife and children, his pets and the ancillary trappings of the Victorian paterfamilias, there lay concealed an iron Darwin determined to press on with the work that to him had the character of a crusade. All he would wait for was the right moment.

8

The Descent of Man

By the later 1860s the time was opportune for a detailed look at the subject, the origin of man and his history, that Darwin had virtually ignored in order to increase the chances for acceptance of *The Origin of Species*. In the 1850s Jacques Boucher de Crèvecoeur de Perthes had discovered in the gravel pits of the Somme Valley flints certainly fashioned by man but found in strata that dated them as within an almost unimaginably distant past. Although they had at first been considered with skepticism, a group of British scientists had visited the site in 1858 and returned convinced of their authenticity. The geologist William Pengelly had shortly afterward made comparable finds in Brixham, Devon, and Sir Joseph Prestwich had subsequently read to the Royal Society his paper on "The Occurrence of Flint Instruments Associated with the Remains of Animals of Extinct Species." These were only the more pertinent of the results now showing that primitive man had lived vast ages ago in France, in Devon and by the shores of the Swiss lakes, as man still lived in Borneo and Central Africa.

Early in 1863 Huxley published *Evidence as to Man's Place in Nature*, consisting of two lectures he had given in Edinburgh on "The Relation of Man to the Lower Animals" and a third he had given in London "On the Fossil Remains of Man." That differences between man and the higher apes in such features as hand, foot and brain were no greater than those between the higher apes and the lower ones was merely one set of facts that Huxley used to put man unequivocally on the evolutionary ladder.

He was given a better reception in Edinburgh than he had expected. But the reaction in the *Witness* a few days later revealed the strength of feeling that still existed and was a warning of what Darwin might expect. "It is surprising," the paper said on January 14, 1862, "that, at the close of the lectures, the hearers refrained from forming themselves into a 'Gorilla Emancipation Society,' and from concerting some prompt measures for humanizing and civilizing their unfortunate brother, as a significant earnest of what they intend to do for the whole fraternity of apes. . . . Will the 'Philosophical' by and by produce in the Hall some apostle of Mormonism? Even this will be a less offensive, mischievous and inexcusable exhibition than was made in the recent two lectures by Professor Huxley."

Later in 1863 Lyell, using geological evidence where Huxley had used anatomical, underlined the link between men and other animals in *The Geological Evidences of the Antiquity of Man*—called by the *Saturday Review* "Lyell's Trilogy on the Antiquity of Man, Ice, and Darwin"—and brought from Darwin the comment that in it he had been too civil to Owen. "By Jove how black Owen will look," he went on. "I am getting more savage against him, even than Huxley or [Hugh] Falconer. He ought to be ostracised by every Naturalist in England." In 1864 Wallace, with "The Origin of Human Races and the Antiquity of Man Deduced from the Theory of 'Natural Selection,' published in the *Journal of the Anthropological Society*, took the step that Darwin had feared to take. Following Wallace there came, in 1865, John Ferguson McLennan's *Primitive Marriage* and Sir Edward Burnett Taylor's *Early History of Mankind*, two further books that linked man dangerously back to the past. It would be unfair to suggest that it was the reception of these other books that determined Darwin to start on *The Descent of Man*. But he felt, quite rightly, that the time was now ready to bring man into the species question. There was also another factor that made the time right.

"I was so much fatigued by my last book that I determined to amuse myself by publishing a short essay on the 'Descent of Man,'" he wrote on July 6, 1868, to Alphonse de Candolle, the former professor of natural history in the University of Geneva, whose *Géographie Botanique Raisonnée* Darwin had used in his studies. "I was partly led to do this by having been taunted that I concealed my views, but chiefly from the interest which I had long taken in the subject. Now this essay has branched out into some collateral subjects, and I suppose will take me more than a year to complete."

He had started on the work the previous year, when he had begun to augment his notes by sending out questionnaires as he had done years earlier when gathering material on the species question. As before, he lobbied his friends for information, writing, typically, to David Forbes, the geologist: "Before leaving you I forgot to remind you that any notes on the idea of human beauty by natives who have associated little with Europeans would be very interesting to me. Also if by any strange chance you should have observed any facts leading you to believe that the women of savage tribes have some influence of determining which man shall steal them or buy them or run away with them I should much like to hear such facts."

He put aside the work for a number of months and only recommenced it in the summer of 1868 when he and the family were on holiday at Freshwater on the Isle of Wight. It was during this break that Darwin called on Tennyson at his home in Farringford and was told: "Your theory of Evolution does not make against Christianity." Darwin's reply, "No, certainly not," was perhaps a trifle overreassuring. But both men had probably been embarrassed by the links between them that had been forged by uninformed public opinion. In particular, those who ignored chronology had often linked *The Origin* with Tennyson's "In Memoriam" and its "Nature, red in tooth and claw . . . finding that of fifty seeds / She often brings but one to bear." Faced with the quotation on one occasion, Tennyson pointed out that "In Memoriam" was written a decade before *The Origin* was published. "Oh, then you are the man," his questioner responded. "Yes, I am the man," Tennyson replied, and then, "I don't want you to go away with a wrong impression. The fact is that long before Darwin's work appeared these ideas were known and talked about."

At Freshwater in 1868 Darwin continued sorting through the notes that he had collected during his species work. In the introduction to *The Descent of Man, and Selection in Relation to Sex,* he made no secret of why they had so far remained unpublished. He had collected them, he said, without any intention of publishing on the subject, "but rather with the determination not to publish, as I thought that I should thus only add to the prejudices against my views." But there was no doubt about the ultimate thrust of those views, and in his "Notebooks on Transmutation of Species" he had written: "Man in his arrogance thinks himself a great work worthy the interposition of a deity. more humble & I think truer to consider him created from animals." And combining recollections of a visit to the zoo with memories of Tierra del Fuego, he had written: "Let man visit Ourang-outang in domestication, hear expressive whine, see its intelligence when spoken [to], as if it understood every word said — see its affection to those it knows, — see its passion & rage, sulkiness & very extreme of despair; let him look at savage [Fuegian], roasting his parent, naked, artless, not improving, yet improvable, and then let him dare to boast his proud pre-eminence." But in the decade that had passed since publication of *The Origin*, Huxley had shown that man differed less in every visible character from the higher apes than he differed from the lower members of the same order of primates. Darwin well knew what an outcry the book would probably cause, writing to St. George Jackson Mivart: "When I publish my book, I can see that I shall meet with universal disapprobation, if not execution. The truth is hard to gain, however much one may try."

It was August 1870 before John Murray received the manuscript, since Darwin had been delayed by his usual tendency to include more than he had initially planned, and by an accident that had taken place in April 1869, when his horse, Tommy, stumbled on Keston Common. Darwin had been rolled on and badly bruised. Although he recovered in three weeks instead of the expected three months, he was obviously shaken and never rode again.

In the manuscript of *The Descent of Man*, which he completed as he recovered, he built up his case, as in *The Origin*, by the steady accumulation of detail, citing references from a huge variety of sources. He showed that man and apes shared certain parasites and certain diseases, and that they were equally susceptible to drugs and other chemical substances. In its early stages of development, the human embryo possessed a tail, just as did the embryo of the ape, thus showing that both had at one time been quadrupeds. There were other vestigial organs to which he drew attention before remarking that "the time will before long come when it will be thought wonderful, that naturalists, who were well acquainted with the comparative structure and development of man and other mammals, should have believed that each was the work of a separate act of creation."

When it came to the mind, to intelligence, the gap between man and the other animals was one of degree, while in some examples man was at a disadvantage. Thus man could make even a stone hatchet only by practice, whereas the beaver, for instance, could "make its dam or canal, and a bird its nest, as well, or nearly as well, the first time it tries, as when old and experienced." As for the emotions: "Happiness is never better exhibited than by young animals, such as puppies, kittens, lambs, &c., when playing together, like our own children. Even insects play together, as has been described by that excellent observer, P. Huber, who saw ants chasing and pretending to bite each other, like so many puppies." Point by point he showed that the claims that had for so long been maintained of differences separating man from the rest of living organisms were based on ignorance. In *The Descent of Man*, moreover, Darwin set down more forthrightly than elsewhere, the aims of his earlier work. "I had two distinct objects in view," he wrote, "firstly, to shew that species had not been separately created, and secondly, that natural selection had been the chief agent of change, though largely aided by the inherited effects of habit, and slightly by the direct action of the surrounding conditions."

In the opening sentences of *The Descent*, Darwin paraded the intentions that had caused him to write the book and that provided its mainspring. He had "put together" the notes gathered for *The Origin* "so as to see how far the general conclusions arrived at in my former works were applicable to man." Thus, he went on, the sole object of his new book was "to consider, firstly, whether man like every other species, is descended from some preexisting form; secondly, the manner of his development; and thirdly, the value of the differences between the so-called races of man."

He began by outlining the evidence for the descent of man from some lower form and followed with two chapters comparing the mental powers of man and the lower animals. After describing the way in which man had developed from a lower form, and the manner in which his intellectual and moral faculties had grown, the races of man were discussed "in the same spirit as a naturalist would any other animal," and the author then turned to sexual selection, the subject that was to occupy two-thirds of his book. Here the secondary sexual characteristics of fishes, birds and mammals in general were treated before Darwin came to those of man. As in the book's other chapters, he illustrated his points with examples culled not only from the literature but also from his wide correspondence with animal breeders and anthropologists. And, as with *The Origin*, he made out his case by piling detail on detail, making few points that were not substantiated by examples that could be simply understood.

The conclusion appeared inevitable, "namely that man is descended from some lowly-organised form," a conclusion that would, he regretted, "be highly distasteful to many persons." We must acknowledge, he ended, "that man with all his noble qualities, with sympathy which feels for the most debased, with benevolence which extends not only to other men but to the humblest living creature, with his god-like intellect which has penetrated into the movements and constitution of the solar system—with all these exalted powers—Man still bears in his bodily frame the indelible stamp of his lowly origin."

Here, indeed, was the light, and a strong one, that he had suggested in *The Origin* would be "thrown on the origin of man and his history."

He was in no doubt about the reaction he could expect, even from those who normally supported him, and to Asa Gray he wrote: "Parts, as on the moral sense, will, I dare say, aggravate you, and if I hear from you, I shall probably receive a few stabs from your polished stiletto of a pen." Huxley, Lyell and Wallace had broken the ice, as it were, but none of them was as successfully persuasive as Darwin. He had, moreover, made no attempt to disguise the implications of what he had written, saying: "if I have erred in giving to natural selection great power, which I am far from admitting, or in having exaggerated its power, which is in itself probable, I have at least, as I hope, done good service in aiding to overthrow the dogma of separate creations."

He was under no illusion as to the probable reactions inside his family. Even while the proofs were being corrected Emma had said: "I think it will be very interesting, but that I shall dislike it very much as again putting God further off."

The *Morning Post*, the *St. James Chronicle* and the *English Churchman* were only three of the publications that had accepted *The Origin*, although with reservations, but that now attacked *The Descent of Man*. The greatest change was to be seen in the *Times*, which on this occasion had no Huxley to point the way, and took five and a half columns, spread across two days, April 7 and 8, to condemn the book. "A man incurs grave responsibility who, with the authority of a well-earned reputation, advances at such a time the disintegrating speculations of this book," it said. "He ought to be capable of supporting them by the most conclusive evidence of facts. To put them forward on such incomplete evidence, such cursory investigation, such hypothetical arguments as we have exposed, is more than unscientific—it is reckless."

Punch, as was customary, continued to make itself heard on any Darwinian topic, writing:

> *"Hypotheses non fingo,"*
> Sir Isaac Newton said
> And that was true, by Jingo!
> As proof demonstrat*ed*
> But Darwin's speculation
> Is of another sort;
> 'Tis one which demonstration
> In nowise doth support.
> . . .

The *Edinburgh Review* was blunter. If Darwin were right, it said, then "most earnest-minded men will be compelled to give up those motives by which they have attempted to live noble and virtuous lives, as founded on a mistake; our moral sense will turn out to be a mere developed instinct . . . and the revelation of God to us, and the hope of a future life, pleasurable daydreams invented for the good of society. If these views be true, a revolution in thought is imminent, which will shake society to its very foundations by destroying the sanctity of the conscience and the religious sense."

The *Edinburgh Review* made yet another point. "In the drawing-room [*The Descent of Man*] is competing with the last new novel, and in the study it is troubling alike the man of science, the moralist and the theologian." In other words, it was making quite as great a furor as *The Origin*. As the *Independent* rather ruefully admitted, Darwinism was spreading among scientists "like measles in a school." There were, moreover, two reasons for its impact being greater than that of *The Origin* on the ordinary mass of readers. For one thing, it affected man himself. It had not been too difficult to maintain that whether or not the ideas of *The Origin* were correct, they did apply only to the birds of the air and the beasts of the field; man was still secure on his own private pinnacle. *The Descent of Man* removed him from it. Second, Darwin was by 1871 a better-known and better-established figure than he had been in 1859, and one whose pronouncements could less easily be dismissed.

An important effect of *The Descent of Man* was that it drove one section of the religious opposition to Darwinism into the position it was to maintain for years: evolution was accepted but natural selection was not, while for others if man himself had at some stage existed on one rung of the evolutionary ladder, he had nevertheless been transformed by a divine touch, at some unknown but distant date, into a being almost sublime. With ingenuity, various permutations and combinations of belief could be found available. In 1871 there was a rallying to the standard of the *People's Friend*, a publication that a decade earlier had postulated two kinds of men: those before and those after the addition of a soul.

The leader of this new and considerable opposition was St. George Jackson Mivart. A Fellow of the Royal Society and of the Linnean, Mivart was a formidable Catholic biologist who in spite of his religious beliefs had initially accepted *The Origin*, although with certain reservations. But starting as a fair critic of Darwin, he ended as a passionate protagonist eager to put the boot in. He had become a personal friend of Huxley's and it was only in 1868, as the inclusion of man in the evolutionary scheme became obvious, however much Darwin might still dissemble about it, that doubts began seriously to worry him. His doubts were encouraged by a Catholic friend, Father W. W. Roberts. "The arguments he again and again urged upon me were the difficulties, or rather the impossibilities, on the Darwinian system, of accounting for the origin of the human intellect, and above all for its moral intuitions—not its moral *sentiments*, but its ethical *judgments* . . ." Mivart later explained.

> For the rest of that year and the first half of the next I was perplexed and distressed as to what line I ought to take in a matter so important, and which more and more appeared to me one I was bound to enter upon controversially.
>
> After many painful days and much meditation and discussion my mind was made up, and I felt it my duty first of all to go straight to Professor Huxley and tell him all my thoughts, feelings and intentions in the matter without the slightest reserve, including what it seemed to me I must do as regarded the theological aspect of the question. Never before or since have I had a more painful experience than fell to my lot in his room at the School of Mines on that 15th of June, 1869. As soon as I had made my meaning clear, his countenance became transformed as I had never seen it. Yet he looked more sad and

surprised than anything else. He was kind and gentle as he said regretfully, but most firmly, that nothing so united or severed men as questions such as those I had spoken of.

Nevertheless no positive breach took place, though the following day, as we were driving homewards together, the conversation became rather sharply controversial. Yet family friendly relations continued. . . .

Mivart now wrote three articles on "Difficulties of the Theory of Natural Selection" for the Catholic journal *The Month*. But despite the difficulties, he was not yet a full-fledged apostate, and he made this clear in *The Genesis of Species*, a book written before the appearance of *The Descent of Man* but published within a few weeks of it. "My first object [in writing the book]," he was later to state, "was to show that the Darwinian theory is untenable, and that natural selection is not *the* origin of species. This was and is my conviction purely as a man of science, and I maintain it upon scientific grounds only. My second object was to demonstrate that nothing even in Mr. Darwin's theory, as then put forth, and *à fortiori* in evolution generally, was necessarily antagonistic to Christianity."

This squaring of the circle was accomplished by giving man, the touchstone of the argument, a two-part ancestry: his body, it was reluctantly admitted, might be an inheritance from the apes, but his soul—a word with which there was somewhat woollily included his mind and his capability for logical thought—was due to a divine and creative act. It was a solution that others had suggested but that no one had previously outlined with the competence of Mivart's sharp mind. It was praised, significantly enough, by Newman, cardinal-to-be, who told Mivart: "Those who have a right to judge speak of it as a first rate book—and it is pleasant to find that the first real exposition of the logical insufficiency of Mr. Darwin's theory comes from a Catholic. In saying this, you must not suppose that I have personally any great dislike or dread of his theory, but many good people are much troubled at it—and at all events, without any disrespect to him, it is well to show that Catholics may be better reasoners than philosophers."

The Descent of Man had shown clearly enough that there could be no compromise between the view of Darwin and those of Mivart and others who sought similar escape routes from the dilemmas with which the evolutionists had faced them. As for Darwin himself, he clearly recognized the formidable nature of the new attack.

"[Mivart's] 'Genesis' at first appeared to me very formidable, on the principle of aggregation," he wrote to Huxley, "but after maturely considering all that he has said, I never before in my life felt so convinced of the *general* truth of the Origin. The pendulum is now swinging against our side, but I feel positive it will soon swing the other way; and no mortal man will do half as much as you in giving it a start in the right direction, as you did at the first commencement."

By this time Huxley, who argued that Mivart was acting "like an Old Bailey lawyer," had already given his first push to the pendulum, replying in the *Contemporary Review* with "Mr. Darwin's Critics" to a forty-page essay in which Mivart had savagely attacked *The Descent of Man* in the *Quarterly Review*. But Mivart was determined and able, and sustained the attack on more than one front. "The Zoological Society," he wrote in *Nature*, "can hardly fail to derive decided material advantage from the publication of Mr. Darwin's 'Descent of Man.' It has been said that already there is a perceptible increase in the visitors to the monkey-house." And he ended his letter uncompromisingly: "Science convinces me that a monkey and a mushroom differ less from each other than do a monkey and a man."

In the United States, the debate went on quite as fiercely, and after Chauncey Wright had written a eulogistic review of *The Descent of Man* in the *North American Review*, Darwin sent a copy to Wallace. "Mivart's book is producing a great effect against Natural Selection, and more especially against me," he said in his covering letter. "Therefore, if you think the article even somewhat good, I will write and get permission to publish it as a shilling pamphlet, together with the MS addition (enclosed), for which there was not room at the end of the review. I do not suppose I should lose more than £20 or £30." Eventually the review, plus further additions, was successfully published as a pamphlet by John Murray.

The virulence of the attacks and counterattacks could not conceal the fact that Mivart had made a number of points that Darwin could not safely ignore. He was busy making additions and corrections to the sixth edition of *The Origin* and used the opportunity to reply. Mivart, he admitted, had illustrated his objections to the theory "with admirable art and force." But he had given no evidence for the other—evolutionary—side. Darwin now filled this gap. It took him nearly thirty pages, and ended by criticizing Mivart's support for saltations, or jumps. Anyone following this belief, he concluded, "will be forced to admit that these great and sudden transformations have left no trace of their action on the embryo. To admit all this is, as it seems to me, to enter into the realms of miracle, and to leave those of Science."

While argument over *The Descent of Man* was in progress, Darwin had been compounding his alleged crime with *The Expression of the Emotions in Man and Animals*. This was a subject on which he had begun taking notes in 1837 and which had further intrigued him after the birth in 1839 of his first son, William, whom he had used as a subject for observation. The reason for his decision to work up some three decades of notes into a book is obvious at more than one point in it. Thus in his introduction he says: "With mankind some expressions, such as the bristling of the hair under the influence of extreme terror, or the uncovering of the teeth under that of furious rage, can hardly be understood, except on the belief that man once existed in a much lower and animal-like condition," and in a final summing-up he said:

> We may confidently believe that laughter, as a sign of pleasure or enjoyment, was practised by our progenitors long before they deserved to be called human; for very many kinds of monkeys, when pleased, utter a reiterated sound, clearly analogous to our laughter, often accompanied by vibratory movements of their jaws or lips, with the corners of the mouth drawn backwards and upwards, by the wrinkling of the cheeks, and even by the brightening of the eyes.
>
> We may likewise infer that fear was expressed from an extremely remote period, in almost the same manner as it is now by man; namely, by trembling, the erection of the hair, cold perspiration, pallor, widely opened eyes, the relaxation of most of the muscles, and by the whole body cowering downwards or held motionless.

As with his botanical books, Darwin was once again using his concern with all organic life to hammer home the lesson of *The Origin*. His detractors often found, as they did here, that having answered the evidence of one book, they were faced with another adding material on yet a fresh aspect of the subject.

He began *Expression of the Emotions* on January 17, 1871, only two days after he passed the final proofs of *The Descent of Man*, using not only the notes he had taken over the years but the replies to questionnaires he had sent to missionaries, physiologists and physicians. Typical was the long list of questions he sent to Dr.

(later Sir) Ferdinand Jacob Heinrich von Müller, government botanist of Victoria, Australia, with the request: "Perhaps you know
some missionary or protector of the aborigines, or some acute
Colonial, in the far interior who wd. take a little trouble to oblige
you. In this case will you have the kindness to forward the enclosed
Queries, & beg your correspondent to make a few observations for
me, as any opportunity may occur, on the expression of the aborigines under the several emotions specified."

His own observations included those of infants, who in later life
would lose the simple sources of their expressions, and of the
insane, who often exhibited strong passions that they did not, or
could not, control. He also used illustrations made by Guillaume
Benjamin Amand Duchenne, who had stimulated into activity the
muscles in the face of an old man, had the expressions photo-
graphed, and then had the prints commented upon by laymen.
Darwin studied paintings and sculptures—but found them of little
use. He studied the reports on primitive people and also "the
expression of the several passions in some of the commoner animals."

All this was evidence of Darwin's customary careful accumulation of facts. But *Expression of the Emotions* also gives some revealing
glimpses of his personal life. "When [his first-born] was about four
months old," he says, "I made in his presence many odd noises and
strange grimaces, and tried to look savage; but the noises, if not
too loud, as well as the grimaces, were all taken as good jokes; and
I attributed this at the time to their being preceded or accompanied by smiles. When five months old, he seemed to understand
a compassionate expression and tone of voice. When a few days
over six months old, his nurse pretended to cry, and I saw that his
face instantly assumed a melancholy expression, with the corners
of the mouth strongly depressed; now this child could rarely have
seen any other child crying, and never a grown-up person crying,
and I should doubt whether at so early an age he could have
reasoned on the subject. Therefore it seems to me that an innate
feeling must have told him that the pretended crying of his nurse
expressed grief; and this through the instinct of sympathy excited
grief in him."

There was also Bob, one of his large dogs who, he wrote,

like every other dog, was much pleased to go out walking. He showed
his pleasure by trotting gravely before me with high steps, head much

raised, moderately erected ears, and tail carried aloft but not stiffly. Not far from my house a path branches off to the right, leading to the hot-house, which I used often to visit for a few moments, to look at my experimental plants. This was always a great disappointment to the dog, as he did not know whether I should continue my walk; and the instantaneous and complete change of expression which came over him, as soon as my body swerved in the least towards the path (and I sometimes tried this as an experiment) was laughable. His look of dejection was known to every member of the family, and was called his *hot-house face.* This consisted in the head drooping much, the whole body sinking a little and remaining motionless; the ears and tail falling suddenly down, but the tail was by no means wagged. With the falling of the ears and of his great chaps, the eyes became much changed in appearance, and I fancied that they looked less bright. His aspect was that of piteous, hopeless dejection; and it was, as I have said, laughable, as the cause was so slight.

For the first time Darwin used photographs to emphasize his points, an innovation that enabled the *Edinburgh Review* to state that "Mr. Darwin has added another volume of amusing stories and grotesque illustrations to the remarkable series of works already devoted to the exposition and defence of the evolutionary hypothesis," a statement Darwin described as "magnificently contemptuous towards myself and many others." However, what came through to Wallace, writing on the book in the *Quarterly Journal of Science*, was Darwin's "insatiable longing to discover the causes of the varied and complex phenomena presented by living things."

Another illustration of that insatiable longing, which was to help give Darwin's work such a broad scientific base, appeared the following year, since he devoted most of 1874 to a book on insectivorous plants. As far back as 1860, he had noticed, when staying with relatives at Hartfield in Sussex, that numbers of insects had been trapped by the leaves of *Drosera*, two species of which grew there in quantity. "I carried home some plants, & on giving them insects," he wrote in his autobiography, "saw the movements of the tentacles, & this made me think it probable that the insects were caught for some special purpose. Fortunately a crucial test occurred to me, that of placing a large number of leaves in various nitrogenous & non-nitrogenous fluids of equal density; & as soon as I found that the former alone excited energetic movements, it was obvious that here was a fine new field for investigation."

Darwin experimented for years with a variety of insectivorous plants, including the famous Venus's-flytrap, the most marvelous plant in the world, as he called it. When, in 1874, he began to write up his notes, he had sufficient material to show that the plants concerned grew in places where there was insufficient nitrogen in the ground for their sustenance. The lack was counteracted by the development of features that enabled them to trap and digest insects whose bodies contained the necessary chemical. *Insectivorous Plants*, like *The Effects of Cross- and Self-Fertilisation in the Vegetable Kingdom* and *The Different Forms of Flowers on Plants of the Same Species*, which followed in 1876 and 1877 respectively, demonstrated how natural selection worked as ubiquitously in the plant as in the animal world.

In the summer of 1876, Darwin was diverted from this preoccupation with evolutionary matters by the invitation of a German editor who asked him for an account of how his mind had developed, together with a brief autobiography. The result was a 40,000-word manuscript, mostly written, an hour at a time, during afternoons between May and August. But although he wrote in response to a suggestion, Darwin had, at the time, little intention of presenting the manuscript for publication. Minor additions were made during the following five years. In the manuscript, Darwin gave a sober outline of his life, exercising his usual caution and taking in good part the attacks that had been made upon him since publication of *The Origin*. "I know that it would have interested me greatly to have read even so short & dull a sketch of the mind of my grandfather written by himself, & what he thought & did & how he worked," he wrote. "I have attempted to write the following account of myself, as if I were a dead man in another world looking back at my own life. Nor have I found this difficult, for life is nearly over with me. I have taken no pains about my style of writing." He also said that he thought that "the attempt would amuse me, & might possibly interest my children or their children."

The autobiography led to considerable argument in the Darwin family when *The Life and Letters of Charles Darwin*, which was to include it, was being edited by his son Francis in the mid-1880s. "Etty [Henrietta] went so far as to *speak* of legal proceedings to stop its publication," Darwin's son Leonard wrote in 1942. "These could only have been against Frank [Francis]. She felt that on religious questions it was crude and but half thought-out, and that in these circumstances it was not only unfair to his memory to publish it, but that he would have objected strongly. I should not be surprised if my Mother, unknown to us all, put in the final word against it [publication of the suppressed passages] to Frank."

Though numbering more than fifty, few of the suppressions were of basic importance. Where Darwin dotted the *i*'s and crossed the *t*'s when he wrote of Christianity, the passages were toned down, although not usually removed. Most excisions concerned only a sentence or two, the only major deletion being some six hundred words that began by maintaining that a belief in a personal God was not essential to leading a good life, and then discussed what religious doubts a man should admit to his wife. Omitted, no doubt on what were in those days considered grounds of good taste, was Darwin's statement that during one controversy he had been consoled by Huxley, who reminded him of Goethe's remark "that every Whale has its Louse." There was a watering down of opinions that Darwin had expressed on other public figures, but the main thrust of the Darwin family's efforts was to reduce his disillusion with religion.

It is evident that Emma felt strongly about this, since she asked Francis to delete from the autobiography Darwin's admonition: "Nor must we overlook the probability of the constant inculcation of a belief in God on the minds of children producing so strong & perhaps an inherited effect on their brains not as yet fully developed, that it would be as difficult for them to throw off their belief in God, as for a monkey to throw off its instinctive fear & hatred of a snake." Francis was told by his mother: "I should wish if possible to avoid the giving pain to your father's religious friends who are deeply attached to him, and I picture to myself the way that sentence would strike them, even those so liberal as Ellen Tollet and Laura [Forster], much more Admiral Sulivan, Aunt Caroline, &c., and even the old servants." When Emma Darwin's letters were privately printed in 1904, eight years after her death, this letter was included. But it was omitted from the public edition published in 1915.

The autobiography occupied only a small amount of Darwin's energies, and in the summer of 1877 he began another line of inquiry. It followed on directly from his book *Climbing Plants* and, like the rest of his work, was designed to supply yet more information on natural selection. ". . . in accordance with the principles of evolution," he was to write, "it was impossible to account for climbing plants having been developed in so many widely different groups, unless all kinds of plants possess some slight power of movement of an analogous kind." He therefore began a long series of experiments, using a wide range of plants in which he traced in detail the movements of the plants' growing tips and of their roots.

Darwin was now sixty-eight and was glad of help from his son Francis in the delicate work that was entailed. "He could dissect well under the simple microscope," Francis has written, "but I think it was by dint of his great patience and carefulness. It was characteristic of him that he thought many little bits of skilful dissection something almost superhuman. He used to speak with admiration of the skill with which he saw Newport [George Newport, the entomologist] dissect a humble bee, getting out the nervous system with a few cuts of a pair of fine scissors." Although dissection was not now essential, the work when carried out demanded care, as Darwin has shown. "A glass filament, not thicker than a horsehair, and from a quarter to three-quarters of an inch in length, was affixed to the part to be observed by means of shellac dissolved in alcohol," he subsequently wrote. "The solution was allowed to evaporate, until it became so thick that it set hard in two or three seconds, and it never injured the tissues, even the tips of tender radicles, to which it was applied. To the end of the glass filament an excessively minute bead of black sealing-wax was cemented, below or behind which a bit of card with a black dot was fixed to a stick driven into the ground. The weight of the filament was so slight that even small leaves were not perceptibly pressed down." Similar ingenious methods were devised for discovering how plant roots found their way around, up, over or across obstacles. Cabbages were the first plants observed. They were followed by dozens of others, from strawberries to runner beans and nasturtiums.

Darwin still showed his habitual dislike of wasting time when at work. "I particularly remember noticing this," Francis has written, "when he was making an experiment on the roots of beans, which required some care in manipulation; fastening the little bits of card upon the roots was done carefully and necessarily slowly, but the intermediate movements were all quick; taking a fresh bean, seeing that the root was healthy, impaling it on a pin, fixing it on a cork, and seeing that it was vertical &c.; all these processes were performed with a kind of restrained eagerness. He always gave one the impression of working with pleasure, and not with any drag."

The outcome of this series of experiments, as Darwin wrote to Alphonse de Candolle, was that he had "succeeded in showing that all the more important great classes of movements are due to the modification of a kind of movement common to all parts of all plants from their earliest youth." The movement, whereby the apex of a growing stem described a counterclockwise and more or less circular spiral path as it grows, Darwin christened circumnutation. While it was primarily caused by the action of light, it was in practice an example of natural selection. Much the same was true of the way in which plants "slept" at night, their movements being not only a reaction to the cold but ensuring them the maximum protection from harmful radiation.

The work was delicate and demanding, and although Darwin had written in its early days to William Turner Thiselton-Dyer of Kew that he was "all on fire at the work," he was becoming despondent by the spring of 1879. "I am overwhelmed with my notes," he said, "and almost too old to undertake the job which I have in hand—i.e. movements of all kinds. Yet it is worse to be idle."

He perked up during the summer, and his daughter Henrietta recalled his enjoyment of a holiday at Coniston in the English Lake District. "My father enjoyed the journey with the freshness of a boy," she has written, "the picnic luncheon, the passing country seen from the train, especially Morecambe Bay, and even missing our connection at Foxfield and being hours late, did not daunt his cheerfulness. . . . One expedition was made to Grasmere. I shall never forget my father's enthusiastic delight, jumping up from his seat in the carriage to see better at every striking moment. . . . Another interest and pleasure in this stay was their making friends with Ruskin. I remember very well his first call on them and his courteous manner; his courtesy even including giving my father the title of 'Sir Charles.' My father perceived by Ruskin's distressed look when he spoke of the new and baleful kind of cloud which had appeared in the heavens that his brain was becoming clouded."

Back at Down House, Darwin was pleased by the publication of *The Power of Movement in Plants*, soon to be recognized as a landmark in botanical research. One reason was that in the end he had been able to demonstrate that movements in response to external stimuli had been developed during the course of evolution and had thus produced an organism better able to survive in the struggle for existence.

By now, Darwin's earlier sins were being remembered less

harshly and even *The Times* devoted to the book an editorial that began, "Of all our living men of science none have laboured longer and to more splendid purpose than Mr. Darwin." The Germans, almost alone, appeared critical. "Many of [them] are very contemptuous about making out the use of organs," Darwin confided to Thiselton-Dyer, "but they may sneer the souls out of their bodies, and I for one shall think it the most interesting part of Natural History."

However, it was German praise for Darwin that now, quite fortuitously, led to a public controversy that deeply worried him, absorbed much energy and time—his friends' and family's as well as his own—and that reveals the strength of his moral rectitude, which formed such a defensive armor in Victorian times.

In February 1879 the German evolutionary journal *Kosmos* published a special issue in honor of Darwin's seventieth birthday. It contained a lengthy essay by a Dr. Ernst Krause on Darwin's grandfather Erasmus, and Darwin wrote to Krause asking for permission to publish an English translation. The reason for this was that Darwin himself was working on a biography of Erasmus, "to contradict flatly some calumnies" in a recent book. Krause agreed, and began to expand his essay before it was translated. While this expansion was continuing, he received from Darwin a copy of Samuel Butler's *Evolution Old and New, or the Theories of Buffon, Dr. Erasmus Darwin and Lamarck Compared with That of Mr. C. Darwin.*

Now, there was a link between the Butler and Darwin families. Butler's grandfather had been headmaster of Shrewsbury School, and Darwin was a pupil there under him with Samuel Butler's father, Thomas. Furthermore, Darwin and the father were fellow undergraduates at Cambridge. Farming in New Zealand in 1859, Samuel Butler had read *The Origin* with delight, as he told Darwin in 1865, since it entered "into so many deeply interesting questions, or rather it suggests so many that it thoroughly fascinated me."

Six years later, when it was rumored that a chapter in Butler's *Erewhon* was an attack on *The Origin*, he was quick to reassure Darwin. "I . . . thought it unnecessary to give any disclaimer of an intention of being disrespectful to the Origin of Species, a book for which I can never be sufficiently grateful, though I am well aware how utterly incapable I am of forming any opinion on a scientific subject which is worth a moment's consideration," he wrote. "However, you have a position which nothing can shake and I know very well that any appearance of ridicule would do your theories no harm whatsoever."

But Butler's views changed during the next decade. He believed that Darwin was trying to banish mind from the universe, and his *Evolution Old and New* was the second of a series of books attacking Darwin's theory of evolution by natural selection. Krause not only read the copy of Butler's book that Darwin sent him but incorporated in his revised essay on Erasmus a number of critical references to it. The chief of these stated: "Erasmus Darwin's system was in itself a most significant first step in the path of knowledge which his grandson has opened up for us, but to wish to revive it at the present day, as has actually been seriously attempted, shows a weakness of thought and a mental anachronism which no one can envy."

Darwin made no reference to any expansions of the *Kosmos* article when he included it in his preliminary note to Krause's book on Erasmus, published by John Murray in November 1879. Early in January he received a letter from Butler, the nub of whose complaint was contained in the words, "your readers will naturally suppose that all they read in the translation [of Krause's essay] appeared in February last, and therefore before 'Evolution Old and New' was written, and therefore independently of, and necessarily without reference to that book."

Darwin replied as best he could, saying that it never occurred to him to state that the article had been modified but that he now regretted he had not done so. Butler was dissatisfied with the answer; so dissatisfied, in fact, that he now wrote a long letter to the *Athenaeum* implying that Darwin had deceived his readers, a letter that Francis Darwin later said "amounted to a charge of falsehood against my father." The letter encouraged Darwin to consult his papers. Among them he found, to his worry, that he had, in fact, sent a note to the printers saying that Dr. Krause had added largely to his original essay, but that the note had eventually been omitted. Should he write to the *Athenaeum* with an explanation? Or would this further complicate an already complicated situation?

Darwin prepared to draft letters to the *Athenaeum*, and these were discussed by members of his family, some of whom felt that no reply at all should be made to Butler. Eventually advice was sought from T. H. Huxley, who proposed that Darwin should let the matter drop for the time being and merely, in the event of a new edition, add a brief note explaining that Krause had expanded his original essay. "Has Mivart bitten him and given him Darwinophobia?" Huxley asked of Butler. "It is a horrid disease & I wd. kill everyone I found running loose with it without mercy." Darwin decided to make no reply, but when Butler raised the matter again in *Unconscious Memory*, published in 1880, he consulted Leslie Stephen. "My opinion about the matter is perfectly distinct and unhesitating," Stephen replied. "I think that you should take no further notice of Mr. Butler whatever."

Darwin had, from the first, been in favor of defending himself. Those members of his family who helped hold him back may, with less ingenuousness and more reality, have felt that Butler had a case. Indeed, Francis Darwin, writing in 1904, two years after Butler's death, said, "after all I now think he had some cause of complaint though he entirely lost his head and behaved abominably."

Darwin's short life of his grandfather was his last book. He disliked the controversy that the argument with Butler had aroused, and after it there set in a black mood made darker by the fact that his eldest daughter, Henrietta Emma, was ailing. "But the worst is that my health is failing much," he wrote to Asa Gray. There is a touching note preserved among his papers, written a year earlier and signed by his seven children. "Dear Father," it said, "We hope that you will let us give you the accompanying fur coat. We know that you will not often wear it and that you will think it too magnificent, but we cannot bear to think that when you *do* travel in winter you should suffer from cold; and so we hope you will forgive this little indulgence of the feelings of your affectionate children." The coat was left, with the letter, on his study table at three one afternoon so that he would find it when he set off for his walk at four. The present, Emma wrote to Leonard Darwin, was "a great success, and though F[rancis] began by thinking it would never be cold enough for him to wear it, he has begun by wearing it so constantly, that he is afraid it will soon be worn out."

By now he was not so much ill as growing increasingly tired. "I literally cannot listen to a novel for 1/2 hour without fatigue," he told Asa Gray. "My good dear wife declares I must go with our whole family (if my girl can be moved) for 2 months to Water Cure; and I fear I must, but it will be quits to all my experiments."

As he had revealed in his autobiography, he was now unable to read a line of poetry and "found [Shakespeare] so intolerably dull that it nauseated me." This distressing state of mind, which was to be discussed when the centenary of his birth was celebrated in 1909, was explained after his death by Frances Julia Wedgwood, a relation of Emma Darwin. "He twice referred to his turning back to books he had read with great interest in youth and finding the interest had gone," she wrote to Francis. "One was Wordsworth's poems, wh. as you know are full of his marks as a young man, & yet he sd. that at the time he spoke (about 1874 or 5) he could not possibly read them, & that he was always finding obscurity where he never remembered any difficulty in the past. I sd. 'I think you must imagine some different kind of understanding from what poetry admits of. Nobody understands poetry in the sense that they can put the meaning of *those* words into *other* words.' He sd. 'Ah, yes, I suppose it is just that, & nobody understands Science unless they can. The habit of looking for one kind of meaning I suppose deadens the perception of another.' " An old friend, Laura Forster, who had herself been seriously ill, has recalled a similar attitude when she was staying at Down House about this time. "I remember his coming into the tea-drawing-room one afternoon and saying: 'The clocks go so dreadfully slowly, I have come in here to see if this one gets over the hours any quicker than the study one does.' Then, as he lay down on the sofa he said regretfully, 'Ah, my dear Laura, how terribly slowly the time must have gone for you all these months.' "

His general pessimism survived even a trip in the summer of 1881 to the Lakes, whence he wrote to Hooker: "I am rather despondent about myself & my troubles are of an exactly opposite nature to yours, for idleness is downright misery to me, as I find here, as I cannot forget my discomfort for an hour. I have not the heart or strength at my age to begin any investigation lasting years, which is the only thing which I enjoy, & I have no little jobs which I can do." And a few weeks later, in an even more despairing letter to Wallace: "What I shall do with my few remaining years of life I can hardly tell. I have everything to make me happy and contented, but life has become very wearisome to me." He had even become depressed about the result of his life's work, since Wallace later wrote: "In one of my latest conversations with Darwin he expressed himself very gloomily on the future of humanity, on the ground that in our modern civilization natural selection had no play, and the fittest did not survive."

Nevertheless, he was still the man who wanted to do and know more, and Francis has recalled how in what was to be the last year of his life he learned to cut sections of roots and leaves. "His hand was not steady enough to hold the object to be cut," he has written, "and he employed a common microtome, in which the pith for holding the object was clamped, and the razor slid on a glass surface. He used to laugh at himself, and at his own skill in section-cutting, at which he would say he was 'speechless with admiration.' "

His mind, also, was still as wide-awake as ever. In the autumn of 1881, Sir Archibald Geikie reported in *Nature* that his geological survey had found a remarkable group of fossils in the lower Carboniferous rocks of Eskdale in southern Scotland. These included specimens of new species of fishes and many well-preserved specimens of an ancient type of scorpion. "As so many scorpions were found," Darwin wrote to Geikie, "one might hope for other terrestrial animals and plants, if some new places were searched by blasting away the overlying rocks. But I daresay you would not think yourself justified in employing the officers of the Survey in such work. This leads me to make an offer, — and I hope and trust that you will not think that I am taking a liberty in doing so, — namely to subscribe £100 or £200 if you can find anyone whom you could trust to send, and if you think it worth while to make further search for the chance of fresh and greater palaeontological treasures being discovered." Geikie assured him that the work would probably be done anyway.

Darwin was well able to offer financial help even though all his books had brought in only a total of about £10,000 during his lifetime. After his elder brother, Erasmus, had died in the summer of 1881, Charles's banker son, William, had written: "I am certain your fortune and 1/2 Uncle Eras' together with No. 6 [Queen Anne Street, Erasmus Darwin's London home] and land will bring you up to at *least* £280,000 *without* mother's. . . . Did you ever expect to be worth over a 1/4 of a million?"

During the first weeks of 1882, Darwin had more than one painful heart attack. In March, walking alone on the grounds of his home, he had a seizure, and it was only with difficulty that he was able to get back to the house. At first he appeared to be recovering, but early on the night of April 18 he had a severe attack, fainted, and on being brought back to consciousness said: "I am not the least afraid to die."

He passed away the following afternoon. The immediate sequel reflected the position that he had occupied. Emma and his sons had planned that he should be buried in the cemetery at Downe, but on April 21, twenty members of Parliament, including Sir John Lubbock, later Lord Avebury, and Henry Campbell Bannerman, the future prime minister, wrote to the dean of Westminster, Dr. George Granville Bradley. "We hope you will not think we are taking a liberty," they said, "if we venture to suggest that it would be acceptable to a very large number of our fellow-countrymen of all classes and opinions that our illustrious countryman, Mr. Darwin, should be buried in Westminster Abbey." His views had no doubt helped to keep from him the distinction of knighthood, but by 1882 his intellectual position was unchallengeable even though his opinions were still debatable. Many no doubt felt as did his friend Leslie Stephen, writing to James Sully: "To me it would seem more congenial to bury the dear old man in that quiet little churchyard close to the house in which he lived and worked so long. Nor can I feel comfortable at the thought of a possible theological brabble over his grave." But Dean Bradley, abroad at the time, telegraphed his agreement to the members of Parliament; and any brabble was avoided. Lubbock emphasized to Francis Darwin that "from a national point of view, it is clearly right that he should be buried in the Abbey." But the family still seem to have favored a local funeral and there were last-minute changes epitomized by the Downe joiner, John Lewis. "I made his coffin just the way he wanted it," Lewis later said, "all rough, just as it left the bench, no polish, no nothin'. But they agreed to send him to Westminster . . . my coffin wasn't wanted and they sent it back. This other one you could see to shave in."

Darwin was buried on April 26, a few feet from the grave of Isaac Newton. Pallbearers included not only Huxley and Wallace, but also James Russell Lowell, the U.S. ambassador; Hooker; William Spottiswoode, the president of the Royal Society; and his old antagonist the Duke of Argyll. They included, as his opponents might ruefully have put it, the past, the present, and a future president of the Royal Society, two dukes (of Devonshire and of Argyll) and an earl (the Earl of Derby). The choir, moreover, sang an anthem especially composed for the occasion by the Abbey organist, the words being taken from the third chapter of the Book of Proverbs and starting: "Happy is the man who finds wisdom and getteth understanding."

Burial in the Abbey was less incongruous than many may have

felt. Although Darwin thought that the description "agnostic"—a person who believes that nothing can be known about the existence of God or of anything except material things—fitted him better than any other, he had in him nothing of the anti-Christian bigot. The views that he held for the greater part of his adult life were well expressed when he wrote in 1873 to a correspondent at the University of Utrecht. "I may say," went his letter, "that the impossibility of conceiving that this grand and wondrous universe, with our conscious selves, arose through chance, seems to me the chief argument for the existence of God; but whether this is an argument of real value, I have never been able to decide. I am aware that if we admit a first cause, the mind still craves to know whence it came from and how it arose. Nor can I overlook the difficulty from the immense amount of suffering through the world. I am, also, induced to defer to a certain extent to the judgment of the many able men who have fully believed in God; but here again I see how poor an argument this is. The safest conclusion seems to be that the whole subject is beyond the scope of man's intellect; but man can do his duty."

The expected eulogies followed the Abbey funeral, many from groups who thirty years earlier had metaphorically cried for Darwin's scalp. More than unwillingness to speak ill of the dead was involved. Carefully considering what they knew personally of the man, many people remembered what Huxley was to call Darwin's "intense and almost passionate honesty by which all his thoughts and actions were irradiated, as by a central fire."

Even in France, which had continued comparatively allergic to Darwin, the radical *Justice* handed out high praise, although this was balanced by the *Univers*, which ended two columns of criticism by stating: "When hypotheses tend to nothing less than the destruction of faith, the shutting out of God from the heart of man, and the diffusion of the filthy leprosy of Materialism, the *savant* who invents and propagates them is either a criminal or a fool. That's what we have to say about monkey-Darwin."

For some, it seemed impossible that a man of Darwin's passionate honesty would wish to die a non-Christian. A deathbed conversion was obviously called for, and if one did not exist, it had to be manufactured. This was done, and with such effect that half a century later the myth was still believed. The Darwin legend, unlike that of the deathbed conversion of Richard Burton, the Arabian explorer, devised by his wife, was created outside the family.

The *deus ex machina* in the case was a Lady Hope, the widow of Admiral of the Fleet Sir James Hope and an evangelist who appears to have preached in Downe during the last years of Darwin's life. Shortly after his death, Lady Hope addressed a gathering of young men and women at the educational establishment founded by the evangelist Dwight Lyman Moody at Northfield, Massachusetts. She had, she maintained, visited Darwin on his deathbed. He had been reading the Epistle to the Hebrews, had asked for the local Sunday school to sing in a summerhouse on the grounds, and had confessed: "How I wish I had not expressed my theory of evolution as I have done." He went on, she said, to say that he would like her to gather a congregation, since he "would like to speak to them of Christ Jesus and His salvation, being in a state where he was eagerly savouring the heavenly anticipation of bliss."

With Moody's encouragement, Lady Hope's story was printed in the Boston *Watchman Examiner.* The story spread, and the claims were republished as late as October 1955 in the *Reformation Review* and in the *Monthly Record of the Free Church of Scotland* in February 1957. These attempts to fudge Darwin's story had already been exposed for what they were, first by his daughter Henrietta after they had been revived in 1922. "I was present at his deathbed," she wrote in the *Christian* for February 23, 1922. "Lady Hope was not present during his last illness, or any illness. I believe he never even saw her, but in any case she had no influence over him in any department of thought or belief. He never recanted any of his scientific views, either then or earlier. We think the story of his conversion was fabricated in U.S.A. . . . The whole story has no foundation whatever." The issue of the *Christian* that printed the denial agreed with her, and added: "Many who followed the investigations of Charles Darwin, and observed his devotion to scientific research, would have been glad to learn that some higher and deeper devotion claimed his soul. If there is no evidence that such was the case, it is well that the facts should be known."

But in the 1880s Darwin had not only reached Westminster Abbey; he had gained such international acceptance that no chance was lost of casting doubt on what he believed.

DECLINE AND RECOVERY

9

Diffusion and Dissent

A RESTING place in the Abbey confirmed Darwin's acceptance as a national figure, and he would no doubt have been mildly amused that this honor had eventually been granted despite the earlier "ecclesiastical bombinations" of the Church. At his death, more than one item in his grand scheme was still under attack, and the next four decades were to witness increased criticism that only evaporated in the 1920s as the latest scientific findings were shown to supplement his basic beliefs rather than contradict them. This phase, which saw the birth and growth of neo-Darwinism, was itself to be followed by an upsurge of criticism not of Darwin's basic beliefs but of the way in which they might be interpreted. These post-Darwinian developments were different in one way from those that had so occupied his life. Darwin himself had relied almost exclusively for his theories on his own observations and those of practicing naturalists and breeders from whom he had collected information for almost a quarter of a century. Now the requirements were changed.

During the century that followed his death, his comparatively simple approaches were, necessarily, complicated by the work of the cellular chemists, of the geneticists who explored the rediscoveries of Gregor Mendel, of the statisticians and biometricians who demanded a new approach to biological mysteries, and of the molecular biologists who in recent decades have pioneered a fresh attack on the problems with which Darwin was, inevitably within the context of his own scientific environment, completely unable to cope.

This fragmentation of the evolutionary attack makes the story of Darwinian survival after 1882 one that, instead of concentrating on Darwin's own efforts, necessarily spreads across a variety of disciplines, each of which had a limited, and sometimes controversial, impact on the theory with which he had shaken the world. To at least some extent, the same had happened with Darwin's predecessors. But even by 1882 there was a difference between Darwin and the rest.

Whereas even the most plausible of the predecessors had seen their claims either ignored or ridiculed, then withering away, his had taken root. It was not entirely because "the moment was ripe" or because of the impressive chapter and verse with which he had supported his views in successive editions of *The Origin*. The character of Darwin himself, the way he behaved, also helped to keep them alive.

Superficially, one clue to that character was provided when Darwin was asked by his cousin Francis Galton, collecting material for *English Men of Science*, whether he had any special talents. "None, except for business as evinced by keeping accounts, replies to correspondence, and investing money very well," he had replied. "Very methodical in all my habits." Both facts were demonstrated by his finances—but they also applied to his works. During the quarter-century that preceded publication of *The Origin*, anything less than the most methodical handling of his material would have ended in chaos.

This humdrum explanation is illuminated best not by Darwin himself but by Sir Arthur Keith. Darwin, he has written, "gave himself to the study of the anatomy and behaviour of mankind with the same assiduity as he gave to the aberrant Barnacles." Yet all of it affected more the substance of Darwin's work than its toleration by many who disagreed with him and their eventual if reluctant admission that there might, after all, be something in what he said. More important in enabling him to weather the early storms was the kindly, conventional nature of the man. Darwin hobnobbing with the local vicar, Darwin the Kent magistrate and careful landowner, known to be worried by the mental anxiety his investigations might cause to others—this was not a man for excoriation but one who should be given the benefit of the doubt however unusual his ideas might be. The champion of evolution was not easily disliked, and in the days before the role had been created, he was his own best public relations man.

On the day of his funeral, *The Times* strikingly admitted the change in the climate of opinion that had taken place since *The Descent of Man* had been published more than a decade previously. "The career of Charles Darwin eludes the grasp of personal curiosity as much as of personal enmity," it said. "He thought, and his thoughts have passed into the substance of facts of the universe." On the Continent, the *Allgemeine Zeitung* reflected the opinion of supporters and opponents alike, who believed, for better or for worse, that "our century is Darwin's century."

Its remaining two decades were to be marked by two somewhat contradictory developments. One was the persistent diffusion of *The Origin*'s ideas into politics, literature and sociology, where their effect might be praised or deplored but could no longer be denied. The second was a more concentrated search for the mechanics of inheritance, whose discovery might reinforce or deflate the importance of natural selection, and at the same time the birth and growth of biometry, the application of mathematics and statistics to biology in general and to inheritance in particular. This scientific work did nothing to undermine belief in evolution, but it did open the way for greater argument over the value of natural selection and over the comparative importance in evolution of small variations and of the "jumps" whose significance Darwin had refused to accept.

The political implications of *The Origin* had been quickly taken up, and as early as May 1860 Darwin had told Lyell: "I have noted in a Manchester newspaper a rather good squib, showing that I have proved 'might is right' & therefore that Napoleon is right & every cheating tradesman is also right." Alphonse Daudet later expanded the idea in his play *La Lutte pour La Vie* to justify robbery and murder. Darwin could afford to take the Manchester squib not too seriously, little realizing the extent to which his biological theories would later be extrapolated into other fields. But Manchester, and even Daudet, were only first signs. During the years that followed Darwin's death, "survival of the fittest" became a catch phrase to explain events as different as the new management of Wall Street after the Panic of 1857—"The change was a fine exemplification of the survival of the fittest, and proved that there was a law of natural selection in financial affairs that superseded old conservatism and sealed its doom," Henry Clews stated in 1888; the Franco-Prussian war; and war in general, with Max Nordau claiming in the *North American Review*: "the greatest authority of all advocates of war is Darwin . . . since the theory of evolution has been promulgated, they can cover their natural barbarism with the name of Darwin and proclaim the sanguinary instincts of their inmost hearts as the last word of science"; and, less questionably, the rise of American industry's "robber barons" after the American Civil War.

All this, and the whole sociological monument that was built under the umbrella of "social Darwinism" sprang as much from Herbert Spencer as from Darwin. Spencer's *Social Statics* had in 1851 argued for the weeding out of the less fit; it was he who had first used the phrase "survival of the fittest"; and his later volumes spread the idea of evolution across the entire sociological field. The impact of the conservative Spencer was greater in the United States than in Britain, and Richard Hofstadter in his survey of social Darwinism in American thought has reported Spencer's influence on such progressives as Theodore Dreiser, Jack London, Clarence Darrow and Hamlin Garland. The extension of evolutionary tenets from one field to others is not surprising. It has been pointed out that the Newtonian synthesis led on to the Age of Reason, that Henry Adams based his philosophy on the thermodynamics of Willard Gibbs; and in more recent times the effect of Heisenberg's Uncertainty Principle has been felt far beyond the realm of physics. So the influence of Spencer and of Darwin was likely to spread. Nevertheless, the mere fact that it was "social Darwinism" and not "social Spencerism" that became the subject under discussion testifies to the far greater impact of *The Origin* than of anything which Spencer wrote.

Darwin would have been eager to disown many of the social statements later made in his name. Yet he did claim, in *The Descent of Man*: "We civilised men, on the other hand, do our utmost to check the process of elimination; we build asylums for the imbecile, the maimed and the sick; we institute poor-laws; and our medical men exert their utmost skill to save the life of every one to the last moment. There is reason to believe that vaccination has preserved thousands, who from a weak constitution would formerly have succumbed to small-pox. Thus the weak members of civilised societies propagate their kind. No one who has attended to the breeding of domestic animals will doubt that this must be highly injurious to the race of man." Writing to William Graham, Professor of Jurisprudence at Queen's College, Belfast, he commented: "I could show fight on natural selection having done and doing more for the progress of civilisation than you seem inclined to admit. Remember what risk the nations of Europe ran, not so many centuries ago of being overwhelmed by the Turks, and how ridiculous such an idea now is! The more civilised so-called Caucasian races have beaten the Turkish hollow in the struggle for existence. Looking to the world at no very distant date, what an endless number of the lower races will have been eliminated by the higher civilised races throughout the world." And he refused when asked in 1877 to give evidence regarding birth control in the Bradlaugh-Besant case, when Charles Bradlaugh and Annie Besant were prosecuted for obscenity after publishing Charles Knowlton's *The Fruits of Philosophy, or The Private Companion of Young Married People*. As he summed up the situation in *The Descent of Man*, "our natural rate of increase, though leading to many and obvious evils, must not be greatly diminished by any means. There should be open competition for all men; and the most able should not be prevented by laws or customs from succeeding best and rearing the largest number of offspring."

From this, and from much more that could be cited, two things seem apparent. The first is that Darwin was either unwilling or unable to think through into human terms the exploitation of the natural laws whose existence he believed to be self-evident. The second, which he stressed more fully elsewhere, was that "the fittest" were not necessarily the strongest or the most brutal but those who were most able to adapt to new circumstances.

In Britain, Walter Bagehot, editor of *The Economist* but better known for his study *The English Constitution*, was the first, other than Spencer, to suggest the targets in economics to which evolutionary theories were leading. As every "scientific conception tends to advance its boundaries and to be of use in solving problems not thought of when it was started," he wrote, "so here, what was put forward for mere animal history may, with a change of form, but an identical essence, be applied to human history." Whatever may be said against the principle of "natural selection" in other departments, he also said, "there is no doubt of its predominance in early human history. The strongest killed out the weakest, as they could. And I need not pause to prove that any form of polity is more efficient than none; that an aggregate of families owning even a slippery allegiance to a single head, would be sure to have the better of a set of families acknowledging no obedience to anyone, but scattering loose about the world and fighting where they stood."

Bagehot's convictions were appropriate during a period of de-

veloping industry and growing competition, where the law of the
jungle was operating relentlessly in Blake's "dark Satanic mills."
This was true not only in Victorian England, but in post–Civil War
America, the era of the Rockefellers, Carnegies, Vanderbilts and
Goulds, where, it has been pointed out, America's "rapid expansion, its exploitative methods, its desperate competition, and its
peremptory rejection of failure," made it "a vast human caricature
of the Darwinian struggle for existence and survival of the fittest."
And if it were felt that a justification was needed for such distortion
of Darwin's ideas, there was always Nietzsche on hand with his
theory of the Superman and the cult of power.

It has recently become fashionable to claim that the economics
of post–Civil War America was more important than the prop of
social Darwinism in creating the overrich, overvulgar top layer of
society that sprouted there during the last quarter of the nineteenth century. Yet Andrew Carnegie asserted that competition
was the "best for the race, because it insures the survival of the
fittest in every department." William Graham Sumner, the economist and philosopher of capitalism on the march, maintained that
millionaires "may fairly be regarded as the naturally selected
agents of society for certain work. They get high wages and live in
luxury, but the bargain is a good one for society. There is the
intensest competition for their place and occupation. This assures
us that all who are competent for this function will be employed
in it, so that the cost of it will be reduced to the lowest terms." And
among those who have studied and analyzed the rise of the robber
barons, few have failed to extrapolate their Darwinian views as an
excuse for climbing the ladder whatever the cost to others.

The implications could easily be carried on to the international
scene. Thus Josiah Strong, discussing the future of America in the
light of Darwin's theories, could write: "Then will the world enter
upon a new stage of its history—*the final competition of races, for which
the Anglo-Saxon race is being schooled* . . . this powerful race will move
down upon Mexico, down upon Central and South America, out
upon the islands of the sea, over upon Africa and beyond. And can
any one doubt that the result of this competition of races will be
the 'survival of the fittest'?"

It is uncertain whether the saddling of Darwin with a Devil-take-
the-hindmost philosophy, an advocacy barren of compassion,
Christian or otherwise, would have had much effect on the long-
term survival prospects of his scientific theories even if unques-

tioned. Yet it was not to remain unquestioned. Both inside and outside the scientific community, counterbalancing assertions were to be made. The first came as early as 1866 by N. D. Nozhin in Russia. Experimental work, he maintained, indicated that "identical organisms do not engage with one another in a struggle for existence, but, on the contrary, strive to combine together, so to speak, to unify their homogenous forces, their interests; and in this process we find . . . co-operation"—a forerunner of E. O. Wilson's argument. The case for cooperation was reiterated in January 1880 by Professor Karl Fedorovich Kessler, then dean of St. Petersburg University, who lectured to a Russian Congress of Naturalists in Moscow "On the Law of Mutual Aid." This, he stressed, "is as much a law of nature as mutual struggle; but for the *progressive* evolution of the species the former is far more important than the latter."

Professor Kessler died soon afterward, before his ideas could be taken further. But among his audience in Moscow there was Prince Kropotkin, the Peter Kropotkin best known for his anarchist writings but in fact a competent naturalist who had already made adventurous expeditions throughout Siberia and Manchuria. Kropotkin disliked the idea of the struggle for existence. "There is," he was to write, "no infamy in civilized society, or in the relations of the whites towards the so-called lower races, or of the 'strong' towards the 'weak', which would not have found its excuse in this formula." In his travels, he was later to write, two aspects of animal life impressed him most. One was the struggle for existence against the forces of nature. "And the other was, that even in those few spots where animal life teemed in abundance, I failed to find —although I was eagerly looking for it—that bitter struggle for the means of existence, *among animals belonging to the same species*, which was considered by most Darwinists (though not always by Darwin himself) as the dominant characteristic of struggle for life, and the main factor of evolution."

While Kropotkin was considering how well Kessler's views chimed in with his own experience, T. H. Huxley published "The Struggle for Existence in Human Society," an "atrocious article," as Kropotkin called it. "I decided to put in a readable form my objections to his way of understanding the struggle for life, among animals as well as among men, the materials for which I had accumulated during a couple of years," Kropotkin later wrote. He approached H. W. Bates, who had worked with Wallace on the

Amazon and was now secretary of the Royal Geographical Society. "That is true Darwinism," Bates responded. "It is a shame to think of what 'they' have made of Darwin's ideas. Write it, and when you have published it, I will write you a letter in that sense which you may publish." Kropotkin then approached James Knowlton, editor of *Nineteenth Century*, which in the early 1890s published a series of his articles on "Mutual Aid among Animals," ". . . among Savages," ". . . among Barbarians," ". . . in the Medieval City," and ". . . among Ourselves."

These articles were incorporated in Kropotkin's *Mutual Aid: A Factor of Evolution*, which at the turn of the century not only presented a fresh debating point for evolutionists but also struck at the heart of the discussion over social Darwinism that was then at its height.

Happily enough [he wrote] competition is not the rule either in the animal world or in mankind. It is limited among animals to exceptional periods, and natural selection finds better fields for its activity. Better conditions are created by the *elimination of competition* by means of mutual aid and mutual support. In the great struggle for life—for the greatest possible fulness and intensity of life with the least waste of energy—natural selection continually seeks out the ways precisely for avoiding competition as much as possible. The ants combine in nests and nations; they pile up their stores, they rear their cattle—and thus avoid competition, and natural selection picks out of the ants' family the species which know best how to avoid competition, with its unavoidably deleterious consequences. Most of our birds slowly move southwards as the winter comes, or gather in numberless societies and undertake long journeys—and thus avoid competition. Many rodents fall asleep when the time comes that competition should set in; while other rodents store food for the winter, and gather in large villages for obtaining the necessary protection when at work. The reindeer, when the lichens are dry in the interior of the continent, migrate towards the sea. Buffaloes cross an immense continent in order to find plenty of food. And the beavers, when they grow numerous on a river, divide into two parties, and go, the old ones down the river, and the young ones up the river—and avoid competition. And when animals can neither fall asleep, nor migrate, nor lay in stores, nor themselves grow their food like the ants, they do what the titmouse does, and what Wallace . . . has so charmingly described: they resort to new kinds of food—and thus, again, avoid competition.

From his conclusions, Kropotkin developed his theory of Solidarism and its plea for human cooperation at all levels. Wallace appears earlier to have held comparable opinions, stating to the Anthropological Society of London on March 1, 1864, that qualities such as the ability to act in concert, sympathy and intelligent foresight would be acted upon by natural selection. "Tribes in which such mental and moral qualities were predominant," he went on, "would therefore have an advantage in the struggle for existence. . . ." But Wallace, and later Kropotkin, were in a minority, and it was the brutalizing possibilities of social Darwinism that won more prominence during the decades that immediately followed Darwin's death.

Even before that death, Leslie Stephen had maintained in the *Fortnightly Review* that Darwin's theory divided the old sociological theory from a new one, while in 1911 the article on sociology in the eleventh edition of the *Encyclopaedia Britannica* was to devote half its space to Darwin.

Just as Darwin, who had a strong sense of "the obligations of enlightened humanity" toward peoples " 'lower in the scale' of human existence," would have been critical of the more extravagant suggestions for "social Darwinism" that followed his death, so was he skeptical of the idea that the development of socialism could be linked with his theory. "What a foolish idea seems to prevail in Germany on the connection between Socialism and Evolution through Natural Selection," he wrote. The belief had been propounded by Virchow, one of the founders of cellular pathology, but seems also to have been held by Huxley, who wrote eight years after Darwin's death, "Have you considered that State Socialism (for which I have little enough love) may be a product of Natural Selection?"

Nevertheless, Darwin was not all Victorian liberal, excoriating slavery, upholding Charles Kingsley in his campaign against child chimney sweeps and perpetually supporting the underdog. He could write in *The Descent of Man*, "In all civilised countries man accumulates property and bequeaths it to his children. So that the children in the same country do not by any means start fair in the race for success. But this is far from an unmixed evil; for without the accumulation of capital the arts could not progress; and it is chiefly through their power that the civilised races have extended and are now everywhere extending, their range, so as to take the place of the lower races." Here, also, he wrote that there was "apparently much truth in the belief that the wonderful progress of the United States, as well as the character of the people, are the results of natural selection."

As for the Communists, they appear to have believed that Darwin's ideas would lead on to a unified science including both man and the rest of nature. The offense taken by much of the Church to *The Origin* tended to make its ideas attractive in Communist eyes, and Darwin had to move deftly to escape the Marxist embrace. As early as December 12, 1859, Engels told Marx: "Darwin, whom I am just now reading, is splendid." The following year Marx noted of *The Origin* to Engels, that although it was "developed in the crude English style, this is the book which contains the basis in natural history for our view," and in 1861 went further in a letter to Lassalle, saying: "Darwin's book is very important and serves me as a basis in natural selection for the class struggle in history. . . . Despite all deficiencies, not only is it a death blow dealt here for the first time to 'Teleology' in the natural sciences but their rational meaning is empirically explained."

It has been claimed that Darwin wrote to Marx on two occasions. He is stated to have thanked Marx in 1873 for sending a copy of his "great work on Capital"; but it now seems possible that this letter was forged by Edward Aveling, the common-law husband of Marx's daughter Eleanor. And a second letter, written in 1880, saying that Darwin would prefer a "Part or Volume" not to be dedicated to him is now thought to have been written not to Marx but to Aveling, and to refer to *The Student's Darwin*, which Aveling was editing. Certainly a letter now displayed in the Marx-Engels Institute in Moscow and allegedly written to Marx himself well illustrates Darwin's attitude to the Church: "Moreover though I am a strong advocate for free thought on all subjects, yet it appears to me (whether rightly or wrongly)," it runs, "that direct arguments against Christianity and Theism produce hardly any effect on the public; and freedom of thought is best promoted by the gradual illumination of men's minds, which follows from the advance of science. It has, therefore, been always my object to avoid writing on religion, and I have confined myself to science. I may, however, have been unduly biassed by the pain which it would give some members of my family, if I aided in any way direct attacks on religion." However, despite Darwin's attempts to keep them at arm's length, the Communists persistently made use of his theories whenever they could be stretched to the Marxist benefit and

Engels, speaking at Marx's graveside in 1883, maintained: "Just as Darwin discovered the law of development of organic nature, so Marx discovered the law of development of human history."

However, sociology and politics were not the only fields in which the results of Darwin's work were to be felt. Twelve years before publication of *The Origin*, when the idea of evolution was already in the air, Disraeli's heroine in *Tancred* had used words that were to be echoed in literature for the rest of the century. "You know, all is development," she averred. "The principle is perpetually going on. First, there was nothing, then there was something; then —I forget the next—I think there were shells, then fishes; then we came—let me see—did we come next? Never mind that; we came at last. And at the next change there will be something very superior to us—something with wings. Ah! that's it: we were fishes, and I believe we shall be crows." Almost a quarter of a century later, Disraeli resumed the argument in *Lothair*, whose Monsignore Berwick found what he called the religion of science. "Instead of Adam, our ancestry is traced to the most grotesque of creatures, thought is phosphorus, the soul complex nerves, and our moral sense a secretion of sugar."

Disbelief and sarcasm were the usual attitudes of novelists to both evolution and the vistas opened up by the new geology. In 1870 Charles Reade in his *Put Yourself in His Place*, had Guy Raby declaiming against "the impudent lies, and monstrous arithmetic, of geology, which babbles about a million years, a period actually beyond the comprehension of the human intellect." Wilkie Collins in 1875 had a character in *The Law and the Lady* dismissively protest: "Oh, the new ideas, the new ideas, what consoling, elevating, beautiful discoveries have been made by the new ideas! We were all monkeys before we were men, and molecules before we were monkeys! And what does it matter? And what does anything matter to anybody?"

Some writers used evolution as a basis for science fiction, and the voyagers in Jules Verne's *Journey to the Center of the Earth* met as living creatures species they had known only as fossils. More than one book centered on the search for the missing link between monkeys and men. R. D. Blackmore, mainly known for *Lorna Doone*, makes the hero of *The Remarkable History of Tommy Upmore* so light that the wind could lift him off the ground—and introduces a doctor who hopes to give him additional weight by the growth of a tail. Bulwer-Lytton stretched fantasy to the limit with *The Coming*

Race, in which tadpoles were the predecessors of a race with limitless intellectual power.

Apart from these sometimes crude attempts to give a topicality to books by invocation of the evolution controversy, there were a number of authors who seriously tried to grapple with the implications of evolution on religious belief. Edward Maitland's *The Pilgrim and the Shrine*, Eliza Lonton's *Under Which Lord*, Winwood Reade's *The Outcast* and Mrs. Humphry Ward's *Robert Elsmere* were only some of them.

These political, social and literary repercussions of Darwinism pervasively seeped into the cultural background of the English-speaking countries and, although more slowly, into that of the rest of the world. At times the idea of evolution itself was conscripted into the nonbiological sciences. Thus the Frenchman Victor-Amédée Meunier and the German Freiherr Karl du Prel maintained that when the nucleus of the solar system was being formed, collisions occurred between stars incapable of separate existence. In the cosmic struggle only those moving in suitable orbits survived. The same argument was used by Johannes Walther, the geologist, in an explanation of mountain ranges: some minerals, he contended, were less affected than others by the environment and these formed the mountains while others were more affected by rain, acids and mechanical forces.

But acceptance of the more conventional implications of the struggle for survival was still often qualified. A good illustration was the case of Rudolf Virchow, who epitomized his beliefs by the famous remark: "All cells arise from cells." As early as 1858, Virchow had said: "Our experiences give us no reason whatsoever for regarding as an eternal rule the immutability of species which at present appears so certain. . . . I must confess that it seems to me to be necessary for science to re-examine the possibility of changes of species into species." Virchow was receptive not only to *The Origin* but to *The Descent of Man* as well. Yet Darwinism was still only a hypothesis, and after Virchow had become a member of the German Reichstag, he voted against the teaching of Darwinism in German schools. The reason was that he, and other scientists, hoped that teaching natural sciences could be greatly increased in state schools. Evolution, he believed, could too easily endanger those plans. "I have spoken as a friend, not an adversary of transformism," he was to say, "and at all times I have approached the immortal Darwin in a friendly, not a hostile way. But

Charles Darwin (1809–1882) and his sister Catherine (1810–1866)
CAMBRIDGE UNIVERSITY LIBRARY

Charles Darwin's brother, Erasmus (1804–1881)
UNIVERSITY COLLEGE, LONDON

H.M.S. **Beagle** *in the Straits of Magellan*
CENTENNIAL BOOK

H.M.S. **Beagle** *being careened off Santa Cruz*
MANSELL COLLECTION, LONDON

Down House, Downe, Kent
CAMBRIDGE UNIVERSITY LIBRARY

Darwin's study, Down House
CAMBRIDGE UNIVERSITY LIBRARY

Darwin outside the front of Down House
CAMBRIDGE UNIVERSITY LIBRARY

Charles Darwin
CAMBRIDGE UNIVERSITY LIBRARY

Emma Darwin (1808–1896)
CAMBRIDGE UNIVERSITY LIBRARY

The Darwin family at Down House: Leonard, Henrietta, Horace, Emma, Elizabeth, Francis, and a schoolfriend called Spitta
CAMBRIDGE UNIVERSITY LIBRARY

Sir Joseph Dalton Hooker (1817–1911)
NATIONAL PORTRAIT GALLERY, LONDON

Asa Gray (1810–1888)
MANSELL COLLECTION, LONDON

Bishop Wilberforce (1805–1873)
NATIONAL PORTRAIT GALLERY, LONDON

Alfred Russel Wallace (1823–1913)
NATIONAL PORTRAIT GALLERY, LONDON

Thomas Henry Huxley (1825–1895), his son Leonard Huxley (1860–1933), and his grandson Julian Huxley (1887–1975)
SIR JULIAN HUXLEY

Punch *cartoon*

Darwin in old age
CAMBRIDGE UNIVERSITY LIBRARY

Charles Darwin's son Francis (1848–1925)
NATIONAL PORTRAIT GALLERY, LONDON

Karl Pearson (1857–1936), left, *and Sir Francis Galton (1822–1911)*
UNIVERSITY COLLEGE, LONDON

George Harrison Shull (1874–1954)
UNITED PRESS

Walter Frank Raphael Weldon (1860–1906)
UNIVERSITY COLLEGE, LONDON

Sir Ronald Aylmer Fisher (1890–1962)
NATIONAL PORTRAIT GALLERY, LONDON

Thomas Hunt Morgan (1866–1945)
UNITED PRESS

William Jennings Bryan (1860–1925), left, *and Clarence Seward Darrow (1857–1938) at the Scopes trial in 1925*
UNITED PRESS

Nicolai Ivanovitch Vavilov (1887–1942/3),
left, *and William Bateson (1861–1926)*
MORAVSKÉ MUSEUM, BRNO,
CZECHOSLOVAKIA

Cyril Dean Darlington (1903–1981)
JOHN INNES INSTITUTE, NORWICH

John Burdon Sanderson Haldane (1892–1964)
SUN PHOTOGRAPH

Sir Julian Sorell Huxley (1887–1975)
UNESCO

Sir Andrew Fielding Huxley (b. 1917)
SIR JULIAN HUXLEY

James Dewey Watson (b. 1928), left, *and Francis Harry Compton Crick (b. 1916), with the model of the double helix*
PHOTOGRAPH A. C. BARRINGTON BROWN

Linus Carl Pauling (b. 1901)
INFORMATION OFFICE, CALIFORNIA
INSTITUTE OF TECHNOLOGY

I have always differentiated between friend and partisan. I can salute and even support a scientific hypothesis, before it is proven by facts. But I cannot become its partisan as long as sufficient proof is lacking." And he voted in favor of reprimanding Hermann Müller, the well-known botanist who had tried to introduce Darwinian ideas into his schoolteaching.

While some of the proevolutionary scientists, of whom Virchow was one, remained cautious in their reactions to Darwin, and while Darwin's influence continued to diffuse throughout political and literary fields, two new methods of investigating evolution began to open up. Until this period it had been almost exclusively the concern of biologists; from now onwards the chemists and the mathematicians were to be brought in, a first hint of the time, a century later, when virtually all the sciences were adding to the knowledge of evolution.

Fresh information about the cell was the first contribution of the chemists, but it was an advance made in conjunction with other technological and industrial progress and one made, it should be stressed, through the work of men in Britain, America, Germany and France. Thus the ability of the microscope to reveal smaller and smaller objects in greater and greater detail was enormously increased by the Abbe substage condenser and the new apochromatic lenses, which could be operated with oil immersion. The use of dead rather than living material, combined with wax embedding and mechanical sectioning, made it possible to see the structure of complete organs that could be sectioned by greatly improved cutting instruments. Equally important were the byproducts of the new synthetic dye industry, which enabled botanists and physiologists to observe more easily the changes that took place during cell division.

Prominent among the cell pioneers was Walther Flemming, who, while working with animal cells, observed that they contained material strongly absorbed by the dye he was using, a material he named chromatin from the Greek word for color. During cell division, the chromatin could be seen to amalgamate into threadlike particles—colored bodies subsequently called chromosomes. The chromosomes next doubled in number, then disentangled themselves to form two groups, one at each end of the cell. The cell then divided into two, a process later called mitosis, each of the two cells now having as many chromosomes as the original cell. Flemming outlined these discoveries in *Cell Substances, Nucleus, and Cell Divi-*

sion. It was published in the year of Darwin's death, ironically so since it paved the way toward an understanding of how inheritance worked, describing the mechanism for which Darwin had been unsuccessfully searching throughout the last forty-five years of his life.

During the following years it was discovered that the cells of all animals and plants—in fact, of all living organisms—contained chromosomes. There was the same number of chromosomes in each specimen of the same species, but the number differed widely from one species to another, ranging up to 100: 20 in corn, 24 in the tomato, 40 in the house mouse, 46 in the potato, and, as was to prove useful thirty years later, a mere 8 in the *Drosophila melanogaster* or fruit fly.

However, Flemming did not realize the full meaning of what he had observed, and Wilhelm Roux, who published a remarkable essay on the subject in 1883, made two proposals, one right and one wrong, that were to confuse ideas of the evolutionary mechanism for a number of years. Roux rightly proposed that the chromosomes must carry the units of heredity, whatever these might be. But he also concluded, wrongly, that at a subsequent cell division, christened meiosis, the split was not necessarily equal, and that at this stage certain characteristics might not be inherited. Roux also put forward an ingenious theory that apparently did something to answer a number of awkward Darwinian problems. This was an extension of the idea of selection to the animal body as a whole. As an instance, the development of blind eyes in cave fish might be explicable if the loss of sight increased the sensitivity of other sense organs.

Although both Flemming and Roux showed that the development of the cell was closely concerned with heredity and therefore formed part of the machinery of evolution, neither supplied a blueprint for the whole machine. This was left to August Friedrich Leopold Weismann, the German biologist who believed that multicellular organisms were analogous to unicellular microorganisms, which divided indefinitely and could therefore be considered to live forever. From the idea came his concept of the "continuity of the germ plasm," invoking an elaborate hierarchy of material bodies including elements of molecular size and not unlike Darwin's pangenes. These were grouped into "determinants," pieces of inheritable matter that themselves formed larger collections on the chromosomes. This germ plasm, according to Weismann, could never be altered by environment but went on repeatedly perpetuating itself—a proposal that brought from Samuel Butler the remark: "a hen is only an egg's way of making another egg."

To prove that characteristics acquired in life could not be inherited, Weismann cut off the tails of nearly 1,600 mice that he bred over twenty-two generations. But the mice were still producing young with normal tails. Despite the result of this experiment, and similar ones, Weismann was constantly attacked on the ground that he was putting forward a theory first and then carrying out experiments rather than doing the experiments first and then forming a theory from the results. He was unrepentant. "To go on investigating without the guidance of theories," he responded, "is like attempting to walk in a thick mist without a track and without a compass. We should get somewhere under these circumstances, but chance alone would determine whether we should reach a stony desert of unintelligible facts or a system of roads leading in some useful direction; and in most cases chance would decide against us."

Insofar as they upheld Darwin's initial view that acquired characteristics could not be inherited, Weismann's ideas might be seen to support Darwin's. Yet they did, in fact, make even more intractable the problem of how variation could take place at all. With the germ plasm continuing unchanged from generation to generation, there would surely be nothing on which natural selection would be able to work. It could be claimed that while natural selection might eliminate the unfit as Darwin said, how did the fit come into existence at all? This awkward problem was theoretically solved by what came to be known as neo-Lamarckianism, very largely a creation of Alpheus Hyatt, the invertebrate paleontologist, and Edward Drinker Cope, the vertebrate paleontologist who had waged a long and bitter professional war with Othniel C. Marsh.

"Before the excellence of a machine can be tested [by natural selection]," Cope wrote in *The Origin of the Fittest*, "it must exist, and before man or nature selects the best, there must be at least two to choose from as alternatives. Furthermore, it is exceedingly improbable that the nicely adapted machinery of animals should have come into existence without the operation of causes leading directly to that end. The doctrines of 'selection' and 'survival' plainly do not reach the kernel of evolution, which is, as I have long since pointed out, the question of 'the origin of the fittest.' The omission of this problem from the discussion of evolution, is to leave Hamlet out of the play to which he has given his name. The law by which structures originate is one thing; those by which they are restricted, directed or destroyed, is another thing."

The neo-Lamarckians filled the gap in the argument with two assumptions Lamarck had made during the previous century: organisms could respond to their environment by developing advantageous characteristics, and could then pass on these characteristics to their offspring. And to these still shaky assumptions they added a variety of mechanisms that, they claimed, showed how the system worked. But at the turn of the century the rediscovery of Gregor Mendel's work revealed that the assumptions were unnecessary.

Before this, however, an alternative was proposed four years after Darwin's death by the Dutch botanist Hugo De Vries. De Vries had read *The Origin* in its German translation, had read the rest of Darwin's publications and included two propositions on Darwin's views in his doctoral dissertation in 1870. The first was that "The hypotheses of Pangenesis cannot explain the variability of species." The second was: "The fact that cross-fertilisation of plants in some cases has a better result than self-fertilisation is only a result of the fact that self-fertilisation is avoided by the shape of the flower, but not its cause." As a plant physiologist, De Vries corresponded with Darwin during the early 1870s. Darwin praised him in his book on climbing plants and in 1878 was happy to meet him in Surrey, where he was staying at his brother-in-law's home, Abinger Hall. During the next few years, De Vries's interests moved from plant physiology to heredity, and his last letter to Darwin, written in October 1881, observed: "I have always been especially interested in your hypothesis of Pangenesis and have collected a series of facts in favour of it, but I am sure that your promised publication will contain much more evidence on all such points, as I would for many years be able to collect."

But Darwin died the following year. De Vries continued collecting. The result was followed by De Vries's *Intracellular Pangenesis*, a short book that ingeniously tried to overcome the limitations of Darwin's pangenesis by postulating an array of units, or pangens, that "are not chemical molecules, but morphological structures, each built up of numerous molecules." The pangens were of two kinds; those that did not pass on changes provoked in them by any of a number of unknown causes; and those that, once changed, passed on the changes to the next generation. "Just as physics and chemistry go back to molecules and atoms," De Vries said in chapter 1 of his book, "the biological sciences have to penetrate to these units in order to explain, by means of their combinations, the phenomena of the living world."

Although intracellular pangenesis foreshadowed more than one feature to be revealed in the twentieth century, it had no longer a life than any of the other proposals for particulate inheritance proposed in the 1880s and 1890s. This was at least partly due to the fact that a curious chance brought De Vries to what he thought was mutation, subsequently found to be a key to evolution.

While collecting material for research on heredity, he found growing outside Amsterdam some groups of the evening primrose *Oenothera lamarckiana*. He cultivated the plants and from about 50,000 obtained some 800 that he classed as separate species. These plants bred true. Thus it appeared that a new species could come into being through methods entirely different from those of natural selection. As De Vries explained in *The Mutation Theory*, "The object of the present book is to show that species arise by saltations [i.e., jumps] and that the individual saltations are occurrences which can be observed like any other physiological process. Forms which arise by a single saltation are distinguishable from one another as sharply and in as many ways as most of the so-called small species and as many of the closely related species of the best systematists, including Linnaeus himself." De Vries could give no reason for these sudden changes but maintained that they were of three types. There were progressive mutations, which produced new characteristics in an organization. But there were also retrogressive and degressive mutations, which involved, respectively, the disappearance of existing characters and the activation of characters that had previously been latent.

There was opposition to De Vriesian mutation—the adjective being necessary, since the word "mutation" was soon to have a different biological meaning—on more than one ground. The American Clinton Hart Merriam surveyed more than 1,000 species and subspecies of North American mammals and birds to discover if any appeared to have arisen by mutation. "My own conviction," he concluded, "is that the origin of species by mutation among both animals and plants is so uncommon that as a factor in evolution it may be regarded as trivial." But quite apart from the lack of supporting evidence, there was the conservative bias of human nature. When Darwinism had appeared on the scene, it had indeed shocked the orthodox; but by now it was an accepted creed that had itself almost been transformed into orthodoxy. "Are we,"

Merriam asked, "because of the discovery of a case in which a species appears to have arisen in a slightly different way [from the Darwinian theory]—for after all the difference is only one of degree—to lose faith in the stability of knowledge and rush panic-stricken into the sea of unbelief, unmindful of the cumulative observations and conclusions of zoologists and botanists?"

In fact, desertion of the by now comparatively respectable Darwinian ideas was unnecessary. In a series of papers from 1910 to 1912, a number of American geneticists showed conclusively that De Vries's so-called mutations of *Oenothera* were the result of an unusual but not mutational pattern of inheritance. What had appeared to be major mutations were in fact complex recombinations of existing character. De Vries continued to uphold his theory until his death in 1935, but general belief in it had died out by the start of the First World War in 1914.

However, while the *Oenothera* were not quite what they had seemed, they had played a part in the unfolding story of evolution by concentrating attention on mutation and the prospects that they held out. "I am reminded," a modern geneticist has said, "by such occurrences that the road to the solution of a scientific puzzle such as that presented by the Oenothera 'mutations' may resemble the way to the solution of a double acrostic or crossword puzzle. It seems that sometimes the important thing is simply to keep on writing in letters (steps in the solution) even when they are wrong and to arrive at a correct solution by serial correction of earlier errors. This means that, in the end, it is more profitable to have errors to correct than a blank page."

It might indeed be so, and it is certainly true that following publication of *The Mutation Theory* (published in Holland in 1901 and translated into English in 1910–11), attention was drawn to the theory of evolution by "jumps," brought about by mutations or sudden changes for which no one could yet account. It is therefore ironic that the validity of De Vries's main evidence, that of the *Oenothera*, should be destroyed just as Morgan in his famous fly room at Columbia was revealing not only the existence of real mutations but many of the ways in which they worked. By that time, however, the controversy between those who believed in Darwin's view of evolution by the accumulation of small variations and those who believed in evolution by "jumps" had been complicated by the introduction into the debate of mathematics and of the statistical approach.

Mathematical Wine for Biological Bottles

THE statistical implications of natural selection had been described more than a decade before Darwin's death by Alfred W. Bennett. In "The Theory of Natural Selection from a Mathematical Point of View," read to Section D of the British Association in September 1870, he had raised a number of awkward points. The most important concerned the extent of a variation before natural selection began to operate. "Suppose," Bennett asked, ". . . that our common brown owl has a *penchant* for mice while moles are abhorrent to its palate; is it conceivable that, supposing a mouse was born approaching a mole by the one-hundredth part in external appearance, say with feet a fraction of a line broader, or eyes slightly deeper set, the shortest-sightest of owls would for a moment mistake *Mus* for *Talpa*? Or, a still more parallel instance: suppose a blue-bottle fly were born blessed with a slightly narrower waist, or a faint band of yellow on its body, will any one maintain that it stands the least chance of escape from destruction by those birds which do not feed on wasps?"

Bennett then went on to argue that in a specific case 1,000 variations would have to be accumulated before an insect passed into a protective form. If the first 20 of the 1,000 steps were required before their accumulation became profitable, then these steps would have to be accumulated by chance. "Let us investigate the value of this chance," Bennett continued. "Suppose there are twenty different ways in which a *Leptalis* [butterfly] may vary, one only of these being in the direction ultimately required, the chance of any individual producing a descendant which will take its place in the succeeding generation varying in the required direction, is 1/20; the chance of this operation being repeated in the same direction in the second generation is $1/20^2$ or 1/400; the chance of this occurring for *ten* successive generations (instead of twenty, as I have assumed above) is $1/20^{10}$, or about one in ten billions."

Bennett's calculations appeared to show that statistical investigation of natural selection was unrewarding, and there followed an interval of some years during which few evolutionists showed much interest in the potential of mathematics to help their work. The lull was in turn followed by the rise of the statistical approach and by anguished arguments between the biometricians, who as a matter of principle applied statistics and mathematics to biology, and those who believed in what might be called the butterfly-net role of the naturalist.

The leader of the new movement was Francis Galton, who had followed up the pangenesis theory with his rabbit-breeding experiments. Galton's dedication to statistics was carried almost to the point of mania by his belief that virtually everything was susceptible to measurement. He studied the effectiveness of prayer by examining the mortality rate of those for whom prayers were said and of those who lacked this luxury. The shipwrecks of vessels carrying missionaries were compared with those of vessels not thus endowed, and he tried to develop a quantitative scale for beauty. Some of these activities stretched statistical ideas dangerously toward the realms of nonsense, but they were in a totally different category from his attempts to conscript statistics to help solve the riddles of heredity—attempts that soon led to the science of biometry, which used statistical analysis for the study of biological data.

Galton based much of his serious work on data sent to him in answer to newspaper advertisements and, later, on the many thousand records taken at the Anthropometric Laboratory that he organized at the London International Health Exhibition of 1884. His results were presented in a series of books, starting with *Hereditary Genius* in 1869, and a stream of papers, reports and lectures. In general, Darwin approved, although one gets the impression that Galton's mathematics were beyond him. "You have made a convert of an opponent in one sense," he wrote after publication of *Hereditary Genius*, "for I have always maintained that excepting fools, men did not differ much in intellect, only in zeal and hard work; and I still think this is an *eminently* important difference. . . ."

Galton's investigations were significant not only in laying the foundations of biometry, but also in stimulating new ideas that could be used in the study of inheritance. One was that of regression, the tendency to move back toward an earlier state. If the regression factor for height was 50 percent, the height of the offspring of a man four inches taller than the average would tend to be two inches above the average. This was further refined into Galton's law of ancestral heredity, which maintained that the two parents, on average, contributed between them one-half of the total heritage of their offspring; the four grandparents one-quarter, the eight great-grandparents one-eighth, and so on.

Galton also showed that the measurements of children depended not only on the measurements of their parents but on those of their race, too. The fact that inheritance was linked not only to parents but also to more diffuse ancestry had some uncomfortable implications. "The more bountifully the Parent is gifted by nature," Galton noted in *Natural Inheritance*, "the more rare will be his good fortune if he begets a son who is as richly endowed as himself, and still more so if he has a son who is endowed yet more largely. But the law is even-handed; it levies an equal succession-tax on the transmission of badness as of goodness. If it discourages the extravagant hopes of a gifted parent that his children will inherit all his powers, it no less discountenances extravagant fears that they will inherit all his weakness and disease."

There was, secondly, the concept of correlation, used when a number of variables change together. In dealing with heredity, it was not possible to separate any one variable from a multitude of others, and Galton was forced into devising a succession of correlation tables that provided a partial solution to this difficulty.

Little of his work could be directly applied to the problem of evolution as it was conceived by Darwin, since Galton's views on the respective parts played by "sports" and by the succession of small variations were radically different from those of his cousin. The progress of evolution, he was to write,

is not a smooth and uniform progression, but one that proceeds by jerks, through successive "sports" (as they are called), some of them implying considerable organic changes, and each in its turn being favoured by Natural Selection.

The same word "variation" has been indiscriminately applied to two very different conceptions, which ought to be clearly distinguished; the one is that of the "sports" just alluded to, which are changes in the position of organic stability, and may, through the aid of Natural Selection, become fresh steps in the onward course of evolution; the other is that of the Variations proper, which are merely strained conditions of a stable form of organisation, and not in any way an overthrow of them. Sports do not blend freely together; variations proper do so. Natural Selection acts upon variations proper, just as it does upon sports, by preserving the best to become parents, and eliminating the worst, but its action upon mere variations can, as I conceive, be of no permanent value in evolution, because there is a constant tendency in the offspring to "regress" towards the parental type.

Here were the ingredients for battles royal in the future. For the biometricians who were to support Galton's statistical approach to evolution were mainly believers in the gradual process, which he saw as "of no permanent value in evolution." By contrast, believers in the overwhelming value of jumps tended to regard the statistical approach as an abomination.

The situation that developed in the 1890s was confused by a number of factors. One was that the statistical evidence produced by Galton and his successors was used to support their own ideas by both the believers in continuous variation and by the saltationists. Yet it was not basically an either/or argument. Neither side genuinely believed that the other side's mechanism did not operate; the point at issue was, rather, the relative importance of continuous and discontinuous change in what was already being seen as an evolutionary process far more complex than had hitherto been imagined. However, this state of affairs was rarely admitted by those involved, the dogmas of evolution by continuous minor variations and by "jumps" being held with all the fervor of Gulliver's Big-Endians and Little-Endians. The dispute was certainly one of opposed beliefs, but it was intensified by a factor that gives an extraordinary air of bitterness to the arguments of the 1890s and the first few years of the twentieth century: this was the strong personal antagonism between the leaders of the two groups. "With co-operation," it was later to be written, "a big advance might have been made in the attack on the problems of evolution, and we might have seen many years earlier that combination of genetics, biometry and statistics, the value of which is being recognised more fully today." Indeed, it has been said that the argument between the two main protagonists delayed a reconciliation of viewpoints for fifteen years.

The two leading opponents were the biologist William Bateson, the champion of Gregor Mendel, the rediscovery of whose work was in 1900 to transform the uncovering of evolution's machinery, and Walter Frank Raphael Weldon, the biologist whose statistical ability was to make him one of the early biometricians. In the early 1880s both men were undergraduates at Cambridge and apparently destined for lives on parallel lines. To Weldon, Bateson admitted owing "the chief awakening of my life. It was through him that I first learnt that there was work in the world which I could do. . . . Such a debt is perhaps the greatest that one man can feel towards another." Yet on Weldon's death in 1906, Bateson could write to Mrs. Bateson: "If any man ever set himself to destroy another man's work, that did he do to me."

Bateson graduated in 1883 with First Class Honours in zoology. Shortly before, he had seen a circular from Johns Hopkins University announcing the discovery by the American morphologist William Keith Brooks of a marine invertebrate, *Balanoglossus*, at the Chesapeake Bay Zoology Station. Although an invertebrate, *Balanoglossus* possessed features that classified it as a chordate. Bateson saw the possibility of discovering its evolutionary relationship with other primitive chordates, and was enabled to spend two spells working at the Chesapeake Laboratory. When he arrived, Brooks was completing a book on heredity, a province Bateson later said was new to him at the time. "Variation and heredity with us [at Cambridge] had stood as axioms," he later wrote. "For Brooks they were problems. As he talked of them the insistence of these problems became imminent and oppressive." Bateson's work on *Balanoglossus* showed that on the accepted canons of morphology this peculiar wormlike creature was in fact related to the vertebrates, a solution to the problem that earned him a Fellowship of St. John's, Cambridge.

Bateson's next attempt to tackle the problem of evolution was made in an unlikely field of operations, the Central Asian steppes. The Aral Sea was becoming increasingly salty, its fauna were believed to be changing, and Bateson felt that here he could test Darwin's theory that a changing environment induced the variations on which natural selection could work. It was expected, he wrote, when asking for permission to work in the area, that the marine inhabitants would be isolated in the various basins that had been formed. The questions he was investigating, he went on, were whether such traces of marine life did exist and, if so, what variations they had undergone.

Bateson was lucky in finding a series of lakes whose salinity varied in an almost continuous series of changes. He studied the fauna in each, particularly one species of shellfish, and found that while the change in salinity appeared to be a continuous process, variations in the shellfish were nevertheless discontinuous. From this he concluded that the initial variations must have been discontinuous and the result not of the environment but of heredity.

On his return to Britain, Bateson began to gather material that would throw light on the nature of variation. His enthusiasm is suggested by the phrase in his *Times* obituary that he "ransacked the field, the museum, and the library" for evidence. The first hint of the way his thoughts were going, and that his view of evolution might be different from Darwin's, came in his paper "On Variations in the Floral Symmetry of Certain Plants Having Irregular Corollas," written with Miss Anna Bateson. "For there is one obvious consideration which makes it difficult to suppose *both* that the process of Variation has been a continuous one, and also that Natural Selection has been the chief agent in building up the mechanisms of living things." The main result of his new researches was revealed in 1894 in a book usually called *Materials for the Study of Variation*. Its full title, however, was *Materials for the Study of Variation Treated with Especial Regard to Discontinuity in the Origin of Species*. Bateson had decided that "jumps" were inherited and that they—if not alone, then to a great extent—were responsible for evolution. In the book, a copy of which he sent to Huxley, he presented 886 cases of what he saw as discontinuous variation. Huxley approved, writing to him on February 20, 1894: "I see you are inclined to advocate the possibility of considerable 'saltus' on the part of Dame Nature in her variations. I always took the same view, much to Mr. Darwin's disgust, and we used often to debate it."

While Bateson had been traveling in the steppes, and then collecting material that might throw light on variation, his old friend Weldon had been concentrating on marine biology, first at the famous Naples biological station and then at the newly opened Marine Biological Association's laboratory at Plymouth, England. Two things were now to draw him away from the morphological and embryological studies with which he was investigating the problems of evolution. One was his growing belief that the study of animals in their natural environment was more likely to provide answers to evolutionary riddles than even the best of laboratory research. The second was the impact of Galton's *Natural Inheritance*. On reading it, Weldon immediately saw that the statistical methods that Galton said could throw light on heredity might as easily be used in evolutionary research. He started with a statistical study of the variation in the common shrimp, followed with a study of selected measurements made on several races of shrimp, and then began a years-long investigation of the crabs of Plymouth Sound, an investigation that was to raise a storm of criticism.

Weldon's work was now at loggerheads with Bateson's for various reasons. Weldon rejected the significance of saltations as firmly as Bateson supported it, and he made his position clear in a bitter and almost derisory review in *Nature* of *Materials for the Study of Variation*. In addition, while Weldon believed that the complexities of inheritance and of evolution could be disentangled only after a sound mathematical foundation had been laid, Bateson believed otherwise, perhaps naturally, since he knew that he was incapable of approaching the problem along such lines. "Mathematics were my difficulty," he wrote of his youth. "Being destined for Cambridge, I was specially coached in mathematics at school. Arrived here I was again coached, but failed. Coached once more I passed, having wasted, not one, but several hundred hours on that study. Needless to say, my knowledge of mathematics is *nil*." A decade or so earlier, there had been a schism between the "field naturalist" school of botanists and the men who had, metaphorically, left the field for the laboratory. Now there appeared a widening rift between the Bateson school, whose members pinned their faith on observation plus deduction, and those who believed that statistics were sufficient to provide the answers.

The new exemplification of the old dichotomy was well described by Bateson himself in *Materials for the Study of Variation*. The data of variation, he wrote,

> attract men of two classes, in tastes and temperament distinct, each having little sympathy or even acquaintance with the work of the other. Those of the one class have felt the attraction of the problem. It is the challenge of Nature that calls them to work. But disgusted with the superficiality of "naturalists" they sit down in the laboratory to the

solution of the problem, hoping that the closer they look the more truly will they see. For the living things out of doors, they care little. Such work to them is all vague. With the other class it is the living thing that attracts, not the problem. To them the methods of the first school are frigid and narrow. Ignorant of the skill and of the accurate, final knowledge that the other school has bit by bit achieved, achievements that are the real glory of the method, the "naturalists" hear only those theoretical conclusions which the laboratories from time to time ask them to accept. With senses quickened by the range and fresh air of their own work they feel keenly how crude and inadequate are these poor generalities, and for what a small and conventional world they are devised. Disappointed with the results they condemn the methods of the others, knowing nothing of their real strength. So it happens that for them the study of the problems of life and of species becomes associated with crudity and meanness of scope. Beginning as naturalists, they end as collectors, despairing of the problem, turning for relief to the tangible business of classification, accounting themselves happy if they can keep their species apart, caring little how they became so, and rarely telling us how they may be brought together. Thus each class misses that which in the other is good.

The split was to last long and to hold back the understanding of how evolution worked, yet it is easy to sympathize with those naturalists who were unable to see statistics as a biological tool. Only a generation later did an analogy drawn from the physical sciences suggest how consideration of populations in the mass might help to explain evolution even before the machinery of inheritance had been fully revealed. "The introduction of a descriptive model of the individual atom with its revolving electrons has been of immense value in the interpretation of the mass phenomena of practical physics," it has been written; "yet research into the behaviour of atoms in the mass—the statistical method of approach—had led to results of far-reaching significance in practical life long before any adequate model of the atom was available. So in the case of the theory of evolution the biometricians realised that the statistical line of attack, involving a study of populations under natural conditions, would lead to results of practical value which need not wait upon the construction and exhaustive testing of any detailed model giving an ordered picture of this process of individual inheritance."

The argument about the use of statistics that split biologists into opposing camps was, however, symptomatic of a wider underlying difference of outlook between Weldon and Bateson. The former believed inheritance to be not only a continuous process but one that depended on the total ancestry of an individual. Bateson, however, gave more weight not only to "jumps," or mutations, but also to the specific inherited contributions from the parents. The battle lines were clearly marked out by Weldon in the first of his papers for the Royal Society on his crab experiments. "It cannot be too strongly urged," he said, "that the problem of animal evolution is essentially a statistical problem: that before we can properly estimate the changes at present going on in a race or species we must know accurately (a) the percentage of animals which exhibit a given amount of abnormality with regard to a particular character; (b) the degree of abnormality of other organs which accompanies a given abnormality of one; (c) the difference between the death rate per cent in animals of different degrees of abnormality with respect to any organ; (d) the abnormality of offspring in terms of the abnormality of parents and *vice versa*. These are all questions of arithmetic; and when we know the numerical answers to these questions for a number of species we shall know the direction and the rate of change in these species at the present day—a knowledge which is the only legitimate basis for speculations as to their past history and future fate."

The opposition to that approach was considerable, in spite of the cachet the approach enjoyed from the link with Galton, but it is unlikely that it would have grown so fast and so successfully had it not been for the support given to Weldon by Karl Pearson. Weldon was a biologist who had taken up statistics solely as a tool of research. Pearson, holding the chair of applied mathematics and mechanics at University College, London, was mathematician first and biologist second, and thus a powerful ally to Weldon in the argument with Bateson. These three protagonists were endowed with considerable powers of sarcasm and did not hesitate to use them. "The term 'controversial,' " Bateson wrote to C. C. Hurst, "is conveniently used by those who are wrong to apply to the persons who correct them. Properly, the word is not applicable in such cases. It has nothing to do with points of fact, but merely with opinion."

In Pearson's view, the importance of Weldon's first paper on the Plymouth crabs could hardly be overestimated, since it was the first to formulate "the view that the method of the Registrar-General [who is responsible for the Census figures] is the method by which the fundamental problems of natural selection must be attacked. . . ." Meanwhile Pearson himself began publishing the first of a series of papers afterward entitled "Mathematical Contributions to the Theory of Evolution." Any fears that the new discipline of biometry might be ignored were removed when, at the end of 1893, the Royal Society set up a Committee for Conducting Statistical Inquiries into the Measurable Characteristics of Plants and Animals. Galton chaired the Committee in the hope that "the numerous bodies engaged in horticulture and zoology might in one aspect of their work, be coordinated by the committee and that research of a scientific kind might be introduced into the proceedings of each of them." In addition, there were probably pious hopes that under his benign influence the increasingly contentious arguments in the evolutionary field might be removed with the minimum of damage. If so, they were false hopes.

After Weldon had scathingly reviewed Bateson's *Materials* in 1894, he had in turn been strongly criticized for his work on crabs. Upon outlining this work to the Royal Society, he was attacked by Sir Ray Lankester, whom he had succeeded as professor of zoology at University College. "Such methods of attempting to penetrate the obscurity which veils the interactions of the immensely complex bundle of phenomena which we call a crab and its environment," wrote Lankester, "appear to me not merely inadequate, but in so far as they involve perversion of the meaning of accepted terms and a deliberate rejection of the method of inquiry by hypothesis and verification, injurious to the progress of knowledge."

"The hypothesis with which I started," Weldon replied, "was, that if natural selection acted upon the frontal breadth of crabs at all, there ought to be a demonstrable difference between the percentage of abnormal frontal breadth in young crabs, and the percentage of the same abnormalities in older crabs; and I proceeded to test this hypothesis by measurement of crabs of different sizes. The result showed that a change in the frequency of abnormal frontal breadth could, in fact, be observed."

The virulence of the argument between the biometricians and the rest was revealed to the world in the columns of *Nature* when in 1895 controversy arose over the origin of cultivated *Cineraria*. The orthodox view was that the plants had originated in a wild species that in the hands of a skilled breeder had been encouraged to accumulate a large number of small variations. Bateson insisted that, on the contrary, they were the result of hybridization between several recognized species. To support his theory, he conscripted the curator of the Botanic Garden at Cambridge. Weldon, backing the continuous accumulation theory, brought forward a number of distinguished botanists such as Botting-Hemanely and Thiselton-Dyer. About a dozen angry letters were printed in *Nature*, their quality being suggested by Thiselton-Dyer, who on May 13 concluded: "I think that in the study of evolution we have had enough and to spare of facile theorising. I infinitely prefer the sober method of Professor Weldon, even if it should run counter to my own prepossessions, to the barren dialectic of Mr. Bateson." In private, the two main contestants were even more outspoken than their supporters. On May 21, after Weldon and Bateson had met to discuss their differences, Bateson recorded: "Weldon's position in writing is therefore that of the accomplice who creates a diversion to help a Charlatan. I cannot at all understand his motives or how he can bring himself to play this part." Weldon replied to Bateson three days after the meeting. "I can do no more," he said. "First, you accuse me of attacking your personal character; and when I disclaim this, you charge me with a dishonest defence of some one else. I have throughout discussed only what appeared to me to be facts, relating to a question of scientific importance. If you insist upon regarding any opposition to your opinions concerning such matters as a personal attack upon yourself, I may regret your attitude, but I can do nothing to change it." With this, the *Cineraria* argument died away. Both Weldon and Bateson were confident that another would soon arise.

Meanwhile, Weldon extended his experiments with the crabs. "The labour involved was excessive," Pearson was later to write of them. "One 'crabbery' consisted of 500 wide-mouthed bottles, each with two syphons for a constant flow of sea water, and each crab had to be fed daily and its bottle cleaned. During the summer of 1897 Weldon spent the whole of his days at the aquarium, and his wife hardly left him except to fetch the needful chop. The sewage experiment was 'horrible from the great quantity of decaying matter necessary to kill a healthy crab.' " What the experiments showed was that the life of a crab was demonstrably affected by the china clay and sewage entering Plymouth Sound, that length of life could be correlated with efficient filtration of water entering the gill chamber, and that the selective death rate resulted in the survival of the fittest—that is, those crabs that had the wider carapace.

Weldon reported his results to the Royal Society's Committee and, shortly afterwards, submitted to it his "Remarks on Variation in Animals and Plants." In the latter, he not only maintained that while "sports" might occasionally affect evolution, continuous variations were more important, but also added: "The questions raised by the Darwinian hypothesis are purely statistical, and the statistical method is the only one at present obvious by which that hypothesis can be experimentally checked." Almost inevitably, Bateson protested, even offering to print four of his letters to Galton and distribute them to members of the Committee. Galton, who agreed with Bateson's views on the discontinuity of evolution, but otherwise seems to have been somewhat allergic to him, decided that drastic measures were necessary. The Committee was therefore reconstituted and renamed the Evolution (Plants and Animals) Committee of the Royal Society. Karl Pearson had been brought in as statistician in 1896, but to balance if not counterbalance him, Bateson was now added, as well as a number of zoologists and breeders. Some of them, Pearson pointed out in his life of Galton, "had small desire to assist quantitative methods of research." Certainly the Committee's attachment to biometry had been weakened. In future, it would not be a few Committee members versus the rest, but two groups pulling in opposite directions.

"The Committee you have got together is entirely unsuited," Galton was warned by Pearson after the first meeting of the new group on February 11, 1897. "It is far too large, contains far too many of the old biological type, and is far too unconscious of the fact that the solutions to these problems are in the first place statistical, and in the second place statistical, and only in the third place biological."

He felt, he said to Galton, that he was "sadly out of place in such a gathering of biologists, and little capable of expressing opinions, which would only have hurt their feelings and not have been productive of real good. I always succeed in creating hostility without getting others to see my views; infelicity of expression is I expect to blame. To you I mean to speak them out, even at the risk of vexing you. . . . The older school of biologists cannot be expected to appreciate these [statistical] methods, e.g. Ray Lankester, Thiselton-Dyer, etc. A younger generation is only just beginning its training in them."

Conditions changed from bad to worse, the artificial barrier between "natural history" and any kind of statistical inquiry leading to numerical results was strengthened, and in 1900 both Pearson and Weldon resigned from the Committee. They were followed a year later by Galton. "Mr. [F. D.] Godman then became chairman and the Reports of the Committee were devoted entirely to the publications of Bateson and his school," Pearson recorded in his life of Galton. "The capture of the Committee was skilful and entirely successful."

It is ironic that the controversy between those who favored a statistical approach to evolution and those who clung to the earlier attitude should move toward a climax as the century ended, since the argument was to be greatly intensified by the developments of the next few years. For once, a new century did mark a genuine watershed in research. Before exploring it, one can conveniently sum up the position of Darwinism four decades after *The Origin* had sent its shock through the world.

It was by now almost unanimously admitted that two separate assumptions were locked together in Darwin's concept of evolution. The first, which was opposed only by a diminishing company of dogmatics, was that evolution had in fact taken place and that all living organisms—with the possible exception of man, whose special creation was still defended by some with a vigor worthy of Custer's last stand—were related to each other through an almost inconceivably long line of descent. The second assumption was that the mechanism powering the process of evolution was that of natural selection. Darwin himself had been careful to stress that, while he regarded this as the most important factor in evolution, he did not consider it to be the only one, a qualification ignored by many of his critics, both scientific and lay. Some, pointing to apparent difficulties in the operation of natural selection, tended almost to rule it out as a factor at all. The need for more information was underlined by Pearson, who in a letter to *Nature* in 1896, wrote: "To demonstrate that natural selection, whether secular or periodic, is actually taking place in any species, and to measure its amount, is in the present state of our knowledge one of the grandest pieces of work that could be done. It would achieve for the Darwinian theory what Hertz achieved for the Maxwellian theory of light."

For those genuinely anxious to support evolution, major riddles still remained after four decades. One concerned the relative significance of the small variations accumulated over long periods, on which Darwin had pinned his faith, and of the "saltations," or jumps, of whose potential importance Huxley had warned Darwin as early as 1859. There was also the fog that covered the way in which characteristics were handed down from one generation to the next. Darwin's pangenesis had been superseded by Weismann's "continuity of the germ plasm," but it had soon been seen that Weismann's theory effectively ruled out the transmission of variations at all, and thus confusion was quickly restored.

The extent of the doubts that still remained at the end of the nineteenth century was stressed by Bateson in a paper on "Problems of Heredity as a Subject for Horticultural Investigation," which he read to the Royal Horticultural Society on May 8, 1900. Speaking of the mechanisms of heredity and variation, he said:

> We *want* to know the whole truth of the matter; we want to know the physical basis, the inward and essential nature, "the causes," as they are sometimes called, of heredity. We want also to know the laws which the outward and visible phenomena obey.
>
> Let us recognise from the outset that as to the essential nature of these phenomena we still know absolutely nothing. We have no glimmering of an idea as to what constitutes the essential process by which the likeness of the parent is transmitted to the offspring. We can study the processes of fertilization and development in the finest detail which the microscope manifests to us, and we may fairly say that we have now a thorough grasp of the visible phenomena; but of the nature of the physical basis of heredity we have no conception at all. No one has yet any suggestion, working hypothesis, or mental picture that has thus far helped in the slightest degree to penetrate beyond what we see. The process is as utterly mysterious to us as a flash of lightning is to a savage. We do not know what is the essential agent in the transmission of parental characters, not even whether it is a material agent or not. Not only is our ignorance complete, but no one has the remotest idea how to set to work on that part of the problem.

No one had the remotest idea. Thus, after forty years of argument, search and exposition, the operational side of evolution remained a mystery. The evidence appeared to be undeniable; but belief in it, demanded, like miracles, an act of faith. The need now was for hard plodding.

"If the work which is now being put into [collecting]," Bateson had already stated, "were devoted to the careful carrying-out and recording of experiments of the kind we are contemplating, the result, it is not, I think, too much to say, would in some five-and-twenty years make a revolution in our ideas of species, inheritance, variation, and the other phenomena which go to make up the science of Natural History. We should, I believe, see a new Natural History created."

But if scientific hurdles still barred the way to a fuller understanding of evolution, there was one credit item that tended to ameliorate the position. This was the view held by a growing number of churchmen that evolution did not necessarily run contrary to religious belief. It was held in varying forms by all manner of church leaders and was well expressed by the Reverend Charles Gore—later the influential Bishop Gore—in a sermon preached in 1894 before Oxford University.

It is quite certain, he said,

that this scientific obstacle [religious objections to Darwinism on the grounds of the argument from design] has been, in the main, removed. In part it has been through the theologians abandoning false claims, and learning, if somewhat unwillingly, that they have no "Bible revelation" in matters of science; in part it has been through its becoming continually more apparent that the limits of scientific "explanation" of nature are soon reached; that the ultimate causes, forces, conditions of nature are as unexplained as ever, or rather postulate as ever for their explanation a Divine mind. Thus if one "argument from design" was destroyed, another was only brought into prominence. No account which science can give, by discovery or conjecture, of the method of creation, can ever weaken the argument which lies from the universality of law, order, and beauty in the universe to the universality of mind. The mind of man looks forth into nature, and finds nowhere unintelligible chance, but everywhere an order, a system, a law, a beauty, which corresponds, as greater to less, to his own rational and spiritual intuitions, methods and expectations. Universal order, intelligibility, beauty, mean that something akin to the human spirit, something of which the human spirit is an offshoot and a reflection, is in the universe before it is in man.

As the twentieth century opened, it was hoped that all was possible. Within a few decades, or perhaps even a few years, was it not even likely that the outstanding scientific riddles might be solved just as the moral problems appeared to have been diluted?

11

First Answers to Inheritance

THE framework of the evolutionary theory was transformed in 1900 by the rediscovery of work by Gregor Johann Mendel, an Austrian monk who had begun his experiments while Darwin was putting his finishing touches to *The Origin* more than forty years earlier. The passing over of Mendel's work for such a long time and its unearthing simultaneously by biologists in the Netherlands, Germany and Austria is one of the more extraordinary stories of science, but perhaps little more extraordinary than the character of Mendel himself.

Born in 1822, he was ordained a priest in 1847 and attached to the Abbey of St. Thomas at Brünn, Bohemia (now Brno, Czechoslovakia). Four years later he was sent to the University of Vienna to study mathematics and science—a training that gave him a distinct advantage when, after returning to Brünn in 1857, he began botanical experiments in the monastery garden. A man of parts, Mendel was an amateur meteorologist who recorded not only the daily rainfall, temperature and humidity but also sunspots and the level of water in the monastery well. He tried to cross different strains of bees, kept mice, and may well have attempted breeding experiments with them. But his religion may have made him cautious of writing about mammalian inheritance, and when he began work in 1857 on a years-long series of experiments, it was pea plants that he chose for study.

However, Gregor Mendel was by no means the semirecluse he is sometimes painted as being. After his appointment as head of the monastery, he ran it with efficient worldly wisdom, started and nourished the local natural history society at which he was to read his seminal paper, and even traveled to London in 1862 with a party of more than one hundred tourists to visit the Great Exhibition being held there eleven years after the more famous exhibition in Hyde Park. Mendel spent a week in London seeing the sights, after a week in Paris on the same activities. A photograph showing him with the rest of the party suggests not so much the recluse as a jovial Friar Tuck.

After the rediscovery of his work, there almost inevitably arose the story that Mendel had visited Darwin during his time in England. Certainly Mendel's library contained a marked German edition of *The Origin* published during the year of his visit. But there is nothing to show that Mendel had even heard of Darwin when he came ashore at Dover. And the dates of his stay, matched against Darwin's known movements, seem effectively to rule out any meeting. A pity.

The experiments in the monastery garden at Brünn to which Mendel returned from London were not the first of their kind. Thomas Andrew Knight, vegetable physiologist, Copley Medalist of the Royal Society and president of the Horticultural Society for more than a quarter of a century, had described in 1823 how he had crossed peas with white and with gray seed coats. The result was uniformly gray-coated seeds, but these produced both grays and whites in the next generation. John Goss, the naturalist, reporting similar experiments the same year, found that the first-generation offspring had seeds like the paternal race. "From these in the next generation he obtained peas of two kinds, one like those of the original grandpaternal race, the others like those of the grandmaternal. Separating these, he found that the blue peas produced in F_3 only blues, and the white peas both blues and whites."

Neither of these two experimenters appreciated the significance of their results, and as Mendel was to write, "among all the numerous experiments made, not one has been carried out to such an extent and in such a way as to permit of the possibility of determining the number of different forms under which the offspring of hybrids appear, or so that these forms may be arranged with certainty according to their separate generations, or that their mutual numerical relations can be definitely ascertained."

This was left to Mendel, whose experiments were made with

some 10,000 pea plants of six varieties. It has sometimes been proposed that the experiments were carried out to disprove Darwin's theory outlined in *The Origin*. No evidence for this has come to light, while Mendel gave his own reason in his paper saying: "Artificial fertilisation, such as is effected with decorative plants in order to obtain new variations in colour, has led up to the experiments which will here be discussed. The striking regularity with which the same hybrid forms always reappeared whenever fertilisation took place between the same species induced further experiments to be undertaken, the object of which was to follow up the developments of the hybrids in their progeny."

Peas were chosen because they had constant traits—notably colour and plant height—that were easily and reliably distinguishable, and because interference from foreign pollen could not easily occur. Over a number of years, Mendel made many thousands of crosses between contrasting varieties, between six-foot plants and one-and-a-half-foot plants and between plants that produced colored blossoms and those that did not.

His method of controlled hybridization was to open a pea flower before it had fully developed and to remove its anthers with a forceps. Using a camel's-hair brush, he would dust its stigma with pollen from the pollen parent he had selected. Then the flower was wrapped in a calico or paper bag to protect it from the visits of insects carrying other pollen.

When he crossed plants having contrasting characteristics he found that only one of these characteristics, which he called dominant, was shown in the hybrids. However, when these hybrids were self-fertilised to produce another generation, three quarters of its members showed the dominant characteristic, and one quarter showed the other characteristic, which Mendel called recessive. About a quarter of these second-generation hybrids resembled, in the characteristic being studied, one pure variety; a quarter resembled the other pure variety; and one half followed, in both looks and breeding characteristics, the first-generation hybrid.

Mendel did not state that the factors governing inheritance, and which he postulated as coming together and separating, were material particles. "For all that we know to the contrary," Thomas Hunt Morgan was to say more than fifty years later, "the good abbot may have had something more spiritual or mystical in mind. Nevertheless, whatever it is that meets and separates, whether spiritual or material, the *process* is in the nature of a physical event."

It was, moreover, a process that appeared to hammer the final nail into the coffin of heavenly direction. All that was now left to God was mutation, that method by which an organism failed to reproduce itself accurately, a method about which little was known during the first years of the century.

Mendel's first conclusions were confirmed by many subsequent experiments and were found to be correct for a large number of characteristics. Differences from the expected ratios were very slight. So much so that it has been suggested more than once that Mendel or some of his helpers tended to record the results expected, a suspicion for which no supporting evidence has been produced. And even had well-wishers metaphorically kept a finger on the balance, Mendelian inheritance has been shown over the years to operate in virtually all forms of life.

"I know that the results I obtained were not easily compatible with our contemporary knowledge," Mendel wrote to the Swiss botanist Karl Wilhelm von Nägeli, "and that under the circumstances publication of one such isolated experiment was doubly dangerous; dangerous for the experimenter and for the cause he represented. Thus I made every effort to verify, with other plants, the results obtained from *Pisum.* A number of hybridisations undertaken in 1863 and 1864 convinced me of the difficulty of finding plants suitable for an extended series of experiments, and that under unfavourable circumstances years might elapse without my obtaining the desired information."

Nägeli, one of the professionals who did not take the amateur Mendel too seriously, could well have been more interested, since he had already accepted the transmutation of species by the time that *The Origin* was published. "External reasons from comparison of floras of successive geological periods, and internal reasons from the physiological and morphological laws of development and from the variability of species," he had written in 1859, "leave little doubt that species have arisen one from another."

Unable to arouse interest elsewhere, Mendel described his work to the local natural history society in the hope of persuading others to follow his lead. He spoke on February 8 and March 8, 1865, to audiences of about forty. There was no discussion, and as far as is known, no one took up the challenge.

But he was asked to publish his paper, and there thus appeared in the *Transactions of the Brünn Natural History Society* for 1866 the paper that was in its own way as significant as Darwin's *The Origin of Species.* Included in it were Mendel's two laws. The first, the Law of Segregation, stated that the two paired units of heredity later segregated into each of the two new cells which were subsequently formed. The second law, that of Independent Assortment, governed the chance distribution to the new cells of the units of heredity in the old cells, the distribution of the units in one pair of cells having no influence on that of the units in the second pair. This independent assortment was in fact qualified by the results of linkage—the association of two units of heredity on one chromosome, an association that tended to make them pass on from one generation to the next as a single unit. But this process was only discovered in the 1900s and was not even suspected in Mendel's day.

Mendel himself seems to have been well aware of the possibilities he had opened up, and after publication of his paper hoped to expand his experiments by studying the *Hieracia,* or hawkweed. However, he did not get very far, for reasons that he humbly explained to Nägeli. "Lack of time is chiefly to blame for this," he wrote, "and I am no longer fit for botanical field trips, for heaven has blessed me with an excess of avoirdupois, which becomes very noticeable during long travels afoot, and, as a consequence of the law of general gravitation, especially when climbing mountains. . . ."

Although 120 copies of the Society's *Transactions* were sent to foreign learned societies, and although Mendel sent many of his own forty offprints to those he felt would be interested, the paper sank with only little trace for more than a third of a century. The offprint sent to the botanist Professor Anton Joseph Kerner von Marilaun of Innsbruck was found after Kerner's death in 1898 but with its pages uncut. However, Wilhelm Olbers Focke, a German hybridizer, mentioned the experiments no less than fifteen times in one paper, George Romanes listed the paper in an article on hybridism in the *Encyclopaedia Britannica*, and there are other, if obscure, mentions in the literature. Mendel was more unappreciated than unknown.

One reason was no doubt the belief that the head of a monastery could be no more than a scientific amateur, a feeling possibly compounded by the anticlericalism of the times. Another factor, still present forty years later, was the belief that natural history was the field for observation rather than for statistics. There was also another, more general, but no less important factor: the fact that heredity tended to be seen during the last third of the nineteenth century mainly in the light of evolutionary theory. "The great ideas of the struggle for existence, the survival of the fittest, and the descent of men, took the centre of the stage," Darlington has pointed out. "And in the orchestra one heard the great theme of 'ontogeny repeats phylogeny' [development during an individual's life repeats evolutionary history], beating out its stately and compelling rhythm. Who then should notice the modest figure of heredity in the background quietly throwing the shuttle of life? To naturalists and to sociologists alike she appeared merely as a part of the decorative backcloth for the heroic realities in whose actions the drama of life and thought seemed to be working itself out."

The situation was dramatically changed in 1900 when three men quite independently read Mendel's previously ignored paper, realized its importance, and wrote their own papers bringing the Austrian monk from obscurity to fame. The first was De Vries, who came upon Mendel's paper in a bibliography, read it, saw the significance of its conclusions, and in a paper on "The Law of Segregation of Hybrids" ended with the words: "From these and numerous other experiments I drew the conclusion that the law of segregation of hybrids as discovered by Mendel for peas finds very general application in the plant kingdom and that it has a basic significance for the study of the units of which the species character is composed."

However, De Vries had earlier sent a shortened version of his paper to the *Comptes Rendus* [*Reports of Proceedings*] of the French Académie des Sciences. It had been read by Carl Franz Joseph Erich Correns, a German botanist who lost no time in repeating Mendel's experiments with other plants and who described them in the same issue of the German journal that printed De Vries's main paper. Correns's paper—"G. Mendel's Law Concerning the Behaviour of Progeny of Varietal Hybrids"—stated that he had found Mendel's laws to apply to various kinds of maize but added a warning that these laws could not be applied universally.

Before the year was out, Erich Tschermak-Seysenegg, an Austrian, had also reported his own success in repeating Mendel's experiments. The following year, Correns suggested that Mendel's laws applied to animals as well as to plants. Within twelve months, Lucien Cuénot reported that experiments with mice showed that their heredity followed these laws and Bateson showed that they also applied to fowls.

Thus within two years it had been demonstrated that inheritance was particulate—in other words, due to the handing on by the cells of specific units or factors that might be concealed for one or more generations but that could reappear at any time for no apparent reason. From the rediscovery of Mendel's work, it was appreciated by most workers in the field that he had only begun to answer the riddle. Indeed, in one way he had added others. "Our problem," Darlington has written of genetics after Mendel, "is less to explain change, which was Darwin's problem, than to account for stability, which, we may recall, was Blyth's problem [in Darwin's day]. The materials for selection are continually present, concealed and stored. They are made visible and flagrantly exposed to selection by the processes of chromosome recombination which Weismann foretold. Selection then leads to change or stability as occasion demands." Yet however complicated the complete answer to the riddle of heredity was to be, Mendel had laid one ghost that had continually worried Darwin. For variations did not, as it were, level themselves out of existence by a process of blending. Short crossed with tall did not simply produce plants of intermediate height. Mendel's revelation that the units passed on from one generation to the next remained constant and unchanged in the descendants, even though their presence remained concealed, removed the problem with which Fleeming Jenkin had been able to belabor Darwin.

Thus Mendel gave a rather old-fashioned look to Galton's belief that every individual was influenced, to greater or lesser degree, by all his ancestors, a quarter of his characteristics coming from each parent, one-sixteenth from each grandparent, and so on. According to Galton's theory, no ancestor could reappear in a pure form in any descendant; according to Mendel, any characteristic could lie dormant for any number of generations before reappearing unadulterated. This of course had widespread implications, not only for scientists but for agriculturalists and farmers, and a commonsense step was taken in 1903 when the American Breeders' Association was formed to bring scientists and breeders together so that "each may get the point of view of the other and that each appreciate the problem of the other."

Darwin could have become acquainted with Mendel's results some sixteen years before his death, and there has often been speculation on how this might have affected his later thoughts. It seems unlikely that the influence would have been very great. Even toward the mathematics of Francis Galton, a man with whom he usually wished to agree, Darwin turned a somewhat questioning eye and an instinctive nonunderstanding of mathematics. The relevance of Mendel could easily have escaped him.

Twenty years after Darwin's death, Galton, Weldon and Pearson were propounding their views that mathematics lay at the root of evolutionary understanding. With the rediscovery of Mendel's work, it might have seemed that the new century had opened with the prospect of a combined attack by biologists and evolutionists on the problems still confronting them. The reverse was to be the case. Mendel's work could be interpreted in two ways: to support the view that evolution operated by a series of small variations accumulating over the generations, as Darwin had forecast, or that it operated through the saltations or major jumps that Huxley had not ruled out in his first letter to Darwin after publication of *The Origin.* The two views were not mutually exclusive. Many biologists appear to have recognized this, and the commonsense judgment might well have predominated but for the personalities of Weldon and Bateson, who sharpened their knives with the help of Mendel's paper and from the first year of the twentieth century waged an increasingly bitter battle that was ended only in 1906 by Weldon's premature death at the age of forty-six.

This battle between the biometricians and the biologists, begun in the 1890s and carried on after Weldon's death by Bateson against Weldon's survivor Karl Pearson, was of considerable significance. No one could by this time challenge Darwin's position as the man who had convincingly shown the existence of evolution to be beyond all reasonable doubt. But how correct was the importance he gave to natural selection? How right had he been to play down the effect of "jumps"? How relevant would his ideas be in the years ahead?

Despite his distaste for the statistical approach, Bateson had increasingly seen the need for data such as Mendel had produced. A paper he read to the Royal Horticultural Society in 1899, "Hybridisation and Cross-Breeding as a Method of Scientific Investigation," revealed that he saw the need for information Mendel had already, in fact, provided. "What we first require is to know," he said, "what happens when a variety is crossed with its *nearest allies.* If the result is to have a scientific value, it is almost absolutely necessary that the offspring of such crossing should then be examined *statistically.* It must be recorded how many of the offspring resembled each parent and how many showed characters intermediate between those of the parents. If the parents differ in several characters, the offspring must be examined statistically, and marshalled, as it is called, in respect of each of those characters separately."

This, of course, was almost exactly what Mendel had done. J. B. S. Haldane, who was to succeed Karl Pearson as Britain's leading biometrician, was later to claim: "If the Proceedings of the Brünn Natural History Society had been a little rarer I suppose that Bateson would now be lying in Westminster Abbey"; and *The Times*, reviewing Bateson's achievements after his death, commented that "had [Mendel's] discovery been delayed a few years the world would now be speaking of Bateson's Law instead of Mendel's."

Bateson first heard of Mendel's work when on May 8, 1900, while traveling from Cambridge to London to read his paper on "Problems of Heredity as a Subject for Horticultural Investigation" to the Royal Horticultural Society, he read the De Vries account that had been published the previous month. So impressed was he that he incorporated the information into the Horticultural Society lecture. "These experiments of Mendel's," he said, "were carried out on a large scale, his account of them is excellent and complete, and the principles which he was able to deduce from them will certainly play a conspicuous part in all future discussions of evolutionary problems."

Once the importance of Mendel's work began to emerge, both Bateson and Weldon tried to invoke it to support their own attitudes and beliefs. To Bateson, particulate inheritance reinforced the case for inheritance by "jumps" to which Darwin had been so opposed. So much so that Bateson unnecessarily stretched his case with not too deep a regard for the facts of history. "With the views of Darwin which at that time were coming into prominence," he wrote, "Mendel did not find himself in full agreement, and he embarked on his experiments with peas." Mendel had, in fact, begun his experiments in 1857, and all the evidence pointed to his having ended them in complete ignorance of the theory that Darwin had by this time shared only with Lyell and Hooker. This backhander at Darwin was later castigated by Ronald Aylmer Fisher—who in 1918 reconciled the biometric and Mendelian approaches to heredity—as a "misrepresentation," a view he later watered down to "misleading."

To Weldon, Mendelism seriously threatened the continuity in

variation that lay at the heart of the Biometrical School's beliefs. A priority was therefore his belittlement of Mendel's work, a task made easier by the recent foundation of *Biometrika: A Journal for the Statistical Study of Biological Problems*, edited, in consultation with Francis Galton, by W. F. R. Weldon, Karl Pearson and Charles B. Davenport. An editorial on page one of the first issue had outlined precisely what the biometricians saw as their task. "The starting point of Darwin's theory of evolution," it said, "is precisely the existence of those differences between individual members of a race or species which morphologists for the most part rightly neglect. The first condition necessary, in order that any process of Natural Selection may begin among a race, or species, is the existence of differences among its members; and the first step in an enquiry into the possible effect of a selective process upon any character of a race must be an estimate of the frequency with which individuals, exhibiting any given degree of abnormality with respect to that character, occur. The unit, with which such an enquiry must deal, is not an individual but a race, or a statistically representative sample of a race; and the result must take the form of a numerical statement, showing the relative frequency with which the various kinds of individuals composing the race occur."

This was not, of course, at all the way in which Mendel had approached matters, and in *Biometrika*, as well as elsewhere, Weldon attacked Mendel on the ground that the characters he had chosen for his experiments could not be expressed in quantitatively definite terms. Each of the terms "green" and "yellow," for instance, included "a considerable range of recognisably different colours, and every known race of peas produces seeds whose cotyledons vary in colour," he wrote. "All that can be inferred from Mendel's statement, therefore, is, that the range of variation in cotyledon colour, which some of his races exhibited, fall entirely within the range of colours called 'green,' while that of other races fell entirely within the range of colours called 'yellow.' "

This line of attack, if not beyond Bateson's view of what was reasonable biological argument, was sufficient to arouse his ire. The outcome was *Mendel's Principles of Heredity: A Defence*, published in 1902 after a report on their latest experiments to the Evolution Committee by Bateson and his assistant, Miss Edith Rebecca Saunders. Neither publication added much to the fundamental argument, although the report to the Committee extended the fields in which Mendel's laws could be seen to apply. In *Mendel's Principles*, however, Bateson began by asserting: "In the Study of Evolution, progress had well-nigh stopped." He then went over to an attack on his opponents that finally ruled out any compromise, personal or, more unfortunately, scientific. "We have been told of late, more than once," he wrote, "that Biology must become an *exact* science. The same is my own fervent hope. But exactness is not always attainable by numerical precision: there have been students of Nature, untrained in statistical nicety, whose instinct for truth yet saved them from perverse inference, from slovenly argument, and from misuse of authorities, reiterated and grotesque."

But this was merely Bateson warming up. After stating that Weldon had omitted the most novel thing in Mendel's paper and poured on it an "undigested mass of miscellaneous 'facts,'" he continued: "To find a parallel for such treatment of a great theme in biology we must go back to those writings of the orthodox which followed the appearance of the 'Origin of Species.'" And of Weldon's statement that he wanted merely to draw attention to a series of facts that suggested fruitful lines of inquiry, Bateson commented: "In this purpose I venture to assist him, for I am disposed to think that unaided he is—to borrow Horace Walpole's phrase —about as likely to light a fire with a wet dish-clout as to kindle interest in Mendel's discoveries by his tempered appreciation." Bateson, it has been said, "actually prepared two even stronger statements for his preface, but Cambridge University Press suggested they be dropped. They were, but Bateson later said he 'rather liked these two bits!'"

One cannot help feeling, wrote G. Udny Yule, the statistician, "that [Bateson's] speculations would have had more value had he kept his emotions under better control; the style and method of the religious revivalist are ill-suited to scientific controversy. It is difficult to speak with patience either of the turgid and bombastic preface to 'Mendel's Principles,' with its reference to Scribes and Pharisees, and its Carlylean inversions of sentence, or of the grossly and gratuitously offensive reply to Professor Weldon and the almost equally offensive adulation of Mr. Galton and Professor Pearson. A writer who indulges himself in displays of this kind loses his right to be treated either as an impartial critic or as a sober speculator." In private, Bateson cast doubt not only on his opponents' ability but their integrity, telling C. C. Hurst that he found it "impossible . . . to believe that they [the biometricians] have made any honest attempt to face the facts"; and he doubted whether they were "acting in good faith as genuine seekers for truth. So I would let them alone. I may *have* to answer Pearson some day in their journal, but I shall not send facts to them." Speaking from the other side, Pearson, it has been said, tended to use "the ugliest means possible" in pointing out errors, and to hit offenders "over the head with a club."

Weldon, moreover, was soon scientifically taking Bateson to task. Bateson and Miss Saunders had crossed the hairy and non-hairy *Lychnis vespertina* (white campion, a flower of the Pink family) and drawn numerous conclusions from the results. But, Weldon pointed out in *Biometrika*, they had conspicuously failed to define the characteristics of the offspring. How hairy, in fact, was hairy? "It is deeply to be regretted," he went on, "that so many interesting experiments, involving so much time and labour, should be recorded in a form which makes it impossible to understand the results actually obtained, and so gives rise to misconceptions both in the minds of the recorders and in others . . . the accumulation of records, in which results are massed together in ill-defined categories of variable and uncertain extent, can only result in harm."

Bateson was unable to reply in *Biometrika*, since its editors had already refused to publish his reply to Weldon on another controversy. On that occasion he had taken an unusual, if not unique, step: he had had his views privately printed—but in the same format as *Biometrika*. This time he attempted to reply in *Nature*. His letter was returned with the firm statement that *Nature* was not willing to continue the discussion.

The argument rumbled on, and when Bateson became president of the British Association's Zoology Section in 1904, it seemed inevitable that a major confrontation would take place at the Association's annual meeting at Cambridge. Bateson's presidential address to the Section set the scene for what could be described as nothing less than a direct attack on the biometricians: "the imposing Correlation Table into which the biometrical Procrustes fits his arrays of unanalysed data is still no substitute for the common sieve of a trained judgment," he declaimed, thus apparently undercutting in a single sentence any trained judgment that his opponents might be able to muster. He was followed in the same vein by Miss Saunders and others who had been working with him in Cambridge.

After an adjournment for lunch, the Section reassembled in the large lecture hall of the new geological building. The room was packed, with members even sitting on the windowsills—much as they had gathered to watch the Huxley-Wilberforce confrontation in Oxford more than forty years previously. Weldon spoke first, passionately and eloquently. Bateson replied, with equal passion and eloquence. There were other speakers. Then Karl Pearson rose. There should be, he suggested, a truce in the great argument for three years. Then the protagonists could meet again, with a better chance of resolving their differences. "On Pearson resuming his seat, the Chairman, the Rev. T. R. Stebbing, a mild and benevolent looking little figure for a great carcinologist, rose to conclude the discussion," R. C. Punnett has written. "In a preamble he deplored the feelings that had been aroused, and assured us that as a man of peace such controversy was little to his taste. We all began fidgeting at what promised to become a tame conclusion to so spirited a meeting, especially when he came to deal with Pearson's suggestion of a truce. But we need not have been anxious, for the Rev. Mr. Stebbing had in him the makings of a first-rate impresario. 'You have all heard,' said he, 'what Professor Pearson has suggested' (pause), and then with a sudden rise of voice, 'But what I say is let them fight it out.' "

It was, for practical purposes, a tactical triumph for Bateson, who from now on was better able to promote evolution by discontinuous "jumps." Furthermore, from 1904 on his standing was consolidated, and his garden at Grantchester, outside Cambridge, began to develop as a center for genetic work and experiment that attracted visitors from all over the world. Late in the year he visited Brno in an attempt to track down Mendel's working papers. He was unsuccessful, but there was no doubt about his rising influence, and in 1908 he at last gained the Chair of Biology in Cambridge. His inaugural lecture was on "The Methods and Scope of Genetics" in which he gave his much-quoted injunction: "Treasure your exceptions! When there are none," he went on, "the work gets so dull that no one dares to carry it further. Keep them always uncovered and in sight. Exceptions are like the rough brickwork of a growing building which tells that there is more to come and shows where the next construction is to be." In this he strikingly followed Darwin, of whom his son Francis has written: "There was one quality of mind which seemed to be of special and extreme advantage in leading him to make discoveries. It was the power of never letting exceptions pass unnoticed. Everybody notices a fact as an exception when it is striking or frequent, but he had a special instinct for arresting an exception. A point apparently slight and unconnected with his present work is passed over by many a man almost unconsciously with some half-considered explanation, which is in fact no explanation. It was just these things that he seized on to make a start from."

Almost half a century later, Bateson was adopting the same principle in his efforts to explain evolution by Darwin's abominated saltations. With Weldon gone in 1906, he carried on the fight with Pearson and the rest of the biometricians. Not until 1921 did he admit that they might have a case, if a poor one. And only in the 1920s did he admit that variations transmitted from one generation to the next could be correlated with the chromosomes, whether the variations were transmitted continuously or intermittently. He believed that inheritance and variation were both due to cell division, but that chromosomes were a secondary, if conspicuous, manifestation of the process. One could not, therefore, expect them to be the "sole effective instruments in heredity." What he demanded in support of a theory was neither convenience nor expectation but evidence; and at the start of the twentieth century, evidence for the chromosome theory was appearing only slowly.

The existence and segregation of chromosomes had, of course, been known long before the rediscovery of Mendel's work. But it was the strength of their link with inheritance, and thus with evolution, that continued under discussion. In 1901 the American zoologist Clarence E. McClung postulated that the so-called accessory chromosome, the sex-determining X chromosome, was male-determining—the first suggestion that a particular characteristic was linked to a particular chromosome. Walter S. Sutton concluded a paper on the chromosomes of the grasshopper *Brachystola magna* with the words: "I may finally call attention to the probability that the association of paternal and maternal chromosomes in pairs and their subsequent separation during the reducing division . . . may constitute the physical basis of the Mendelian law of heredity."

Yet even then, two years after the rediscovery of Mendel's experiments, extraordinarily little was known about the unit of heredity itself. Bateson made this dramatically clear when he spoke at the Third International Conference on Genetics. "But ever in our thoughts the question rings, what *are* these units the presence or absence of which in their orderly distributions decide so many and perhaps all of the attributes or faculties of each creature before it is launched into separate existence?" he asked. "Colour, shape, habit, power of resistance to disease, and many another property that might be named, have one by one been analyzed and shown to be alike in the laws of their transmission, owing their excitation or extinction to . . . such units or factors. Upon them the success or failure of every living thing depends. How the pack is shuffled and dealt we begin to perceive: but what are they—the cards? Wild and inscrutable the question sounds, but genetic research may answer it yet."

Mendel with his peas and beans had been followed by Cuénot with his mice and Bateson with his fowls. As well as these leaders, there were other biologists who had produced their own confirmatory results, and during the first years of the twentieth century it became more and more likely that Mendel's basic principles of segregation and combination could be applied across the whole spectrum of living things, even up to and including man.

Whether evolution was mainly dependent on Darwin's accumulation of innumerable small changes or on larger "jumps," or saltations, was still in dispute. Opinions were, and continued to be, strongly held. "Whoever studies the distinctions of geographical varieties closely and extensively," it was written in 1903, "will smile at the conception of the origin of species *per saltum*." Yet ten years later, Bateson was still averring in *Problems of Genetics*: "The transformation of masses of population by imperceptible steps guided by selection, is, as most of us now see, so inapplicable to the facts, whether of variation or of specificity, that we can only marvel both at the want of penetration displayed by the advocates of such a proposition, and at the forensic skill by which it was made to appear acceptable even for a time."

Inheritance was without much doubt controlled by particulate factors, soon being described as genes. But genes themselves were still regarded with suspicion by some biologists, since there was no more hard evidence of their existence than there was of the protons and electrons that, according to Ernest Rutherford, made up that building brick of matter men knew as the atom. Only a few years previously, the atom had been what Rutherford had called "a nice hard fellow, red or gray in colour according to taste"; by now it was a miniature solar system of innumerable particles, and suspected of containing more unsolved mysteries. A comparable transformation was soon to affect the gene, although while Rutherford had changed a simple concept into a complicated one, geneticists were to change a nebulous concept into the picture of a physical entity.

Further support for the reality of inheritance based on Mendel's laws soon came from the medical profession, and came, moreover, in a way that confirmed them to be as applicable to the human race as to peas or wheat. Since the early days of *The Origin*, the sticking point with many scientists, as with many laymen, had been the problem of including man in the evolutionary program. But as far back as 1873 an American, Dr. Joseph G. Richardson, had suggested to a medical class at the University of Pennsylvania that natural selection might be allowed to limit the spread of certain diseases in which it was the tendency toward them rather than the disease itself that was inherited. "As race or family peculiarities descend from parent to child," he said according to one report, "so may *microscopic peculiarities* of formation. For example, congenital smallness of the arteries supplying blood to the feet may be the direct cause of senile gangrene, or a predisposition to consumption might be discovered in an abnormal distension of the bronchial arteries. It will not be out of place to state that the author is by no means an adherent of Darwinism in natural science; but for that very reason his testimony as to its value in the science with which he is best acquainted will have all the more weight."

Mendelism threw further light on the way in which human characteristics might be inherited, and in *Mendel's Principles of Heredity*, Bateson explained how the mating of first cousins could enable a rare recessive factor to explain the disease of alkaptonuria, a congenital disorder of metabolism in which the patient's urine turns a dark brown. Man was apparently at the mercy of the same laws that governed the fortunes of the good Abbot's peas.

This was also noted by the British doctor Archibald E. Garrod. "At that time," a friend of his has said, "nearly all diseases were thought to be due to infective agents, and alkaptonuria was supposed to be caused by an organism in the intestines which disturbed the metabolism of tyrosine, and was thus responsible for the excretion of homogentisic acid. One afternoon while walking home from the Hospital thinking about these problems, it suddenly occurred to him that alkaptonuria might be due to a chemical error on the part of the body, which might be present throughout life. The proof of this hypothesis was unexpectedly easy as the mother of one of his alkaptonuric patients was pregnant."

The new child was also an alkaptonuric, the parents were first cousins, and only the siblings were affected—one out of every four —facts that provided the first proof of Mendelian inheritance in man. The cause, Garrod suggested, was a gene defect that resulted in inactivity of a specific enzyme that would normally take a step in a sequence of chemical reactions. "If any one step in the process fails, the intermediate product in being at the point of arrest will escape further change, just as when the film of a biograph is 'brought to a standstill the moving figures are left foot in air.' " Garrod, later recognized as the originator of biochemical genetics, found that albinism, cystinuria and a handful of other diseases were caused by similar "inborn errors of metabolism," as he called them.

Bateson, still reluctant to believe in the physical existence of genes—much as Ernst Mach and Wilhelm Ostwald had been unwilling to believe in the physical existence of atoms as late as the end of the nineteenth century—continued seeking more evidence. The first to be uncovered appeared merely to confuse the situation. Working with his young assistant Punnett on sweet peas, Bateson found that two Mendelian factors were connected in some unknown way. Crossing produced some plants with purple flowers and some with red; it also produced plants with long pollen and those with round pollen, the purple color and the long pollen being the result of the Mendelian factors that were dominant. But these two dominant factors were transmitted together more frequently than chance would have allowed. Bateson called this "coupling," on the grounds that the factors governing certain characteristics appeared to hold together as though coupled and were therefore likely to be passed on together to future generations. But why this was so remained entirely unknown until "linkage" provided the answer.

The work that followed the rediscovery of Mendel's experiments quickly gave rise to a new vocabulary, which is still growing. Mendel had used the word *"Merkmal"* ("mark," "characteristic") throughout his paper to describe the determinants of the different characteristics such as tallness or shortness produced in his experiments. The first report to the Evolution Committee of the Royal Society in 1902 described Mendelian factors as "physiological units of as yet unknown nature," and Bateson initially used the word "factor." Then, on April 18, 1905, he wrote to Adam Sedgwick, remarking that there was need for a specific name for the study of heredity. "No single word in common use quite gives this meaning," he went on. "Such a word is badly wanted, and if it were desirable to coin one, 'Genetics' might do."

The following year, reviewing J. P. Lotsy's "Lectures on the Theories of Descent with Special Regard to the Botanical Aspect of the Question Delivered at the Free University in Leiden," in *Nature*, he recommended that the new branch of science should be named. "Studies in 'Experimental Evolution' or in the 'Theory of Descent' strike a wrong note," he said, "for, theory apart, the physiology of heredity and variation is a definite branch of science, and if we knew nothing of evolution that science would still exist. To avoid further periphrasis, then, let us say genetics."

In 1909 Wilhelm Johannsen began to use the word "gene" for the unit of heredity, itself a derivative from Darwin's pangenesis and De Vries's pangen, which sprang from it. Earlier, in 1902, Bateson and Saunders had produced the word "allele" to describe characters that are alternative to one another in Mendelian inheritance. Later, in 1912, Morgan and Cattell used "crossing over" to describe the occurrence of new combinations of linked characters, while Johannsen introduced "genotype" to describe the entire genetic constitution of an organism, and "phenotype" to describe the sum total of an organism's characteristics.

As genetics was being built up into a new branch of science during the early years of the twentieth century, an entirely new concept not only of evolution but of life itself was seriously put forward by Svante August Arrhenius, the Swedish chemist who in 1903 had been awarded the Nobel Prize for his theory of the connection between chemical affinity and electrical conductivity. Having added to chemical knowledge, Arrhenius turned to the larger mysteries, and in *Worlds in the Making*, published in 1908, he proposed that life had reached earth in the form of living spores from other parts of the universe. The idea was not entirely new. A few years after Pasteur had shown that spontaneous generation of life did not appear to take place on earth, Sir William Thomson had suggested, in an address to the British Association in 1871, that the first living organisms might have reached the earth in a meteorite. "The hypothesis that [some] life [has actually] originated on this Earth through moss-grown fragments from the ruins of another world may seem wild and visionary," he said; "all I maintain is that it is not unscientific [and cannot rightly be said to be improbable]". Scientific or not, it was given little respect by

Huxley, who asked Hooker: "What do you think of Thomson's 'creation by cockshy'—God Almighty sitting like an idle boy at the seaside and shying aerolites (with germs), mostly missing, but sometimes hitting a planet!" Three years later Hermann Helmholtz, the German physiologist and physicist, had also suggested that this was possible.

But Arrhenius went further, devoting the entire last chapter of his book to the spreading of life through the universe by a process he christened panspermia. The theory was not given much credence but could not be entirely ignored and was to be revived more than half a century later when some of the initial objections had been removed by the early explorations of space.

Arrhenius's panspermia was not taken too seriously. But with the believers in evolution trying in the 1900s to incorporate the implications of Mendelism, although uncertain how best to do it, their world remained in a state of somewhat confused change when the centenary of Darwin's birth and the fiftieth anniversary of *The Origin*'s publication arrived in 1909. Even three years after the celebrations, Karl Pearson, giving the Cavendish Lecture on "Darwinism, Medical Progress and Eugenics," was forced to admit somewhat apologetically: "I belong to a school which still believes that Darwin taught us the truth," and to add: "I think it is rather the fashion nowadays to dismiss its views, not by meeting its arguments, but by describing it as 'mid-Victorian.'"

In Cambridge, the celebrations in 1909 included an impressive three-day program with dinners, luncheons, awards of honorary degrees and throwing open to visitors the rooms Darwin had occupied eighty years previously. The Darwin celebrations yielded more than one story that, if possibly apocryphal, had an air of truth. John Lubbock, by now Lord Avebury, recalled at the Linnean Society how one of Darwin's friends, asking after his health, was told by the gardener that he had been ill. "I often wish he had something to do," the man went on. "He moons about in the garden, and I have seen him stand doing nothing before a flower for ten minutes at a time. If he only had something to do I really believe he would be better." And it was possibly the same gardener who was reported as saying to his master: "That might be alright in a book, sir, but it wouldn't be much good in the potting shed."

In the United States, the American Philosophical Society fittingly celebrated the anniversaries and Columbia University organized a series of public lectures, in one of which John Dewey emphasized the more general, nonbiological, implications of Darwin's work. "In laying hands upon the sacred ark of absolute permanency," he said, "in treating the forms that had been regarded as types of fixity and perfection as originating and passing away, the 'Origin of Species' introduced a mode of thinking that in the end was bound to transform the logic of knowledge, and hence the treatment of morals, politics, and religion."

In London, the main qualifying note was struck by *The Times*, whose leading article on February 12, following the announcement of the celebrations coming in the summer, was questioning enough to bring a long critical letter from the zoologist Sir Ray Lankester, a passionate Darwin supporter and a man who was, as the *Dictionary of National Biography* puts it, "a man of strong feelings which he did not hesitate to express." *The Times* had begun by noting: "The popular view still is that Darwin discovered, or perhaps invented, evolution," and said of *The Origin* that "as usually happens in such cases, the book became a sort of badge or trophy in the name of which the combatants belaboured one another with such hearty good will that they had little time to inquire precisely what it contained." The article went on to point out that while the physicists had traced evolution in the nonliving world and biologists had done the same in the world of living organisms, "in neither of these august evolutionary processions do we find any explanation of the evolution of the living from the non-living." As for the "jumps" of De Vries, "we seem to be brought once more perilously near to the dreaded special act of creation," while recent speculations about them "have no positive value, but . . . are negatively significant as showing that the Darwinian hypothesis is losing its hold upon men's minds."

Sir Ray protested, with some justification, that this leading article, an important one in an important place, gave a misleading impression of current informed opinion. Nevertheless, compared with the euphoria of the Cambridge celebrations, it did strike the note of caution needed as the biometricians and the geneticists continued to question the methods by which Darwinian evolution took place.

There was one other point, again of caution rather than criticism, raised in *The Times Literary Supplement*. Making one of its rare excursions outside pure literary criticism, the journal published a leading article under the heading "Literature and Science" that was to be echoed half a century later by C. P. Snow's strictures on the growth of the two cultures. "It would have seemed strange to Virgil, stranger still to Dante," it began, "to suppose that there could be any antagonism or incompatability between the scientific and the artistic mind." It then quoted the sentences from Darwin's autobiography in which he stated: "But now for many years I cannot endure to read a line of poetry: I have tried lately to read Shakespeare, and found it so intolerably dull that it nauseated me. I have also almost lost any taste for pictures or music."

Yet science and art need not be in conflict, the article continued. When Darwin had described his work as grinding out general laws, it could just as well be described as the ability "to take the sudden imaginative leap, seizing the exact moment which justifies it, from the particular to the general." And it reached a conclusion that reflects, if obliquely, on Darwin's ability to remain a living force, saying of art and science, "They have diverged, it appears, so far that they seem doomed to regard each other to the end of the chapter as in essence mutually exclusive. Fragments may float from one side of the gap to the other, but their faces are set in opposing directions. We cannot change the directions, but possibly we may learn to refuse the choice as yet imposed upon us, of following one and disregarding the other. At any rate, if there is any hope of a union and a reconciliation, it must lie in the spread of the intellectual temper which characterised the most far-reaching, it may be, of all the great spirits who first saw the light in that wonderful year, now a century past."

Darwin's stroke of imaginative genius had left plenty of problems, and Mendel had compounded rather than removed them. Within less than a decade, many were to be solved in Columbia University by Thomas Hunt Morgan.

12

The Fly Room

BETWEEN 1907 and 1917 man's knowledge of the mechanism of heredity was transformed by Thomas Hunt Morgan. A critic of much that was in *The Origin*, he provided the material that was eventually used to reconcile the attitude of the biometricians and that of their opponents. Without Morgan there might well have been no neo-Darwinism that successfully combined the theory of natural selection with the discoveries of Mendelian genetics.

An embryologist at Bryn Mawr College, Pennsylvania, at the turn of the century, Morgan became fully converted to the study of heredity and its impact on evolution during a visit to De Vries in Amsterdam a few years later. "No one can see his experimental garden, as I have had the opportunity of doing," he wrote, "without being greatly impressed, for here on all sides are new species that have suddenly appeared, fully equipped, from a known original parent form, living now side by side with its group of descendants."

So impressed was Morgan with what he had seen that within a few years he felt that "we are beginning to see the process of evolution in a new light." He went on:

> Nature makes new species outright. Amongst these new species there will be some that manage to find a place where they may continue to exist. How well they are suited to such places will be shown, in one respect, by the number of individuals they can bring to maturity. Some of the new forms may be well adapted to certain localities

and will flourish there; others may eke out a precarious existence, because they do not find a place to which they are well suited, and cannot better adapt themselves to the conditions under which they live; and there will be others that can find no place at all in which they can develop, and will be unable even to make a start. From this point of view the process of evolution appears in a more kindly light than when we imagine that success is only attained through the destruction of all rivals. The process appears not so much the result of the destruction of vast numbers of individuals, for the poorly adapted will not be able to make even a beginning. Evolution is not a war of all against all, but it is largely a creation of new types for the unoccupied, or poorly occupied places in nature.

When in 1904 Morgan joined Columbia University as professor of experimental zoology he was still a convinced "saltationist" and so he remained for a number of years. Like Bateson, he was skeptical of continuous variation, but unlike Bateson he had, at the start, little faith in Mendelism, writing sarcastically as late as 1909 that "in the modern interpretation of Mendelism, facts are being transferred into factors at a rapid rate." The point seems to have been, wrote Alfred H. Sturtevant, one of his pupils who became a distinguished collaborator, "that he felt the Mendelian factors to be arbitrary inventions made up to fit the facts, with no independent evidence for their existence and not capable of experimental demonstration." Thus it is ironic that it was Morgan who was eventually to provide so much of the evidence, and that the citation of his Nobel Prize for Physiology and Medicine in 1933 should read: "for his discoveries concerning the function of the chromosome in the transmission of heredity."

With his skepticism about Mendelian factors, it was natural that Morgan should concentrate his work on a search for mutations, for changes in the factors that governed transmission of characteristics from one generation to the next, which took place for reasons that were not understood. First he used mice, then rats. But it was only after he had chosen for study *Drosophila melanogaster* that the way ahead began to open up. Also known as the vinegar fly—Morgan's favorite name—the fruit fly, the pomace fly and the banana fly, *Drosophila* had many advantages as a tool for experimental genetics. It could be bred by the thousand in milk bottles. It was easy to find, needed little space, cost little and lived on simple food. But there were two other advantages even more important. A *Drosophila* egg hatched, turned into an adult, and was itself producing more eggs within ten days. And it had only four chromosomes, which made Morgan's work easier than it would otherwise have been.

Not that ease would have attracted Morgan. "I once heard him say, semi-seriously," a colleague wrote, "that the only book worth writing was one in a field that was developing so rapidly that the book would soon be out of date." He was a hard-headed man, rather like Bateson, always calling for evidence, who "took no stock in the pseudophilosophical mumbo jumbo rampant among many biologists even in the era immediately following Darwin, and would not let himself be over-awed by the air of mystery surrounding such subjects as regeneration, embryology, heredity and evolution." He thought that experience had shown, he once said, "that in an undeveloped subject such as ours progress has come less from unverified speculations about living things than by putting every new idea to the test of a critical experiment on the material itself before regarding a new idea as a serious contribution to science." So he began, from about 1908, to seek evidence in the fly room, at Columbia, trying to induce mutations in generations of *Drosophila* by changing temperatures, by the use of salts, sugars, acids, alkalis, radium and X rays.

The fly room was only 16 feet by 23 feet, and into it were crowded eight desks. Morgan's was in the middle of the room, and he usually worked standing up at it, examining his flies with a jeweler's glass. Calvin B. Bridges, whom Morgan had initially hired as a bottle washer and who developed into one of America's leading geneticists, had little need for such aids; washing a discarded bottle, he spotted an unusual orange-eyed fly with his naked eye, a discovery that made Morgan aware of his potentialities in the fly room. Like most other men working under Morgan, Bridges could turn his hand to most things, and was quite willing to do so. He changed Morgan's primitive method of isolating flies through consecutive empty bottles; standardized the feeding system; constructed constant-temperature incubators; and generally brought the mechanical side of the fly room into line with the early twentieth century.

Changes were certainly necessary. For the picture of the fly room, where some of the most crucial steps toward understanding human existence were being taken, has more than a passing "string-and-sealing wax" resemblance to that room in Manchester

University where Ernest Rutherford was at the same time preparing to shake the world with his concept of the nuclear atom. To start with, the fly room had no incubators; a bookcase and a wall case rigged up with electric light bulbs and a cheap thermostat had to suffice. Identification of the flies in the bottles—"accumulated by various more or less unorthodox methods"—was by paper slips stuffed into the bottle tops and frequently consisting of Morgan's current correspondence. In a corner of the room, there was food for the flies, often a bunch of bananas, only later replaced with a mixture of agar, cornmeal, molasses and yeast.

As Sturtevant has written, the group worked as a unit. "Each carried on his own experiments but each knew exactly what the others were doing, and each new result was freely discussed. There was little attention paid to priority or to the source of new ideas or new interpretations. What mattered was to get ahead with the work. There was much to be done; there were many new ideas to be tested, and many new experimental techniques to be developed. There can have been few times and places in scientific laboratories with such an atmosphere of excitement and with such a record of sustained enthusiasm. This was due in large part to Morgan's own attitude, compounded of enthusiasm combined with a strong critical sense, generosity, open-mindedness and a remarkable sense of humor. No small part of the success of the undertaking was also due to [Edmund B.] Wilson's unfailing support and appreciation of the work—a matter of importance partly because he was head of the department."

The first crossings of *Drosophila* were made in 1907, but for more than two years nothing of particular scientific interest appeared, and one visitor recalls Morgan waving his hand toward rows of bottles and saying: "There's two years' work wasted. I've been breeding those flies for all that time and have got nothing out of it." Then, early in 1910, Morgan noted something important. In one of his *Drosophila* stock bottles there buzzed one male fly that had white eyes rather than the normal red eyes. Morgan bred the white-eyed male with a red-eyed female and noted that all the offspring were red-eyed, an indication that the white-eyed condition might be due to a Mendelian recessive factor. When first-generation offspring were crossed with each other, the resulting F_2 generation consisted of one white-eye to three red-eye, a further indication that white-eye was caused by a Mendelian recessive, since three to one was the ratio to be expected from a cross between two hybrids. However, all the white-eyes were male. It seemed clear to Morgan that this stable genetic mutation—but a mutation very different from those of De Vries—was associated in some basic way with sex inheritance.

It had been discovered as far back as 1890 that while chromosomes in an organism were normally present in pairs, there was one exception to this. A chromosome at first called the accessory chromosome and later called the X chromosome was not always matched by an identical double. While female organisms contained a pair of X chromosomes, males contained one X chromosome and another, called the Y chromosome, which was never present in a female. With the white-eyed male now available, Morgan embarked on a series of experiments that showed that the gene on the chromosome producing white-eye must in fact be present on the single X chromosome.

The white-eye became famous, and legend maintains that Morgan's wife, visited by him in the hospital where she had just given birth to a daughter, greeted him with, "Well, how is the white-eyed fly?" Morgan, it is said, replied with great enthusiasm and at some length before suddenly stopping to ask: "And how is the baby?"

It soon became clear that the gene producing white-eye must lie on the chromosome that governed sex, and this example of sex-linked inheritance, the first of the major discoveries made with *Drosophila*, was described by Morgan in July 1910. The implications were noted, and Morgan observed early in 1911 that color blindness in man "follows the same scheme as does white eyes in my flies."

However, white-eye was not the only characteristic produced by a gene that could be shown to lie on the sex-determining chromosome. Short wings, discovered on a series of flies named subimentary, was another, while by 1912 Morgan had published thirteen papers on the occurrence and behavior of some twenty-six sex-linked mutants in *Drosophila*. When flies with two different sex-linked features were interbred the two features were normally both passed on together from generation to generation. However, it was not always so. The most likely explanation was that the portion of the chromosome carrying one or more genes had crossed over and changed places with one of the *Drosophila*'s other three chromosomes. Morgan soon extrapolated from these ideas, which were confirmed experimentally, the essence of the modern chromosome theory of heredity. The nearer together the relevant genes lie on the chromosome, the greater the chance of their being inherited together; and the greater their distance on the chromosome, the greater the chance of their being separated by the process of crossing over when a part of one chromosome changes places with part of another.

From this observation, applied to the wide range of mutants that became available as breeding expanded, Morgan and his fellow workers slowly began to transform what was known about the variations on which Darwin's natural selection could operate. When they started breeding *Drosophila*, it was known only that the chromosomes played some vital part in transmitting certain features from one generation to the next. As for genes, soon to be considered the ultimate units of inheritance, lying like beads on the chromosome, they were, in 1909, being granted only a shadowy existence. "The conception of the gene as an organoid, a little body with independent life and similar attributes," wrote Johannsen, coining the word "gene" in 1909, "is no longer to be considered. Assumptions which could make such a conception necessary fail utterly." Yet by the time that Morgan's *The Mechanism of Mendelian Heredity* was published in 1915, it was possible to say that certain physical features of a fly being studied were due to genes—the word rather reluctantly adopted by Morgan—that were present at certain places on a specific chromosome.

The recording of results was made simpler by the use of a tall four-sided box known as the "Totem Pole" and designed by Bridges. Each side represented one of the *Drosophila*'s four chromosomes. A series of horizontal lines ran across each face of the box, representing different positions on the chromosomes. Onto the box there were pushed, as information increased, white enamel thumbtacks, each standing for one particular kind of mutant. The tacks were moved from right to left as the increased usefulness of the mutation became known, and were moved up or down as the place of the gene on the chromosome became more accurately located. "At a glance," Morgan was to write, "one sees how far the location of all the genes has been worked out. Some remain on the right side because they were lost before accurate data were obtained, or because they were too poor in viability or phenotype to permit accurate location."

The ability to estimate the relative positions of specific genes was soon being used to discover in further detail how heredity worked. First, it was found that certain genes tended to remain together and to be passed on together to successive generations. In other words, they did not follow Mendel's second law, that of independent assortment. The strength of this linkage between genes, which Bateson and Punnett had called reduplication, depended on their nearness to each other on the chromosome. Secondly, there was crossing over, the process in which part of a chromosome, possibly carrying a whole chain of genes, would be interchanged with part of a corresponding chromosome.

The importance of these two processes was evident to Morgan. "Both linkage and crossing-over are . . . part of the system of heredity, and must be taken into account when dealing with the theory of evolution," he wrote. "Linkage insures that certain characters will more frequently be transmitted together, while crossing-over means that characters, that first appear linked together, may be separated in the course of successive generations. The chances of such separation follow a definite numerical law, constant for specific pairs but different for different pairs of characters."

Almost a third of a century after these discoveries had been made, their importance was seen to be even greater than they appeared at the time, since it was then realized that the effect of a gene depended at least to some extent on the actions of its neighboring genes. "However much the story of the formative period of the *Drosophila* work may be re-written and re-appraised in the future," Morgan's assistant Hermann J. Muller wrote in 1946, "there must remain agreement in regard to the fact that Morgan's evidence for crossing over and his suggestion that genes further apart cross over more frequently was a thunderclap, hardly second to the discovery of Mendelism, which ushered in that storm that has given nourishment to all of our modern genetics."

The advance soon led to the production of the first chromosome maps. This idea occurred to Sturtevant in 1911 when he was discussing with Morgan a paper in which William E. Castle had published diagrams to illustrate the interrelationships of genes affecting the color of rabbits. "I suddenly realized," Sturtevant has written, "that the variations in strength of linkage, already attributed by Morgan to differences in the spatial separation of the genes, offered the possibility of determining sequences in the linear dimension of a chromosome. I went home and spent most of the night (to the neglect of my undergraduate homework) in producing the first chromosome map, which included the sex-linked genes *y, w, v, m*, and *r*, in the order and approximately the relative spacing that they still appear on the standard maps." By 1913, Sturtevant had mapped the position of six genes on *Drosophila* chromosomes and within another two years the number had increased to thirty-six. "A parallel to the maps," Morgan later wrote, "is found in a railroad timetable, where the number of minutes between stations is given. From such a table one can judge accurately the sequence of the stations and roughly the actual number of miles between them. Knowledge of the normal speed of the train and the condition of the road bed and of the grades would make it possible to judge more accurately the number of miles between the stations from the number of minutes between the stations."

But as work continued, so was the complexity of genetics seen as constantly growing. It was not only the single gene that was involved in producing any particular characteristic. "I may state," wrote Morgan in 1917, "that we have found about 50 eye-color factors, 15 body-color factors, and at least 10 factors for length of wing in *Drosophila*." Eventually, moreover, it was possible to say that so much of the difference in average wing length between two groups of *Drosophila* was due to genes on one chromosome, so much to genes on another, so much to interaction between the two.

The importance of the work was that it began to show beyond reasonable doubt not only that the chromosome theory was correct but also that each of the large number of genes that lay on the chromosomes was responsible for some specific characteristic. Moreover, as the findings from the fly room were taken as the basis for experiments elsewhere, and with other material, it became increasingly clear that the chromosome theory was applicable to all living organisms. So now, a decade and a half after Mendel had been rediscovered, it became possible to compound Darwin's scandalous theory that man was linked to the apes. His stature, the color of his eyes—in fact, all his physical attributes and perhaps even his intellectual ability—were governed by minute discrete particles. They were too small to be seen, yet as real, and as significant, as those even smaller particles on whose existence Rutherford was preparing to postulate a new kind of world.

Some biologists still found it impossible to follow Morgan all the way, or to concede that *The Mechanism of Mendelian Heredity*, written by him and his colleagues and published in 1915, was a successful attempt to interpret the whole field of genetics in terms of the chromosomal theory. Morgan was well aware of these objections. One, he wrote in 1916, was that he and his group were "dealing with artificial and unnatural conditions. It has been more than implied that results obtained from the breeding pen, the seed pan, the flower pot and the milk bottle do not apply to evolution in the 'open,' nature at large, or to wild types. To be consistent, this same objection should be extended to the use of the spectroscope in the study of the evolution of the stars, to the use of the test tube and the balance by the chemist, of the galvanometer by the physicist. All these are unnatural instruments used to torture Nature's secrets from her. I venture to think that the real antithesis is not between unnatural and natural treatment of Nature, but rather between controlled or verifiable data on the one hand, and unrestrained generalization on the other."

Among the objectors was Bateson, apparently overawed into incredulity by the implications of the work in the fly room. When reviewing *The Mechanism of Mendelian Heredity* in *Science*, he wrote: "it is inconceivable that particles of chromatin or of any other substance, however complex, can possess those powers which must be assigned to our factors [i.e., genes]. . . . The supposition that particles of chromatin, indistinguishable from each other and indeed almost homogeneous under any known test, can by their material nature confer all the properties of life surpasses the range of even the most convinced materialism." He paid professional tribute to the work of the fly room; but he felt forced to add a reservation: "We are provided with a sketch—a vigorous and impressionist sketch—of the facts as the authors see them, but we want a much nearer view. Pending this, judgment must be suspended."

Privately, Bateson admitted his ambiguous feelings in two letters to Carl Emil Hanson Ostenfeld. "I am just through a long course in *Drosophila* and have sent my article on it to 'Science,' " he wrote on July 16, 1916. "Beginning with a strongly sceptical feeling I have come around so far as to see that the suggestion is, to say the least, very attractive. They have left themselves however too many 'boltholes'—and until these are stopped we shall not know what the truth is. The theory of 'crossovers' is to me the least promising part, but even if that has to go there will be a great deal left as the result of their work." Within less than twelve months he was having second thoughts. "I get further and further away from the chromosome hypothesis and Morgan and his friends," he wrote to the same correspondent in June 1917. "Last year I did hesitate somewhat, but I can't apply it to the everyday facts of heredity at all."

The Mechanism of Mendelian Heredity had in fact shown that the variations upon which Darwin had based his theory of natural selection were dependent upon the submicroscopic factors known as genes. Yet this appeared only to make more unresolvable another problem that had been raised by the work of the biometricians. Galton with his Law of Ancestral Inheritance, and Pearson with his more finely tuned version of a similar machine, had produced numerical correlations between numbers of different families for various characteristics such as height. These predictive correlations between relatives were well established for continuously varying characters; but there was no indication that they could be explained in Mendelian terms. Indeed, Pearson had already maintained that it was not possible. So it appeared that Darwin's natural selection of continuous small variations could still not be reconciled with the statistical products of Mendel's theory.

Bateson's reluctance to accept the implications of Morgan's experimental evidence only indicated the crosscurrents that had increasingly affected evolutionary thought as Mendel's laws were confirmed by practical example in Morgan's fly room. The overall reaction was one of disillusion with Darwin's belief in natural selection as the main process controlling evolution. D. H. Scott, giving the presidential address to the Botany Section of the British Association in 1921, expressed the view clearly. "It may be that the theory of Natural Selection, as Darwin and Wallace understood it, may some day come into its own again," he said; "certainly it illuminated, as no other theory has yet done, the great subject of adaptation, which to some of us is, and remains, the chief interest of Biology. But in our present total ignorance of variation and doubt as to other means of change, we can form no clear idea of the material on which Selection has had to work, and we must let the question rest. For the moment, at all events, the Darwinian period is past; we can no longer enjoy the comfortable assurance, which once satisfied so many of us, that the main problem had been solved—all is again in the melting-pot. By now, in fact, a new generation has grown up that knows not Darwin."

However, not all the dismay was on the part of the Darwinians. One of their problems had been to argue away, if possible, the evening primroses that De Vries had cited as proof that evolution could take place by large "jumps," or mutations. Now the job was done for them by George Harrison Shull, Otto Renner and Ralph Erskine Cleland, who in a series of papers, started in 1913, had shown that the changes in the plants were due to the particular complexity of their genetic make-up and not to mutation as the word was then understood.

It is symptomatic of the current confusion in the evolutionary field that while the demise of Darwin's beliefs was being announced by Scott, the leading paleobotanist of his day, a thesis that was to show Darwin's natural selection as complementary to Mendelism was already gaining support. It had been written by Ronald Aylmer Fisher, a young Englishman who had studied statistical mechanics at Cambridge. Fisher had become interested in evolutionary and genetical controversies and appears to have felt, as much by intuition as by anything else, that it would be possible to resolve the problems. In June 1916, Fisher told Karl Pearson: "I have recently completed an article on Mendelism and Biometry which will probably be of interest to you. I find on analysis that the human data is as far as it goes, not inconsistent with Mendelism. But the argument is rather complex." Pearson replied to other points in Fisher's letter but made no mention of the paper. Anything that gave support to Mendelism could barely be acknowledged, even if it came from someone other than Bateson.

In Fisher's words, he had "attempted to ascertain the biometrical properties of a population of a more general type than has hitherto been examined, inheritance in which follows this [Mendelian] scheme. It is hoped that in this way it will be possible to make a more exact analysis of the causes of human variability."

He had started with Pearson's own data on human stature, and similar measurements, and had then gone on to show that the correlations derived from them on the basis of blending inheritance could as well be derived from a basis of particulate inheritance such as Mendel's experiments had brought to light. This contradicted the established biometric view; yet at the same time it was supported by mathematics that were beyond the comprehension of many a Mendelian. The difficulties became obvious when Fisher sought publication. There was virtually no chance of this in Pearson's *Biometrika*, and Fisher therefore submitted it to the Royal Society. One of the two assessors was Pearson, who started his report with the words: "I have not examined in detail the results of this paper, as I am overfussed with other work," before continuing: "I do not think in the present state of affairs that the paper is wide enough to be of much interest from the biometric standpoint for its hypotheses need some observational basis." The second assessor was R. C. Punnett, who began with the admission: "I have had another go at this paper but frankly I do not follow it owing to my ignorance of mathematics." After a few kindly but critical remarks, he concluded: "However, whatever its value from the standpoint of statistics & population I do not feel that this kind of work affects us biologists much at present. It is too much of the order of problem that deals with weightless elephants upon frictionless surfaces, where at the same time we are largely ignorant of the other properties of the said elephants and surfaces."

Neither referee recommended that publication should be turned down. But the chairman of the Sectional Committee for Zoology wrote to Fisher, and the paper was withdrawn. More than half a century later, it was possible to consider objectively the effective blocking of what was later seen to be a seminal paper. Both Pearson's and Punnett's faint praises appear to have originated from "reservations as to its scientific status, as opposed to its mathematical status," wrote Bernard Norton and E. S. Pearson, Karl Pearson's son. "Their common stated objection was largely philosophical. Pearson suggested that the hypothesis adopted 'is only one of a very large number that would lead to similar results,' and, in his view, the use of a large number of Mendelian factors would 'carry that character out of the range of experiment by Mendelian methods.' Punnett wondered whether this assumption of a large number of factors 'could be tested by experiment.' Certainly, neither of the reports went carefully into Fisher's work." It seemed that Darwin's natural selection would, as far as the biometricians and the Mendelians were concerned, remain a bone for argument.

The situation was saved in 1918 when the Eugenics Education Society, prodded on by Darwin's son Leonard, agreed to sponsor publication through the Royal Society of Edinburgh. Fisher submitted the paper in June and read it in July. Publication came in October, and the paper was quickly acknowledged as having successfully begun to synthezise what had since 1900 developed into two conflicting approaches to heredity and the problems of evolution, the Darwinian and the Mendelian.

Fisher completed the reconciliation of the two beliefs a decade later in *The Genetical Theory of Natural Selection*, whose importance was to be cogently described by the zoologist and evolutionist Gavin de Beer. In the book, De Beer noted, Fisher "demonstrated that the mechanism of particulate inheritance of Mendelian genes which remain uncontaminated, segregate, re-combine, self-copy, and occasionally mutate, provides exactly what Darwinian selection theory requires to explain the source of variation; that Selection provides exactly what Mendelian theory requires to explain why some genes become dominant, others recessive, and others again suppressed; and that no mechanism other than selection will explain all the facts." Fisher also showed that the control of visible characteristics by the genes was more complex than had been thought. At first it had been believed that any specific characteristic was due to the presence of one particular gene; later it became evident that the cause might be interaction of a group of genes within the organism. Fisher demonstrated, in particular, that the characteristics of dominance or recessiveness might thus be governed.

In 1920 some men still held out against Fisher's mathematically derived theories. Among them was Karl Pearson, who wrote to Fisher, from whom he received a copy of the paper. "Many thanks for your memoir which I hope to find time for," he said. "I am afraid I am not a believer in cumulative Mendelian factors as being the solution of the heredity puzzle."

Nevertheless, Fisher's paper was the first—and in some respects a decisive—shot in a campaign to be carried on not only by himself but also by Sewall Wright in America and J. B. S. Haldane in Britain. The result was the pure neo-Darwinism that successfully merged the genetic beliefs of the *Drosophila* group with those of the biometricians. The development came at a critical moment, for the cytological analysis of Shull, Cleland and Renner now showed that the allegedly different species of De Vries's *Oenothera*s were not different species at all. "By 1919," it has been pointed out, "De Vries's mutation theory was scrapped and neo-Darwinism prevailed. The *Drosophila* group no longer had contenders and had now become spokesmen for the dominant viewpoint of genetics."

Even Bateson eventually capitulated. In 1921 he visited Morgan. Soon afterward, addressing the American Association for the Advancement of Science, honesty forced him to recant. "We have turned still another bend in the track and behind the [egg and the sperm cells] we see the chromosomes," he admitted. "For the doubts—which I trust may be pardoned in one who had never seen the marvels of cytology, save as through a glass darkly—can not as regards the main thesis of the *Drosophila* workers, be any longer maintained. The arguments of Morgan and his colleagues, and especially the demonstrations of Bridges, must allay all scepticism as to the direct association of particular chromosomes with particular features of the zygote [the fertilized ovum before it undergoes cleavage]. The transferable characters born[e] by the gametes [reproductive cells] have been successfully referred to the visible details of nuclear configuration." In other words, the visible characteristics of an organism were directly linked to invisible units on the chromosome.

SURVIVAL OF
THE FITTEST

13

Toward a New Darwinism: Development and Repercussions

FISHER's paper, published as the world awaited the 1918 armistice, came at the start of three decades that spread across the years between the two world wars and into the years following the second. The most important development in evolution was the growth of a new synthesis, at least partly founded on Fisher's work, that reconciled the importance Darwin had given to natural selection with the particulate facts of genetics as built upon Mendel's discoveries. This was augmented by the growth of population genetics, which revealed that the laws governing evolution in large populations were different from those governing evolution in individuals. But this inexplicable difference was complicated by the discovery that radiation had a definite, but only partly understood, effect on the machinery of inheritance. And it was yet further complicated as investigation of the gene itself showed that the machinery was more complex than had been appreciated.

From this background of accumulating knowledge there stood out two developments that respectively encouraged and discouraged Darwin's basic conclusion that the world's species had evolved rather than been separately created according to the Bible story. The first was the practical exploitation of genetic knowledge in both the United States and Russia to tackle one of the most persistent threats to the human race, the shortage of grain, whose production had failed to keep pace with the continuing, and almost explosive, increase in the world's population. The second was the growth, particularly in the United States, of fundamentalist religious thought. If in some areas the First World War had destroyed many of the simple faiths by which men had steered their lives, there were others where it had seemed more necessary to support the alleged home truths of the Bible and the story it told of how the world had been created. Thus evolution began to come under attack once again, by opponents of smaller intellectual caliber than the bishop of Oxford and those who supported him, but opponents of strong dogmatic beliefs.

The idea of crossing different breeds of grain to produce larger and better crops had arisen long before Darwin and his successors began to give it scientific foundation. Cotton Mather, the American largely remembered for his notorious part in the trials of the Salem witches, had written on the subject in 1716, and James Logan, governor of Pennsylvania, had carried out experiments along the proposed lines a few years later. The early nineteenth century had witnessed some success in Europe. In Germany, where it had been found that the sugar in mangel-wurzel, a large beet grown for cattle fodder, was the same as the sugar in sugar cane, selective breeding increased the sugar content by 50 per cent. In England, Thomas Knight, "the father of modern plant breeding," originated new varieties of potatoes, apples and pears. In 1860 the *Gardeners' Chronicle*, which had reproduced Huxley's review of *The Origin* from *The Times*, suggested that the quantity and quality of crops grown in the British colonies might be improved if Darwin's ideas were taken to heart.

Forty years later, De Vries brought the forecast up to date, writing, "Knowledge of the principles of mutation will certainly at some time in the future enable a fully planned artificial induction of mutations, i.e., the creation of new properties in plants and animals. Moreover, it is likely that man will be able to produce superior varieties of cultivated plants and animals by controlling the origin of mutations."

There was also to be a direct link between Darwin and production of the hybrid corn that was to revolutionize American agriculture in the twentieth century. Darwin had told Asa Gray of his experiments in crossing plants even before he described them in print, and Gray had discussed the subject with one of his former students, William Beal, then of Michigan State College. Beal planted together varieties of flint and stent corn and removed the tassels—the pollen-bearing male clusters—from one variety before the pollen was shed. The female flowers of the emasculated plants then received their tassels from the other variety. The seed borne on the detasseled plants, being a crossed breed, produced only hybrid plants when planted the following season.

There were disadvantages in this method, and two further steps had to be taken. The first came with George H. Shull, working at the Carnegie Institution's Station for Experimental Evolution. Shull produced by inbreeding a number of pure lines of corn. They had little vigor but were quite uniform in their number of kernel-rows. Shull correctly believed that he had produced a series of pure lines—comparable to the pure lines of beans produced by Wilhelm Johannsen. When these pure lines were crossed, their products not only remained uniform but were also of a surprising vigor—so much so that hybrid corn was frequently known as mule corn, being as vigorous as the mule, the hybrid from a horse and an ass.

Shull reported his results in two papers in 1908 and 1909. But the inbred strains were themselves unproductive, and once again the utilization of "hybrid vigor" was found too expensive to be practical. The problem was resolved by Donald Jones at the Connecticut Agricultural Experiment Station. His solution was to use seed from a double cross instead of a single cross. The situation, it has been said, "was transformed from Shull's magnificent design to practical reality when Jones' method of seed production made it feasible and his theory explaining hybrid vigor made it plausible."

Before the end of the First World War, hybrid-corn breeding had been introduced into many states. By 1920, heterosis—the name given by Shull to hybrid vigor—was appearing in American textbooks of genetics. By 1933, hybrid corn was in commercial production and giving vastly increased yields, while today it accounts for some 96 percent of U.S. corn acreage.

Hybrid corn is possibly the most spectacular example of genetic engineering applied to agriculture, but there are many similar by-products from the search for an understanding of how evolution works. Corn has been developed with several small ears instead of one large one in order to ease mechanical harvesting. Sorghum with short stems and slender heads has been bred for the same reason, while the production not only of vegetables but of cattle, sheep, pigs and turkeys to definite specifications has become commonplace.

Although the exploitation of genetic knowledge increased greatly in America in the 1920s, it was in Russia that the major change was to take place. Here it was the disastrous famine of 1920 that turned attention toward the subject and the opportunity it offered of producing improved varieties of domestic plants and animals. "The famine to prevent," Lenin is claimed to have said, "is the next one and the time to begin is now." As a result, money was diverted from famine relief funds to build the Institute of Applied Botany in Leningrad. In charge was Nikolai Vavilov, who was to introduce more than 25,000 foreign varieties of cultivated plants into Russia, and during the next few years was to turn the Institute into one of the greatest plant breeding and seed selection centers in the world. Vavilov offered Hermann J. Muller, who had worked in Morgan's fly room, the directorship of the Genetics Laboratory in his Institute, and Muller arrived shortly afterward, bringing with him not only thirty-two different strains of *Drosophila* but 10,000 glass vials, 1,000 bottles and a suitcase filled with the flies and equipment for making their food. Within a few years the Institute had become the greatest theoretical research center in the subject outside the United States. Almost as important was the work carried out with Muller's contribution of *Drosophila* by Sergei S. Chetverikov. He had become interested in the variation in natural populations and the relation between population size and evolutionary potential. As a result he started crossbreeding Muller's *Drosophila* with wild stocks collected outside Moscow. From this there developed the study of population genetics and the discovery that the rules governing the genetic structure of a population are different from those governing the genetics of individuals, "just as rules of sociology are distinct from physiological ones, although the former are in the last analysis integrated systems of the latter." This was not as surprising as it may at first sound, since the factors governing the rules are different in the two cases.

Conventional Darwinism was still accepted in Russia and when Bateson visited the country in 1925 on the occasion of the bicentenary of the Russian Academy of Sciences, he found that the Darwin Museum, created to illustrate the theory of evolution, was flourishing. "Zinovieff [the Russian leader who had presided over the Third International] . . . speaks in the same breath of the 'discovery' of Karl Marx and the 'discovery' of Charles Darwin," he reported.

The enthusiastic acceptance of genetics in postrevolutionary

Russia was the result of something more than a realization that it might help to keep starvation at bay. The new government was constitutionally favorable toward Darwin on account of what was considered to be his materialistic, nonreligious standpoint. During the 1920s a new edition of all his works was issued in Moscow, complete with introductory essays evaluating the current status of each work and defending each against what were seen as the more dangerous attacks. The arguments themselves no doubt helped to impress authority, since they could be carried on in the language of dialectic materialism.

While the benefits of evolutionary research to agriculture was being exploited in countries as differently governed as the United States and Russia, and as its implications for medicine were slowly being appreciated, the antievolutionary movement began to flex its muscles. Its foundation was still the Christian Church, as it had been after publication of *The Origin*, but it had some unexpected supporters. In Britain, one of them was George Bernard Shaw, who wrote in his preface to *Back to Methuselah* that at first one did not realize all that Darwinism involved, and it therefore seemed simple. "But when its whole significance dawns on you," he continued, "your heart sinks into a heap of sand within you. There is a hideous fatalism about it, a ghastly and damnable reduction of beauty and intelligence, of strength and purpose, of honor and aspiration, to such casually picturesque changes as an avalanche may make in a mountain landscape, or a railway accident in a human figure. To call this Natural Selection is a blasphemy, possible to many for whom Nature is nothing but a casual aggregation of inert and dead matter, but eternally impossible to the spirits and souls of the righteous. If it be no blasphemy, but a truth of science, then the stars of heaven, the showers and dew, the winter and summer, the fire and heat, the mountains and hills, may no longer be called to exalt the Lord with us by praise: their work is to modify all things by blindly starving and murdering everything that is not lucky enough to survive in the universal struggle for hogwash."

But it was in North America that the antievolutionists mustered their greatest strength, opposing under the Fundamentalist banner any suggestion that the story told in Genesis was less than the literal truth. And here they were now aided, quite fortuitously, by the unlikely figure of William Bateson.

In 1921 the American Association for the Advancement of Science met in Toronto, and here Bateson delivered one of his most famous papers, "Evolutionary Faith and Modern Doubts." He stressed his belief in evolution. But he then continued: "In dim outline evolution is evident enough. From the facts it is a conclusion which inevitably follows. But that particular and essential bit of the theory of evolution which is concerned with the origin and nature of *species* remains utterly mysterious. We no longer feel as we used to do, that the process of variation, now contemporaneously occurring, is the beginning of a work which needs merely the element of time for its completion; for even time can not complete that which has not yet begun. The conclusion in which we were brought up, that species are a product of a summation of variations, ignored the chief attribute of species first pointed out by John Ray that the product of their crosses is frequently sterile in greater or less degree. Huxley, very early in the debate pointed out this grave defect in the evidence, but before breeding researches had been made on a large scale no one felt the objection to be serious. Extended work might be trusted to supply the deficiency. It has not done so, and the significance of the negative evidence can no longer be denied."

It was, of course, no more than the truth. But that Bateson was insufficiently aware that the antievolutionists were waiting, like watchers in the slips, to field any remark of use to them was evident as he continued: "The survival of the fittest was a plausible account of evolution in broad outline, but failed in application to specific difference. The Darwinian philosophy convinced us that every species must 'make good' in nature if it is to survive, but no one could tell how the differences—often very sharply fixed—which we recognize as specific, do in fact enable the species to make good. The claims of natural selection as the chief factor in the determination of species have consequently been discredited."

Bateson admitted that his confessions enabled "the enemies of science [to] see their chance." Yet he wrote to his wife: "Only a line to say last night's address ["Evolutionary Faith and Modern Doubts"] went well. I had to announce my conversion on the main point 'that chromosomes are definitely associated with the transferable characters' is how I express it. Much enthusiasm over this of course, but as a candid man I don't see how any other view can now be maintained." And judging by the letters to his wife, he was surprised by such American headlines as "Darwinism Disproved." He seems, moreover, to have been innocently unaware that when he derided Darwin's theory of continuous evolution, only a sleight of expression was needed to discredit evolution altogether.

Speeches like the Toronto address—and Bateson's later statement in *Nature* that "The variations by which [species] have arisen are not yet known to us, but we are satisfied that the particular account of their origin which is the one Darwin chiefly favoured is incorrect"—were quickly seized by the Fundamentalists in the United States. Their movement had come into being in the mid-nineteenth century as scholarly studies began to question the literal truth of the Bible, and had been formalized after the Niagara Bible Conference of 1905. It culminated in 1919 with a World Bible Conference in Philadelphia, whose outcome was the World Christian Fundamentalist Association. Suppression of free thought on evolution was one of its aims, and in this aim it had allies. One was the postwar mood in America and elsewhere. The ending of the First World War had been followed not only by libertarian outbreaks but by a conservative counteraction. A number of state legislatures passed laws prohibiting the use in state schools of textbooks that were "seditious, defamatory of the Founding Fathers, or in any other way disloyal to the nation and to its heritage." In New York State the Lusk laws decreed that schoolteachers "must obtain 'certificates of qualification' testifying to their moral character, loyalty to the government, and conservative political views." If this upsurge of moral rectitude was a factor that made it easier to limit free thought on the contentious subject of evolution, another almost as important was the presence of William Jennings Bryan, lawyer, orator and a regular if unsuccessful candidate for the Democratic nomination for the presidency. Bryan was not only a fluent and passionate speaker but also a leading Fundamentalist who by the early 1920s was organizing antievolutionist movements in twenty states, and he was always willing to reassert: "It is better to trust in the Rock of Ages, than to know the age of the rocks; it is better for one to know that he is close to the Heavenly Father, than to know how far the stars in the heavens are apart."

In 1922 Bryan descended upon Kentucky. Soon afterward a state bill to prohibit the teaching of "Darwinism, Atheism, Agnosticism, or the theory of Evolution as it pertains to man" was lost by a single vote. The following year the Oklahoma state legislature forbad the use in public schools of any text-book offering "a materialistic conception of history, that is, the Darwin theory of creation versus the Biblical theory of creation." Although the law was repealed two years later, it was clear that the Fundamentalists were making headway. In Delaware, it is true, a bill banning the teaching of "the theory that man evolved from a lower order of animals," was facetiously referred to the Committee on Fish, Game and Oysters, but elsewhere attempts to limit the teaching of biology continued.

It was in Tennessee that such legislation now found its way onto the statute book. In 1932 the state enacted a law in these words: "It shall be unlawful for any teacher in any of the universities, teachers' colleges, normal schools or other public schools of the State which are supported, in whole or in part, by the public school funds of the State, to teach any theory that denies the story of the divine creation of man as taught in the Bible, and to teach instead that man descended from a lower order of animals."

Approval of what became known as the "Monkey Law," which would have gravely limited the education of Tennessee's children had it been fully implemented, and which was to make the state a laughingstock throughout the world, appears to have followed horsetrading by a governor who also passed a number of enlightened educational measures. "The law," a close friend of the governor has said, "was the result of cheap politics. Governor [Austin] Peay would have vetoed the measure, but he needed the votes of the anti-evolutionists to put through his education program. Had he known the ridicule the measure was going to bring on the State he would have acted differently." Even so, it appears to have been chance as much as anything else that brought matters to a head.

Early in the summer of 1925, John Thomas Scopes, a twenty-four-year-old football coach and high-school science teacher in the small town of Dayton, Tennessee, was discussing the new law with George W. Rappelyea, a young mining engineer who was the superintendent of the local coal mines. Rappelyea agreed that it was crazy for Scopes to have textbooks on evolution but to be forbidden to use them. "Why don't I have you arrested for teaching evolution from that text and bring the whole thing to an end?" he asked, encouraged no doubt by the fact that the American Civil Liberties Union had already offered to defend any teacher who would test the law. Scopes was duly charged—but it was to be forty-two years before the "Monkey Law" was brought to an end by repeal.

Despite the furor that *The Origin* had created in the 1860s, its implications had not before been seriously debated in the courts.

By 1925, the fact of evolution was accepted by most educated men and women, even though its mechanism was still debated, and this itself would have made the case newsworthy and Dayton notorious. But the Civil Liberties Union briefed for the defense Clarence S. Darrow, the most famous criminal lawyer of his generation. If there was a possible challenger to Darrow's position, it was Bryan. Bryan immediately offered his services to the Tennessee prosecution. Thus the stage was set for a ready-made drama. It was no longer to be either Scopes or Darwin on trial but the state of Tennessee.

Darrow always attracted an audience of crime reporters. Bryan drew both the political and the religious pundits. To have them facing each other on such a fundamental issue as the descent of mankind inevitably transformed the trial into a set-piece entertainment. It also transformed the hitherto almost unknown township of Dayton. The roads were hung with posters demanding "Where Will You Spend Eternity?" and declaiming "You Need God in Your Business" or "Sweethearts Come to Jesus." Hot dog, lemonade and sandwich stands sprang up along the sidewalks, says one account of the scene. "Little cotton apes appeared in windows, and stores offered pins reading 'Your Old Man's a Monkey.' " Nor was it only reporters who descended upon Dayton by the score. Circus performers, hoping to give evidence, arrived with two chimpanzees. Cranks, zealots and publicity seekers included Lewis Levi Johnson, "Absolute Ruler of the Entire World, without Military, Naval or other Physical Force"; the flat-earther Wilber Glenn Voliva; and Elmer Chubb, who claimed that he could withstand the bite of any venomous serpent.

Passions ran high, and Darrow and his legal team had difficulty in finding accommodations. George Rappelyea, giving an impromptu address in favor of evolution at a public meeting, was confronted by the town barber, who shouted: "You can't call my family monkeys," and then sank his teeth in the unfortunate mining engineer.

When the trial began on July 10, Darrow found that Judge John T. Raulston was sitting under a banner that read: "Read Your Bible Daily." Then Scopes succeeded in bringing out the fact that eleven of the twelve jurors were Fundamentalists. All of them admitted that they knew little about science or evolution, and one said that the only Darwin he had heard of ran a local store. Another revealed that he could neither read nor write.

The first defense move was an attempt to quash the indictment on the grounds that it violated the constitution of Tennessee and a section of the Fourteenth Amendment of the Constitution of the United States. In addition, it was stated to be contrary to a Supreme Court decision that "The law knows no heresy, and is committed to the support of no dogma, nor to the establishment of any sect."

Darrow failed to have the indictment quashed but remained in his usual ebullient form. "If today you can make teaching of evolution in the public schools [the state schools] a crime," he told the jury, "tomorrow you can make it a crime to teach it in the private schools. At the next session of the Legislature you can ban books and newspapers. You can set Catholic against Protestant, and Protestant against Protestant, when you try to foist your own religion upon the minds of men. If you can do the one, you can do the other. After a while, Your Honor, we will find ourselves marching backward to the glorious days of the 16th century when bigots lighted the fagots to burn men who dared to bring any intelligence and enlightenment to the human mind."

Darrow now tried to call the first of his expert witnesses. His attempt was met by an impassioned plea from the state's attorney, who protested that no such witnesses were necessary. Support came from Bryan, who showed to the jury the textbook Scopes had been using. One page included a drawing in which man was shown in a circle with other mammals. "Talk about putting Daniel in the lions' den," Bryan declaimed. "How dare these scientists put man in a little ring with lions and tigers and everything that smells of the jungle. . . . One does not need to be an expert to know what the Bible says. . . . Expert testimony is not needed!"

This was the first of two tactical mistakes Bryan made during the trial. He was answered by Dudley Field Malone, one of Darrow's supporting team, not only a great courtroom orator but a Catholic. "I have never seen greater need for learning than is exhibited by the Prosecution which refuses information offered by expert witnesses . . ." he said. "Why this fear of meeting the issue? Mr. Bryan has said this is to be a duel to the death. I know little about dueling, Your Honor, but does it mean that our only weapon, the witnesses, is to be taken away while the Prosecution alone carries the sword? This is not my idea of a duel. . . . We do not fear all the truth they can present as facts. We are ready. We stand with progress. We stand with science. We stand with intelligence. We feel that we stand with the fundamental freedoms in America. We are not afraid. Where is the fear? We defy it."

Then he turned and, pointing to Bryan, uttered the words: "There is the fear!" The crowd cheered so long and so loudly— even in Dayton—that the court had to be cleared for fifteen minutes. When it reassembled, the judge ruled that the witnesses were not to give evidence. This, one commentator later declared, was a wise decision. "If a great state has decided by law that twice two are five, it would be foolish to allow mathematicians to testify."

Darrow countered by telling the witnesses to go to the stenographers' room and prepare a statement for the press outlining what their evidence would have been. When, as he had no doubt expected, the judge tried to bar the move on the ground that it "might reach the jury," Darrow replied with an answer that he knew would make the headlines. The judge could do what he pleased with the jury. "You can lock it up, but you cannot lock up the American people. The testimony will be released."

Bryan now made his second tactical error. He agreed to go into the witness box "as a biblical witness" and be cross-examined by Darrow. The result was devastating. Bryan's evidence was struck out from the record on the orders of the judge, but this did not prevent it from being sent round the world by the scores of journalists who between them telegraphed some 175,000 words during each day of the trial. They included H. L. Mencken, at his bitter best in such a situation, who wrote of the Dayton citizens as "anthropoid rabble" and "Gaping primates." Bryan had patently failed to convince all who were not already convinced and had done the Fundamentalist cause a good deal of harm.

When the judge ruled out Bryan's damaging evidence as irrelevant, he said that the only question was "What did Scopes teach?" At this—and having won a considerable moral victory over Bryan —Darrow rose. "Your Honor," he said, "we are wasting time. You should call the jury and instruct it to bring in a verdict of guilty." The judge did so, and after the jury had found for a verdict of "Guilty," fined Scopes $100, this being thrown out a few months later by the Tennessee Supreme Court, since the amount should have been decided by the jury rather than the judge. Scopes himself accepted a scholarship to the University of Chicago, funded by grateful scientists, and eventually became a geologist.

One result of the sudden closing of the case by Darrow was that Bryan was unable to make his own prepared speech in court. However, it was published shortly afterward and illustrated the effect on Bryan of Bateson's speech in Toronto. "It is less than four years ago that Prof. Bateson came all the way from London to Canada to tell the American scientists that every effort to trace one species to another had failed—every one. He said he still had faith in evolution but had doubts about the origin of species. But of what value is evolution if it cannot explain the origin of species?"

Immediately after the end of the trial, Bryan drove to nearby Winchester, stayed there with friends, and began editing the undelivered speech for publication. To the editor of the Chattanooga *Daily News* he declared: "I feel this is the mountain peak of my life's efforts." The following day, he died. Various causes were given. Some said he had died "of mental assassination at the hands of that atheist Darrow, but perhaps more accurately the consequence of diabetes and an exceedingly large chicken dinner on a hot summer's day."

The Scopes case had not, as Rappelyea had hoped, brought "the whole thing to an end," and not until 1967 did it once again become legally possible to teach evolution in Tennessee. Moreover *Biology for Beginners*—today the popular and retitled *Modern Biology*—carried at the time of the Scopes trial a frontispiece portrait of Charles Darwin. It was omitted from the next edition.

However, the trial had one result that shocked many Fundamentalists. "No attempt at repression has ever backfired so impressively," wrote one of the uncalled expert witnesses. "Where one person had been interested in evolution before the trial, scores were reading and inquiring at its close. Within a year the prohibitive bills which had been pending in other states were dropped or killed. Tennessee had been made to appear so ridiculous in the eyes of the nation that other states did not care to follow its lead." A few in fact did so, but not many.

But there was another and broader way in which the Scopes trial gave a shot in the arm to evolution and helped to foster Darwin and Darwinism between the two world wars. George Marsden, in his deep study of Fundamentalism and American culture, has noted:

> The central theme [of the trial] was, inescapably, the clash of two worlds, the rural and the urban. In the popular imagination there were on the one side the small town, the backwoods, half-educated yokels, obscurantism, crackpot hawkers of religion, fundamentalism, the

South, and the personification of the agrarian myth himself, William Jennings Bryan. Opposed to these were the city, the clique of New York–Chicago lawyers, intellectuals, journalists, wits, sophisticates, modernists, and the urbane agnostic Clarence Darrow. These images evoked the familiar experiences of millions of Americans who had been born in the country and moved to the city or who were at least witnessing the dramatic shift from a predominantly rural to a predominantly urban culture. *Main Street*, Sinclair Lewis's famous portrait of the dullness of smalltown America, had since its publication in 1920 furnished a potent symbol of the rural America from which people of education and culture escaped. Dayton surpassed all fiction in dramatizing the symbolic last stand of nineteenth-century America against the twentieth century.

From now on, it was increasingly difficult to deny that a belief in evolution was part of the twentieth century.

There were exceptions. The Bible Crusade, the Bryan Bible League, the World Christian Fundamentalist Association, the Supreme Kingdom and the Defenders of the Christian Faith were some of the groups roused to fresh effort by the confrontation in Dayton. But of a dozen antievolution bills immediately following the Scopes trial, only those in Mississippi and Arkansas were passed, while Oklahoma repealed the state law restricting the use of textbooks.

Undeterred by the ridicule that had met the Scopes case, Fundamentalists in Arkansas petitioned in these terms for their own "monkey law." "We, the undersigned citizens, voters and taxpayers of the State of Arkansas and County of Randolph, believing in the Mosaic account of creation, and believing the Darwinian theory of the origin of man to be erroneous, false, and misleading, and calculated in its nature to lead men from the truth of God and to instill in the spirit of infidelity; Do, therefore, petition your honorable body to enact a law, similar to the 'Tennessee Anti-Evolutionary Law' with just such changes and modifications as will make it applicable to the state of Arkansas." Although widely disobeyed, it stayed on the state books unchallenged until 1965.

In retrospect it can clearly be seen that the fame of the Scopes trial arose more from the confrontation between Darrow and Bryan than from the controversies within a subject of which most laymen were fundamentally ignorant. Yet throughout the long weekend between the two world wars the status of Darwin and

Darwinism continued to arouse strong passions. This was partly the result of a new, questioning approach to religion and ethics, which was a by-product of the general disillusion following the First World War. It was partly the result of genetic research continuing throughout the world, which increasingly provided a physical matrix within which a solution to the riddles of heredity and evolution might be sought. Added to this there was the instinctive feeling, not entirely dispersed by such sensational headlines as "Scientist Discovers Secret of Life," that important revelations about the mechanisms of life were only just over the horizon.

That headline came in England after Julian Huxley, T. H.'s grandson, had carried out in Oxford an intriguing experiment that was to be quoted more than half a century later when the conventional view of evolution was again under attack. The experiment was with two axolotls, amphibians found in a number of Mexican lakes. In the distant past a branch of the axolotl family was shown by the fossil record to have developed into the salamander. In the twentieth century, however, it retained the gills and other features of its early tadpole state for the whole of its life. In other words, it appeared never to grow up.

Now it was known to Huxley, who had recently been appointed Oxford University's Senior Demonstrator in Zoology, that the metamorphosis of frog tadpoles could be speeded up by the use of mammalian thyroid gland, or thyroid extracts. Would it, Huxley asked himself, be possible to use the same substance to bring about the metamorphosis of an axolotl, an event that had only taken place before the creature had evolved into its twentieth-century form? On November 30, 1919, he began feeding two axolotls a diet of ox thyroid. The animals, 11.5 cm and 12.7 cm long respectively, and believed to be between six months and a year old, were given the special diet at first three times, and later twice, a week. Within fifteen days they had begun to change in color, and their gills and fin had begun to be reabsorbed into the body. Four days later, the penultimate stage had been reached, and when one of the animals was taken from the tank of water in which it had been living, it had no difficulty in walking. Thus a change in hormonal balance appeared to have produced the equivalent of an evolutionary effect. A comparable environmental change of balance, it was to be speculated in the 1970s, might have enabled man to evolve from the ape by an analogous process.

In Britain, where the headlines following the axolotl experiments encouraged Huxley to describe his experiment in layman's terms and subsequently to embark on popular science writing, there was no equivalent to Fundamentalism. The nearest approach to it came from the stalwarts of the Victoria Institute and from isolated writers. Thus as late as 1927 the influential *Nineteenth Century* could publish "The Case Against 'Evolution,' " in which George H. Bonner could write: "There is not a shred of conclusive evidence for the animal ancestry of man: the whole structure of its colossal delusion rests upon certain similarities between the physical nature of man and that of the animals—similarities which are easily explainable without postulating any descent of man from the apes."

By contrast, there came in the late 1920s two avowals of support for Darwin that were important not so much for their content as for the context within which they were made. The first came from Sir Arthur Keith, the eminent anthropologist whose *The Antiquity of Man* twelve years earlier had discussed all known human fossil remains. That Keith should speak out in support of Darwin was no cause for surprise: his anthropological studies had long led him to claim a greatly longer ancestry for man than was generally admitted, and he was known to be a keen evolutionist. However, it was the occasion of his declaration that gave it weight.

In 1927 Keith assumed the presidency of the British Association for the Advancement of Science, and on August 31 gave the presidential address to the Association's meeting in Leeds. Richard Owen had in his presidential address of 1858 mentioned the Darwin and Wallace papers read to the Linnean Society. The following year Charles Lyell had reported on *The Origin* that was soon to break upon the world. But there had been no presidential equivalent of the Huxley-Wilberforce confrontation of 1860. Presidents had tended to be cautious; it was, after all, the Association's aim to attract as many members as possible, and when evolution had been dealt with at presidential level the tendency, sometimes lighthearted, had been to keep the subject at arm's length. In 1871 Thomson had gone so far as to say in his presidential address of the origin of species by natural selection: "I have always felt that this hypothesis does not contain the true theory of evolution, if evolution there has been, in biology." Lord Salisbury, president in 1894, had chaffed the believers in natural selection, saying that he did not wonder that they needed 100 million years to show progress. "Of course if the mathematicians are right, the biologists cannot have what they demand," he went on. "The jelly-fish would have been dissipated in steam long before he had had a chance of displaying the advantageous variation which was to make him the ancestor of the human race."

The attitude was maintained at subpresidential level, and when the position of Darwinism was discussed at a joint meeting of the Botanical and Zoological sections in 1922, John T. Cunningham, while supporting the idea of evolution, thought that natural selection was "as extinct as the dodo." Keith was thus introducing something of an innovation when in 1927 he gave his address on "Darwin's Theory of Man's Descent As It Stands Today." It was not only the supporters of the Victoria Institute who still maintained the literal accuracy of Genesis; throughout Britain—as, indeed, throughout the Western world—there remained a sluggish wash of opinion that preferred not to think about Darwinism at all or, if it were forced to, preferred to give the equivalent of a Scottish "not proven" verdict. Keith would allow no such thought to linger. At the end of an hour-long recapitulation of the evidence that had accumulated following the appearance of *The Origin*, he concluded: "Was Darwin right when he said that Man, under the action of biological forces which can be observed and measured, has been raised from a place amongst anthropoid apes to that which he now occupies? The answer is Yes! and in returning this verdict I speak but as foreman of the jury—a jury which has been empanelled from men who have devoted a lifetime to weighing the evidence." By this time, there was little opposition among scientists, even though they still disputed exactly how the raising had taken place; but to the large mass of scientifically interested laymen with ambivalent views on the subject, unqualified affirmation from a man of Keith's reputation, given in a presidential address to the British Association, was a heavy weight in the scales.

Within less than a month another, and from a religious standpoint more worrying, declaration had been made by Ernest William Barnes, bishop of Birmingham. That Barnes should defend evolution was to be expected. Seven years earlier, preaching to members of the British Association in Cardiff Parish Church on "The Christian Revelation and Scientific Progress," he had asked: "Can we accept the idea that man and the gorilla have sprung from a common stock and yet hold that man has an immortal soul?" and had continued: "I answer emphatically that we can." A week later, he had reiterated his convictions in a sermon in Westminster Abbey on "Evolution and the Fall."

Barnes had preached along similar lines more than once in the 1920s, but his sermon in Westminster Abbey on September 25, 1927, aroused particular controversy. "Darwin's assertion that man has sprung from the apes has stood the test of more than half a century of critical examination . . ." he said. "The stories of the creation of Adam and Eve, of their primal innocence and of their fall, have become for us folk-lore. . . . Darwin's triumph has destroyed the whole theological scheme." He ended by concluding "that on the whole the modern scientific view of the origin of man's body and mind agrees well with Christ's teaching. But it cannot be reconciled with certain statements of St. Paul, nor with a belief in the infallibility either of the Bible or the Church, nor with the acceptance of some of the main strands of traditional Catholic theology." The sermon, said a leader in the *Morning Post*, which also devoted four news columns to it, would, it was almost certain, "provoke controversies and raise doubts by which the whole structure of revealed religion must be severely tested." The *Church Times* criticized the sermon in a leading article of more than three columns headed "The Over-Bold Dr. Barnes," while the *British Israelite* described Barnes as a pagan.

There was a counterbalance to Bishop Barnes in the Bishop of Exeter, who in an article in the *Hibbert Journal* declared: "The equality of men is a Christian ideal, but one which should prove subversive to all evolutionary development." The Bishop, remarked *Nature*, "lays his finger upon two implications of Darwinism which appeal to many as subversive of social tendencies as they exist today, and as they have been encouraged especially by Christianity." One was the struggle for existence, seen as a policy of destruction. The second was the encouragement of classes with specialized functions.

By the 1930s Darwin and Darwinism could be used, with little difficulty, as a weapon in almost any battle—by either side or by both.

14

The New Synthesis Develops

WHILE theologians and others were speculating on evolution and the various alternative ways in which it might work, if it worked at all, the body of evolutionary knowledge was being added to by scientists throughout the world. At the same time it was gradually being synthesized into a coherent whole that—for a while at least —satisfied the cytologists, the geneticists and the paleontologists as well as workers in other specialized biological fields.

A number of the most important developments took place in the United States, and in the same year that Keith and Bishop Barnes metaphorically threw their hats into the public ring on behalf of evolution, H. J. Muller, back in America, was making a series of disturbing discoveries. As far back as 1904, De Vries had suggested that since X rays, discovered by Wilhelm Roentgen in 1895, and the radioactivity reported three years later by the Curies, were "able to penetrate into the interior of living cells, [they might] be used in an attempt to alter the hereditary particles in the germ cells." By the 1920s numerous biological effects of both X rays and radiation had been reported. Some workers had suggested that radium treatment affected the chromatin in the chromosomes, and others believed that either radium or X rays could be used to break them up. Morgan, and others, had experimented with *Drosophila*, but while this work produced a number of mutations, there was no conclusive evidence that they had been produced by the treatment. As Muller was to put it, "the work [had] been done in such a way that the meaning of the data, as analyzed from a modern genetic standpoint, has been highly disputatious at best; moreover what were apparently the clearest cases have given negative or contrary results on repetition." However, during the early 1920s evidence continued to accumulate that living matter was affected by many kinds of high-energy radiation, and in 1926 Muller began a concentrated attempt to discover the effect of X rays in producing mutations in *Drosophila.*

Already some of the mysteries and uncertainties of mutation were being cleared away. As more had become known about the gene, the elementary building block of heredity, it had been necessary to make a stricter definition of the word "mutation." This had for long been a rather woolly blanket word to cover almost any change in the material of heredity. Some changes were special cases of Mendelian recombination, some were due to abnormalities in entire chromosomes on which the genes lay. Others were due to changes in individual genes, and from the mid-1920s on the sense of the word "mutation" tended to be limited to this third meaning, an alteration in a specific gene, and it was this kind of change that Muller began investigating. A few years previously, he told an international congress in New York: "Beneath the imposing structure called Heredity there has been a dingy basement called Mutation." Now it was to be made clear what secrets lay in the basement.

One problem had arisen from the fact that mutations had appeared to be exceedingly rare. Such mutations, it was being increasingly realized, formed the basis for variations on which natural selection worked to bring about evolution, and this became clearer as it was shown by Muller that while a mutated gene incorporated a genetic error, the error was passed on to subsequent generations. The property of replication was not altered, whatever the importance of the gene concerned and, as it has been said, "The recognition of this feature of error copying transformed the 19th century outlook of 'heredity *and* variation' to the 'heredity *of* variation.' " The fact that the gene was autocatalytic was seen by the Russian Sergei S. Chetverikov as presenting a new line of inquiry: why should it not be possible to analyze wild populations of animals and plants and to evaluate their powers of passing on heritable variability to their offspring? It was not only found possible but was to underscore the realization that the rules governing the genetic structure of a population were distinct from those governing the genetics of individuals.

It began to be realized, moreover, that there were other ways in which the genetic control of heredity was more complex than had been appreciated. While certain specific genes did control certain specific characteristics, some appeared to work only in concert with others. Many of the first mutations that had been studied were lethal, and it had been assumed that this was usually so. However, it slowly became clear that there were others that were neutral or might even have beneficial results.

The situation was, in fact, even more complicated, since it was possible for a mutation to be advantageous in one set of circumstances and disadvantageous in another. One of the most famous examples is that of the British peppered moth, which exists in two forms, the gray moth known as *Biston betularia* and a dark melanic form known as *carbonaria*, controlled by a single dominant Mendelian gene, and with skin cells containing the dark-brown pigment called melanin. A century ago the *carbonaria* formed fewer than 1 per cent of peppered moths in Britain's industrial areas, since its black shape made it easily seen by predators while the gray variety merged in with the lichens covering the tree bark on which it rested. During the second half of the nineteenth century, however, the industrial revolution continued to produce more carbon dust, and this killed off the lichen and blackened the tree bark. The *carbonaria* was thus provided with protection, while the lighter variety stood out against the blackened bark. Natural selection now began to operate in the industrial areas against the gray variety and in favor of the darker moths. The result is that today *carbonaria* form 99 percent of the population. Figures suggest, furthermore, that while it survives 10 percent better than the gray variety in polluted areas, it survives 17 percent less well in clean areas.

Quite apart from the fact that the effect of a mutated gene might depend on nonbiological changes in the environment or climate, there was another complicating factor that became more evident during the years between the two world wars. This was that the gene, mutated or otherwise, did not always operate in the same way; it might have one effect when still on its original chromosome and yet a different effect when it had taken up another position due to crossing over. Muller himself was to estimate that during twenty years of *Drosophila* work in which 20 million flies had been examined, only 400 spontaneous visible mutations had been recorded, one mutation for every 50,000 flies. However, Muller emphasized the vast number of combinations of genes that could arise by mutation and recombination. As his biographer has remarked: "It was the essential pruning of the unfavored combinations which made the utterly improbable become commonplace."

In 1926 Muller soon obtained startling results from his experiments with X rays. Several hundred mutants were obtained from flies subjected to X rays, and more than 100 of the mutant genes were followed through three, four or more generations. The results, which were to reveal a new and potentially revolutionary tool for the investigation of heredity, were described in a few sentences of Muller's report in *Science.* "When the heaviest treatment was given to the sperm, about a seventh of the offspring that hatched from them and bred contained individually detectable mutations in their treated X-chromosome. Since the X forms about one fourth of the haploid chromatin, then, if we assume an equal rate of mutation in all the chromosomes (per unit of their length), it follows that almost 'every other one' of the sperm cells capable of producing a fertile adult contained an 'individually detectable' mutation in some chromosome or other. Thousands of untreated parent flies were bred as controls in the same way as the treated ones. Comparison of the mutation rates under the two sets of conditions showed that the heavy treatment had caused a rise of about fifteen thousand per cent in the mutation rate over that in the untreated germ cells."

A few weeks after publication of this first report, Muller gave fuller details to an international congress in Berlin. The implications were considerable, not to say ominous. "If, as seems likely on general considerations," he had concluded in his earlier report, "the effect is common to most organisms, it should be possible to produce, 'to order,' enough mutations to furnish respectable genetic maps, in their selected species, and, by the use of the mapped genes, to analyze the aberrant chromosome phenomena simultaneously obtained. Similarly, for the practical breeder, it is hoped that the method will ultimately prove useful." He then added: "The time is not ripe to discuss here such possibilities with reference to the human species."

Almost twenty years earlier, Bateson had warned that as soon as it becomes common knowledge, "not philosophical speculation, but a certainty—that liability to a disease, or the power of resisting its attack, addiction to a particular vice, or to superstition, is due to the presence or absence of a specific ingredient; and finally that these characteristics are transmitted to the offspring according to definite, predictable rules, then man's views of his own nature, his conceptions of justice, in short his whole outlook on the world, must be profoundly changed." Garrod was even then starting to trace the link between heredity and certain diseases, and year by year the possibility of what is now called genetic engineering was becoming more substantial. "Genetic research," Bateson had said as president of the British Association in 1914, "will make it possible for a nation to elect by what sort of beings it will be represented not very many generations hence, much as a farmer can decide whether his byres shall be full of shorthorns or Herefords. It will be very surprising indeed if some nation does not make trial of this new power. They may make awful mistakes, but I think they will try." Now, in 1927, the cloud on the horizon was growing larger. Might it, in the not-so-distant future, be possible to produce genetically controlled characteristics at will? As for mutations produced by the radiations that followed nuclear disintegration of the atom, that was a prospect too distant and too unnerving to be contemplated—especially if their effects were similar in one way to those of X rays, of which Muller wrote in 1930 that "the frequency of the mutations produced is exactly proportional to the energy of the dosage absorbed (as indicated by the amount of induced ionisation). There is, then, no trace of a critical or threshold dosage beneath which the treatment is too dilute to work."

After the *Drosophila* experiments, barley was next found to be susceptible to artificial mutations produced by X rays, and Muller's forecast that most organisms would respond in the same way soon began to be confirmed. As it has been said, between 1927 and 1930, "the Coolidge tube [an early form of X-ray apparatus] proved to be a cornucopia from which the riches of lethal mutations, recessive visible mutations, ever-sporting displacements, gross structural rearrangements and minute structural rearrangements poured in generous quantities."

The discovery that X rays—and, as it was soon found, other radiations—could have such radical effects on the gene, and therefore on the transmission of characteristics from one generation to the next, tended to widen scientific considerations of what was possible. Increasingly, it was realized that investigating the gene was almost comparable to opening a series of Chinese boxes, with each stage revealing yet further mysteries beyond. It was difficult to rule out any theory, and in 1933 the concept of "the hopeful monster"—the organism whose mutation-produced characteristics enabled it to fit a vacant niche in life—was revived by Richard B. Goldschmidt.

In the 1920s Goldschmidt had challenged the prevailing gene theory with the assumption that genes were enzymes—those proteins that produce chemical change without themselves being affected—and that apparently similar genes could differ in quantity rather than quality. This supposition was exchanged early in the 1930s for the idea that each chromosome consisted of a single long molecule, separate parts of which were available for specific genetic functions, the gene itself no longer being looked upon as a particulate corpuscle. The supposition was accepted no more readily than its predecessor. Goldschmidt also believed for a while that the protein in the gene, or its equivalent, was the genetic material carrying information from one generation to the next and that the nucleic acid already found in the cellular material was merely the scaffolding for structural material—the opposite of what is known today to be the truth.

These assumptions, while subsequently found to be wrong, were no worse than justifiable deductions in a period when information about the genetic processes formed mere islands in an ocean of speculation and ignorance. Goldschmidt was, furthermore, a highly respected figure. Even so, his case for hopeful monsters went against the grain when he first mentioned them in public. Darwin had briefly discussed them in *The Origin* but had ruled out their importance in evolution. "We have also what are called monstrosities; but they graduate into varieties," he had written. "By a monstrosity I presume is meant some considerable deviation of structure in one part, either injurious to or not useful to the species, and not generally propagated. If monstrous forms of this kind ever do appear in a state of nature and are capable of reproduction (which is not always the case), as they occur rarely and singly, their preservation would depend on unusually favourable circumstances. They would, also, during the first and succeeding generations cross with the ordinary form, and thus their abnormal character would almost inevitably be lost."

Goldschmidt was not the first to believe that this proposition should be qualified. As far back as 1895, E. Bonavia, M.D., Brigade Surgeon in the Indian Army, had included a complete chapter, "Monstrosities as Probable Factors in the Creation of Species" in his *Studies in the Evolution of Animals*. "The majority, no doubt, became extinct from unfitness in the battle of life," he wrote, "but now and again a monstrous individual may have been fitted, not perhaps to carry on the *same* life as those which bred it, but that very monstrosity may have enabled it to acquire a different habit of life, which may have left it *without* competitors, and so enabled to live. Then if it bred with the others out of which it evolved, it would *sometimes* transmit the monstrosity to which it may have owed its life, and so by degrees a new type of animal would come into existence. Having more or less the same habits, they would congregate together and interbreed, and thus *fix* that monstrosity, so called."

By 1933 Goldschmidt had come to believe that, while the variations on which Darwin had placed so much faith could account for microevolution, something more drastic was needed for macroevolution—the great changes visible in fossils from geological ages separated by millions of years. "The solution," he later wrote, "was the existence of macromutants, which, in rare cases, could affect early embryonic processes so that through the features of embryonic regulation and integration at once a major step in evolution could be accomplished and fixed under certain conditions. I spoke half jokingly of the hopeful monster in my first publication on the subject, a lecture read by invitation in 1933 at the World's Fair in Chicago."

However jokingly Goldschmidt may have made his original suggestion, it grew within the next few years, and *The Material Basis of Evolution*, an extension of his 1939 Silliman Lectures, maintained that mutants producing monsters might "have played a considerable role in macroevolution." Furthermore, he spelled out the details. "A monstrosity appearing in a single genetic step might permit the occupation of a new environmental niche and thus produce a new type in one step," he wrote. "A Manx cat with a hereditary concrescence of the tail vertebrae, or a comparable mouse or rat mutant, is just a monster. But a mutant of Archaeopteryx producing the same monstrosity was a hopeful monster because the resulting fanlike arrangement of the tail feathers was a great improvement in the mechanics of flying. A fish undergoing a mutation which made for a distortion of the skull carrying both eyes to one side of the body is a monster. The same mutant in a much compressed form of fish living near the bottom of the sea produced a hopeful monster, as it enabled the species to take to the life upon the sandy bottom of the ocean, as exemplified by the flounders. A dog with achondroplastic bow-legs was a monstrous mutant until man found the proper niche for it—to follow the badger (dachs) into its den—and selected the hopeful monster as a dachshund."

Goldschmidt's "hopeful monsters" became something of a joke, which was rather unfair, since Darwin himself had recalled the ram lamb born in Massachusetts in 1791 that had short crooked legs and a long back like a turnspit dog. "From this one lamb," he noted, "the *otter* or *ancon* semi-monstrous breed was raised. . . ."

If there were doubts about progress in genetics, they came at a different level and from a different source. During the 1920s there had begun the revolution in physics that was to encompass Heisenberg's uncertainty principle, Schrödinger's wave mechanics and Bohr's complementarity principle. Together, they created a somewhat misty confusion for all but professional physicists. This was particularly so in the case of geneticists, who had hitherto been able to congratulate themselves that they had followed the precepts of the physical sciences and were now buttressing their theories with the solid results of experiment. Morgan was one of those who well expressed the worries that the new physics—and the new cosmology—had raised.

> I am aware, of course, that biologists who in the past have relied on [the appeal to experiment] had supposed that in the physical sciences they had an anchor to windward. Recent developments in physics have been so extraordinary that, today, the biologist is left wondering whether he has anchored on a safe bottom. He is flattered for the moment, when the eminent mathematician and philosopher, Whitehead, discovers that the biological conception of organism is far more important for physicists than their traditional but narrow point of view, and when a mathematician and astronomer, Jeans, concludes that the Universe is Mind. Now the *human mind* is something that the biologist had hoped some day to study by the experimental approach. He would be immensely flattered to be told that he would then be engaged in the elucidation of something that extends out beyond the farthest star, were it not that he has become a little skeptical regarding the adequacy of metaphysical solutions of the cosmos based on introspection.

Despite Morgan's skepticism, one repercussion of the new physics was indirectly to affect the growth of evolutionary knowledge in a dramatic way. In 1932 Niels Bohr discussed biological indeterminacy in a paper published in *Nature.* Heisenberg had recently shown that due to the dual particle/wave nature of matter it was impossible accurately to determine simultaneously both the position and the momentum of a particle. Bohr suggested a biological corollary: that an organism could only be studied properly while it was alive but that this prevented a proper study of its components. Could the study of biological phenomena, he asked, lead to new laws in chemistry and physics? Some years later the physicist Erwin Schrödinger took up the question in his *What Is Life?* and asked whether classical physics might have to change once again to account for biological problems. And it was to be Schrödinger's *What Is Life?* that helped guide Crick and Watson toward the double helix of the 1950s.

However, the philosophical question raised by the new physics did nothing to inhibit the new evolutionary synthesis, as it was to become known. The phrase was introduced by Julian Huxley, grandson of "Darwin's bulldog," in *Evolution: The Modern Synthesis,* published in 1942, and was used there to describe the general acceptance over recent years of two propositions: that gradual evolution could be explained in terms of mutations and their recombination, which produced genetic variation worked on by the process of natural selection; and that evolutionary phenomena, including the macroevolutionary processes and speciation revealed by paleontology, could be explained in terms of the known genetic mechanisms.

This synthesis was the result of work not only by geneticists but also by cytologists, by systematicists, whose classification of living organisms stressed their evolutionary connections, by botanists and by paleontologists. In each field there was disagreement about the correct interpretation of fresh experimental results, as well as about the results in other fields. The United States, Britain, France and Germany each produced their own individual pattern of emphasis, while over all there hung the obfuscating fact, more prominent here than in most sciences, that a single word could have a widely different variety of meanings for different people. With all these factors at work, it is hardly surprising that even today there remains disagreement about the exact course of the evolutionary synthesis and even about the date of its beginning.

Nevertheless, it is difficult not to give prime importance to Fisher's paper of 1918, which not only reconciled Darwin's view of natural selection with the Mendelian laws but put beyond doubt the value of mathematics in finding a way through the genetic maze.

Meanwhile, statements about evolution and also about the raw materials of genetics or the effects of evolution were increasingly given quantitative support. Thus it was soon being estimated that there were about 4,000 genes in a *Drosophila melanogaster*. The chromosomes on which they were arranged were estimated to be some 7.5 microns in length and about 0.2 microns in breadth, while the genes themselves were estimated to be about sixty-thousandths of a micron in diameter—a micron being one-millionth of a meter. When it came to the effects of evolution, J. B. S. Haldane, the British geneticist and mathematician, felt confident in making numerous estimates, among them being his suggestion in *Biometrika* that the increase in the tooth length of the horse during its evolution since the Eocene Age was roughly 4 percent per million years.

It was a new departure for geneticists. As the British geneticist E. B. Ford has emphasized, "Most of the earlier Darwinian zoologists (including Wallace, Lankester, and Poulton) were extremely unmathematical, and they felt Mendelism could be an intrusion of mathematics into biology. I once," he continued, "spent part of an afternoon trying to explain p^2: $2pq$: q^2 to William Bateson. Not only could he not understand it but he could see no possible point in it."

This attitude was slowly eroded by Fisher, whose mathematical approach was outlined most fully in his *Genetical Theory of Natural Selection*, published in 1930, and by J. B. S. Haldane, whose mathematical approach to genetics was supplemented by a rare ability to say what he meant in simple words. Haldane's *Causes of Evolution*, published in 1932, contained a lengthy and remarkable mathematical appendix that not only spelled out Fisher's views but also reconciled them with those of Sewall Wright, the American whose "Evolution in Mendelian Populations" had suggested that Fisher's theories would in practice tend to remove the variations on which natural selection operated.

The mathematical attack showed, particularly in Fisher's work, that although the mutation rates in *Drosophila*, on which the crucial work had been done, were relatively low, and although selective advantages created would be only mild, the great age of the earth had been enough to allow the gradual accumulation of new favorable attributes. Thus it tended to lay the ghost, at least for the time being, of the need for saltations in which Bateson had placed so much faith. Just as important, Fisher, Haldane and Wright showed that the genetic structure of a population was governed by rules distinct from those governing the genetics of individuals. While Morgan had begun to discover this in the Columbia fly room, its theoretical basis now began to emerge. As Theodosius Dobzhansky has neatly expressed it, "Haldane, Wright, and Fisher are the pioneers of population genetics whose main research equipment was paper and ink rather than microscopes, experimental fields, *Drosophila* bottles, or mouse cages. Theirs is theoretical biology at its best, and it has provided a guiding light for rigorous quantitative experimentation and observation." There was, and is, much support for the view. Haldane ended the appendix to *The Causes of Evolution* with the forecast: "The permeation of biology by mathematics is only beginning, but unless the history of science is an inadequate guide, it will continue, and the investigations here summarised represent the beginning of a new branch of applied mathematics." At a symposium on the mathematical challenges to the neo-Darwinian interpretation of evolution more than thirty years later the late Alfred North Whitehead was quoted as saying: "I will not go so far as to say that to construct a history of thought without profound study of the mathematical ideas of successive efforts is like omitting Hamlet from the play which is named after him; that would be claiming too much. But it is certainly analogous to cutting out the part of Ophelia. This simile is singularly exact, for Ophelia is quite essential to the play. She is very charming and a little mad." There was a contrary view, current in Haldane's heyday and expressed at the symposium on mathematical challenges in 1966 by the noted geneticist C. H. Waddington. "The whole real guts of evolution—which is, how do you come to have horses and tigers, and things—" he said, "is outside the mathematical theory."

Nevertheless, the mathematical work carried out between the two world wars made it possible to predict what naturalists might find in the field, a possibility followed up most vigorously by the Russians under Sergei Chetverikov, who was to be so important in launching experimental population genetics.

It has also been maintained that Chetverikov's importance lay in his influence not only on population genetics but, if more indirectly, on Theodosius Dobzhansky, whose *Genetics and the Origin of Species* was to spread the gospel of the evolutionary synthesis in the United States as vigorously as Julian Huxley's *Evolution: The Modern Synthesis* in Britain.

However true the belief that it was the mathematical geneticists who had succeeded by the 1930s in supplying a theoretical base for much of the evolutionary synthesis, it is no less true that their efforts were supplemented from other fields. Important contributions were certainly made by the cytologists, who before the First World War had begun to demonstrate that De Vries's *Oenothera* had not, in fact, produced new species as believed, showing, in the words of Ernst Mayr, that De Vries's *Oenothera* mutations were "a horrible mixture of segregates of balanced chromosomal complexes, cases of polyploidy, and a few cases of true gene mutations. It took the evolutionists some forty or fifty years to free themselves of the albatross that De Vries had hung around the neck of the term mutation." Cyril Darlington was even more scathing in his condemnation that De Vries's *Oenothera* "had given rise to a false theory of evolution, as well as a false theory of mutation and a false theory of heredity and chromosome behavior. Indeed, if we talk about scientific research blocking the progress of a science, *Oenothera* was the imperishable example."

The truth about the plants was important because the existence of the false theory had inevitably made it difficult to accept unequivocally any theory of evolution by gradual change. But there was another way in which cytologists had by the early 1930s removed a barrier to forward movement. Until that period it had remained difficult to think of genes in terms of physical entities—much as it had been difficult to think of nuclear particles in such a manner until Rutherford's experiments during the first decade of the twentieth century. By 1930, however, the work of Morgan's team in the Columbia fly room, as well as that of workers elsewhere, had demonstrated not only that genes existed but also that they were to be found at specific places on the chromosome.

Another influence on the evolutionary synthesis was the resolution of the problem that many paleontologists had seen as presented by the fossil record. Darwin had always been ambivalent about this, admitting that there were huge gaps in the record of the rocks, but bringing forward a variety of explanations to account for it. The argument had gone on throughout the years, but many—possibly a majority of—paleontologists continued to require an explanatory mechanism for macroevolution different from the mechanisms postulated by geneticists to explain the evolution that could be studied in the laboratory or in the field. Here the synthesis was to come largely from the work of George Gaylord Simpson, who presented, in *Tempo and Mode in Evolution*, an argument that accounted for macroevolution while using no more than the models geneticists were already using.

It is difficult to pin down the date at which these developments in a variety of biological sciences began to be seen as a new synthesizing approach to evolution, but the approach was certainly visible in *The Science of Life*, published in 1931, and written by Julian Huxley, H. G. Wells and Wells's son G. P. Wells. Three years before this, the trend could have been noted in Huxley's brief *Stream of Life*; it was to be emphasized in his *New Systematics* and, overwhelmingly, in his *Evolution: The Modern Synthesis*. Whatever the relative importance of the various synthesizers, which the historians of science are likely to debate for many more years, it had become clear by the end of the Second World War that Darwin's essential theory had not been shaken. Natural selection had been restored to an importance it had lost in the first years of the century, while if evolution by "jumps" did operate in some areas, it did so by methods that, when analyzed, showed more similarity to the methods of microevolution than had previously been suspected. Darwin and Mendel, natural selection and the mechanisms of genetics were in most cases mutually supportive rather than mutually exclusive.

But there was one exception within this climate of Darwinian approval. In Russia, whose leaders had in 1921 seized the results of genetic research to improve the country's agriculture, a change was increasingly noticeable in the official attitude. One reason for this had been the clinging by the Russian establishment to the orthodoxy of Marx and Engels. Both had approved of Darwin when, in his later years, he had swung toward at least some of Lamarck's ideas. In the West, this trend had by the 1920s been seen to be little more than a temporary aberration. The transmission from one generation to the next of characteristics acquired as a result of environment—an idea pleasing to those who hoped to redirect the lot of man—had been shown in Morgan's fly room, as elsewhere, to be no more than a dream. But the Russian party line continued to take the Darwinian view that had been abandoned in the twentieth century and, inevitably, excoriated the modern Western synthesis that incorporated genetics as well as natural selection.

"Under the new Stalin régime, after 1928," Cyril Darlington has written, "Marxist orthodoxy became more important. Party members of research institutes began to find it profitable to intrigue for promotion. Philosophical exegisis began to intrude more frequently into the papers of young scientists. Western influence became suspect. A screen was gradually drawn between Russia and the outside world. English summaries were reduced in scientific papers. Visits abroad became restricted to those who left hostages behind. Too many of the leading Soviet scientists, geneticists, as well as others, who went abroad were hesitating to return."

In genetics the process was exemplified by the overshadowing —and eventual death in Siberia—of Nikolai Vavilov, and the rise of Trofim Denisovich Lysenko, a scientist who could claim: "Genetics is merely an amusement, like chess or football." Lysenko had first claimed that by treating wheat grains before they germinated, the plants could be induced to mature more quickly. If the theory proved correct the process, known as vernalization, would obviously be of immense aid to Russian farmers who would be enabled to grow wheat in districts farther north. Next, Lysenko maintained that other crops could be treated with similar success and that yet others, by treatment, could be made to transmit acquired characteristics. Following up the work of Ivan Vladimirovich Michurin, he said that he could change the character of all plants by grafting. Moreover, plants that had never been crossed, could, he claimed, be crossed to produce fertile hybrids; by the use of mixed pollen it was even possible to change rye into wheat.

The abandoning in Russia of classical genetics took place progressively over nearly two decades. As early as August 1931 a decree "On Plant Breeding and Seed Production," issued on behalf of Lysenko, testily ordered potato breeders to change to improved varieties within four to five years rather than the ten to twelve years that had been regarded as minimal. Four years later he declared that southern Russia could become self-sufficient in production of potato tubers by the simple method of planting in midsummer. "Potato specialists must have gaped in astonishment at this announcement," it has been said. "It was first presented to them not in a technical journal but at the Second Congress of Collective Farm Shock-Brigade Workers, with Stalin interjecting 'Bravo, Comrade Lysenko!' A little later the official newspaper of the Commissariat of Agriculture presented Lysenko's claims, and without the tag 'For discussion' that would have made it possible to disagree. Lysenko presented summer planting as his discovery, failing to mention—much less evaluate—the experience of farmers who had long practiced various forms of it in scattered parts of the U.S., France and his native Ukraine."

By 1937 the situation had become so bad that Muller, who had been working in Moscow since 1932, decided to leave the country. As he wrote to his friend Julian Huxley:

> The narrowness of biologists (in the U.S.S.R.) on the one hand and of most of the economic and political progressives on the other hand, together with the inability of most people to see two things at a time, has led to a widening rift between one group, which believes in biological (genetic) improvement, and another, which believes in social betterment. There is no reason at all why these two methods should be mutually exclusive: on the contrary, each is really conducive to the other. Some people might term such an interaction "dialectic," and I regard the antithesis that is usually set up as most unfortunate, and have done my utmost to play upon the psychology of the socially advanced group—for I expect them really to control work, or be prevented from it by the effect of the campaign of Lysenko and Prezent (crazy Lamarckists, who, however, deny being Lamarckists). . . . It might help your understanding of the situation to know of the attitude of the leading party people in fields connected with [genetics]. . . . Bauman [Head of Science for the party] accused me of trying to carry over biological principles directly into the social level, and said we couldn't apply genetics to man that way. Yacovlev [Head of Agriculture] maintained that the genes of man had been changed by the environment of civilisation, and therefore primitive races existing today have inferior genes. But, he said, about three generations of socialism will so change the genes as to make all races equal.

The Seventh International Congress on Genetics was to have been held in Moscow in 1938. It was canceled, then finally held in Edinburgh in 1939; but by that time the Russians had signed the Nazi-Soviet Pact, and the Soviet delegation failed to arrive. A letter from Vavilov, sent privately to Haldane, made it clear that Vavilov was acting under duress. During the Second World War it became known that he had died after banishment to Siberia.

But Vavilov had not been the first prominent biologist to suffer for his views. The details of this black period in Russian history are still uncertain; but as evidence mounted after the war for what had at first been unsubstantiated fact, it became clear that many geneticists had been banished to Siberia and that many had died there. Others simply disappeared. All this was in line with the pattern described by Sir Eric Ashby, who spent a year in Russia in 1945. "Work may be condemned by Lysenko and his disciples," he wrote, "not on any intrinsic weakness it may have, but because it falls into any one of several heresies. The chief heresies are: any sort of idealism founded on the work of Berkeley or Kant; any formalism founded on the work of Mendel or Weismann; any work done under the influence of capitalism (Lysenko's assistant, Prezent, talks about 'the enormous social-class significance of our controversy'); any work tainted with 'theism' (that Mendel was a priest is sufficient to discredit his experiments); 'fascism' (i.e. any theory which presupposes an innate heterogeneity of people or plants is fascist); and finally 'abiologism,' which is the application to biology of inappropriate techniques, such as mathematics."

Any lingering doubt that Darwin was being sacrificed to ideology was removed in 1948. First Lysenko addressed the Lenin Academy of Agriculture with a 15,000-word diatribe. In this, Darwin was reprimanded for accepting the theory of the struggle for existence. The overwhelming majority of Western biologists were claimed to have "debased Darwinism and smothered its scientific foundation." Weismann's idea of a hereditary substance was said to represent a "frankly idealistic, essentially mystical concept," while Weismann, Mendel and Morgan were described as "the founders of modern reactionary genetics."

The following month, official approval was given to these perversions of fact when the Presidium of the USSR Academy of Sciences passed twelve resolutions in August that abolished existing laboratories; called for the removal from scientists' councils of those who supported "Morgano-Weismannite genetics"; and asked for the popularization of a "critical exposure of the pseudoscientific Morgano-Weismannite tendency." Furthermore, it was claimed that "Michurin's materialistic direction in biology is the only acceptable form of science because it is based on dialectical materialism and on the principle of changing nature for the benefit of the people." Five years later, Lysenko revealed the extent to which politics had taken over genetics. "Comrade Stalin," he wrote in *Pravda*, "has shown the ways to develop the theory of Michurinist materialist biology. . . . He personally edited the draft of the report on the 'Situation in Biological Science,' explained to me in detail the corrections which he had made, and gave directions concerning the presentation of some parts of the report."

It is inconceivable that the politically inspired actions even of a state as powerful as the Soviet Union could at this date have permanently stopped the advance that had been started by Darwin almost a century previously. But the seriousness of the situation in Russia had already been indicated by letters from H. J. Muller and from Sir Henry Dale, a former president of the Royal Society, both of whom had resigned from the USSR Academy of Sciences following the 1948 meeting.

Muller said that he was resigning because of the dropping of notable geneticists, and the Academy's actions "in abolishing the Laboratory of Cytogenetics of your most eminent remaining geneticist, Dubinin, in announcing your support of the charlatan, Lysenko, whom some years ago you had stooped to take into your membership, and in repudiating, at his insistence, the principles of genetics." Sir Henry Dale was even more critical. "Though Darwin's work is still formally acknowledged in the U.S.S.R.," he said, "his essential discovery is now to be rejected there. The whole great fabric of exact knowledge, still growing at the hands of those who have followed Mendel, Bateson and Morgan, is to be repudiated and denounced; and the last few, who were still contributing to it in the U.S.S.R., have now been deprived of position and opportunity."

But Russia was to pay a heavy price for political obduracy. "[Lysenko's] activities on behalf of fantasy," it has been rightly said, "crippled Soviet agriculture to an extent that made him possibly the greatest ally of the Western nations in the struggles of the post–World War II decade."

15

Molecular Biology Takes Over

WHILE Russian genetics was being bludgeoned by dialectical materialism into maintaining, if necessary for the good of the party, that black was white, a very different and immeasurably more important process was taking place in America and Europe: the merging of genetics and biochemistry into molecular biology—"the search for explanations of the behaviour of living things in terms of the molecules that compose them." If statistics had been the queen of the sciences used by evolutionists during the heyday of Pearson, Fisher, Haldane and Sewall Wright, it was now to be replaced by molecular biology, which during the decades that followed the end of the Second World War began to answer some of the most worrying riddles that had puzzled Darwin and his successors.

It was also to lead on, during the second half of the twentieth century, to increased questioning of neo-Darwinism and of the belief that natural selection occupied a place in the evolutionary machinery as important as Darwin had maintained; or, more accurately, as important as he was often stated to have maintained— for he was frequently quoted without the qualifications and limitations with which he cautiously hedged many of his pronouncements. The relative importance of "jumps" and of continuing minor variations, the roles that each played respectively in macroevolution—which dealt with major changes throughout geological eras—and in microevolution—which concerned the accumulation of imperceptible changes on which Darwin had put such weight— were discussed in the light of new evidence. The evolutionary story was seen to be even more complex than had been realized, while the gene, first given a relatively clear chemical outline by the molecular biologists, was later seen to hide mysteries that had not even been suspected. Throughout all this, Darwin's position was very largely governed by the eye of the beholder. To those for whom the primary biological achievement of the nineteenth century was the establishment of evolution as a process forever operating on organic matter, his role was still unique and unchallenged. To those who concentrated on the mechanisms of evolution, seen by Darwin within the limitations of his time, the temptations of iconoclasticism were often too great, and Darwin was condemned for being wrong in detail however right in broad principle.

Many factors—important among them being technological improvements—combined to bring about the postwar new look at Darwin and Darwinism, but the work of the molecular biologists was preeminent. The story had really started in the last third of the nineteenth century when the Swiss biochemist Johann Friedrich Miescher discovered that the nucleus of living cells consisted mainly of a substance containing nucleic acid and basic proteins. This was chromatin, revealed by Miescher first in the nuclei of pus cells and then in the nuclei of fish sperm. The substance was found to exist not randomly in the nucleus but in the chromosomes, which had been considered, soon after their discovery, to be the messengers carrying specific characteristics from one generation to the next. The implications were spelled out by the American Edmund B. Wilson, who wrote in 1895 that one thus reached "the remarkable conclusion that inheritance may, perhaps, be effected by the physical transmission of a particular chemical compound from parent to offspring."

From that point on, one line of research into inheritance, and thus into evolution, began to concentrate on chemical possibilities. As Morgan and his team in the fly room at Columbia began to discover the way in which characteristics were genetically transmitted, chemists began to search for the composition of chromatin. Miescher's work had itself triggered off a series of discoveries. Altman found a method of taking the protein from the nuclein in yeast, and thus isolated pure nucleic acid for the first time. Albrecht Kossel discovered that nucleic acid contained four organic bases—the chemicals adenine, guanine, thymine and cytosine—whose molecules were half a century later found to hold the key to variation in living organisms. Then it became known that there were two kinds of nucleic acid. One was deoxyribonucleic acid, now known as DNA, containing the sugar deoxyribose; the other was ribonucleic acid or RNA, with the sugar ribose in place of deoxyribose. In addition to the different kind of sugar, RNA contained uracil as one of its four bases instead of the thymine of DNA.

However, of the two constituents in chromatin, it was not clear whether the nucleic acid or the protein carried the genetic information. For long it was taken for granted that the protein was responsible, a conclusion reached after Garrod had shown in his medical work not only that alkaptonuria, the disease in which a patient's urine turned brown, was inherited as if due to a single Mendelian recessive gene but that its physical cause appeared to be the absence of a special enzyme. Bateson and Punnett found comparable examples in their work on flowers, and there slowly grew up the theory of "one gene: one enzyme," according to which there was a direct relationship between particular genes and specific enzymes.

The belief that the protein in nucleoprotein carried the genetic information rested largely on the belief that while protein molecules had molecular weights of up to several million, consisted of up to 20 different amino acids, and therefore appeared to offer an almost limitless variety of inheritable possibilities, DNA had a comparatively small molecular weight of about 1,500. This theory was demolished after Hermann Staudinger's discovery of polymerized macromolecules—molecules of large molecular weight formed by the chemical union of similar molecules of smaller weight—led in the late 1920s to new methods of investigation. Using these methods, researchers found that the DNA molecule had a molecular weight of up to one million. It was, in fact, complex enough to carry the required amount of genetic information.

Even so, it was not until 1944 that experiments at the Rockefeller Institute by Drs. Oswald T. Avery, Colin M. MacLeod and Maclyn McCarty showed conclusively that the nucleic acid was in fact the carrier. The breakthrough was finally made by taking two different strains of pneumonia bacteria, both of which bred true and both of which could be easily identified. By mixing the nucleic acid from the two strains, it was found possible to transform one type of bacteria into another; more importantly, the transferred bacteria passed on to following generations its newly acquired characteristics. "This result," it has been said, "startled the researchers as much as if they had transformed a duck into a dog."

The researchers themselves were more cautious, but they could say: "The evidence presented supports the belief that a nucleic acid of the desoxyribose type is the fundamental unit of the transforming principle of Pneumococcus Type III."

Avery had, moreover, written to his brother Roy even before the experiments were completed, making it clear that he knew the full significance of what he and his colleagues were demonstrating. "If we are right, and of course that's not yet proven," he wrote, "then it means that nucleic acids are *not* merely structurally important but functionally active substances in determining the biochemical activities and specific characteristics of cells—and that by means of a known chemical substance it is possible to induce *predictable* and *hereditary* changes in cells. This is something that has long been the dream of geneticists."

The paper by Avery and his fellow workers was published the following year. Erwin Chargaff, who was to play a crucial part in the story of DNA, commented, "It would have been difficult to say more in so few words, for this discovery established the chemical nature of the genes, or at any rate of some genes. In a certain sense, it meant that classical biochemistry had come to an end."

There had been a strangely comparable change in the physical sciences a third of a century earlier. Ernest Rutherford had then propounded his idea of the nuclear atom, a concatenation of minute particles forever circling the nucleus in their comparatively immense seas of empty space. Comparably, the fundamental unit of genetics had previously been the invisible and abstract gene; now it was a chemical molecule, soon to be revealed as a structure of daunting complexity.

Complexity was inevitable, since whatever the mechanism for passing on characteristics from one generation to the next, it had to be capable of dealing with the near-infinite varieties of living organisms. This was certainly true of the nucleic acids, as became increasingly evident during the decade that followed Avery's announcement. But major campaigns were to be needed both in Europe and the United States before their structure and their methods of operation could be established. It is doubtful if this work could have been accomplished without the developments in scientific research that had been brought about by the Second World War. One radical break with the past was the replacement by the team of the solitary genius working alone. Another was the greater importance of technicians, and a scientific team was rarely viable without its backup group of technicians. There were also subtle human changes. Scientists had achieved a new status during the war. They could be, and were, more ambitious than their counterparts before 1939. They tended to be more competitive, and the race for results tended to be run more intensely.

In addition, considerable technological advances had taken place. The availability of radioisotopes, a natural by-product of nuclear research on both sides of the Atlantic, opened up entirely new prospects. In 1944, partition chromatography had been introduced for the easier separation and identification of biochemical substances. The photoelectric ultraviolet spectrophotometer had followed. These and other developments made it possible for geneticists to work with ever smaller and shorter-lived organisms, a matter of considerable importance. Morgan's fruit flies numbered only a few thousand individuals, and some twenty days passed between generations. Microorganisms such as bacteria or bacterial viruses allowed an experimenter to use billions of individuals, and only a few minutes passed between each generation. "One can therefore perform in a test tube in 20 minutes," it has been pointed out, "an experiment yielding a quantity of genetic data that would require, if humans were used, the entire population of the earth. Moreover, with microorganisms special tricks enable one to select just those individuals of interest from a population of a billion. By exploiting these advantages it becomes possible not only to split the gene but also to map it in the utmost detail, down to the molecular limits of its structure." As C. H. Waddington was to put it in 1966, "The great advances in modern genetics have just come from being able to work in 10^9 organisms instead of having to fiddle around with 100 or so mice."

With these advantages over their predecessors, the molecular biologists of the late 1940s set about answering the question that Erwin Schrödinger had used as a title for his short but seminal book of 1945, *What is Life?* Schrödinger, the Viennese physicist who in the 1920s had helped evolve wave mechanics, and who could stride effortlessly across the frontiers separating science and the humanities, had asked in his little book: "How can the events *in space and time* which take place within the spatial boundary of a living organism be accounted for by physics and chemistry?" He had gone on to present the idea of a code controlling inheritance and pointed out that "the number of atoms in [a gene] need not be very large to produce an almost unlimited number of possible arrangements. For illustration, think of the Morse code. The two different signs of dot and dash in well-ordered groups of not more than four allow of thirty different specifications. Now, if you allowed yourself the use of a third sign, in addition to dot and dash, and used groups of not more than ten, you could form 29,524 different 'letters'; with five signs and groups up to 25, the number is 372,529,029,846,191,405. . . . What we wish to illustrate is simply that with the molecular picture of the gene it is no longer inconceivable that the miniature code should precisely correspond with a highly complicated and specified plan of development and should somehow contain the means to put it into operation."

The possibility of a chemical coding being responsible for the variations to be observed in living organisms had in fact been suggested half a century earlier by Johann Friedrich Miescher. "In the huge molecules of albumen compounds or in the yet more complicated molecules of haemoglobin, etc.," he wrote to his uncle Professor Wilhelm His in December 1892, "the many asymmetric carbon atoms provide a colossal amount of stereo-isomerism [differences in chemical compounds having the same molecular formula, the differences being due to different arrangements of the atoms in the three-dimensional space within the molecule]. In them all the wealth and variety of hereditary transmissions can find expression, just as all the words and concepts of all languages can find expression in twenty-four to thirty alphabetic letters. It is therefore quite superfluous to make the egg and sperm cell a storehouse of countless chemical substances each of which carries a particular hereditary quality (the Pangenesis of de Vries). My own research has convinced me that the protoplasm and the nucleus, far from consisting of countless chemical substances, contain quite a small number of chemical individuals [compounds] which are likely to be of a most complicated chemical structure."

Miescher's belief remained undisclosed in the archives until the mid-1960s, but *What Is Life?* was read by Francis H. C. Crick, one of the three men to be awarded the Nobel Prize for unraveling the structure of DNA. Crick was impressed by the idea that fundamental biological problems "could be thought about in precise terms, using the concepts of physics and chemistry." However, that was not all. A greater stimulus to research on the subject came from religion, he has written. He was, he went on, an atheist who wanted "to try to show that areas apparently too mysterious to be explained by physics and chemistry, could in fact be so explained."

He expanded this view in his application for a research studentship. "The particular field which excites my interest is the division between the living and the non-living, as typified by, say, proteins, viruses, bacteria and the structure of chromosomes," he wrote. "The eventual goal, which is somewhat remote, is the description of these activities in the terms of their structure, i.e., the spacial distribution of their constituent atoms, in so far as this may prove possible. This might be called the chemical physics of biology."

Crick was awarded a research studentship and subsequently joined the Medical Research Council's unit in the Cavendish Laboratory, Cambridge. Here he began work with James D. Watson, an American who had intended to become an ornithologist but had been encouraged into genetics by H. J. Muller. In addition to this Cavendish team, there was another working on the problem at King's College, London. Its leading members were Maurice Wilkins, a New Zealander who like Crick had been turned toward biological problems by Schrödinger's book, and Rosalind Franklin. Their speciality was X-ray crystallography, and Franklin's pictures of the X-ray refraction pattern of DNA were among the first to give clues to the discovery of its structure. In the United States, there was Linus Pauling, at the California Institute of Technology, who had already uncovered the structure of proteins and was correctly thought by the two English teams, soon working together, to be nearing a solution to the DNA problem.

Thus during the early 1950s there were three teams of exceptionally able scientists, quite apart from their departmental heads and colleagues such as Erwin Chargaff and Max Perutz, all seeking —it is hardly an exaggeration to say desperately seeking—an answer if not to the question "What is life?," then at least to "How does inheritance work?" The answer involved a number of disciplines, and a complex scientific situation was made ever more complex by natural rivalry. The personal story has been told by Watson in *The Double Helix*, the detailed scientific story with its triumphs and disasters by Robert Olby in *The Path to the Double Helix*.

In the summer of 1952, Pauling and Crick met at the International Biochemical Congress in Paris and discussed the situation in some detail. Only in the autumn did further work encourage each to prepare a paper for *Nature* on the subject of *a* keratin, the fibrous protein that is the main constituent of wool, hair, horn and hoofs. The journal was, and is, one of the main international fields for staking claims to priority—so much so that in 1939 the nuclear fission team at the Collège de France in Paris had rushed a vital paper to London by air to forestall publication of results from America. And now, in 1952, a curious sequence of events recurred. Crick's paper, dated October 22, 1952, appeared in the November 22 issue. That from Pauling, dated October 14, did not appear until January 10, 1953. The British paper, Watson has written, "was quickly drafted and given to Bragg [Sir Lawrence Bragg, then head of the Cavendish Laboratory] to send on to the editors, with a covering note asking for speedy publication. If the editors were told that a British article was of above-average interest, they would try to publish the manuscript almost immediately. With luck, Francis' [Crick's] coiled coils would get into print as soon as if not before Pauling's." Yet British chauvinism was not entirely the reason for success, since Pauling's paper was supported by three diagrams for which blocks had to be made, and Crick's demanded none. However, comparison of the dates of other papers in the January 10 issue, it has been pointed out, "shows that Pauling's paper was not delayed, but that Crick's paper was pushed ahead."

With Pauling known to be working on the structure of DNA, the gentlemanly competition of scientists searching for fundamental truths was soon augmented by an increasingly passionate desire to win the race. The stakes were high, and Francis Crick, jubilant as they breasted the tape, exaggerated only slightly when he announced that the team had found the secret of life.

Before this, there had been one nasty moment. Pauling was reported to have solved the problem. He had, moreover, sent a copy of his coming paper to his son Peter, then working in Cambridge. "Only those who have experienced the trauma of competition in research will know how Watson and Crick must have felt with Peter Pauling in the room, the manuscript from his father sticking out of his pocket," Robert Olby has reflected. "Had Pauling really discovered the secret? Did he know all? Was this, as they feared, just a repetition of the a-helix affair, this time with DNA? Many years later Watson had not forgotten how his 'stomach sank in apprehension at learning that all was lost.' " But on being shown the paper Watson and Crick both decided—correctly, as it turned out—that Pauling's solution, incorporating three entwined helical chains, must be wrong. Work on a viable alternative was redoubled. And on April 25, 1953, a communication to *Nature* by Watson and Crick announced the famous double helix, the model of DNA that, as they said, "has novel features which are of considerable biological interest."

The DNA molecule consisted of two helical chains of phosphate sugars coiled round the same axis and linked by pairs of the four bases that had been found in DNA many years previously. "The novel feature of the structure," continued the paper, "is the manner in which the two chains are held together by the purine and pyrimidine bases. The planes of the bases are perpendicular to the fibre axis. They are joined together in pairs, a single base from one chain being hydrogen-bonded to a single base from the other chain, so that the two lie side by side with identical z-co-ordinates. One of the pair must be a purine and the other a pyrimidine for bonding to occur."

The paper concluded with what has been called "one of the most coy statements in the literature of science." It had not escaped their notice, it said, "that the specific pairing we have postulated immediately suggests a possible copying mechanism for the genetic material."

The following month Watson and Crick expanded on this tantalizing statement in a further communication to *Nature.* Although considerable evidence suggested that DNA was the material that passed on information from one generation to the next, there had so far been no evidence as to how it carried out "the essential operation required of a genetic material, that of exact self-duplication." The double helix, however, and the manner in which its two chains were held together, might allow such an operation to take place. "The phosphate-sugar backbone of our model is completely regular, but any sequence of the pairs of bases can fit into the structure," said Watson and Crick. "It follows that in a long molecule many different permutations are possible, and it therefore seems likely that the precise sequence of the bases is the code which carries the genetical information. If the actual order of the bases on one of the pair of chains were given, one could write down the exact order of the bases on the other one, because of the specific pairing. Thus one chain is, as it were, the complement of the other, and it is this feature which suggests how the desoxyribonucleic acid molecule might duplicate itself." Before duplication, the hydrogen bonds were broken and the two chains of the helix unwound and separated. Each chain then acted as a template for the formation onto itself of a new companion chain, so that eventually there were two pairs of chains where before only one had existed. Moreover the sequence of the pairs of bases was the same as in the original chains.

The revelation solved one problem that had bedeviled evolution for almost a century. A molecule of DNA was estimated to contain as many as ten million bases, while the sequence of bases in a haploid mammalian cell was estimated to be about three billion sequences. These can theoretically be arranged in a number of different ways equaling four raised to the power of about three billion, a number larger than the estimated number of elementary particles in the universe, and corresponding to infinity. If the genetic information passed on by DNA depended on the sequence of the bases, the number of these sequences was sufficient to account for the almost infinitely large number of variations in living organisms.

But two important matters were completely unresolved. One was the method by which the "information" in the DNA was taken up and utilized by the cell. The other was the meaning of the base sequences in DNA, the "code" by which they operated. These problems were only solved in the 1960s, and then solved slowly and by the lengthy study and testing of new concepts. "Many of the essential ideas were first proposed in informal discussions on both sides of the Atlantic and were then quickly broadcast to the cognoscenti by private international bush-telegraph," it has been stated. "Months and often years elapsed before a new idea was committed to print, and then very often it was not by the person who had thought of it. Nevertheless, it can hardly be doubted that here too Watson and Crick played a dominant role, as well as Seymour Benzer, then at Purdue University."

The picture that emerged of the process by which the DNA was put to use was even more complicated than anticipated and was found to be a two-stage operation. In the first stage, called transcription, a strand of RNA duplicates the bases in a strand of DNA, turning the adenine, guanine, cytosine and thymine of the DNA into the adenine, guanine, cytosine, and uracil of the RNA. The second stage, called translation, is accomplished by intracellular particles called ribosomes. The ribosomes "read" the transcribed RNA bases three at a time, and convert each trio of bases into one of the twenty amino acids of which proteins are composed. Thus cytosine, uracil and adenine are converted into the amino acid leucine; guanine, uracil and adenine into the amino acid methionine. The sequences of the DNA bases thus control the build-up in the cell of the acids of which the proteins are formed.

The uncovering of the method by which information from the amino acids was transmitted into proteins was soon followed by a discovery with equally important implications: the discovery that this was a one-way process and that the proteins could not transmit their characteristics back to the nucleic acids. Information acquired during the life of an organism could never be slipped back for future use in the next generation. Soft inheritance, the transmission of acquired characteristics, all the multitudinous efforts of Lamarckianism and neo-Lamarkianism had disappeared forever from the realm of the necessary.

Once it had become clear that the sequence of DNA bases governed the acids that produced proteins, the search began for identifications of the code. The first success came in 1961 when Marshall W. Nirenberg announced at the International Congress of Biochemistry being held in Moscow the results of work showing that in the genetic code the uracil-uracil-uracil (or in DNA the equivalent thymine-thymine-thymine) trio represented the amino acid phenylalanine. Other identifications followed, and during the 1960s the bulk of the genetic code was revealed.

Quite as significant was the fact that the genetic code was found to be, for most practical purposes, the same in all organisms, even the most primitive. This was a support, totally unsuspected even in the 1950s, for the view that all life, however apparently unrelated, had evolved from one single origin. Thus within a decade of the double helix being sprung upon the world, it appeared that molecular biology had produced a tidy answer to more than one of the riddles that had worried Darwin. Variations of what were in practice an infinitely large number could be passed on from one generation to the next. Moreover, the fact that the ribosomes "read" the code in groups of three increased the chance of an error in translation and thus the chance of a mutation. An accident—such as the impact of the radiation with which Muller had experimented—had only to delete one of the bases as they were being read in threes by the ribosome, and the following triplets would be affected. The possibility of mutations, as well as the creation of variation, was thus far greater than had been thought likely. Nor was this all. For it was found, perhaps not unexpectedly, that it was not only the impact of radiation that could cause specific effects on the replication process. Certain dyes were found to cause certain deletions in the series of bases. Mustard gas would remove the base guanine, while other chemicals were found to cause certain bases to behave, contrarily, like others.

While these and comparable discoveries were being made concerning the ways in which the genetic material worked, other research began to reveal the effect of changes in genetic coding. Spectacular in its potentials was Vernon Ingram's work at the Massachusetts Institute of Technology in the 1960s, which showed that the position of one amino acid, responsible for the difference between sickle-cell and normal hemoglobin, followed the substitution of one base in the corresponding section of DNA. Thus a single "typographical error" in replicating the code could have enormous human consequences. "This and other examples," Garland Allen has written, "suggested that even the mechanism of evolution could be taken down to the molecular level and understood in the same terms that accounted for the processes of genetic transmission, transcription, translation, and embryonic differentiation. The unit of biology, sought after for so long, seemed to be finally at hand."

All this, however, was only one side of the coin. As chemistry came to the aid of biology, the evolutionary debate was widening out over other fields and against new oppositions.

16

Old Problems,
New Challenges

WHEN Sir Andrew Huxley, grandson of "Darwin's bulldog," gave his presidential address to the British Association in 1977, he speculated on "what topic could, in the second half of the 20th century, generate emotions as strong as those which arose over evolution in the early 1860s." Events were, in fact, already suggesting that, once again, evolution itself was to be the topic. New theories and speculations about evolution and the origin of life, possibly aroused by the success of space travel and by the continuing progress of molecular biology, began to come two-a-penny from the publishers. The controversy over whether evolution occurred gradually or by "jumps" increased to a point where it began to split the biological community down the middle, as did a new method of taxonomic classification that aroused passions reminiscent of the Wilberforce-Huxley debate. Simultaneously, the Fundamentalists, who had survived the dramatic comedy of the Scopes trial half a century earlier, reappeared in creationist form and in the United States developed serious attempts to limit the teaching of evolution and to replace it with a belief in the literal truth of the Book of Genesis.

In an age of space travel it was hardly surprising that some speculations should consider evidence from the extraterrestrial world. Darwin, it will be remembered, was seriously worried by the claims of Lord Kelvin that the history of the earth was too short to allow of evolution by natural selection, a view later made untenable by the discovery of radioactivity. In the twentieth century it has been claimed that more than one series of extraterrestrial events may have actually played a part in evolution, the most credible factor proposed being a change in the amount of ionizing radiations reaching the earth. Since Muller's work in 1927, it has been accepted that these can cause mutations and thus, without doubt, affect the progress of evolution to lesser or greater extent. It is also known that the earth is continuously submitted to a background of radiation from the rest of the solar system. The significance and dangers of this background radiation have been the subject of considerable argument, which increased after the "natural" radiation was augmented by the explosion of nuclear weapons—although the effect of this on the rate of evolution is still quite uncertain.

The position was further complicated in the late 1950s. Artificial satellites and space probe experiments revealed in 1958 the existence of the Van Allen radiation belts, consisting of charged particles trapped within the earth's magnetic fields. It was proposed that, in the geological past, radiation from these belts might have spilled over onto the earth. The result could, over an indefinite but possibly long period, have been mutation rates in living organisms many times higher than those caused by contemporary background radiation. This, in turn, could have meant a speeding up of the evolutionary process, which would justify the "jumps" view of evolution. While the idea went against the Darwinian grain, it would help explain one point that had continued to worry Darwin until his death: the long gaps in the fossil record and the failure of the paleontologists to find in it many of the intermediate species that theory suggested should be present. The "missing link" had remained missing. However, the problem of the missing link is not quite the same as it was in Darwin's day. Many gaps in the record —such as those between fish and amphibians, reptiles and mammals, reptiles and birds, apes and man—have been filled in. Gaps do still remain, but this is hardly surprising when one remembers that although the coelacanth, the "fossil fish" of which a specimen was found living in 1938, has been in existence for 100 million years, not a single coeleacanth fossil has been discovered.

Another extraterrestrial factor that, it was suggested, might have affected evolution in the distant past was reversal of the magnetic field's polarity. A third of all living species are believed to have become extinct at the close of the Cretaceous period, a time when there are known to have been polarity reversals following a long period of normal magnetic activity, and much work has been done in an effort to discover the mechanism by which such reversals could affect evolution. A paper on the "Influence of Ancient Solar-Proton Events on the Evolution of Life" pointed out in *Nature* that solar protons are normally guided by the geomagnetic field toward high geomagnetic latitudes. This influence is weakened, or disappears, during polarity reversals, and the result is that in certain areas radiation can increase considerably. "Such increases," it is stated, "would inevitably have some effect on simple freshwater micro-organisms, many of which at present seem to be living close to their maximum tolerance of ultraviolet radiation." Another mechanism has been suggested by Vlado Valkovic; the magnetic field, he says, affects the concentration of trace elements needed in approximately the right strengths by certain organisms, and "low magnetic fields can result in toxic supply of some essential trace elements."

The explosion of intragalactic supernovae may also have had its effect on the course of evolution. In 1979 two Czech biologists made an estimate of the radiations these might have produced over lengthy periods; even after their reduction by passage to the earth, the radiations might, they maintained, have had a significant mutagenic action. The more frequent but more distant supernovae explosions were considered of most importance for montane organisms, while maritime organisms were more likely to be affected by secondary radiation products.

Potential influences on evolution have been traced back even farther, and in the Bakerian Lecture for 1981 on the "Natural Selection of the Chemical Elements," R. J. P. Williams has traced the reasons which have led organisms to utilize certain elements, rather than others, to perform specific functions. "Once primitive life had emerged, the choice of one element rather than a similar one for a particular functional role," he concludes, "must have been dictated partly by the energy cost of getting the element, i.e. considerations of availability, partly by the ability to retain it, and partly by relative functional advantages."

The various postulated links between organic evolution and the distant past have been accompanied by a development of the theory of panspermia that Arrhenius had proposed in the early 1900s. While he was a respected chemist, his knowledge of biology was slight and his theory was given little serious consideration. But in 1973, no less a scientist than Francis Crick, co-discoverer of the double helix, not only revived Arrhenius's idea but with Leslie E. Orgel developed it further. The earth, they proposed, might have been deliberately seeded by intelligent beings from elsewhere in the solar system who had evolved ahead of the earth's inhabitants. This process was called directed panspermia, and after reviewing recent knowledge gained in space research, which showed radiation in space to be less damaging than previously thought, Crick and Orgel used the ubiquity of the genetic code to support the idea. It had been explained in various orthodox ways, they said, but none was generally accepted as completely convincing. "It is a little surprising," their argument continued, "that organisms with somewhat different codes do not co-exist. The universality of the code follows naturally from an 'infective' theory of the origins of life. Life on Earth would represent a clone derived from a single extraterrestrial organism. Even if many codes were represented at the primary site where life began, only a single one might have operated in the organisms to infect the Earth." Within the foreseeable future, the authors concluded, "we could, if we wished, infect another planet, and hence that it is not out of the question that *our* planet was infected."

Basically, they were maintaining only that the evolutionary record showed that there has been time for directed panspermia to have taken place. It was a speculative theory that was neither provable nor disprovable, but it had at least a background of genetic plausibility.

Something very different was subsequently maintained in *Evolution from Space* by the astronomer Fred Hoyle and his colleague Chandra Wickramasinghe. "In our view," they said, "the arrival at the Earth of living cells, and of fragments of genetic material more generally, is a continuing ongoing process that directs the main features of biological evolution. It is this process which does the job that is usually attributed to Darwinism." Here was no plea for a reordering of the mechanism that had produced man from the mud, no minor proposed change in the priorities that should be given to "jumps" or to continuous evolution, but a revolutionary claim that the whole evolutionary hypothesis should be replaced by something different.

Once it could be maintained that microorganisms could arrive on earth, Hoyle saw this as possibly providing an answer to what *Nature* called a number of biological oddities that he had cited— the fact that *Drosophila* responded to ultraviolet light of wavelengths too short to be found on earth, that *Vicia fabia* of the pea family makes hemoglobin, the red oxygen-carrying substance in the blood, and that some bacteria were immensely resistant to radiation. Criticism concentrated on the fact that the authors rejected the Darwinian explanation of complex adaptation on the ground that the possibility of life arising on earth, defined as needing 2,000 enzymes, each with an average of 200 amino acids, would be $10^{-40,000}$, a figure that for practical purposes ruled out such a chance. However, the Darwinian theory maintained that complex combinations arose differently, by the piecemeal accumulation of small changes to previously existing, and simpler, structures. "This calculation [of Fred Hoyle and Chandra Wickramasinghe] is nonsense," it was pointed out. "$10^{-40,000}$ is an estimate of the chance that 2000 enzymes will be formed simultaneously from their component amino acids on a single specified occasion. The relevant probability is the chance of some far simpler self-replicating system, capable of development by natural selection, being formed at any place on the earth's surface, at any time within a period of the order of 10^8 years; the expectation of such an event is unknown since we know neither the nature of the hypothetical self-replicating system nor the composition of the 'primaeval soup,' but it is very much greater than $10^{-40,000}$ and may approach infinity."

Acceptance of "evolution from space" demanded considerable faith, as did other theories that rested mainly if not exclusively on unverifiable data from the past. It seemed unlikely to undermine the survival of Darwin's views of evolution, and the same was true of the equally revolutionary idea put forward by Rupert Sheldrake in *A New Science of Life: The Hypothesis of Formative Causation.* This was the proposal that the form and the behavior of living organisms were dependent not so much on the physical genes passed down from one generation to the next as on morphogenetic fields— invisible fields transmitted across space and time by previous generations.

The hypothesis of formative causation led to predictions that even the author admitted might seem so improbable as to be absurd. "Thus, for instance, if thousands of rats were trained to perform a new task in a laboratory in London, similar rats should learn to carry out the same task more quickly in laboratories everywhere else. If the speed of learning of rats in another laboratory, say in New York, were to be measured before and after the rats in

London were trained, the rats tested on the second occasion should learn more quickly than those tested on the first. The effect should take place in the absence of any known type of physical connection or communication between the two laboratories."

To the obvious objections, Sheldrake had an obvious answer. "Morphic resonance," he wrote, "is non-energetic, and morphogenetic fields themselves are neither a type of mass nor energy. Therefore there seems to be no *a priori* reason why it should obey the laws that have been found to apply to the movement of bodies, particles and waves. In particular, it need not necessarily be attenuated by either spatial or temporal separation between similar systems; it could be just as effective over ten thousand miles as over a yard, and over a century as an hour."

Reaction to such a theory was generally critical. "Anyone tempted to take formative causation or morphic resonance seriously should ask themselves why," commented the distinguished zoologist Professor D. R. Newth in the columns of *Nature*. "A world haunted by messages from the past, some, like those from morphic units of extinct species, destined to vibrate eternally and in vain while seeking a morphic germ with which to resonate, may have a poetic appeal. Unfortunately, it may also appeal to a perverse fear of scientific understanding." After saying that Sheldrake's book was the best candidate for burning for many years, *Nature* maintained that it should, nevertheless, not be burned "but, rather, put firmly in its place among the literature of intellectual aberrations."

Neither the idea of evolution being dependent on outer space, nor that of morphogenetic fields with its mystical overtones were likely to send tremors through the Darwinian framework. Nor were the views of Pierre Teilhard de Chardin, the Jesuit who appears almost like a twentieth-century echo of St. George Jackson Mivart —but a writer lacking Mivart's biological training. Teilhard de Chardin's concept of evolution, leaning on faith rather than science, put man in a special niche, and like that of Herbert Spencer, encompassed more than the biological world. Teilhard de Chardin's prose, in the works that, because of his Jesuit vows, could only be published after his death in 1955, ensured him an immediate hearing. But scientific opinion was bitterly split. Julian Huxley, who praised him for trying, if unsuccessfully, to bridge the gap between scientific humanism and religion, wrote an introduction to the English edition of *The Phenomenon of Man*. But Peter Medawar, addressing a meeting of biologists in the United States, commented: "Many of you will have read with incredulous horror the kind of pious bunk written by Teilhard de Chardin."

The methods by which extraterrestrial events were believed to have affected evolution, the speculations on formative causation, and Teilhard de Chardin's construction of a universal scheme in which evolution could sit as comfortably as a laid egg in the nest, were all ideas that were debated almost in isolation from the working lives of biologists concerned with the day-to-day investigation of evolution in the study or in the field. At a totally different level of biological plausibility were two concepts put forward in recent years that raised, and still do raise, heated controversy. One dealt with classification, or taxonomy, the other with the perenially debatable conflict between minor variations and "jumps" as the main power behind evolution.

In *The Origin* Darwin had stated: "From the first dawn of life, all organic beings are found to resemble each other in descending degrees, so that they can be classed in groups under groups. This classification is evidently not arbitrary like the grouping of the stars in constellations." However, although not arbitrary, classification depended to lesser or greater extent on the background and experience of the classifier. In an attempt to reduce subjective judgments, there grew up in the late 1950s the use of the computer to quantify the similarities and differences between organisms and the development of numerical phenetics. The innovation met with limited success but was superseded by a more controversial system of classification known as cladistics, introduced by the German biologist Willi Hennig. Cladistics, which gained popularity after Hennig's paper outlining the scheme had been translated into English in the 1960s, has had the effect of a large stone thrown into a small pool, arousing some biologists to denounce it as having Communist implications and others to maintain that it supports the case that the antievolutionary creationists have been making for years. Hennig's cladistics, a name derived from the Greek word for shoot or branch, attempts—its supporters would say, successfully attempts—to reflect the evolutionary relationships of organisms. Its methods have rarely been outlined more accurately and simply than by Professor Maynard Smith in his account of the contemporary state of evolutionary studies. Hennig made, he says, two suggestions as to how one should deduce evolutionary history. "The first is that for each species, X, in a set of species, one should attempt to find a 'sister group' Y, such that X and Y have a common ancestor more recently in the past than either do with any other member of the set. The second is that, in identifying sister groups, one should pay attention, not equally to all similarities, but specifically to similarities in derived traits ('apomorphisms') rather than in primitive traits ('plesiomorphisms'). Thus men, bats and lizards have five fingers, but this is not evidence of close relationship, because the condition is primitive in land vertebrates. Horses and zebras have one finger; this *is* evidence of close relationship, because to have one finger is not primitive. The argument is convincing; its critics point out, however, that it is not always so easy to decide which state is primitive and which derived." Using these assumptions, it is possible to construct "cladograms," or branching patterns of classification, that can be compared to the family trees used for more conventional systems.

Cladistics, as originally conceived by Hennig in the 1950s, was subsequently developed into the even more controversial "transformed cladistics," in which the branching system is considered as the record of existing groups rather than as a record of how they have evolved—an approach that tends to be anathema to many Darwinians. "As the theory of cladistics had developed," Colin Patterson of the British Museum of Natural History, a transformed cladist, has explained, "it has been realised that more and more of the evolutionary framework is inessential and may be dropped. . . . [That cladistics] is not necessarily about evolution—speciation, ancestry and such things. It is about a simpler and more basic matter, the pattern in nature—groups, hierarchies or nested sets of groups and characters of groups."

A main advantage claimed for cladistics is that it forces the taxonomist to decide which are the important features of living organisms on which their classification depends, and principally for this reason its use has spread throughout both Europe and the United States since the early 1960s. Yet it has also raised considerable opposition. The paleontologist Stephen Jay Gould has written: "I do not see how the cladistic system can serve as a reasonable basis for classification. It produces wildly unbalanced and unstable higher taxa (any change of opinion about branching sequences early in the history of a group forces a recalibration of all ranks). It also explicitly ignores the biologically important fact that differential amounts of evolution characterise the different forks of a branch (I refuse to abandon the useful notion of 'fish' because coelacanths are closer cladistic relatives of humans than of trout).''

On the other side Colin Patterson, faced at a conference on the subject with the cladistic view that a lungfish is more closely related to a cow than to a salmon, answered: "Yes, I cannot see what is wrong in that.''

While controversy has continued, support for the theory has been increased by the development of fresh ideas about continental drift, first suggested by Alfred Wegener early in the twentieth century. The position of the continents was for long generally assumed to have been static throughout the geological past. But in 1915 there arose the theory that in Carboniferous times there had existed a single massive land mass called Pangaea. This mass had eventually split into the northern Laurasia and the southern Gondwanaland; the latter had then split again and drifted apart to form Asia and North America; and, to the south, Africa, South America and Australia. This splitting was claimed by the supporters of cladistics to be reflected in the branching patterns of many groups of animals and plants. The supposition was then taken further by Gareth Nelson and Norman Platnick, who suggested that the splitting apart of Gondwanaland some eighty million years ago could be correlated with the development of human races, a suggestion that many biologists refuse to take seriously.

Arguments about the relevance of cladistics rumbled on in professional circles throughout the 1970s, but it was only in 1980 that they broke into the open. The catalytic events were two exhibitions at Britain's Museum of Natural History in London. The first, on dinosaurs, was accompanied by the publication in 1979 of the Museum's booklet, *Dinosaurs and Their Living Relatives*. The following year there came an exhibition on Man, for which there was published *Man's Place in Evolution*. The exhibitions and the booklets prompted to a sometimes bitter correspondence that continued in the pages of *Nature* for eight months, prompted the journal to publish a leading article headed "Darwin's Death in South Kensington," induced Sir Andrew Huxley to upbraid *Nature* for its criticism of the Museum, and opened up the argument of evolution versus creationism by that time being waged with increased vigor in the United States.

The first shot in the battle was fired by Dr. L. B. Halstead of Reading University's Department of Zoology and Geology, who pointed out that both Natural History Museum booklets described the exhibitions in cladistic terms. If that on dinosaurs appeared to contradict what had been learned from the fossil record over the years, that on the evolution of man was even more revolutionary. In the section on *Homo erectus*, and under the heading "Not our direct ancestors," it stated, "The *Homo erectus* people were not quite like us . . . the *Homo erectus* skull has several characteristics that the modern skull does not share. Because of these special characteristics we think that the *Homo erectus* people were not our direct ancestors." The implications of this statement, with its echo of the Owen-Huxley controversy more than a century earlier, were spelled out by Halstead. "This," he wrote, "presents the public for the first time with the notion that there are no actual fossils directly antecedent to man. What the creationists have insisted on for years is now being openly advertised by the Natural History Museum."

He, and others, objected not so much to the exposition of cladistics in the Museum's exhibits and booklets as to the way in which it was presented without being balanced by the Darwinian alternative. This viewpoint was answered by the Museum's Colin Patterson with the statement: "Cladistics is not about evolution, but about the pattern of character distribution in organisms, or the recognition and characterization of groups."

However, evolution was not the only subject for argument. Cladistics supported, both implicitly and explicitly, the notion of evolution by "jumps," a notion in complete contradiction to the gradualist conception that had been part of the evolutionary synthesis. Why should the notion of gradualism, the alleged target of the cladists, arouse such passionate intensity, Halstead asked in his letter criticizing the Museum's policy. The question further extended the controversy, since it was claimed that the answer was to be found in the political arena. Just as social Darwinism had a century earlier divided the Left from the Right, so was cladistics now seen as being politically motivated. "There are basically two contrasting views with regard to human society and the process of change through time," wrote Halstead; "one is the gradualist, reformist and the other is the revolutionary approach. The key tenet of dialectical materialism, the world outlook of the Marxist-Leninist party according to J. V. Stalin, is in the recognition of 'a development in which the qualitative changes occur not gradually but rapidly and abruptly, taking the form of a leap from one state to another' (Engels). This is the recipe for revolution. If this is the observed rule in the history of life, when translated into human history and political action it would serve as the scientific justification for accentuating the inherent contradictions in society, so that the situation can be hurried towards its appropriate 'nodal point' and a qualitative leap supervenes."

But Engels and Lenin, Halstead continued, were content to see in evolution only gradual change. "This has always been a matter of some disquiet for Marxist theorists," he went on. "If it could be established that the pattern of evolution was a saltatory one after all, then at long last the Marxists would indeed be able to claim that the theoretical basis of their approach was supported by scientific evidence."

After this assertion, the opponents of cladistics found themselves fighting on both the scientific and the political fronts. A controversy that already included Museum policy and the best use of the unique building that housed the Natural History Museum, was yet further extended. The relevance of politics to the saltation versus gradualism argument was soon both ridiculed and emphasized. When a sentence starting "If the theory of evolution is true" was quoted from one of the Museum booklets, there was considerable horror: that is, until it was pointed out that Darwin had used the same words in *The Origin*. Karl Popper, quoted as disbelieving in the testability and the logical status of natural selection, revealed that he had changed his mind, a recantation that cut some of the ground from beneath the creationists and, by implication, the cladists.

These disparate side issues tended to confuse an already confused issue that continues to be argued out with unabated vigor. Even the most dedicated cladists—although not the transformed cladists—maintain that the most their theory involves is a development of, rather than a denial of, Darwinian evolution, a claim their opponents decline to take at its face value. However, the cladistic debate would not have been waged so vigorously had not evolutionists also been divided over "punctuated equilibria," a theory that gave a new cutting edge to the perennial argument between evolution by continuing small changes and evolution by "jumps."

Although the new synthesis, with its assumption of evolution by small gradual changes, had by the end of the Second World War gained general acceptance, there were those who insisted on qualifications. One was Ernst Mayr, who in 1942 had argued that some birds, those living in small concentrations, had evolved rapidly in "jumps," a proposition he developed twelve years later.

Mayr's advocacy of "jumps," at least in small isolated communities, received much support, but it was only in the early 1970s that punctuated equilibria, as it was christened, began to take hold. It was first outlined in 1971 by Niles Eldredge and then, in the following year, by Eldredge and Stephen Jay Gould, two paleontologists who had been prominent in giving a new importance to paleontology as a discipline in the evolutionary field.

Although the significance of "jumps" as described by punctuated equilibria was different from that speculated upon a century earlier, the new theory did not have the anti-Darwinian force that some were anxious to foist upon it. In the fourth edition of *The Origin*, Darwin had suggested that evolution did not go on continuously: "it is far more probable that each form remains for long periods unaltered, and then again undergoes modification." The periods "during which species have been undergoing modification, though very long measured by years," he went on, "have probably been short by comparison with the periods during which these same species remained without undergoing change." The name *Stufenreihe* was given to such steplike evolution, and in later decades George Gaylord Simpson elaborated on it as "quantum evolution."

However, punctuated equilibria was an idea independently arrived at on the basis of intensive paleontological research. During the previous decade there had been a considerable increase in the number of paleontologists concentrating on evolution. This was partly due to the huge mass of new evidence that had been produced since Marsh and Cope had raced each other to the telegraph during the 1880s in their efforts to be first with new paleontological discoveries. But it was due, also, to the growth of a new school of paleontologists who believed that the fossil record offered a far greater chance of solving evolutionary riddles than had previously been suspected. In another field, J. J. Thomson at the start of the century in Cambridge, England, had been the center of a brilliant group who were to reveal the nuclear structure of the atom. Forty years later, a comparable air of dedicated excitement and enthusiasm suffused the corridors of America's Radiation Laboratory at the Massachusetts Institute of Technology and Britain's Telecommunications Research Establishment at Malvern, where radar was being brought to life. During the 1970s something of the same atmosphere pervaded the paleontological groups in Chicago and Harvard. In fact, Gould asserted with much justification that "our profession now wears the glass slipper and, if not the queen of the evolutionary ball, at least cuts a figure worth more than a passing glance."

There was, of course, ample space for them. Darwin had in his day been unhappy about the failure of the fossil record to give more than slight, and then only occasional, support to the theory of evolution. It is true that there was the archaeopteryx as well as Marsh's fossil horses, but these were exceptional cases; and even though Darwin knew that only parts of any organism would be preserved as fossils, and then only in favorable environments, the lack of paleontological evidence worried him to the end of his life.

The situation had changed since Darwin's day, and is illustrated by one example. "The fate of the more than 400 fossil genera . . . at the turn of the century, had such a long fossil record that each of them was considered a case of 'arrested evolution,' " says Thomas J. M. Schopf. "As the decades passed and additional taxonomic characters were revealed by new methods of study (for example by thin sections), the taxa were subdivided, and the very long stratigraphic ranges were reduced. Indeed by the time the Treatise on Invertebrate Paleontology was written from the 1950s into the 1970s, the average duration of these genera was half what it had been half a century earlier."

Yet Schopf himself emphasized the enormous gaps that remain in the fossil record and, by implication, the need to correlate the paleontological evidence with that on which the evolutionary synthesis had been built. "So prevalent are missing blocks of time in oceanic sediments (the best and most complete of any geologic sections)," he has written, "that one correlates by means of the missing portions (!), and it is called 'hiatus stratigraphy.' " As an example of missing evidence he cites the order Multituberculata, the longest-lived mammalian order. "It is considered to range from the middle Jurassic to the end of the Eocene, 160 m[illion] y[ears'] duration. On a stage by stage basis, fossils of this order are known to occur in stages whose cumulative duration is only 87 m.y., just 54 percent of the duration of the order. That is, 46 percent of the time the Multituberculata existed, there has not yet been discovered a record of the order anywhere in the world. This simply underscores the vagaries of preservation and fossilization. Given the very uneven occurrence of particular taxa during times when they are supposed to occur, it is no wonder that even orders have the aspect of appearing 'suddenly' in the fossil record. . . .

Owing to the enormous incompleteness of the fossil record, when it comes to evaluating continuity of taxa through time, regardless of categorical rank, the 'sudden' appearance of any taxon is almost guaranteed—it could hardly be otherwise!"

It was the suddenness of the appearance and the lack of intermediate forms, the "missing links" of popular imagination, that led Eldredge and Gould to work out their explanatory theory of punctuated equilibria. "We believe," they said, "that an inadequate picture has been guiding our thoughts on speciation for 100 years. We hold that its influence has been all the more tenacious because paleontologists, in claiming that they see objectively, have not recognized its guiding sway. We contend that a notion developed elsewhere, the theory of allopatric speciation [speciation having different areas of distribution], supplies a more satisfactory picture for the ordering of paleontological data."

Their proposition was that a species occupying a small area peripheral to its main location underwent change in isolation and subsequently invaded the main area and replaced the occupying and ancestral species. Since the newer species had evolved in an isolated peripheral location, no signs of the development might be found. Evolution itself, moreover, was said to take place in sudden spurts that punctuated long periods during which there were no adaptations, no changes and few intermediate forms to be found in the fossil record. More than a century after T. H. Huxley had criticized Darwin for loading himself "with an unnecessary difficulty in adopting *Natura non facit saltum* so unreservedly," the paleontologists had removed the load with the wave of an idea. But in its place there had appeared the problem of *stasis*, the almost equally mysterious lack of change.

"Paleontologists," ended the lengthy paper that introduced punctuated equilibria to a surprised world in 1972, "should recognize that much of their thought is conditioned by a peculiar perspective that they must bring to the study of life: they must look down from its present complexity and diversity into the past; their view must be retrospective. From this vantage point, it is very difficult to view evolution as anything but an easy and inevitable result of mere existence, as something that unfolds in a natural and orderly fashion. Yet we urge a different view. The norm for a species or, by extension, a community is stability. Speciation is a rare and difficult event that punctuates a system in homeostatic equilibrium. That so uncommon an event should have produced such a wondrous array of living and fossil forms can only give strength to an old idea: paleontology deals with a phenomenon that belongs to it alone among the evolutionary sciences and that enlightens all its conclusions—time."

Within a decade, alterations to the theory were to be proposed, but it remained a subject of controversy. To some, it was among the worst of anti-Darwinian heresies, since it so developed the saltationist theory that Darwin had continued to reject despite all of Huxley's pleadings. To others, the fact that it answered some of the questions raised by the gaps in the fossil record that had so worried Darwin, that it buttressed the very idea of evolution, brought it within the body of the true faith. Much of the difference between punctuated equilibria and Darwin's claim of evolution by small variations boils down to how "sudden." "For example," R. J. Berry has said, "genetical change up to the specific level can occur in a few tens or, at most, hundreds of generations (neglecting 'instant speciation' as produced by such mechanisms as polyploidy), while Eldredge and Gould quote examples based on fossils separated in time by intervals of a hundred thousand years. . . . The issues raised by [them] are important for interpreting the relative significance of different mechanisms that have produced evolutionary change; they are in no way important as major criticisms of evolution itself."

However, there were significant implications of punctuated equilibria. If species did continue without change for lengthy geological periods, what were the causes of the sudden outbursts of change that did take place? Was it possible that there was no cause in the usual meaning of the word? Was chance, after all, the great arbiter of evolution? These were some of the questions raised in the aftermath of punctuated equilibria's birth. At the same time the limitations of the fossil record, in particular the smaller chance of finding the short-lived rare species in comparison with the more abundant, were once again emphasized.

For some years supporting evidence for punctuated equilibria was slight. Then, early in 1981, there came a striking report from, of all places, the Galápagos; and on, of all things, one species of Darwin's finches. In 1975 two ornithologists from Montreal's McGill University, Peter T. Boag and Peter R. Grant, began to study the population of Darwin's medium ground finch on the 100 acres of Daphne Major, one of the smaller Galápagos Islands. More than 1,500 birds were color-banded and measured for seven external morphological characters. Continuous records were kept of the banded birds, of the rainfall, and of the birds' feeding habits, and it was established that the population was stable. Then, in 1977, a severe drought struck the island, and the rainfall dropped from 127 mm to 24 mm. The following year plant seed production dropped alarmingly, and 85 percent of the medium ground finches starved to death, only one of the 388 nestlings banded in 1976 surviving into 1978. The survivors were the heavier birds with the larger beaks, which enabled them to use the only food available. As a result, their average weight was 15 percent more than it had been before the drought, and the beaks were 17 percent larger. Had the drought gone on for a number of years, the increases would have continued and a new subspecies adapted to a new food supply would have quickly emerged.

"Our results," Boag and Grant wrote, "are consistent with the growing opinion among evolutionary ecologists that the trajectory of even well-buffered vertebrate species is largely determined by occasional 'bottlenecks' of intense selection during a small portion of their history. More specifically, given the many small, isolated, relatively sedentary, and morphologically variable populations of Darwin's finches and the high spatial and temporal variability of the Galápagos, this type of event provides a mechanism for rapid morphological evolution." The episode, claim the supporters of punctuated equilibria, illustrated the sudden burst of evolution following a period of stability, which is the core of their theory. At the least, it did illustrate the extreme variability in the rate of evolution that could sometimes be observed.

This aspect of punctuated equilibria, like many other developments in the story of evolution, has been regularly twisted by the creationists to support their beliefs. "The beneficial effect of widespread acceptance of the Gould-Eldredge . . . theory is already well recognised," a writer in the procreationist journal Contrast commented. "Their admission of the reason they were forced to devise such a theory which predicts no intermediate forms gives strong support to creation theory which also predicts the gaps." Yet both Gould and Eldredge are among the most doughty proponents of evolution.

Indeed, any threat to the survival of Darwin's basic beliefs comes today not from the ranks of the scientists but from the creationists, who in the United States have threatened the teaching of Darwinism in schools and who have ardently seized on any new assessment of how evolution works to proclaim that it does not work at all. For although the Scopes case had in the 1920s made Tennessee the laughingstock of much of the world, Bryan had had a powerful following, and his defeat, emphasized emotionally by his subsequent death, caused a reaction. Between the 1920s and 1970, in fact, no less than seventy-two attempted legal actions designed to regulate the teaching of evolution in twenty-seven states were introduced in America. However, only seven of them were adopted, and in 1968 the U.S. Supreme Court, adjudicating in a case brought against an Arkansas law banning the teaching of evolution, decreed that such laws were unconstitutional.

However, this legislative victory for the proevolutionary forces has been only one factor in creating the situation that exists today. Another, at least as important, is the influence of state and local boards of education, whose rulings can be as significant as legislative action. By means of outright, if local, prohibition of evolutionary teaching, by control of biological textbooks, and by demands that when biology is taught Fundamentalist theories should be given equal time with those of evolution, they have been part of a continuing attempt to remove the teaching of evolution from the educational curriculum. The extent of their influence can be judged from the fact that "A Chronology and Analysis of Regulatory Actions Relating to the Teaching of Evolution in Public Schools," a thesis finished by Richard David Wilhelm in 1978, runs to some 200,000 words.

The growth of the creationist influence in modern times, particularly from the mid-1960s onward, is partly due to the strong Fundamentalist beliefs that characterized much of America during its pioneering frontier period of the early and mid-nineteenth century. It has perhaps been supported by the common human frailty of wishing to hedge one's bets: even Einstein could tell with understanding of how a resolutely agnostic uncle, chided when going to the synagogue in full formal dress, replied: "Ah, but you never know."

During the years between the two world wars, and throughout the course of the Second, as the repercussions of Morgan's work in the Columbia fly room spread throughout the world, as Muller made his ominous discovery that radiations can affect the gene and therefore the machinery of inheritance, the increasingly hard evidence for the facts of evolution continued to make little impact on the general public. As late as 1942, a national survey in the United

States indicated that less than half of America's high-school biology teachers even mentioned evolution in their courses. In 1959, Muller was able to state that biological teaching in the United States was still dominated by " 'antiquated religious traditions' and . . . barely referred to modern research in population genetics and related areas that increasingly refined and supported the concept of evolution." This was despite the *Humani Generis* encyclical of Pope Pius XII, which in 1950 had seemed to open the way, at least for Roman Catholics, toward a more liberal consideration of evolution. "1. In any discussion of evolution the Catholic must take for granted the spiritual soul of men," it stated. "2. Otherwise, such a discussion is left open by the Church. 3. However, such a discussion is for experts in science and theology, and reasons for and against must be gravely weighed. The Catholic must be ready to submit to the judgment of the Church. 4. People should not take it for granted that evolution is a proved fact and should not act as if there were no theological reasons for reserve or caution in their discussion." Although far from being the green light for acceptance of evolution, this was very different from the slick certainties being preached by the creationists.

The comparatively low-key level of the argument between the evolutionists and the creationists was drastically changed in 1957. The signal for change came, incongruously, from the country that had acclaimed Darwinism in the aftermath of the First World War and had then tried to extirpate it with the rise of Lysenkoism; for Russia's sputnik, shooting into space in October 1957, was to have repercussions in the United States. One was the realization that if Russia's dedication to science could give her such a lead in the exploration of space, then it might be advisable to strip from the American educational system the limitations that arose when religious views circumvented scientific training. There followed a seven-million-dollar Biological Sciences Curriculum Study supported by the National Science Foundation, part of a larger plan to awake the United States to the potentials of science in the contemporary world.

The Curriculum Study, which successfully defeated more than one attempt to maintain that its textbooks supporting evolution were unconstitutional, had a limited success. But, in line with Newton's warning that every action produces an equal reaction, the creationist movement began to flourish. It was spearheaded by the Creation Research Society, which in 1963 was formed out of the

American Scientific Affiliation. The first three points in its "Statement of Belief," to which all members have to subscribe, typify the attitude of the movement from the 1960s until the present day. "The Bible is the written Word of God," says the first point, "and because it is inspired throughout, all its assertions are historically and scientifically true in all the original autographs." To the student of nature this means that the account of origins in Genesis is a factual presentation of simple historical truths.

"All basic types of living things, including man, were made by direct creative acts of God during the Creation Week described in Genesis," the "Statement" continues. "Whatever biological changes have occurred since Creation Week have accomplished only changes within the original created kinds. The great Flood described in Genesis, commonly referred to as the Noachian Flood, was a historic event worldwide in its extent and effect." Even Bishop Wilberforce at his most evangelical might have avoided quite such a dogmatic creed.

To the Creation Research Society there were subsequently added the Institute for Creation Research, a division of the Christian Heritage College in San Diego; the Creation Science Research Center in San Diego; and the Bible Science Association of Caldwell, Idaho. In Britain, where supporters are numbered in hundreds rather than thousands, there is the Bible Creation Society; the Creation Science Movement, renamed from the Evolution Protest Movement of 1932; and the Newton Scientific Association. All avoid some of the larger lunacies of the American movement, and their influence is far less, although whether the two facts are linked is uncertain.

In the United States, the debate has increasingly revolved around the creationists' claim that, since the teaching of evolution cannot easily be constitutionally banned, following the decision against Arkansas in 1968, equal time should be given for the teaching of creationism. "This will presumably require," *Scientific American* has said of the claim, "that such competing theories as the story given in Genesis and Aristotle's theory of spontaneous generation be taught along with Darwinism."

The issue has been complicated by the First Amendment of the U.S. Constitution. "Congress shall make no law respecting an establishment of religion, or prohibiting the free exercise thereof. . . ." This has on occasion led the creationists to claim the status of a science for their beliefs and—sometimes simultaneously—to claim that belief in evolution is held as a religion. The result was that by the end of 1980 bills requiring that creationism be presented as a scientific model alongside evolution had been introduced and debated in Florida, Georgia, Illinois, Iowa, Kentucky, Louisiana, Minnesota, New York, South Carolina, Tennessee and Washington. Decisions varied, from rejection to compromise. To generalize, evolution seemed to have been regaining some of the ground it lost during the previous decade. Thus in Mississippi a law making it illegal "to teach that mankind ascended or descended from a lower order of animals" was overthrown by the state supreme court. And in Indiana a judge ruled that use of the alternative textbook *Biology: A Search for Order in Complexity*, written by members of the Creation Research Society, violated state law, the Indiana constitution and the First Amendment.

The outcome of the battle on a national basis is still in doubt, as a random choice of significant pointers will show. As late as June 1981, Laurie R. Godfrey, who teaches physical anthropology at the University of Massachusetts, could write that "Many scientists are baffled that such poor science [as that provided by scientific creationists] can be so easily swallowed, and that creation is being taught as science in some schools around the country. Scientific creationism may be poor science, but it is powerful politics. And politically, it may succeed."

An alternative view is put forward by the American geneticist William Provine, who, to the surprise of some, maintained before an audience at Corning, New York, in November 1981 that creationism should be taught in schools. "I do not believe that natural scientists should suppress the creationist point of view and keep it out of the science classroom when creationism is a viable, understandable and plausible theory for the creation point," he said. "It is my opinion that it is a wrong theory, and the reason why I should like it discussed, particularly in the science classroom, is that when we put it against evolutionism in the science classroom, creationism will gradually die out. Students will accept evolutionism rather than creationism."

Early in 1980 there came an attempt by the Illinois senator Robert Mitchler to make compulsory the teaching of creationism in state schools side by side with evolution. It brought reactions typical of those that were to be increasingly witnessed in other states during the next few years. The Chicago *Tribune* argued that there was not, nor should there be, any "established religion" in the United States and continued: "The attempt to legislate the teaching of religious dogma in the public schools is contrary to our national laws and institutions, whatever the dogma might be." It added that schools should use undogmatic science to teach about creation rather than the sacred writings of Christian or Jew, Hindu or Buddhist. One reader pointed out that the proposed law would ignore the Norse, Babylonian and Aztec stories of creation and another asked, "How about the Hopi Indians. Aren't they entitled to equal space?"

Supporters for the other side maintained that evolution as it was being taught needed "some good stiff competition to clean up all the bad science it has picked up," and maintained that the teaching of creationism would meet this need. More neutral was the position of the writer Joan Beck, who in a column-length article in the Chicago *Tribune* gave a rational explanation of the support for creationism that for a short while appeared to be gaining ground against the evolutionists.

> When presented as more than just religious dogma, creationism appeals to many people who don't necessarily believe literally in Genesis but find it takes a leap of faith to account for the origin and wonder of life and the multiplicity of species simply by evolution alone. They argue that believing in evolution involves so much doctrine that it constitutes a sort of Godless religion. Implying that there is no God is as much a religious statement as believing God exists, they contend.
>
> Some of those who advocate creationism are also troubled by the moral implications of evolution. They fear it fosters ideas of elitism— individual and racial. They are concerned that it can be used, perhaps subconsciously, to justify not only racism, but lack of care for endangered species and a turning away from massive efforts to help the less physically and mentally able at the expense of the fittest. And they worry about deliberately using genetic engineering to further evolution.

These were understandable reasons, even if their intellectual content was minimal.

Later in the year the creationists had the good luck, organized or otherwise, to have on the platform of a Fundamentalist rally held in Dallas on August 22, 1980, no less a person than Ronald Reagan, then the Republican contender in the coming presidential election. And of evolution, Reagan stated before the enthusiastic crowd: "It's a scientific theory, and in recent years has been challenged in the world of science."

The Chicago *Tribune* asked four days later: "Since [Reagan] is campaigning to be a President of all the people, why does he go out of his way to identify himself with factional causes that have nothing to do with the Presidency?" And a reader of the paper, after pointing out that Genesis contained two quite incompatible versions of creation, asked: "Would Mr. Reagan have teachers stop discreetly at Genesis 2:4, after the first account, which, broadly interpreted, can sound compatible with Darwinism? Or would he have them go boldly, literally on, until after the Flood, when all the living non-aquatic species have been safely landed from Noah's Ark?"

That the battle against evolution is as real and earnest as it was when Clarence Darrow reduced Bryan to incoherence in Dayton more than half a century earlier was shown in the spring of 1981 when Kelly L. Segraves, director of the Creation Science Research Center in San Diego, charged the state with violating the religious rights of its children by refusing to allow science classes to consider the creationist theory. To give evidence, he called his thirteen-year-old son, Kasey Segraves, who said he was being taught that man evolved from apes, an idea that was contrary to his religious beliefs. "I believe that God created man and put him on the earth," he said.

After nearly a week of testimony, given by experts who traversed the various theories of creation and evolution—including the seeding of the earth by organisms from outer space—the case ended in a compromise, the judge simply directing the state to reemphasize the already existing policy. "The verdict," commented the New York *Times*, "leaves evolution where it belongs, the dominant theory in biology. And it leaves creationism where it belongs—a belief worth discussing outside the science curriculum."

By contrast, an argument in Livermore, California, the home of the Lawrence Livermore Laboratory, where scientists work on the latest nuclear weapons, was won by evolutionists who discovered that their children were being taught creationism at the local primary school. After a long acrimonious debate, the local board of education agreed to stop the teaching.

Perhaps more insidious in the fight against evolution than the demands for equal time is the censorship being exercised by pressure groups to tone down, or omit, from school textbooks, significant references to evolution. This is part of a wider campaign, and a national censorship study, sponsored by the American Library Association, the Association of American Publishers and the Association for Supervision and Curriculum Development, has revealed that a quarter of school administrators and librarians had reported challenges to a wide variety of teaching materials in the 1978–80 school years. Inevitably, the teaching not only of biology but of geology has been affected. In California, the statement in one textbook that "slowly, over millions of years, the dinosaurs died out" was changed by deletion of "over millions of years"— many creationists still put the age of the earth as no more than 10,000 years. "As reptiles evolved from fishlike ancestors" became, in the same textbook, "If reptiles evolved from fishlike ancestors, as proposed in the theory of evolution." In California in 1973 it was noted of science textbooks for the elementary grades that those on life and on heredity do not mention—not even once anywhere in the text, the vocabulary, or the index—the word "evolution" or any form of the word "evolve."

The power of those who challenge evolution was for long exemplified by the situation in Texas, where the fifteen-member Textbook Committee recommends textbooks for the entire state based on certain criteria. Here, a key section included a requirement that books treating the theory of evolution must identify it as only one of several such theories. As in twenty-two other states that select textbooks at state level, the 1,152 school districts in Texas can purchase only those on the state-approved list. Moreover, with Texas being the second-largest textbook buyer in the United States, taking about 8 percent of the nation's purchases, a book not approved by Texas is unlikely to be a financial success.

As a result, some publishers have begun self-censoring their publications. Thus Eugene Frank, a publishing executive of Laidlaw (a division of Doubleday), was quoted as saying: "You're not going to find the word 'evolution' in the new textbook *Experiences in Biology.*" The reason, he said, according to the organization People for the American Way, was "to avoid the publicity that would be involved in a controversy over a textbook." Another publisher removed the word "evolution" from the latest edition of its only biology textbook. As Dr. Wayne A. Moyer, executive director of the National Association of Biology Teachers, wrote of the situation which existed until the spring of 1984, "Thus in one sweep the Texas Board of Education has equated theory with speculation; confused evolution and natural selection; and worst of all, failed to distinguish between explanations verified by observation and those verified by faith."

The situation was altered only in the spring of 1984, when biology textbook adoption lists were selected, as happens every eight years, and the Texas Board of Education repealed the requirement that biology and science textbooks used in the state's public schools describe evolution as "only one of several explanations" of the origin of human beings. The board's action came after the Texas attorney general stated that the rule was unconstitutional and that he would not, therefore, defend the board against any suits on the issue.

The censorship threat, which if continued elsewhere in the United States could lead to a rising percentage of young Americans growing up biologically ignorant, comes largely from the creationists. Their response to fresh scientific evidence has been to echo the response of the flat-earthers to the first satellite pictures showing the curvature of the earth; like Admiral Nelson at Copenhagen responding to the signal to withdraw, they have tended to say, "I do not see it."

Nevertheless, it is not only the creationists who have been mounting a threat to the survival of Darwinism. Disillusion with science in general has left its mark. As for the textbook critics, it has been pointed out they have been "part of the romantic resistance to science that is reflected in the popularity of astrology, mystical cults, and the imaginary cosmologies of Immanuel Velikovsky and Erich Von Daniken. They are also part of a political resistance to science that is reflected in increased social action against innovation and in the demands for lay participation in scientific and technical decisions. As questions that are normally resolved by professional consensus are brought into the political arena, and as democratic values such as freedom of choice, equality and fairness enter into science policy, the consequences of such resistance to science may be painful."

However, a reaction has already started. In March 1981, the authorities in the state of Arkansas approved the Balanced Treatment for Creation—Science and Evolution—Science Act. The bill, which called for equal importance to be given to the theories of evolution and creation, was followed by similar bills in seventeen other states, and it was clear that its fate would be of crucial importance. Thus there was much satisfaction in scientific circles when Judge William R. Overton ruled that the bill violated the constitutional separation of church and state and said: "Both the concepts and wording . . . convey an inescapable religiosity." To the claim that the creationists were propounding a scientific theory, Overton ruled that this could not be so of "a theory that is by its own term dogmatic, absolutist and never subject to revision." Moreover, "no group," he added, "no matter how large or small, may use the organs of government, of which the public schools are the most conspicuous and influential, to foist its religious beliefs on others."

The dogmatism of the creationists has been counterproductive in other ways. For some while it was claimed that Karl Popper's beliefs on the verifiability of evidence put evolution out of court as a subject for scientific study in his view. But this claim was pressed so hard that in 1980 Popper felt it necessary to set matters straight. "Some people," he said, "think that I have denied scientific character to the historical sciences, such as paleontology or the history of the evolution of life on Earth or to, say, the history of literature, or of technology, or of science. This is a mistake, and I here wish to affirm that these and other historical sciences have in my opinion scientific character; their hypotheses can in many cases be tested."

In the summer of 1982 the New York City Board of Education, reacting to the more liberal climate, decided that *Experiences in Biology* would "no longer be approved for listing and purchase in the New York City Public Schools." The reason was that "the text does not contain a treatment of the theory of evolution" and, specifically, omitted reference to eight listed topics. Prentice-Hall's *Life Science* was disapproved on similar grounds, since the book was "threaded with expressions implying that evolution is less widely accepted as a scientific theory than is creation." A third textbook was disapproved at the same time, and in a blistering editorial the New York *Times* proclaimed: "Censorship is shameful but bowdlerization is ridiculous. Textbook publishers commit both when, in surrender to certain fundamentalists, they put out texts on biology that soft-pedal its unifying explanatory system, the theory of evolution."

Thus, a century after Darwin died, the truth and relevance of his "unifying explanatory system" has once again been supported in the battle against neolithic obscurantism.

This growing, if latter-day, appreciation that—at its very lowest level—any muffling of the evolutionary argument can create an intellectual national handicap is one encouraging pointer to the long-term survival of Darwin and all that he stood for. More important still is the vigor with which the bulk of scientists and their lay supporters have continued to accept the basic assumptions of evolution, whatever their arguments over detail. This, however, is hardly surprising. No plausible alternative to evolution has been proposed that could account for the huge body of biological evidence that is augmented almost weekly. Stasis, it is true, tends to supplant "jumps" as a problem. Recent advances in molecular biology suggest that natural selection may operate at the genetic level, and there is no doubt that the acknowledged complexities of evolution and of life itself will continue to increase.

But neither the contemporary upsurge of interest in creationism nor the arguments among today's biologists about the evolutionary mechanism have changed the lasting import of Darwin's work. The first has been largely the result of well-orchestrated publicity, and the second have been complicated enough to confuse many laymen. Nevertheless, conceptions of biology, and of what T. H. Huxley called man's place in nature, still remain indisputably pre- and post-Darwinian.

During the century since he was laid to rest in the Abbey, the way in which evolution operates has, it is true, been the subject of complex discussion. This is hardly surprising. Mendel's work, made widely known at the turn of the century, opened the door on to mechanisms about which Darwin knew nothing, however much he may have suspected. Technological advance has since enabled information to be gained from organisms whose lifespans are short enough to be followed through successive generations, but whose size had until recently greatly limited such work. The development of increasingly sophisticated mathematical techniques has enabled the workings of inheritance, and its evolutionary potential in large populations, to be investigated in great detail. Molecular biology has produced fresh facts bearing on the ways in which natural selection operates, and is continuing to operate. The result has been not to destroy Darwin's ideas but to qualify them, just as Einstein's Special Relativity did not overthrow Newton but showed that Newtonian ideas were valid only in certain circumstances.

The prodigious amount of work on evolution carried out during the last few decades has been concerned very largely with the validity of the evolutionary synthesis and with the relevance of punctuated equilibria and cladistics to Darwin's work. Writing of the evolutionary synthesis, the evolutionist Ernst Mayr has said: "A glance at the current evolutionary literature shows how much disagreement in the interpretation of certain specific problems of evolution still exists. Yet the opposing viewpoints do not question any of the basic theses of the synthetic theory; they merely have different answers for some of the pathways of evolution." Andrew Huxley, grandson of T. H., has written equally sagely after asking whether evolution goes progressively, with the whole of a species changing more or less simultaneously and continuously, or by the process of punctuated equilibria, and whether cladistics is anti-Darwinian: "These are interesting and important questions but I regard them as being questions within the Darwinian framework —they do not give rise to doubts as to whether Darwinism is right or not. They are really cases where it is not a question of available explanations being inadequate, it is a question of there being too many explanations: there are alternative explanations and the question is which one is right, or rather, how great are their respective contributions?"

The picture, therefore, is not of the evolutionary scene fading, as a badly washed photographic print can fade over the years, but of further detail being constantly added. This may change parts of the picture, but the overall pattern is as clear as when T. H. Huxley and the Bishop of Oxford thundered at each other in Oxford a century and a quarter ago.

References

Full details of the sources quoted, manuscript and printed, are given with bibliographical information in the Bibliography, pp. 397–418.

1   A Young Country Gentleman

PAGE

3   "nothing but a great aptitude": The Comte de Buffon, quoted Marie Jean Hérault de Séchelles, "Voyage à Montbar," p. 15.

4   "As far as I can judge of myself": Charles Darwin, MS of "Recollections of the Development of My Mind and Character dated 1876, May 31," p. 56, The Darwin Papers, Cambridge University Library, Cambridge, England, there numbered DAR. 26 [afterward referred to as Auto].

4   "Darwin's bull-dog": Thomas Henry Huxley quoted Leonard Huxley (ed.), *Life and Letters of Thomas Henry Huxley*, 2 vols., here 1:363 [afterward referred to as *Huxley L.L.*].

6   "You care for nothing but shooting": Dr. Robert Waring Darwin, quoted Auto., p. 6.

6   "It doesn't matter": Quoted Ronald W. Clark, *Einstein: The Life and Times*, p. 10.

6   "to reduce the facts": Erasmus Darwin, *Zoonomia, or the Laws of Organic Life*, 2 vols., here 1:1.

7   "I recollect my mother's gown": Darwin, "Fragment of an autobiography 'written August 1838,' " DAR. 91.

7   "I . . . invented some great falsehoods": Ibid.

7   "except most trifling ones": Ibid.

7   "as a means of education": Auto, p. 5.

8   "I am dying by inches": Darwin–William Darwin Fox, June 1828, Fox Letters, Christ's College, Cambridge, England, quoted from a set of Xerox copies held at Cambridge University Library [afterward referred to as Fox Letters].

8   "I really hardly know anything in this life": Darwin–Fox, September 20, 1862, Fox Letters.

PAGE

8   "That was the proudest moment": Darwin–unnamed visitor to Down, DAR. 112.

8   "one day, on tearing off some old bark": Auto., p. 34.

8   "I discovered, though unconsciously": Ibid., p. 53.

9   "My first recollections": Entry for June 1822, "Darwin's personal journal (1809–81)," DAR. 158.

9   "My father kept to the end of his life": Henrietta E. Litchfield, *Emma Darwin, Wife of Charles Darwin: A Century of Family Letters*, 2 vols.; here 1:180 [afterward referred to as *Century of Letters*].

9   "as all the world knows": Darwin–Fox, Wednesday, December 24 [incorrectly dated 25], 1828, Fox Letters.

9   "He was very fond of all the Owens": *Century of Letters*, 1:309.

10   "used to dread going in": A sister, quoted Francis Darwin, "Reminiscences of My Father's Everyday Life" [afterward referred to as Francis Darwin, "Rems."], printed Francis Darwin (ed.), *The Life and Letters of Charles Darwin*, 3 vols.; here 1:108–60; here p. 136 [afterward referred to as *Darwin L.L.*]. MS of "Recollections of Charles Darwin by Francis Darwin" is in DAR. 140 (3).

10   "I became convinced": Auto., p. 11.

10   "Caught a sea mouse": Entry for February 9, 1826, "Diary for 1826, with entries about birds, beasts and flowers seen on walks," DAR. 129.

10   "Caught an orange coloured (Zooptuti?)": Entry for February 15, 1826, ibid.

10   "was literally covered with Cuttle fish": Entry for March 2, 1826, ibid.

11   "A great many Seamice": Entry for March 11, 1826, ibid.

11   "Mr. Darwin communicated to the Society": Entry for March 27, 1827, Minute Book of the Plinian Society [held in Edinburgh University Library], quoted Professor J. H. Ashworth, F.R.S., "Charles Darwin as a Student in Edinburgh, 1825–27," p. 103.

11   "Having procured some specimens": Entry for April 20, 1827, "Early Notebook, containing Observations made by Darwin when he was at Edinburgh, March 1827," DAR. 118.

11   "I asked for some time to consider": Auto., p. 25.

12   "It never struck me": Ibid., p. 26.

12   "became slightly acquainted": Entry for 1831, "Darwin's personal journal (1809–81)," DAR. 158.

12   "Continued to collect insects": Entry for Christmas 1830, ibid.

12   "The marks of *design*": William Paley, *Natural Theology*, p. 473.

13   "The logic of this book": Auto., p. 29.

13   "getting up Paley's Evidences": Darwin–Francis Galton, May 28, 1873, quoted Karl Pearson, *The Life, Letters and Labours of Francis Galton*, 4 vols.; here 2:179 [afterward referred to as *Galton L.L.*].

13   "God's great plough": Louis Agassiz, quoted Edward Lurie, *Louis Agassiz: A Life in Science*, p. 98.

14   "on a large scale": William Smith, quoted John Phillips, *Memoirs of William Smith*, p. 8.

14   "I have lately read": Darwin–Joseph Dalton Hooker, August 6, 1881, DAR. 95.

15   "of the most placid": J. W. Heaviside–Francis Darwin, September 15, 1882, DAR. 112.

PAGE

15 "What a fellow that Darwin is": Professor Henslow, quoted J. M. Rodwell reminiscence, n.d., DAR. 112.

15 "the same opportunity of drilling my mind": Entry for December 13, 1831, Charles Darwin, "The Journal of a Voyage in H.M.S. Beagle," MS at Down House, Downe, Kent. From facsimile edition published 1979 by Genesis Publications [afterward referred to as Journal]; here Journal, p. 23.

15 "No common person or gamekeeper": Game law quoted by Darwin, "Early notes on guns and shooting," DAR. 91.

15 "An unqualified person can only be convicted": Ibid.

15 "Special talents, none" and "Somewhat nervous temperament": Questionnaire enclosed Darwin–Galton, May 28, 1873, quoted *Galton L.L.*, 2:178.

15 "I hope it arises from your being 10 fathoms deep": Darwin–Fox, August 1828, Fox Letters.

16 "men thus endowed": Auto., p. 28.

16 "after a day or two": Darwin–Professor T. McK. Hughes, May 24, 1875, quoted John Willis Clark and Thomas McKenny Hughes, *The Life and Letters of the Reverend Adam Sedgwick*, 2 vols.; here 1:380 [afterward referred to as *Sedgwick L.L.*].

16 "came on some strange wild places": Auto., p. 46.

16 "it would be the greatest misfortune": Ibid., p. 44.

17 "a burning zeal to add": Ibid., p. 42.

17 "There may be metal": Robert FitzRoy in 1830, quoted Sir Gavin de Beer, *Charles Darwin: Evolution by Natural Selection*, p. 22 [afterward referred to as De Beer, *Darwin*].

18 "Capt. F. wants a man": John Stevens Henslow–Darwin, August 24, 1831, DAR. 97.

18 "the pursuit of Natural History": Josiah Wedgwood–Dr. Robert Darwin, August 31, 1831, DAR. 97.

18 "a discouraging letter from my Captain": Darwin–Fox, September 6, 1831, Fox Letters.

19 "I like what I see of him": Captain Robert FitzRoy–Captain Francis Beaufort, n.d., quoted Nora Barlow, "Robert FitzRoy and Charles Darwin," *The Cornhill Magazine*, p. 494 [afterward referred to as Barlow, *Cornhill*].

19 "[He] says the stormy sea": Darwin–Miss Susan Darwin [September 5, 1831], DAR. 154.

19 "Darwin is a very sensible": FitzRoy–Beaufort, March 5, 1832, quoted Richard Darwin Keynes (ed.), *The Beagle Record*, p. 42 [afterward referred to as Keynes].

19 "against assenting hastily": Captain Robert Fitz-Roy, *Proceedings of the Second Expedition, 1831–1836, under the Command of Captain Robert Fitz-Roy, R.N.*, Vol. II of Robert Fitz-Roy (ed.), *Narrative of the Surveying Voyages of His Majesty's Ships Adventure and Beagle*, 3 vols.; here 2:682 [afterward referred to as FitzRoy, *Narrative*].

20 "It is a pity": Darwin–Sir Charles Lyell [December 5, 1859], Francis Darwin and A. C. Seward (eds.), *More Letters of Charles Darwin*, 2 vols.; here 1:129 [afterward referred to as *Darwin M.L.*].

20 "J. S. Henslow to his friend C. Darwin": Inscription in vols. 1 and 2 [bound together], Third edition, 1822, Alexander von Humboldt, *Personal Narrative of Travels to the Equinoctial Regions of the New*

PAGE

Continent, during the Years 1799–1804, Darwin Archive, Cambridge University Library.

20   "I was also troubled with palpitations": Auto., p. 54.

2   *The Voyage of Discovery*

21   "Although I like": Darwin–a sister, n.d., quoted Barlow, *Cornhill*, p. 496.

22   "to define a species": Darwin–Joseph Dalton Hooker, n.d., quoted H. Graham Cannon, review of Jean Rostand, *Charles Darwin* (Paris: Gallimard, 1947), in *Nature* 162, no. 4126 (November 27, 1948): 831.

22   "I look at the term species": Charles Darwin, *On the Origin of Species by Means of Natural Selection* (1st ed., 1859), p. 52 [afterward referred to as *Origin*].

22   "We see all living nature": William Bateson, "Hybridisation and Cross-Breeding as a Method of Scientific Investigation," p. 59 [afterward referred to as Bateson, "Hybridisation and Cross-Breeding"].

23   "It would be profitless": L. H. Bailey, "Systematic Work and Evolution," pp. 532–33.

23   "We should always keep in mind": Thomas Hunt Morgan, *Evolution and Adaptation*, p. 33.

23   "the general pattern": Thomas J. M. Schopf, "Evolving Paleontological Views on Deterministic and Stochastic Approaches," p. 344.

23   "the 'Truth' of any given": Ibid.

23   "While St. Clement": Emanuel Rádl, *The History of Biological Theories*, p. 1 [afterward referred to as Rádl].

24   "Nature which governs the whole": Marcus Aurelius Antoninus, *The Twelve Books of Marcus Aurelius Antoninus, the Emperor*. Seventh Book, p. 102.

24   "Nature, as the saying goes": Joanne Raio [John Ray], *Methodus Plantarum nova*, Preface.

24   "Nature is varied": Oliver Goldsmith, *An History of the Earth, and Animated Nature*, 8 vols., here 2:301.

25   "Organic Life beneath the shoreless waves": Erasmus Darwin, *The Temple of Nature*, p. 26.

25   "At the end of many successive generations": J.B.P.A. de M. de Lamarck, *Philosophie Zoologique*, 2 vols., here 1:62.

26   "to complete the survey": Charles Darwin, *Journal of Researches into the Natural History and Geology of the Countries Visited during the Voyage of H.M.S. Beagle Round the World under the Command of Capt. FitzRoy, R. N.* (2d ed., 1845), p. 1. [afterward referred to as *Journal of Researches* (1845)].

27   "I have just room to turn round": Darwin–Henslow, October 30, 1831. Original Letters from Charles Darwin to Professor J. S. Henslow, 1831–1837, The Royal Botanic Gardens Kew (Library), England [afterward referred to as Kew Library].

27   "The narrow space at the end": Admiral Sir James Sulivan–Francis Darwin, n.d., quoted *Darwin L.L.*, 1:218.

27   "We worked together for several years": Admiral J. Lort Stokes–Editor of *The Times*, April 25, 1882, *The Times*, April 27, 1882.

PAGE

27   "at times, when I have been officer of the watch": Alexander Burns Usborne reminiscence, n.d., quoted *Darwin L.L.*, 1:224.

27   "As far as I can judge": Darwin–Miss Caroline Darwin, April 25, 1832, DAR. 154.

28   "Farewell, dear Fitzroy": Darwin–FitzRoy, 1846, quoted Keynes, p. 42.

28   "I am become quite a Gaucho": Darwin–Miss Caroline Darwin, September 20 [1833], DAR. 154.

29   "Fidler and Boy to Poop Cabin": Sir Gavin de Beer (ed.), "Some Unpublished Letters of Charles Darwin," p. 14 [afterward referred to as De Beer, "Unpublished Letters"].

29   "I do not think it just": Darwin–Miss Catherine Darwin, May 22, 1833, DAR. 154.

29   "now make a fine collection": Darwin–Miss Catherine Darwin, May 22, 1833, continuation of June 6, DAR. 154.

29   "Birds from Galapagos Archipelago": Note, DAR. 29 (iii).

29   "are a fine set of fellows": Darwin–Henslow, October 30, 1831, Kew Library.

29   "One of the former is lined": Darwin–Henslow, November 12, 1833, Kew Library.

30   "But I maintain that no person": Darwin–Henslow, August 15, 1832, Kew Library.

30   "But Geology carries the day": Darwin–Fox, May 1832, Fox Letters.

30   "I am quite charmed with Geology": Darwin–Henslow, March 1834, Kew Library.

30   "His [Dr. Darwin's] son is doing admirable work": Rev. Adam Sedgwick–Dr. S. Butler, November 7, 1835, *Sedgwick L.L.*, 1:380.

31   "The following is a copy": Sir Horace Darwin, "Copy No. 1 of Typescript of Charles Darwin's Diary" (Cambridge, 1891), DAR. 217.3.

31   "The most curious fact": "M.S. Notes made on board H.M.S. 'Beagle,' 1832–6, on: (i) animals," DAR. 29 (i).

32   "will afford me many hours": Entry for January 10, 1832, Journal, p. 55.

32   "Many of these creatures": Entry for January 11, 1832, ibid.

32   "notwithstanding our smiles": FitzRoy, *Narrative*, 2:107.

32   "This like the last . . . was caught in the forest": Entry for June 1832, "Diary of observations on zoology of the places visited during the voyage [of HMS *Beagle*]," DAR. 30 (i).

33   "I have drawn my pen through those parts": Entry for January 17–18, 1832, "Diary of observations on the geology of the places visited during the voyage. Part I," DAR. 32 (i).

33   "greatest event of the day": Entry for March 21, 1832, Journal, p. 127.

33   "the feat could not have been performed": Philip Gidley King, "The Beagle's Voyage," DAR. 107.

33   "run the risk of being eat up alive": Darwin–Henslow, November 12, 1833, Kew Library.

33   "The Minute I landed": Darwin–Miss Caroline Darwin, October 23, 1833, DAR. 154.

PAGE

33   "It was something new to me": Darwin–Miss Susan Darwin, July
      14, 1832, continuation of August 7, 1832, ibid.

33   "Darwin, did you ever see a Grampus": Bartholomew James Suli-
      van quoted in Entry for April 1, 1832, Journal, p. 130

34   "the unspeakable pleasure": Entry for January 19, 1832, Journal,
      p. 67.

34   "The delight one experiences": Entry for February 28, 1832,
      ibid., p. 115.

34   "The day has passed delightfully": Entry for Feb. 29, 1832, ibid.

34   "I am sorry to see": [Brother] Erasmus Darwin–Darwin, August
      18, [1832], DAR. 204.6(1).

35   "a request to the Chaplain of Buenos Ayres": Robert Hamond–
      Francis Darwin, September 19, 1882, DAR. 112.

35   "I have already found beds": Entry for August 5, 1834, Journal,
      p. 468.

35   "This grand range": Charles Darwin, *Geological Observations on
      South America*, Part III of *The Geology of the Voyage of the Beagle, under
      the Command of Capt. Fitzroy, R.N., during the Years 1832 to 1836*, p.
      247.

35   "But, on the other hand": Entry for March 19, 1835, Charles
      Darwin, *Journal of Researches into the Geology and Natural History of
      the Various Countries Visited by H.M.S. "Beagle," under the Command
      of Captain Fitzroy, R.N., from 1832 to 1836* (1st ed., 1839),
      p. 386 [afterward referred to as *Journal of Researches* (1839)].

36   "Every animal in a state of nature": *Journal of Researches* (1845),
      p. 175.

36   "At an elevation from 10–12,000 ft.": Darwin–Henslow, April 18,
      1835, Kew Library.

36   "It looked as though God had caused": Fray Tomás de Berlanga
      in 1535, quoted David Lack, *Darwin's Finches*, p. 6 [afterward
      referred to as Lack].

37   "nothing but loose Rocks": Woodes Rogers, diary entry for May
      20, 1709, *A Cruising Voyage Round the World*, p. 207.

37   "Nothing could be less inviting": *Journal of Researches* (1839), p.
      454.

37   "I frequently got on their backs": Ibid., p. 465.

37   "differed from the different islands": *Journal of Researches* (1845),
      p. 394.

38   "When I recollect the fact": "Ornithology–Galapagos," "M.S.
      Notes made on board H.M.S. 'Beagle', 1832–6, on: (ii) birds,"
      DAR. 29 (ii).

38   The truth . . . in a fifty-three-page paper: Frank J. Sulloway,
      "Darwin and His Finches: The Evolution of a Legend" [afterward
      referred to as Sulloway] pp. 1–53.

38   "Seeing this gradation and diversity": *Journal of Researches* (1845),
      p. 380.

38   "small finch-like beaks": Lack, p. 11.

38   "All the birds that live": Captain FitzRoy quoted Nora Barlow–Ed-
      itor of *Nature*, n.d., *Nature* 136, no. 3436 (September 7, 1935): 391.

39   "the focus for a considerable legend": Sulloway, p. 5.

39   "most of the specimens of the finch tribe": *Journal of Researches*
      (1845), p. 395.

PAGE

39   "After he left Charles Island": Sulloway, p. 19.

39   "Unfortunately I did not": Charles Darwin (ed.), *The Zoology of the Voyage of H.M.S. Beagle, under the Command of Captain Fitzroy, R.N., during the Years 1832 to 1836*, 5 parts; here Part III: *Birds*, by John Gould, p. 99.

39   "Amongst other things, I collected every plant": Darwin–Henslow, January 1836, Kew Library.

39   "I have always felt": Auto., p. 49.

40   "I never was intended": Darwin–Henslow, January 1836, Kew Library.

40   "There is only one sorrowful drawback": Darwin–Dr. Robert Darwin, February 10, 1832, DAR. 154.

40   "but how great a difference between this": Darwin–Miss Caroline Darwin, September 20 [1833], ibid.

40   "I never see a Merchant vessel": Darwin–Miss Caroline Darwin, February 14, 1836, ibid.

40   "if nothing unforeseen happens": Darwin–Henslow, March 1834, Kew Library.

40   "enough alone to make me long": Darwin–Miss Catherine Darwin, July 20, 1834, P.S., quoted Nora Barlow, *Charles Darwin and the Voyage of the Beagle*, p. 104 [afterward referred to as Barlow, *Voyage*].

40   "long been grieved & most sorry": Darwin–Miss Catherine Darwin, November 8, 1834, DAR. 154.

40   "I am heartily glad of it": Darwin–Henslow, March 1835, Kew Library.

40   "I loathe, I abhor the sea": Darwin–Miss Susan Darwin, August 4 [1836], DAR. 154.

41   "the most memorable event": Entry for June 8–15, 1836, Journal, p. 740.

41   "never talked much": Auto., p. 78.L.

41   "I allude to that mystery of mysteries": John Herschel–Lyell, February 20, 1836, quoted Walter F. Cannon, *The Impact of Uniformitarianism*, p. 305.

41   "I arrived here yesterday morning": Darwin–FitzRoy, October 6 [1836], *Darwin L.L.*, 1:269.

42   "flycatcher" and "stone-pounder": Caroline Fox diary entry for October 3, 1836, Horace N. Pym (ed.), *Memories of Old Friends*, p. 8.

3   Evolution of an Idea

44   "The idea of the Pampas going up": Lyell–Darwin, December 26, 1836, Mrs. [Katharine Murray] Lyell (ed.), *Life, Letters and Journals of Sir Charles Lyell*, 2 vols; here 1:475 [afterward referred to as *Lyell L.L.*].

44   "you stand the first": Lyell–Darwin, December 26, 1836, ibid.

44   "Darwin is a glorious addition": Lyell–Sedgwick, April 21, 1837, *Sedgwick L.L.*, 1:484.

44   "in support of my heretical doctrines": Lyell–Leonard Horner, March 12, 1838, *Lyell L.L.*, 2:39.

45   "The author concluded by remarking": Darwin, "On the Formation of Mould," p. 576.

PAGE

45   "I could somehow see nothing all around me": Darwin–William
      Darwin, n.d., DAR. 153.

45   "the hardy wielders of the hammer": J. W. Judd, "Darwin and
      Geology," in A. C. Seward (ed.), *Darwin and Modern Science*, pp.
      337–84; here p. 363.

45   "Finished paper on Glen Roy": Entry for September 6, 1838,
      "Darwin's personal journal (1809–81)," DAR. 158.

45   "If Agassiz or Buckland": Darwin–Horner, August 10, 1846, Ka-
      tharine M. Lyell (ed.), *Memoir of Leonard Horner*, 2 vols.; here 2:104
      [afterward referred to as *Horner Memoir*].

46   "Your arguments seem to me": Darwin–Thomas Francis Jamie-
      son, September 6 [1861], National Library of Scotland, Edin-
      burgh.

46   "neither of us saw a trace": Auto., p. 46.

46   "though very good humoured": Ibid., p. 78.D.

47   "almost at the top": Sir Archibald Geikie, "Charles Darwin: Part
      II," p. 74.

47   "feel like a knight": Darwin–Richard Owen, December 19, 1836,
      Fitzwilliam Museum, Cambridge, England.

47   "It is a sorrowful": Darwin–Fox, March 1837, Fox Letters.

47   "I miss a walk in the country": Darwin–Rev. Leonard Jenyns [Rev.
      L. Blomefield, by this time], April 10, 1837, *Darwin L.L.*, 1:282.

48   "Now the scheme [is]": Darwin–Henslow, March 28, 1837, Kew
      Library.

48   "that by following the example of Lyell": Auto., p. 87.

48   "long reflected": Ibid., p. 60.

48   "During the voyage of the 'Beagle' ": Ibid., p. 85.

49   "— Had been greatly struck from about Month": Entry for July,
      1837, "Darwin's personal journal (1809–81)", DAR. 158.

49   "determined to collect blindly": Darwin–Hooker [January 11,
      1844], DAR. 114.

49   "I continue to collect all kinds": Darwin–Fox [January 25, 1841],
      P.S., Fox Letters.

49   "I shd . . . be very glad": Darwin–Fox, May 7, 1855, ibid.

49   "I have done the black deed": Darwin–Fox, July 22, 1855, ibid.

49   "Is the Rabbit wild": Darwin–Laurence Edmondston, September
      11 [1856], De Beer, "Unpublished Letters," p. 30.

49   "Now you will think me": Darwin–Henry Tibbats Stainton, Feb-
      ruary 18, 1858, British Museum (Natural History), Department of
      Entomology Library, London.

50   "breeds of fowls": Sir Gavin de Beer, Introduction to Charles
      Darwin, "Questions about the Breeding of Animals [1840]," p.
      vii [afterward referred to as "Questions"] (1839 is suggested as
      a more probable date by R. B. Freeman and P. J. Gautrey in
      "Darwin's 'Questions about the Breeding of Animals,' with a
      Note on 'Queries about Expression,' " p. 221.)

50   "If the cross offspring": 1st Query, "Questions," p. 1.

50   "Do you know instances": 15th Query, "Questions," p. 5.

50   "Where any animal whatever": 17th Query, "Questions," p. 6.

50   "I hope that some of your readers": Darwin–Editor of the *Garden-
      ers' Chronicle*, n.d., *Gardeners' Chronicle and Agricultural Gazette*, Janu-
      ary 21, 1860, p. 49.

51   "had occurred when populations": Gavin de Beer, Introduction, Sir Gavin de Beer (ed.), "Darwin's Notebooks on Transmutation of Species. Part II: Second Notebook (February to July 1838)," p. 77.

51   "by 'my theory' ": De Beer, ibid.

51   "I worked on true Baconian principles": Auto., p. 87.

52   "We have seen Darwin several times": Horner–Mrs. Katharine M. Lyell, August 20, 1837, *Horner Memoir*, 1:337.

52   "If I live till I am eighty years old": Darwin–Henslow, November 4, 1837, Kew Library.

53   "Did He cause the frame": Charles Darwin, *The Variation of Animals and Plants under Domestication*, 2 vols.; here 2:431 [afterward referred to as *Variation*].

53   ". . . death of species": Darwin, " 'B' Notebook dealing with evolutionary theory 'commenced . . . July 1837,' " DAR. 121.

53   "I came to the conclusion": Darwin–Alfred Russel Wallace, April 6, 1859, *Darwin M.L.*, 1:118.

53   "for amusement": Auto., p. 88.

54   "It may safely be pronounced": Rev. Thomas Malthus, *An Essay on the Principle of Population*, (5th ed. 1817), 3 vols., here 1:9.

54   Some 230 pages were eventually recovered: Sir Gavin de Beer, M. J. Rowlands, and B. M. Skramovsky (eds.), "Darwin's Notebooks on Transmutation of Species: Part VI: Pages Excised by Darwin," p. 131.

54   comparing the scissor marks: ibid., p. 132.

54   "We ought to be far from wondering": "Excised leaf p. 134 from Darwin's 'D' Notebook dealing with evolution theory, 'July 15th 1838. Finished October 2nd,' " DAR. 208. (Darwin's " 'D' Notebook" is in DAR. 123. The two excised leaves, p. 134 and p. 135, were found later and are now contained in an envelope numbered DAR. 208. They have not been reinstated into the actual notebook.)

54   "Population is increase[d] at geometrical ratio": "Excised leaf p. 135 from Darwin's 'D' notebook," ibid.

55   Silvan S. Schweber, "The Origin of the 'Origin' Revisited," pp. 229–316.

55   "being well prepared to appreciate": Auto., p. 88.

56   "can we doubt": *Origin* (1st ed., 1859), p. 80.

56   "a little nudge": Ernst Mayr, "Darwin and Natural Selection," p. 322.

56   "Towards close I first thought": Inside Front Cover, "Darwin's 'D' notebook," DAR. 123.

56   "As soon as I had become": Auto., p. 105.

56   "I think I shall avoid": Darwin–Wallace, December 22, 1857, *Darwin L.L.*, 2:109.

57   "some little light": *Origin* (1st ed. 1859), p. 199.

57   "thought it best": Auto., p. 106.

57   "It would have been useless": Ibid.

57   "In regard to the origination": Lyell–Darwin, June 1, 1838, quoted Leonard G. Wilson, *Charles Lyell, the Years to 1841*, p. 439.

57   "the idea struck me": Ibid.

58   "disbelief crept over me": Auto., p. 64.

58   "& have never since doubted": Ibid.

58   "There is grandeur in this view of life": *Origin* (1st ed., 1859), p. 490.

58   "by the Creator": *Origin* (2d ed., 1860), p. 490.

58   "speculated much about 'Existence of Species' ": Entry for February 25, 1838, "Darwin's personal journal (1809–81)," DAR. 158.

58   "Frittered these foregoing days": Entry for September 14, 1838, ibid.

58   "became unwell": Entry for December 24, 1839, ibid.

58   "did very little": Entry for April 26, 1839, ibid.

58   "wasted some time": Entry for November and December 1838 to the end of year, ibid.

58   "when well enough": Entry for November 14, 1840, ibid.

59   "His ailments were felt": Sir Arthur Keith, *Darwin Revalued*, p. 26, [afterward referred to as Keith].

59   "been a bitter mortification for me": Darwin–Lyell, June 1841, *Darwin L.L.*, 1:272.

59   "From July to end of year": Entry for 1848, "Darwin's personal journal (1809–81)," DAR. 158.

59   "I thought all this winter": Darwin–Syms Covington, March 30, 1849, quoted "Original Letters of Charles Darwin to an Australian Settler," contributed by Alfred McFarland, *The Sydney Mail* 38, no. 1257 (August 9, 1884): 254–55, here p. 254 [afterward referred to as "Darwin-Covington Letters"].

59   "best month since April 1850": Comment for September 1851, Darwin's "Diary of Health, 1849–1854," Down House Archive.

59   "I think I am not so strict": Comment for August 1853, ibid.

59   "Very little fatigue": Darwin–Colonel Edward Sabine, June 28 [1854], Royal Society MSS. Sa.386, The Royal Society, London.

59   "gone back latterly to my bad ways": Darwin–Horner, December 23, 1860, *Horner Memoir*, 2:299.

59   "so liable to illness": Horner–Mrs. Katharine M. Lyell, February 17, 1863, ibid., p. 357.

59   "I would ask him to Down": Darwin–Wallace, June 25, 1869, quoted James Marchant, *Alfred Russel Wallace: Letters and Reminiscences*, 2 vols.; here 1:245 [afterward referred to as *Wallace L&R*].

60   "I have hardly crawled": Darwin–Hooker, June 22, 1869, DAR. 94.

60   "Ill people suspected of hypochondria": P. B. Medawar, "Darwin's Illness," p. 528.

60   "I am inclined to agree with [Dr.] Minoprio": George Gaylord Simpson, *Concession to the Improbable*, p. 172.

61   "I have taken up": Darwin–Wallace, September 2, 1872, *Wallace L&R*, 1:300.

61   "The trouble was that": Gwen Raverat, *Period Piece: A Cambridge Childhood*, pp. 121–22.

61   "endeavoured to make it clear": John Tyndall–Darwin, October 9, 1868, DAR. 106.

PAGE

62 "I was introduced": Sir Joseph Hooker notes to Francis Darwin, n.d., *Darwin L.L.*, 2:19.

62 "I used to sleep with the sheets": Ibid., p. 20.

63 "Charms of music and female chit-chat": Charles Darwin, "This is the Question, 'Marry' and 'Not Marry,' " DAR. 210.10.

63 "Never mind, trust to chance": Ibid.

63 "I marvel at my good fortune": Auto., p. 74.

63 "borne with the utmost patience": Ibid.

63 "cheerful comforter throughout life": Ibid.

63 "I propose to do for Emma": Josiah Wedgwood II–Dr. Robert Darwin, November 15, 1838, *Century of Letters*, 1:415.

63 "I was quite ashamed of myself today": Darwin–Emma Wedgwood, January 20, 1839, ibid., p. 438.

64 "used to laugh over the ugliness": Henrietta Darwin reminiscence, n.d., DAR. 112.

64 "that is, for him to have the disposal": Darwin–Miss Caroline Darwin, April 29, 1836, DAR. 154.

65 "I went to the Captain's": Darwin–Miss Susan Darwin, April 1839, quoted Barlow, *Cornhill*, p. 500.

65 "Most people (who know anything of the subject)": FitzRoy–Darwin, November 16, 1837, DAR. 164.F. Pt. II.

67 "that his book has been a very great treat": Horner–Mrs. Horner, May 20, 1838, *Horner Memoir*, 1:361.

67 "I like Darwin's Journal much": J. E. Davis–Hooker, n.d., Leonard Huxley (ed.), *Life and Letters of Sir Joseph Dalton Hooker*, 2 vols.; here 1:66, n. 1 [afterward referred to as *Hooker L.L.*].

68 *"charged* me to keep a book": Darwin–Hooker, June 29, 1845, DAR. 114.

68 "Seeing what von Buch": "Darwin's 'D' Notebook," DAR. 123.

68 "First Pencil Sketch of Species Theory . . . 1842": DAR. 6.

68 "during my stay at Maer": Entry for June 15, 1842, "Darwin's personal journal (1809–81)," DAR. 158.

68 Peter J. Vorzimmer . . . noted: Peter J. Vorzimmer, "An Early Darwin Manuscript: The 'Outline and Draft of 1839.' "

68 In 1982 this theory was assailed: David Kohn, Sydney Smith and Robert C. Stauffer, "New Light on 'The Foundations of the Origin of Species.' " pp. 419–42.

69 "the mysterious 13-page ink manuscript": Ibid, p. 427.

69 "This was sketched in 1839": On "Table of Contents," "Sketch of species theory, 1844. Fair copy of DAR. 7 [Original MS], annotated by Darwin," DAR. 113.

69 "It puts my extracts (written in 1839 . . .)": Darwin–Wallace, January 25 [1859], *Darwin L.L.*, 2:146.

69 "I gained much by my delay": Auto., p. 96.

69 "Extracts from a MS. work": Charles Lyell and Joseph D. Hooker–J. J. Bennett, Secretary of the Linnean Society, June 30, 1858, (read July 1, 1858), printed *Journal of the Proceedings of the Linnean Society: Zoology* 3 (1859): 45–46; here p. 45.

69 "in which he repeats his views": Ibid.

70 "With equal probability": "First Pencil Sketch of Species Theory, . . . 1842," DAR. 6.

PAGE

4   The Influence of Down

71   "My father came home": John Lubbock [1st Lord Avebury],
        quoted Horace G. Hutchinson, *Life of Sir John Lubbock, Lord Ave-
        bury*, 2 vols.; here 1:15 [afterward referred to as *Lubbock Life*].

71   "resist his future career": Darwin–James Dwight Dana, Septem-
        ber 27, 1853, Daniel C. Gilman, *The Life of James Dwight Dana*, p.
        310 [afterward referred to as *Dana Life*].

72   "We could hold the Hensleighs": Darwin–Miss Catherine Darwin
        [July 1842], *Darwin M.L.*, 1:33.

72   "A most deceptious property": Bricklayer, quoted Darwin–Miss
        Susan Darwin, n.d., DAR. 92.

72   "It is really surprising": Darwin–Miss Catherine Darwin [July
        1842], *Darwin M.L.*, 1:32.

72   "Forgive me for one bit more trouble": Darwin–Asa Gray, June
        10 [1862], Historical Records Survey, *Calendar of the Letters of
        Charles Robert Darwin to Asa Gray*, p. 42 [afterward referred to as
        Darwin-Gray Letters].

73   "an invaluable treasure": *Century of Letters*, 2:63.

73   "a long hilly stage of 10 miles": Darwin–Richard Owen [1848],
        "Unpublished Letters of Charles Darwin in the Collection of
        Charles F. Cox, New York," DAR. 135(18).

73   "he spent most of his life": R. J. Berry, "Happy is the man that
        findeth wisdom," p. 7.

73   "I hope by going up to town": Darwin–Fox [December 9, 1842],
        Fox Letters.

74   "We are now undertaking": Darwin–Miss Susan Darwin, Septem-
        ber 3, 1845, *Century of Letters*, 2:83.

75   "farmer": "Householders in Downe," Samuel Bagshaw, *History,
        Gazetteer, and Directory of the County of Kent*, 2 vols.; here 1:695.

75   "tired with haymaking": Darwin–Lyell [July 1845], *Darwin L.L.*,
        1:338.

75   "To Boil Rice": Entry in Charles Darwin's handwriting in "Emma
        Darwin's Recipe Book (started May 16, 1839)," DAR. 214.

75   "I think of a sound": Henrietta Litchfield, *Century of Letters*, 2:181.

75   "Thanks for the very curious story": Darwin–Rev. J. Brodie
        Innes, May 29, 1871, quoted Robert M. Stecher, "The Darwin-
        Innes Letters," p. 237 [afterward referred to as "Darwin-Innes
        Letters"].

75   *"hot house face"*: Charles Darwin, *The Expression of the Emotions in
        Man and Animals*, p. 60 [afterward referred to as *Emotions*].

76   "The two subjects which moved my Father": a son's reminiscence
        [unidentified], January 14, 1883, DAR. 112.

76   "You ask my opinion": Darwin–Professor Ray Lankester, March
        22, 1871, *Darwin L.L.*, 3:200.

76   "every one has heard of the dog": Darwin, *The Descent of Man, and
        Selection in Relation to Sex*, 2 vols [1st ed., 1871]; here 1:40 [after-
        ward referred to as *Descent of Man* (1871)].

76   "the soul by consent of all": "Darwin's 'B' Notebook," DAR. 121.

76   "We are sharers": Asa Gray, *Natural Science and Religion*, p. 54.

77   "A being so powerful": Auto., p. 69.

77   "hearing that a farmer": William Erasmus Darwin speaking at
        banquet in Cambridge, quoted James Crichton-Browne–Editor

PAGE

of *The Times*, June 30, 1909, *The Times*, July 8, 1909.

77   "that he should never have": Francis Darwin, "Rems.," p. 110.

77   "since it would horrify them": Darwin–George John Romanes, April 7, [1875], in P. Thomas Carroll (ed.), *An Annotated Calendar of the Letters of Charles Darwin in the Library of The American Philosophical Society*, p. 164 [afterward referred to as Carroll, *Am. Phil. Soc. Calendar*].

77   "We never thoroughly agreed": Rev. J. Brodie Innes, Statement in his handwriting, n.d., quoted "Darwin-Innes Letters," p. 256.

77   "I am not a convert": Innes–Darwin, February 24, 1871, "Darwin-Innes Letters," p. 235.

78   "I hope that you will admit": Darwin–The Members of the Down Friendly Club, February 19, 1877, DAR. 138 (5).

78   "We have just had a curious scene": Darwin–Innes, August 23, 1880, "Darwin-Innes Letters," p. 247.

79   "I attended the Bench": Darwin–Hooker, November 21, 1859, DAR. 115 (i).

79   "long walks, romps with the children": Sir Joseph Hooker, Notes to Francis Darwin, n.d., *Darwin L.L.*, 2:26.

79   "an established rule": Ibid., p. 27.

79   "I cannot endure to think": Darwin–Fox, September 4, 1850, Fox Letters.

79   "I hate schools & the whole system": Darwin–Fox, "24th" [1852], Fox Letters.

80   "I remember him throwing it once": George Darwin reminiscences, n.d., DAR. 112.

80   "I am sorry that you cannot 'grind' ": Darwin–William Darwin, n.d., DAR. 153.

80   "You will surely find": Darwin–William Darwin, October 3, 1855, ibid.

80   "A young man may here slave": Darwin–Covington, November 23, 1850, "Darwin-Covington Letters." p. 254.

80   "To what shall you bring up your boys?": Darwin–Covington, February 28, 1855, ibid.

81   "I looked into this hole": Darwin's "Précis of his Field Notes on Humble Bees, May, 1872," quoted R. B. Freeman, "Charles Darwin on the Routes of Male Humble Bees," p. 181.

81   "I could only follow them": Ibid, p. 182.

81   "I was able to prove this": Ibid, p. 182.

81   "How on earth do bees": Comment July 26, 1856, Darwin's "Original Field Notes on Humble Bees, 1854–1861," quoted ibid., p. 186.

82   "Yesterday, after writing to you": Darwin–Mrs. Emma Darwin, April [1858], DAR. 154.

82   "to make him a tank": John Lewis, quoted in "A Visit to Darwin's Village: Reminiscences of Some of His Humble Friends," *The Evening News* (London), February 12, 1909, p. 4 [afterward referred to as "Lewis"].

82   "About noon every day": George Darwin reminiscences, n.d., DAR. 112.

82   "rejoicing if the post was a light one": Francis Darwin, "Rems.," p. 112.

PAGE

83   "I should like extremely to see you": Darwin–Fox, October 26, 1865, Fox Letters.

83   "I should wish to get back here": Darwin–Hooker, Sat. [June] 29th, 1844, DAR. 150.

83   "that no tour whatever": Darwin–Dana, November 25, 1852, *Dana Life*, p. 309.

84   "His dissecting table": Francis Darwin, "Rems.," p. 146.

84   "The drawers [of the dissecting table] were labelled": Francis Darwin, "Rems.," p. 146.

84   "a very presumptuous work": Darwin–Hooker, January 11, 1844, DAR. 114.

84   "gleams of light": Ibid.

85   "It is no great boldness": [Robert Chambers] *Vestiges of the Natural History of Creation*, p. 219.

85   "If the book be true": Sedgwick–Lyell, April 9, 1845, *Sedgwick L.L.*, 2:82.

85   "the writing and arrangement": Darwin–Hooker [1844 ?], *Darwin L.L.*, 1:333.

86   "Nevertheless, it is a grand piece of argument": Darwin–Lyell, October 8 [1845], *Darwin L.L.*, 1:344.

86   "gradually come . . . to see": Auto., p. 62.

86   "There is a simple grandeur": Darwin, "Sketch of species theory, 1844, original MS," DAR. 7.

87   "If I have said more than some": Lyell–George Poulett Scrope, June 14, 1830, *Lyell L.L.*, 1:271.

87   "I have just finished my sketch": Darwin–Mrs. Emma Darwin, July 5, 1844, DAR. 154.

88   "the next best": Ibid.

88   "On these visits": Hooker–W. E. Darwin, February 19, 1905, *Hooker L.L.*, 2:459.

89   "which differed so much from all other": Auto., p. 83.

89   "The general conclusions": Darwin–Jenyns [Blomefield], October 12 [1845], *Darwin L.L.*, 2:32.

90   "Your father had Barnacles on the brain": Hooker–Francis Darwin, December 31, 1885, *Hooker L.L.*, 2:299.

90   "three stages in his career": Ibid.

90   "I remember, in the course of my first interview": Huxley, "On the Reception of 'The Origin of Species,'" *Darwin L.L.*, 2:179–204; here p. 196 [afterward referred to as Huxley, "Reception of 'Origin' "].

90   "never did a wiser thing": Huxley, quoted *Darwin L.L.*, 1:347.

90   "Like the rest of us, he had": Ibid., pp. 347–48.

91   "for the last half-month": Darwin–FitzRoy, n.d., *Darwin L.L.*, 1:349.

91   "I have lost for the last 4 or 5 months": Darwin–Owen [1849], "Unpublished Letters of Charles Darwin in the Collection of Charles F. Cox, New York," DAR. 135 (18).

91   "I have lately got a bisexual cirripede": Darwin–Hooker, May 10, 1848, DAR. 114.

92   "quite a nugget": Darwin–Covington, March 9, 1856, "Darwin-Covington Letters," p. 255.

PAGE

92 "But I shall now in a day or two": Darwin–Hooker, September 7 [1854], DAR. 114.

92 "I am getting on splendidly with my pigeons": Darwin–Willy [William Darwin], n.d., DAR. 153.

92 "Those who cavalierly reject": [Herbert Spencer] "The Development Hypothesis."

93 "I took my stand upon two grounds": Huxley, "Reception of 'Origin,'" p. 188.

93 "While we think of evolution": Herbert Spencer, *First Principles* (2d ed., 1867), p. 545.

93 "be looked at as by far the greatest living philosopher": Darwin–Lankester, March 15 [1870], *Darwin L.L.*, 3:120.

94 "With the exception of special points": Darwin–J. Fiske, December 8, 1874, ibid., p. 193.

94 "the Survival of the Fittest": *Origin* (5th ed., 1869), p. 92.

94 which Spencer had used: Herbert Spencer, *The Principles of Biology*, 2 vols.; here 1:444.

94 "Your remarks on the general argument": Darwin–Spencer, November 25 [1858], *Darwin L.L.*, 2:141.

94 "It would be quite justifiable": Ernst Mayr, *The Growth of Biological Thought*, p. 386 [afterward referred to as Mayr].

5   The Making of The Origin

95 "I am hard at work on my notes": Darwin–Fox, March 19, 1855, Fox Letters.

95 "a sudden flash of insight": Wallace, receiving the first Darwin-Wallace Medal at the Linnean Society, July 1, 1908, quoted *Wallace L&R*, 1:113.

96 "I well remember the excitement": Alfred Russel Wallace, *The Wonderful Century*, p. 137.

96 "gather facts . . . 'towards'": Henry Walter Bates, Preface, *The Naturalist on the River Amazons*, 2 vols.; here 1:[iii].

96 "my early letters to Bates": Alfred Russel Wallace, *My Life: A Record of Events and Opinions*, 2 vols.; here 1:257 [afterward referred to as Wallace, *Life*].

96 "We must at the outset": Alfred Russel Wallace, "Note for Organic Law of Change," in "Notebook, 1855–1859," pp. 35–36, A. R. Wallace's MSS, MS. 180, The Linnean Society of London.

97 "The following law may be deduced": Alfred R. Wallace, "On the Law Which Has Regulated the Introduction of New Species," p. 186.

97 "Granted the law": Ibid., p. 196.

97 "What think you of Wallace's paper": Edward Blyth–Darwin, December 8, 1855, DAR. 98.

98 "With Darwin": Charles Lyell, "Scientific Journal No. I," p. 137, in Leonard G. Wilson (ed.), *Sir Charles Lyell's Scientific Journals on the Species Question*, p. 54 [afterward referred to as *Lyell Sc. J.*].

98 "Genera differ in the variability": Ibid.

98 "The reason why Mr. Wallace['s]": "Scientific Journal No. I," p. 138, *Lyell Sc. J.*, p. 55.

98 "When Huxley, Hooker and Wollaston": Lyell–Charles J. F. Bunbury, April 30, 1856, *Lyell L.L.*, 2:212.

PAGE

98 "I hardly know what to think": Darwin–Lyell, May 3 [1856], *Darwin L.L.*, 2:67.

98 "I am fixed against any periodical or Journal": Darwin–Hooker, May 9 [1856], DAR. 114.

99 "the heterodox conclusion": Darwin–Gray, July 20 [1856], *Darwin-Gray Letters*, p. 7.

99 "Began by Lyell's advice": Entry for May 14, 1856, "Darwin's personal journal (1809–81)," DAR. 158.

99 "This I have begun to do": Darwin–Fox, June 10, 1856 [postmarked], quoted *Lyell Sc. J.*, p. xlviii.

99 "Sometimes I fear I shall break down": Darwin–Fox, November 1856, *Darwin L.L.*, 2:72.

99 "This summer will make the 20th year(!)": Darwin–Wallace, May 1, 1857, ibid., p. 95.

100 "a strange act of wilfulness": Edmund Gosse, *Father and Son*, p. 119.

100 "I assume that each organism": Philip Henry Gosse, *Omphalos: An Attempt to Untie the Geological Knot*, p. 111.

100 "I venture to suggest": Ibid., p. vi.

101 "It may be objected": Ibid., p. 347.

101 "Who will say": Ibid.

101 "give up the painful and slow conclusion": Charles Kingsley–Philip Henry Gosse, May 4, 1858, quoted Edmund Gosse, *The Life of Philip Henry Gosse*, p. 281.

101 "what rational man": Charles Kingsley, *Glaucus; or, the Wonders of the Shore*, p. 14 n.

101 "a riddle wrapped in a mystery": Winston Spencer Churchill, radio broadcast, October 1, 1939.

102 "he has pointed out to me": Darwin–Hooker, July 14, [1857 ?], DAR. 114.

102 "You have done me the greatest possible service": Darwin–Lubbock, [July] 14 [1857], *Darwin L.L.*, 2:104.

102 "It is enough": Darwin–Lubbock, ibid.

102 "This was sent to Asa Gray": *Darwin L.L.*, 2:120 n.

102 "Why I think that species": Darwin–Gray, September 5 [1857], ibid., pp. 121 and 123.

103 "This sketch is *most* imperfect": Ibid., p. 125.

104 "I have for some years": Darwin–Covington, May 18 [1858], "Darwin-Covington Letters," p. 255.

104 "You would laugh if you could know": Darwin–Hooker, June 8, 1858, DAR. 114.

104 "He is now preparing for publication": Wallace–Bates, January 4, 1858, *Wallace L&R*, 1:67.

104 "Vaguely thinking over the enormous": Wallace, *Life*, 1:362.

105 "From the effects of disease": Ibid.

105 A long round of research: John Langdon Brooks, *Just Before the Origin: Alfred Russel Wallace's Theory of Evolution* (1984).

106 "Your words have come true": Darwin–Lyell, [June] 18 [1858], *Darwin L.L.*, 2:116.

106 "I would far rather burn my whole book": Darwin–Lyell [June 25, 1858], ibid., p. 117.

PAGE

107 "half a letter" and "[giving] up all priority to him": Darwin–Hooker, July 13, 1858, DAR. 114.

107 "to send some MS to them": Darwin–Wallace, April 6, 1859, P.S., *Wallace L&R*, 1:137.

107 "the interests of science": Charles Lyell and Joseph D. Hooker–J. J. Bennett, Secretary of the Linnean Society, June 30, 1858 (read July 1, 1858), printed *Journal of the Proceedings of the Linnean Society: Zoology*, 3 (1859): 45–46; here p. 45.

107 "Most fortunately my paper had to give way": George Bentham–Francis Darwin, May 30, 1882, DAR. 112.

107 "Extract from a MS. work on Species": Minute of Special Meeting, July 1, 1858, *Proceedings of the Linnean Society of London*, pp. liv–lvi, here p. lv, bound in *Journal of the Proceedings of the Linnean Society: Botany* 3 (1859).

108 "But in truth it shames me": Darwin–Hooker, July 5 [1858], DAR. 114.

108 "the only very brief thing": Darwin–Gray, July 4, [1858], *Darwin-Gray Letters*, p. 14.

108 "I am MUCH *more* than satisfied": Darwin–Hooker, July 13, 1858, DAR. 114.

108 "the subject [was] too novel": Hooker–Francis Darwin, October 22, 1886, *Hooker L.L.*, 2:301.

109 "The year which has passed": Thomas Bell, presidential address to the Linnean Society on the anniversary of Linnaeus's birth, May 24, 1859, *Proceedings of the Linnean Society of London*, pp. viii–xx, here p. viii, bound in *Journal of the Proceedings of The Linnean Society: Botany* 4 (1860).

109 "assuming, as is probable": Richard Owen, presidential address, *Report of the Twenty-eighth Meeting of the British Association for the Advancement of Science; held at Leeds in September 1858*, pp. xlix–cx; here pp. xci–xcii.

109 "founded upon the imaginary probable": [Rev.] Arthur Hussey, Rottingdean, February 1859, "The Tendency of Species to form Varieties," p. 6474.

109 "The salvation of man": Review of Hugh Miller, *The Testimony of the Rocks*, *The Dublin Review* 44, no. 88 (June 1858): 375–95; here pp. 379–80.

109 "the weight of authority": Rev. Professor [Samuel] Haughton, address delivered at Adjourned Anniversary Meeting of the Geological Society of Dublin, February 9, 1859, *Journal of the Geological Society of Dublin* 8 (1857–60): 137–56; here p. 152.

110 "writing with a series": H. B. Tristram, "On the Ornithology of Northern Africa," pp. 415–35; here p. 429.

110 "a monument to the natural generosity": Julian S. Huxley, "Alfred Russel Wallace (1823–1913)," p. 547.

110 "mutual nobility": Loren Eiseley, *Darwin's Century*, p. 292.

110 "This assures me the acquaintance": Wallace–his mother, October 6, 1858, *Wallace L&R*, 1:71.

110 "without [his] knowledge": Wallace–A. B. Meyer, November 22, 1869, quoted A. B. Meyer, "How Was Wallace Led to the Discovery of Natural Selection?," p. 415.

PAGE

111   "The action of [natural selection]": Alfred Russel Wallace, "On the Tendency of Varieties to Depart Indefinitely from the Original Type," p. 62.

111   "might have occurred": Gregory Bateson, *Mind and Nature*, p. 43.

111   "July 20th to August 12th at Sandown": Entry for July 20 to August 12, 1858, "Darwin's personal journal (1809–81)," DAR. 158.

111   "It seems a queer plan": Darwin–Hooker, [July] 30 [1858], DAR. 114.

111   "Wallace's impetus seems to have set Darwin": Huxley–Hooker, September 5, 1858, *Huxley L.L.*, 1:159.

111   "but without you lived with me": Darwin–Hooker, November 23, 1858, DAR. 150.

111   "That confounded Leguminous paper": Ibid.

112   "was its moderate size": Auto., p. 96.

112   "I will condense to utmost": Darwin–Hooker, July 21 [1858], DAR. 114.

112   "I think [this] will be better in many respects": Darwin–Hooker, December 24 [1858], DAR. 114.

112   "The book *ought* to be popular": Darwin–John Murray, March 1859, quoted George Paston, *At John Murray's*, p. 168 [afterward referred to as Paston].

113   "On the strength of this information": John Murray–Darwin, April 1, 1859, John Murray Archives, London.

113   "declared that the Darwinian theory": Paston, p. 170.

113   "More than ever": Rev. Whitwell Elwin–John Murray, November 10, 1885, Warwick Elwin (ed.), *Some XVIII-Century Men of Letters*, 2 vols.; here 1:354.

113   "After you had the kindness": Rev. Whitwell Elwin–Murray, May 3, 1859, Murray Archives.

116   "It is my deliberate conviction": Darwin–Murray, May 6, 1859, ibid.

116   "There is no end": Darwin–Gray, April 4 [1859], *Darwin-Gray Letters*, p. 16.

116   "I can see daylight": Darwin–Fox, [March] 24 [1859], Fox Letters.

117   "made some splendid strokes!": Darwin–William Darwin, [May 3, 1858], *Century of Letters*, 2:185.

117   "does me a deal of good": Darwin–Fox, [March] 24, [1859], Fox Letters.

117   "I find the style incredibly bad": Darwin–Murray, June 14 [1859], *Darwin L.L.*, 2:159.

117   "I have fairly to blacken": Darwin–Hooker, June 22, 1859, DAR. 115 (i).

117   "I had no business to send": Darwin–Murray, n.d., Murray Archives.

117   "the best materials": Joseph Dalton Hooker, *The Botany of the Antarctic Voyage of H.M. Discovery Ships "Erebus" and "Terror" in the Years 1839–1843*, Part I: *Flora Antarctica*, "Summary of the Voyage," pp. v–xii; here p. xii.

118   "insanely strong wish to finish": Darwin–Hooker, September 1, 1859, DAR. 115 (i).

118   "I corrected last proof yesterday": Darwin–Hooker, [September] 11, 1859, ibid.

118   "On this difficult and mysterious subject": Sir C. Lyell, introductory address by the president of Section C, Geology Section, "On the Occurrence of Works of Human Art in Post-pliocene Deposits," *Report of the Twenty-ninth Meeting of the British Association for the Advancement of Science, held at Aberdeen in September 1859*, pp. 93–95; here p. 95 [afterward referred to as Lyell, Br. Ass. address, 1859].

118   "I have just finished your volume": Lyell–Darwin, October 3, 1859, *Lyell L.L.*, 2:325.

119   "God knows what the public will think": Darwin–Wallace, November 13, 1859, *Wallace L&R*, 1:139.

119   "Murray has printed": Darwin–Lyell, September 30 [1859], *Darwin L.L.*, 2:171.

6 On the Mystery of Mysteries

120   "Light will be thrown": *Origin* (1st ed., 1859), p. 488.

120   "When two races of men": Darwin, " 'E' Notebook dealing with evolution theory, 'July 15th 1838. Finished October 2nd.,' " DAR. 124.

121   "*Our* ancestor was an animal": Darwin–Lyell, January 10 [1860], P.S., *Darwin L.L.*, 2:266.

121   "But with regard to the material world": W. Whewell, *The Bridgewater Treatise III: On Astronomy and General Physics*, p. 356, quoted Darwin on October 1, 1859, *Origin* (1st ed., 1859), page opposite title page.

121   "Darwin was publicly satisfied": Edward S. Reed, "Darwin's Evolutionary Philosophy," p. 203.

121   "With respect to Design": Darwin–Gray, December 11 [1861], *Darwin L.L.*, 2:382.

121   "I objected in my 'Antiquity of Man' ' ": Lyell–the Duke of Argyll, September 19, 1868, *Lyell L.L.*, 2:431.

122   "I cannot possibly believe": Darwin–Gray, November 11, [1859,] *Darwin L.L.*, 2:13.

122   "I do not think I am brave enough": Darwin–Lyell, December 2 [1859], ibid., p. 238.

122   "I rejoice profoundly": Darwin–Lyell, November 23 [1859], ibid., p. 230.

122   "When I reflect": Darwin–William Benjamin Carpenter, June 17, 1861, Down House Archive.

122   "I shall be very grateful for any criticisms": Darwin–Jenyns [Blomefield], November 13, 1859, *Darwin L.L.*, 2:220.

123   "I rest on the fact": Darwin–Gray, December 24, [1859], *Darwin-Gray Letters*, p. 20.

123   "That seems to me the turning point": Darwin–Gray, May 11, [1861], ibid., p. 35.

124   "individuals of the same variety": *Origin* (1st ed., 1859), p. 7.

124   "an entangled bank": Ibid., p. 489.

124   "Light will be thrown": Ibid., p. 488.

124   "This morning, I heard . . . from Murray": Darwin–Lyell, November [24, 1859], *Darwin L.L.*, 2:234.

PAGE

124 "I am very glad of 3,000 copies": Darwin–Murray, December 4, 1859, Murray Archives.

125 "And as to the curs": Huxley–Darwin, November 23, 1859, *Huxley L.L.*, 1:176.

125 "I was too anxious": Huxley–Francis Darwin, n.d., quoted *Darwin L.L.*, 2:255.

125 "to such dreamers": [Huxley] review of Charles Darwin, *On the Origin of Species* (1859), *The Times*, December 26, 1859.

125 "as greedy of cases and precedents": Ibid.

125 "The old fogies will think": Darwin–Huxley, December 28 [1859], *Darwin L.L.*, 2:253.

125 "It will do grand service": Darwin–Hooker, December 28, 1859, DAR. 115 (i).

125 "provided us with the working hypothesis": Huxley, "Reception of 'Origin,' " p. 197.

126 "You have loaded yourself": Huxley–Darwin, November 23, 1859, *Huxley L.L.*, 1:176.

126 "As in first cases distinct species inosculate": Darwin "Red Notebook," p. 130, Down House Archive.

126 "From the first time that I wrote": Huxley–Kingsley, April 30, 1863, *Huxley L.L.*, 1:239.

126 "In my earliest criticisms of the 'Origin' ": Huxley, "Reception of 'Origin,' " p. 198.

126 "Those who think the natural geological record": *Origin* (1st ed., 1859), p. 310.

126 "were perhaps somewhat slow": Archibald Geikie, *A Long Life's Work, an Autobiography*, p. 71 [afterward referred to as Geikie, *Auto.*].

127 "the history of science hardly presents": [A. R. Wallace] review of Sir Charles Lyell, *Principles of Geology*, 10th ed., 1867 and 1868, and *Elements of Geology*, 6th ed., 1865, *The Quarterly Review* 252 (April 1869): 359–94; here p. 381.

127 "you may well believe": Lyell–Thomas S. Spedding, May 19, 1863, *Lyell L.L.*, 2:376.

127 "We may compare [it]": Sir Archibald Geikie, *Charles Darwin as Geologist*, p. 52.

128 "passed beyond the bounds of the study": Review of Richard Owen, *Paleontology; or a Systematic Summary of Extinct Animals and Their Geological Relations*, *The Saturday Review* 9 (1860): 573–74; here p. 573.

128 "Everybody has read Mr. Darwin's book": [Thomas Henry Huxley] review of Charles Darwin, *On the Origin of Species* (1860), *The Westminster Review*, n.s. 17, no. 2 (April 1860): 541–70; here p. 541 [afterward referred to as Huxley, review of *Origin* (1860)].

128 "Trusting to your desire": Patrick Matthew–Editor of *The Gardeners' Chronicle*, March 7, 1860, *The Gardeners' Chronicle and Agricultural Gazette*, April 7, 1860, p. 312.

129 "There is a law universal in Nature": Patrick Matthew, *On Naval Timber and Arboriculture*, Appendix Note B., p. 364.

129 "I freely acknowledge that Mr. Matthew": Darwin–Editor of *The Gardeners' Chronicle*, n.d., *The Gardeners' Chronicle*, April 21, 1860, p. 362.

PAGE

129   "To me the conception of this law": Matthew–Editor of *The Gardeners' Chronicle*, May 2, 1860, *The Gardeners' Chronicle*, May 12, 1860, p. 433.

130   "scarcely fair in alluding": Matthew–Editor of *Saturday Analyst and Leader*, n.d., quoted " 'Natural Selection'—Whose Is It?" *Saturday Analyst and Leader*, November 24, 1860, p. 959.

130   "an obscure writer": Darwin–Professor J. L. A. de Quatrefages, June [no day], 1860, quoted William J. Dempster, *Patrick Matthew and Natural Selection*, p. 30.

130   "One of the subjects discussed": John Claudius Loudon, review of Patrick Matthew, *On Naval Timber and Arboriculture* in The Gardeners' Magazine, December 1832, quoted ibid., p. 23.

131   "very clever, odd, wild fellow": Darwin–Hooker, May 10, 1848, DAR. 114.

131   Blyth contributed three articles: Edward Blyth, "An Attempt to Classify the 'Varieties' of Animals," "Observations on the Various Seasonal and Other External Changes Which Regularly Take Place in Birds," and "On the Psychological Distinctions between Man and All Other Animals."

131   "May not, then, a large proportion": Blyth, "On the Psychological Distinctions Between Man and All Other Animals," p. 135.

131   "In the course of his argument": Cyril Darlington, *Darwin's Place in History*, p. 34 [afterward referred to as Darlington, *History*].

131   "It was Darwin's contribution": Loren C. Eiseley, "Charles Darwin, Edward Blyth, and the Theory of Natural Selection," p. 100.

131   "No one, whatsoever may be his personal ideas": Review of *The Origin of Species* (1859), *The English Churchman* 17, no. 883 (December 1, 1859): 1152.

132   "that Mr. Darwin will yet be enabled": Ibid.

132   "Only let our scientific friends": Answer to correspondent, Rhiwenian, *The Family Herald* 19, no. 956 (August 24, 1861): 268.

133   "She once said to my sister": *Century of Letters*, 2:6.

133   "Half a dozen schemes of harmony": *The British and Foreign Evangelical Review* 10 (1861): p. 627.

133   "The 'man' who is without the 'living soul' ": Leader, *The Morning Advertiser*, September 4, 1863.

133   "We should advise Mr. Darwin to assume": [Asa Gray], "Darwin and His Reviewers," p. 413.

133   "Consequently we must look to *forces*": William B. Carpenter, *Nature and Man*, p. 110.

134   "I quite agree with you": Lyell–Darwin, May 5, 1869, *Lyell L.L.*, 2:442.

134   He believed that God had intervened: Rádl, p. 35.

135   "Mr. Darwin's work has done the cause": Review of Charles Darwin, *On the Origin of Species* (1859), *The Dublin Review* 48, no. 95 (May 1860): pp. 50–81; here p. 78.

135   "I am the more pleased": Darwin–Horner, March 20, 1861, *Horner Memoir*, 2:301.

135   "In spite of difficulties": Rev. Fenton John Anthony Hort–Rev. B.F. Westcott, March 10, 1860, P.S., Arthur Fenton Hort, *Life and Letters of Fenton John Anthony Hort*, 2 vols.; here 1:414.

135   "But *the* book which has most engaged me": Hort–Rev. John

PAGE

Ellerton, April 3, 1860, ibid., p. 416.

135   "a most delightful [book]": The Duke of Argyll–Lyell, February 29, 1860, quoted the Dowager Duchess of Argyll (ed.), *George Douglas, Eighth Duke of Argyll*, 2 vols.; here 2:482.

136   "She asked me a good deal": Lyell–Lady Lyell, May 7, 1863, *Lyell L.L.*, 2:369.

136   "an animated conversation on Darwinism": Lyell–Darwin, January 16, 1865, ibid., p. 385.

136   "a worthy daughter of her father [Prince Albert]": Ibid.

136   "To investigate fully and impartially": "Objects of the Victoria Institute," *Journal of the Transactions of the Victoria Institute, or Philosophical Society of Great Britain*, 1 (1866): vi [afterward referred to as *Victoria Institute Trans.*]

136   "that it is impossible for the Word of God": "The Declaration of Students of the Natural and Physical Sciences," *The Times*, September 20, 1864.

136   "were quite confident that the Word of God": The Earl of Shaftesbury, at first General Meeting of the Victoria Institute, May 24, 1866, *Victoria Institute Trans.* 1 (1866): 71.

137   "a good working hypothesis": George Warington, "On the Credibility of Darwinism," 2 (1867): ibid., p. 61.

137   "On the contrary": James Reddie, ibid., p. 62.

137   "It is clear to me": Huxley–Kingsley, September 23, 1860, The Huxley Papers, 19.169, Imperial College of Science and Technology, London [afterward referred to as Huxley Papers].

137   "I trembled before him like a boy": Kingsley–Lubbock, May 27, 1867, *Lubbock Life*, 1:92.

137   "One cannot look at this Universe": Darwin–Sir John Herschel, May 23, 1861, Royal Society MSS, H.S. 6.17, The Royal Society, London.

138   "In the plainest and *coarsest* Language": Marginal comment by Darwin on proof of E. Vansittart Neale, "On Typical Selections, as a Means of Removing the Difficulties Attending the Doctrine of the Origin of Species, by Natural Selection," *Proceedings of the Zoological Society*, January 8, 1861, Darwin Offprint Collection No. R.45, Cambridge University Library.

138   "the brain of an ant": Charles Darwin, *Descent of Man* (1871), 1:145.

138   "many other facts, which are so obscure": Charles Darwin, *The Effects of Cross- and Self-Fertilisation in the Vegetable Kingdom*, p. 458.

138   "they have six pairs of beautifully constructed natatory legs": *Origin* (1st ed., 1859), p. 441.

138   "used to laugh at him": Francis Darwin, "Rems.," p. 155.

138   "I propose . . . that the triumph": Walter F. Cannon, "The Bases of Darwin's Achievement: A Revaluation," p. 109.

138   ". . . I have read your book with more pain": Sedgwick–Darwin, December 24, 1859, *Sedgwick L.L.*, 2:356.

139   "Each series of facts is laced": [Sedgwick,] "Objections to Mr. Darwin's Theory of the Origin of Species," *The Spectator*, March 24, 1860, p. 285.

139   "I do not think my book": Darwin–Sedgwick, November 26, 1859, *Sedgwick L.L.*, 2:359.

PAGE

139   "I have read Darwin's book": Sedgwick–Miss Gerard, January 2, 1860, ibid.

139   "Sedgwick's [paper] was not very fair": Darwin–Henslow, April 2, 1860, DAR. 93.

140   "Critics exclusively trained in classics": Huxley, review of *Origin* (1860), p. 566.

140   "The line of argument often pursued": Darwin, " 'D' Notebook," DAR. 123.

140   "How odd it is that anyone should not see": Darwin–Henry Fawcett, September 18, 1861, quoted Leslie Stephen, *Life of Henry Fawcett*, p. 101.

140   "I shd. really much like to know": Darwin–Henslow, May 8 [1860], DAR. 93.

140   "No other work of mine": Auto., p. 76.

141   a long review of *The Origin* written by Fleeming Jenkin: *The North British Review* 46, no. 92 (June 1867): 277–318 [afterward referred to as Jenkin, review of *Origin*].

141   "I had . . . during many years": Auto., p. 94.

141   "Watchfulness and work": "Samuel Wilberforce," *Chambers's Encyclopaedia*, 10:654.

142   "of being a first-class controversialist": Huxley–Francis Darwin, June 27, 1891, *Huxley L.L.*, 1:187.

142   "did not see the good of giving up": Ibid.

142   "and have [his] share": Ibid., p. 188.

142   "a working and a causal hypothesis": Bishop Samuel Wilberforce, quoted Rev. W. Tuckwell, *Reminiscences of Oxford*, p. 53.

143   "begged to know": [Mrs. Isabella Sidgwick,] "A Grandmother's Tales," p. 433 [afterward referred to as "Grandmother's Tales"].

143   "If any one were to be willing": quoted Rev. Adam Story Farrar, D.D. (1826–1905)–Leonard Huxley, July 12, 1899, Huxley Papers, 16.13.

143   "The Lord hath delivered him": Huxley–Sir Benjamin Collins Brodie, quoted Huxley–Francis Darwin, June 27, 1891, *Huxley L.L.*, 1:188.

143   "If, then, said I": Huxley–Frederick Daniel Dyster, September 9, 1860, Huxley Papers, 15.115.

143   "*I* would rather be the offspring": Huxley quoted G. Johnstone Stoney–Francis Darwin, May 17, 1895, DAR. 107.

144   "I swore to myself that I would smite": Hooker–Darwin, July 2, 1860, *Hooker L.L.*, 1:526.

144   "I knew of this theory": Hooker quoted Henry Fawcett, "A Popular Exposition of Mr. Darwin on the Origin of Species," p. 92.

144   "Mr. Huxley, with the look on his face": "Grandmother's Tales," p. 434.

144   "From all that I hear from several quarters": Darwin–Huxley, July 20, 1860, Huxley Papers, 5.125.

144   "(which I am sure I never could do)": Darwin–Hooker [July 2, 1860], DAR. 115 (i).

145   "scientific attainments": [Bishop Samuel Wilberforce,] review of *Origin of Species* (1860), *The Quarterly Review* 108, no. 215 (July 1860): 225–64; here pp. 225–26.

145   "really charming writing": Ibid., p. 230.

PAGE

145   "if Mr. Darwin can . . .": Ibid., p. 231.

145   "First, then, he [Darwin] not obscurely declares": Ibid., p. 257.

146   "Is it credible that all favourable varieties": Ibid., p. 239.

146   "It is uncommonly clever": Darwin–Hooker [July 1860], *Darwin L.L.*, 2:324.

146   "By the way the Bishop makes": Darwin–Lyell, August 11 [1860], *Darwin L.L.*, 2:332.

146   "very clever and I am quizzed": Darwin–Murray, n.d., quoted Paston, p. 175.

146   "uncommonly clever": Darwin–Gray, July 22, [1860], *Darwin-Gray Letters*, p. 29.

146   "Did you see the Quarterly Review?": Darwin–Innes, December 28 [1860], "Darwin-Innes Letters," p. 207.

146   "I am glad he takes it in this way": Wilberforce–Innes, quoted Innes's statement in own handwriting, n.d., ibid., p. 256.

146   "For once reality and his brains": Huxley–John Tyndall, July 30, 1873, Huxley Papers, 9.72; 8.151.

146   "In justice to the Bishop": Huxley–Francis Darwin, June 27, 1891, *Huxley L.L.*, 1:188.

147   "Lines written on hearing that Professor Huxley had said that 'he did not care whether his grand-father was an Ape' ": Samuel Wilberforce Papers, Bodleian Library, Oxford, quoted Richard W. Wrangham, "Bishop Wilberforce; Natural Selection and the Descent of Man," p. 192.

147   "My book has stirred up the mud": Darwin–Gray, July 3, [1860], *Darwin-Gray Letters*, p. 27.

148   "speaking generally": Major-General Edward Sabine, presidential address, Anniversary Meeting, November 30, 1864, *Proceedings of the Royal Society* 13, no. 69 (1863–64): 497–517; here p. 508.

148   "beyond the province of our Society": George Bentham, presidential address, Anniversary Meeting, May 24, 1862, *Journal of Proceedings of the Linnean Society: Zoology* 6 (1862): lxvi–lxxxiii; here p. lxxxi.

148   "scarcely within the legitimate scope": George Bentham, presidential address, Anniversary Meeting, May 25, 1863, *Journal of Proceedings of the Linnean Society: Zoology* 7 (1864): xi–xxix; here p. xvi.

148   "during all my experience": Dr. John Edward Gray, "Revision of the Species of Lemuroid Animals," p. 134.

148   "One day I was at work": Roland Trimen, quoted De Beer, *Darwin*, p. 161.

149   "perfectly valid...": Darwin–Dana, February 20 [1863], *Dana Life*, pp. 314–15.

149   "goes far with me": Darwin–Gray, March 8, 1881, *Darwin-Gray Letters*, p. 76.

149   "No one could, until he had enlarged his gullet": Ibid.

149   "I never expected to convert people": Darwin–Innes, December 28 [1860], "Darwin-Innes Letters," p. 207.

149   "I feel not a shade of surprise": Darwin–unknown correspondent, March 14, 1861, quoted George Sarton, "Darwin's Conception of the Theory of Natural Selection," p. 338.

PAGE

150   "The laws governing inheritance": *Origin* (1st ed., 1859), p. 13.

150   "The laws governing inheritance": *Origin* (6th ed., 1872), p. 10.

150   "the Survival of the Fittest": *Origin* (5th ed., 1869), p. 92.

150   dropped "On": *Origin* (6th ed., 1872), title page.

150   "The second edition was little more than": Darwin, "Additions and Corrections to the Sixth Edition," *Origin* (6th ed., 1872), p. [xi].

150   "The third edition was largely corrected": Ibid.

150   "Of the 3,878 sentences": Morse Peckham (ed.), *"The Origin of Species" by Charles Darwin: A Variorum Text*, p. 9.

150   "There is grandeur in this view of life": *Origin* (1st ed., 1859), p. 490.

151   "by the Creator": *Origin* (2d ed., 1860), p. 490.

151   "I got some mathematician": Darwin–Lankester, April 15 [1872], *Darwin M.L.*, 1:336.

151   "with widely open mouth": *Origin* (1st ed., 1859), p. 184.

151   "I can see no difficulty in a race of bears": Ibid.

151   "been of no avail": *Origin* (6th ed., 1872), p. 421.

151   "An Historical Sketch of the Recent Progress of Opinion": *Origin* (3d ed., 1861), pp. xiii–xix.

152   "there was a stampede of my's": Samuel Butler, *Luck, or Cunning*, p. 237 [afterward referred to as Butler].

152   "Buffon planted": Ibid, p. 291.

152   "[His genius] consists in taking up": Leader, *The Times*, May 25, 1931.

152   "veritable rubbish": Darwin–Hooker, 1844, *Darwin L.L.*, 2:29.

152   "absurd though clever work": Darwin–Hooker [Wed. September, n.d.], ibid., p. 39.

152   "extremely poor": Darwin–Lyell, October 11 [1859], ibid., p. 215.

153   "This comes of tinkering": Butler, p. 186.

153   "on the whole most probable": Professor W. Thomson, "On the Age of the Sun's Heat," p. 393.

153   "The limitation of geological periods": Sir William Thomson, "Of Geological Dynamics," p. 222.

153   "I should rely much on pre-Silurian time": Darwin–Wallace, July 12, 1871, *Wallace L&R*, 1:268.

153   "probably one of the gravest as yet advanced": *Origin* (6th ed., 1872), p. 409.

154   "How this will please the geologists": Darwin–George Darwin, October 29 [1878], *Century of Letters*, 2:290.

154   "Is man an ape or an angel?": Benjamin Disraeli, Speech at Meeting of the Society for Increasing Endowments of Small Livings in the Diocese of Oxford, at the Oxford Diocesan Conference, November 25, 1864, *The Times*, November 26, 1864.

154   "Darwinism, on the contrary": Leslie Stephen, "An Attempted Philosophy of History," p. 672.

154   "I was proud to welcome him": Leslie Stephen–C. E. Norton, May 5, 1877, Frederic William Maitland, *The Life and Letters of Leslie Stephen*, p. 300 [afterward referred to as *Stephen L.L.*].

7   Darwinism Takes Root

155   "human dignity and human feeling": Leader, *Daily Telegraph*, September 25, 1861.

156   "a being of that hideous order": Paul B[elloni] Du Chaillu, *Explorations and Adventures in Equatorial Africa*, p. 71.

156   "I do not believe": Huxley–Hooker, April 27, 1861, *Huxley L.L.*, 1:191.

156   "a poetical squib": Huxley–Mrs. T. H. Huxley, April 16, 1861, ibid.

156   "Am I a Man and a Brother?": Sir Philip Egerton, "Monkeyana," *Punch*, May 18, 1861, p. 206.

156   "speaks volumes for Owen's perfect success": Huxley–Hooker, April 30, 1861, *Huxley L.L.*, 1:192.

156   "My working men stick by me": Huxley–Mrs. T. H. Huxley, March 22, 1861, ibid., p. 190.

157   "The case at present": *Origin* (1st ed., 1859), p. 308.

157   "The fossil bird with the long tail": Darwin–Dana, January 7, 1863, *Dana Life*, p. 312.

157   "completed the series of transitional forms": T. H. Huxley, "The Coming of Age of 'The Origin of Species,' " p. 3.

158   "is the most wonderful thing": Huxley–Mrs. T. H. Huxley, August 11, 1876, *Huxley L.L.*, 1:463.

158   "He then informed me": O. C. Marsh, "Thomas Henry Huxley," p. 181.

158   "that were there no other evidences of evolution": J. L. Wortman, "Othniel Charles Marsh," p. 564.

158   "afforded the best support": Darwin–Marsh, August 31, 1880, *Darwin L.L.*, 3:241.

158   George Gaylord Simpson calculation: British Museum (Natural History), *A Handbook on Evolution*, p. 24.

159   "Every single word": Darwin–Gray, July 22 [1860], *Darwin-Gray Letters*, p. 28.

159   "outlive this mania": Louis Agassiz–Sir Philip de Grey Egerton, n.d., quoted Charles Frederick Holder, *Louis Agassiz: His Life and Work*, p. 181.

159   "I hope you will at least": Darwin–Louis Agassiz, November 11 [1859], *Darwin L.L.*, 2:215.

159   "This is truly monstrous!": Agassiz marginal note on his copy of *The Origin*, quoted Edward Lurie, "Louis Agassiz and the Idea of Evolution," p. 92.

159   "growls over [Darwinism]": Gray–Hooker, Jan. 5, 1860, quoted A. Hunter Dupree, *Asa Gray, 1810–1888*, p. 269.

159   "Far from agreeing with [the view of Darwin]": "Professor Agassiz on the Origin of Species," Book Notices, *The American Journal of Science and Arts* 2d ser. 30, no. 88 (July 1860): 142–54; here p. 143.

159   "I shall therefore consider": Ibid. p. 154.

160   "The more I think of Darwin's ideas": William James–Henry James, March 9 [1868], Ralph Barton Perry, *The Thought and Character of William James*, 2 vols.; here 1:265.

160   "Our visit to the Galapagos": Agassiz–Professor B. Peirce, July 29 [1872], Elizabeth Cary Agassiz (ed.), *Louis Agassiz: His Life and Correspondence*, 2 vols.; here 2: 762.

PAGE

161   "I am inclined to think": James McCosh, Lecture II, *Christianity and Positivism*, p. 42.

161   "That this principle": Lecture III, ibid., pp. 63–64.

161   "I regard evolution": Henry Ward Beecher, *Henry Ward Beecher in England*, p. 94.

161   "I hold that Evolution": Ibid, p. 95.

162   "conspiracy of silence": Huxley, "Reception of 'Origin,' " p. 186.

162   *De l'Origine des Espèces, ou Des lois du progrès chez les êtres organisés*: Title of *Origin* translated by Mlle. Clémence-Auguste Royer from the third edition, with preface and notes by the translator.

162   "The doctrine of M. Darwin": Mlle. Clémence-Auguste Royer, Preface, *De l'Origine des Espèces*, p. lxiii.

162   "a little dull book against me": Darwin–Wallace, n.d., quoted *Darwin L.L.*, 3:30.

162   "At last Mr. Darwin's work has appeared": [Marie Jean] P[ierre] Flourens, *Examen du livre de M. Darwin sur l'Origine des espèces*, p. 65.

162   "The conclusion is that": Dmitri Pisarev, quoted James Allen Rogers, "Russia: Social Sciences," in Thomas F. Glick (ed), *The Comparative Reception of Darwinism*, pp. 256–68; here p. 258.

163   "To express doubts": S.S. Glagol'ev in *Bogoslovskii vestnik* 3 (1912): 651, quoted George L. Kline, "Darwinism and the Russian Orthodox Church," p. 309, [afterward referred to as Kline].

163   "I do not at all like that you": Darwin–Ernst Haeckel, May 21, 1867, *Darwin L.L.*, 3:69.

163   "You are still discussing in England": Arch[ibald] Geikie, "The Meeting of German Naturalists and Physicians at Innsbruck, Tyrol," p. 23.

163   "The question we have first to consider": Professor Rokitansky, quoted ibid.

163   "opened the gates": D. Gregorio Chil y Naranjo, *Estudios Históricos, Climatológicos y Patológicos de las Islas Canarias.* Part I: *Historia*, 3 vols.; here 1:14.

165   "I think this little volume" and "It will perhaps serve": Darwin–Murray, September 24, 1861, *Darwin L.L.*, 3:254.

166   "I have found the study of Orchids": Darwin–Hooker, May 14, 1862, DAR. 115 (ii).

166   "When I think of my beloved Orchids": Darwin–Gray, n.d., *Darwin-Gray Letters*, p. 94.

166   "to the conclusion in my speculations": Auto., p. 100.

166   "quite unique—there is nothing": Hooker–Brian Hodgson, December 6, 1862, *Hooker L.L.*, 2:32.

167   "Orchids manufacture their intricate devices": Stephen Jay Gould, *The Panda's Thumb*, p. 20.

167   "And now I am going to tell you": Darwin–Hooker, December 24, 1862, DAR. 115 (ii).

167   "Hot house is ready": Darwin–Hooker, February 15, 1863, DAR. 115 (iii).

168   "and if I had should probably have made a mess": Darwin–Lubbock, n.d., Down House Archive.

168   "I am getting very much amused": Darwin–Hooker, July 14 [1863], DAR. 115 (iii).

168   "The only approach to work": Darwin–Hooker, apparently March 1864, *Darwin L.L.*, 3:315.

PAGE

168   "In treating the several subjects": Introduction, *Variation*, 1:14
       fn.4.

169   "I cannot tell you how sorry I am": Darwin–Murray, January 3,
       1867, *Darwin L.L.*, 3:59.

169   "But I feel that the size": Darwin–Hooker, January 9, 1867, DAR.
       94.

169   "call attention to the rare": *The Pall Mall Gazette*, February 10, 15
       and 17, 1868; here February 10, 1868.

169   "a very rash and crude hypothesis": Darwin–Huxley, May 27
       [1865 ?], *Darwin L.L.*, 3:44.

169   "fearfully imperfect": Darwin–Hooker, November 17 [1867],
       DAR. 94.

169   "a mad dream": Darwin–Gray, October 16 [1867], *Darwin-Gray
       Letters*, p. 58.

169   "a relief to have some feasible explanation": Darwin–Wallace,
       February 27 [1868], *Darwin L.L.*, 3:80.

170   "I assume that cells": *Variation*, 2:374.

170   "It may be a defect of power": Richard Owen, *On the Anatomy of
       Vertebrates*, 3 vols.; here vol. 3 (Mammals), p. 813 n.

170   "the gamekeeper of natural selection": C.D. Darlington, "Pur-
       pose and Particles in the Study of Heredity" in E. Ashworth
       Underwood (ed.), *Science, Medicine and History*, 2 vols.; here 2:474.

170   "but that Darwin's theory": Jenkin, review of *Origin*, p. 318.

171   "I do not doubt your judgement": Darwin–Huxley, July 12
       [1865 ?], *Darwin L.L.*, 3:44.

171   "Towards the end of the work": Auto., p. 105.

171   "As Whewell, the historian": *Variation*, 2:357.

172   "Approaching the subject": Darwin–Huxley, quoted De Beer,
       Darwin, p. 208.

172   "I fully believe that each cell": Darwin–Hooker, February 28
       [1868], DAR. 94.

172   "much despised child": Darwin–Lankester, March 15 [1870],
       Darwin L.L., 3:120.

172   "None of [them] will speak out": Darwin–Wallace, February 27,
       1868, *Wallace L&R*, 1:197.

173   "I want to make some peculiar experiments": Galton–Darwin,
       December 11, 1869, *Galton L.L.*, 2:157.

173   "I have not said one word about the blood": Darwin–Editor of
       Nature, April 27, 1871, *Nature* 3 (April 27, 1871): 502–3; here p.
       502.

173   "my former groom": Darwin–Galton, May 27 [1872 ?], *Galton
       L.L.*, 2:168.

173   "The experiments were thorough": Francis Galton, *Memories of
       My Life*, p. 297 [afterward referred to as Galton, *Memories*].

174   "No good news": Galton–Darwin, March 17, 1870, *Galton L.L.*,
       2:158.

174   "Good rabbit news": Galton–Darwin, May 12, 1870, ibid., p. 160.

174   "F. Galton's experiments about rabbits": Mrs. Emma Darwin–
       Henrietta Darwin, March 19 [1870], *Century of Letters*, 2:230.

174   "Do you want one more generation?": Darwin–Galton, Novem-
       ber 8 [1872?], *Galton L.L.*, 2:175.

PAGE

174 "The experiments have, I quite agree": Galton–Darwin, November 15, 1872, ibid.

8 The Descent of Man

176 "It is surprising": Leader, *The Witness*, January 14, 1862.

176 "Lyell's Trilogy on the Antiquity of Man, Ice, and Darwin": *The Saturday Review* 15, no. 384 (March 7, 1863): 311–12; here p. 311.

176 "By Jove": Darwin–Lyell, February 4, 1863, in Carroll, *Am. Phil. Soc. Calendar*, p. 107.

176 "I was so much fatigued by my last book": Darwin–Alphonse Louis Pierre Pyrame de Candolle, July 6, 1868, *Darwin L.L.*, 3:98.

177 "Before leaving you I forgot to remind": Darwin–David Forbes, March 1868, The Pushkin Library, Moscow, quoted De Beer, "Unpublished Letters," p. 33.

177 "Your theory of Evolution": Tennyson–Darwin, "My Mother's Journal," entry for August 17, 1868, Hallam Tennyson, *Alfred, Lord Tennyson, a Memoir*, 2 vols., here 2:57.

177 "No, certainly not": Darwin–Tennyson, ibid.

177 "Oh, then you are the man": Dr. Grove, quoted Edward Bagnall Poulton, *Charles Darwin and "The Origin of Species*," p. 9. [afterward referred to as Poulton].

177 "Yes, I am the man" and "I don't want you": Tennyson, quoted ibid.

177 "but rather with the determination": Introduction, *Descent of Man* (1871), 1:1.

178 "Man in his arrogance": Darwin, " 'C' Notebook dealing with evolution theory, February–July 1838," DAR. 122.

178 "Let man visit Ourang-outang": Ibid.

178 "When I publish my book": Darwin–St. George Jackson Mivart, April 23, [ca. 1869–71], in Carroll, *Am. Phil. Soc. Calendar*, p. 137.

178 "the time will before long come": *Descent of Man* (1871), 1:33.

179 "make its dam or canal": Ibid., p. 39.

179 "Happiness is never better exhibited": Ibid., p. 39.

179 "I had two distinct objects in view": Ibid., p. 152.

179 "put together" and "so as to see how far": Ibid., p. 2.

179 "to consider, firstly": Ibid., p. 2.

179 "in the same spirit": Ibid., p. 215.

180 "namely that man is descended": *Descent of Man* (1871), 2:404.

180 "be highly distasteful": Ibid., p. 404.

180 "that man with all his noble qualities": Ibid., p. 405.

180 "Parts, as on the moral sense": Darwin–Gray, n.d., *Darwin L.L.*, 3:131.

180 "if I have erred": *Descent of Man* (1871), 1:153.

180 "I think it will be very interesting": Mrs. Emma Darwin–Henrietta Darwin, n.d., quoted *Century of Letters*, 2:229.

180 "A man incurs grave responsibility who": *The Times*, April 7 and 8, 1871; here April 8, 1871.

181 " '*Hypotheses non fingo*' ": "Darwin and Pickwick," *Punch*, 69 (April 8, 1871): 145.

181 "most earnest-minded men": Review of Charles Darwin, *The Descent of Man* (1871), *The Edinburgh Review*, 134 (July 1871): 195–235; here p. 195.

PAGE

181 "In the drawing-room: Ibid.

181 "like measles in a school": *The Independent*, 23 (March 16, 1871): 6.

182 "The arguments he again and again urged": St. George [Jackson] Mivart, "Some Reminiscences of Thomas Henry Huxley," p. 994.

182 "For the rest of that year": Ibid., p. 995.

183 "My first object [in writing the book]": St. George Mivart, "Evolution and Its Consequences," p. 168.

183 "Those who have a right to judge": Newman–Mivart, December 9, 1871, quoted Jacob W. Gruber, *A Conscience in Conflict*, p. 73.

184 "[Mivart's] 'Genesis' at first appeared": Darwin–Huxley, September 21, 1871, Huxley Papers, 5.279.

184 "like an Old Bailey lawyer": Huxley, quoted Auto., p. 99.

184 "Mr. Darwin's Critics": T. H. Huxley, "Mr. Darwin's Critics," *Contemporary Review*, 18 (November 1871): 443–76.

184 a forty-page essay: [Mivart] review of Charles Darwin, *The Descent of Man* (1874), *The Quarterly Review*, 131 (July 1871): 47–90.

184 "The Zoological Society can hardly fail": St. George Mivart, "Ape Resemblances to Man," p. 481.

184 "Science convinces me": Ibid.

184 "Mivart's book is producing a great effect": Darwin–Wallace, July 9, 1871, *Wallace L&R*, 1:264.

184 "with admirable art and force": *Origin* (6th ed., 1872), p. 176.

185 "will be forced to admit": Ibid., p. 204.

185 "With mankind some expressions": Darwin, Introduction, *Emotions*, p. 12.

185 "We may confidently believe": Ibid., p. 361.

186 "Perhaps you know some missionary": Darwin–Dr. F. Müller, n.d., DAR. 92.

186 "the expression of the several passions": Introduction, *Emotions*, p. 17.

186 "When [his first-born] was about four months old": Ibid., p. 359.

186 "like every other dog": Ibid., pp. 57 and 60.

187 "Mr. Darwin has added another volume": Review of Charles Darwin, *The Expression of the Emotions in Man and Animals* (1872) in *The Edinburgh Review*, 137 (April 1873): 492–528; here p. 492.

187 "magnificently contemptuous": Darwin–Alexander Bain, October 9, 1873, *Darwin L.L.*, 3:173.

187 "insatiable longing to discover": Alfred R. Wallace, review of Charles Darwin, *The Expression of the Emotions in Man and Animals*, "Notices of Books," *The Quarterly Journal of Science*, n.s. 3 (January 1873):113–18; here p. 113.

187 "I carried home some plants": Auto., p. 109.

188 "I know that it would have": Ibid., p. 1.

188 "the attempt would amuse me": Ibid.

188 "Etty [Henrietta] went so far as to *speak*": Leonard Darwin–Nora Barlow, 1942, quoted Introduction, Nora Barlow (ed.), *The Autobiography of Charles Darwin, 1809–1882*, p. 12.

189 "that every Whale has its Louse": Goethe, quoted Huxley, quoted Auto., p. 111.C.

189 "Nor must we overlook": Ibid., p. 72.

PAGE

189 "I should wish if possible": Mrs. Emma Darwin–Francis Darwin, 1885, *Century of Letters*, 2:360.

189 ". . . in accordance with the principles": Auto., p. 111.C.

190 "He could dissect well": Francis Darwin, "Rems.," p. 110.

190 "A glass filament, not thicker than a horsehair": Charles Darwin, *The Power of Movement in Plants*, p. 6.

190 "I particularly remember noticing this": Francis Darwin, "Rems.," p. 144.

191 "succeeded in showing that all": Darwin–A. de Candolle, May 28, 1880, *Darwin L.L.*, 3:333.

191 "all on fire at the work": Darwin–W. T. Thiselton-Dyer, n.d., quoted ibid., p. 329.

191 "I am overwhelmed with my notes": Darwin–Thiselton-Dyer, [spring 1879], quoted ibid., p. 332.

191 "My father enjoyed the journey": Henrietta Litchfield, *Century of Letters*, 2:299.

192 "Of all our living men of science": Leader, *The Times*, November 20, 1880.

192 "Many of [them] are very contemptuous": Darwin–Thiselton-Dyer, November 28, 1880, *Darwin L.L.*, 3:334.

192 "to contradict flatly": Darwin–Reginald Darwin [cousin], March 27, 1879, ibid., p. 219.

192 "into so many deeply interesting questions": Samuel Butler–Darwin, October 1, 1865, DAR. 106.

192 "I . . . thought it unnecessary": Butler–Darwin, May 11, 1872, ibid.

193 "Erasmus Darwin's system": Ernst Krause, "The Scientific Works of Erasmus Darwin," pp. 131–216; here p. 216 in *Erasmus Darwin*, translated from the German by W. S. Dallas, with a Preliminary Notice by Charles Darwin.

193 "your readers will naturally suppose": Butler–Darwin, January 2, 1880, DAR. 92.

193 "amounted to a charge of falsehood": Francis Darwin in *Darwin L.L.*, 3:220.

194 "Has Mivart bitten him": Huxley–Butler, n.d., DAR. 92.

194 "My opinion about the matter": Stephen–Darwin, January 12, 1880, ibid.

194 "after all I now think he had some cause": Francis Darwin–Henrietta Litchfield, January 23, 1904, quoted Barlow, "The Darwin-Butler Controversy," p. 216.

194 "But the worst is that my health": Darwin–Gray, February 17, 1881, *Darwin-Gray Letters*, p. 73.

194 "Dear Father, We hope that you will": 7 children–Darwin, January 17, 1880, DAR. 99.

194 "a great success": Mrs. Emma Darwin–Leonard Darwin, n.d. [January 1880], *Century of Letters*, 2:303.

194 "I literally cannot listen to a novel": Darwin–Gray, February 17, 1881, *Darwin-Gray Letters*, p. 73.

194 "found [Shakespeare] so intolerably dull": Auto., p. 115.

195 "He twice referred to his turning back to books": F. Julia Wedgwood–Francis Darwin, October 3, 1884, DAR. 139.

195   "I remember his coming into the tea-drawing-room": Laura Forster–Francis Darwin, November 16, 1885, DAR. 112.

195   "I am rather despondent about myself": Darwin–Hooker, June 15, 1881, DAR. 95.

195   "What I shall do with my few remaining years": Darwin–Wallace, July 1881, *Darwin L.L.*, 3:356.

195   "In one of my latest conversations": Alfred Russel Wallace, *Studies, Scientific and Social*, 2 vols.; here 1:509.

196   "His hand was not steady enough": Francis Darwin, "Rems.," p. 110.

196   "As so many scorpions were found": Darwin–Geikie, November 1881, Geikie, *Auto.*, p. 192.

196   "I am certain your fortune": William Darwin–Darwin, September 18, 1881, quoted Sir Hedley Atkins, *Down, the Home of the Darwins*, p. 100 [afterward referred to as Atkins, *Down*].

196   "I am not the least afraid to die": quoted *Darwin L.L.*, 3:358.

197   "We hope you will not think": 20 Members of Parliament–Dr. Bradley, Dean of Westminster, April 21, 1882, Appendix I, ibid., p. 360.

197   "To me it would seem more congenial": Stephen–James Sully, April 22, 1822, *Stephen L.L.*, p. 346.

197   "from a national point of view": Sir John Lubbock–Francis Darwin, April 25, 1882, Appendix I, *Darwin L.L.*, 3:361.

197   "I made his coffin": John Lewis, quoted "A Visit to Darwin's Village: Reminiscences of Some of His Humble Friends," *The Evening News* (London), February 12, 1909, p. 4.

198   "I may say that the impossibility": Darwin–N. D. Doedes, April 2, 1873, DAR. 139.

198   "intense and almost passionate honesty": T. H. Huxley, Introductory Notice, *Charles Darwin Memorial Notices Reprinted from "Nature,"* p. xi.

199   "How I wish I had not expressed my theory": Darwin, quoted Atkins, *Down*, p. 51.

199   "would like to speak to them of Christ Jesus": Darwin, quoted ibid.

199   "I was present at his deathbed": Mrs. R. B. Litchfield, "Charles Darwin's Death-Bed: Story of Conversion Denied," *The Christian*, February 23, 1922, p. 12.

199   "Many who followed the investigations": Ibid.

9 Diffusion and Dissent

203   "ecclesiastical bombinations": J. B. S. Haldane, Introduction, *The Causes of Evolution*, p. 3.

204   "None, except for business": Darwin–Galton, May 28, 1873, "Answers to Mr. Galton's Questions," *Darwin L.L.*, 3:179.

204   "gave himself to the study": Keith, p. 150.

205   "The career of Charles Darwin": Leader, *The Times*, April 26, 1882.

205   "I have noted in a Manchester newspaper": Darwin–Lyell, May 4, 1860, P.S. [facsimile of original letter], John C. Greene, *The Death of Adam*, p. 308.

205   "The change was a fine exemplification": Henry Clews, *Twenty-eight Years in Wall Street*, p. 6.

PAGE

205   the Franco-Prussian war: J[acques] Novicow, *La Critique du Darwinisme Social*, pp. 12–15.

205   "the greatest authority of all": Max Nordau, "Philosophy and Morals of War," p. 794.

206   "We civilised men, on the other hand": *Descent of Man* (1871), 1:168.

206   "I could show fight on natural selection": Darwin–W. Graham, July 3, 1881, *Darwin L.L.*, 1:316.

207   "our natural rate of increase": *Descent of Man* (1871), 2:403.

207   "scientific conception tends to advance": Walter Bagehot, *Physics and Politics*, p. 43.

207   "there is no doubt of its predominance": Ibid., p. 24.

208   "rapid expansion": Richard Hofstadter, *Social Darwinism in American Thought, 1860–1915*, p. 30.

208   "a vast human caricature": Ibid.

208   "best for the race": Andrew Carnegie, "Wealth," p. 655.

208   "may fairly be regarded": William Graham Sumner, "The Concentration of Wealth: Its Economic Justification" (1902) in *The Challenge of Facts*, p. 90.

208   "Then will the world enter": Josiah Strong, *Our Country: Its Possible Future and Its Present Crisis*, pp. 213 and 214.

209   "identical organisms do not engage": N. D. Nozhin in "Knizhnii vestnik," no. 7 (1866): 173 ff., quoted Kline, p. 309.

209   "is as much a law of nature as mutual struggle": Professor Kessler, Lecture to Russian Congress of Naturalists, quoted P. Kropotkin, *Memoirs of a Revolutionist*, 2 vols.; here 2:317 [afterward referred to as Kropotkin, *Memoirs*].

209   "There is no infamy in civilized society": Ibid.

209   "And the other was": P. Kropotkin, *Mutual Aid: A Factor of Evolution*, p. vii [afterward referred to as Kropotkin, *Mutual Aid*].

209   "atrocious article": Kropotkin, *Memoirs*, 2:317.

209   "I decided to put in a readable form": Ibid.

210   "That is true Darwinism": H. W. Bates, quoted Kropotkin, *Memoirs*, 2:318.

210   "Happily enough . . . competition is not the rule": Kropotkin, *Mutual Aid*, p. 74.

211   "Tribes in which such": Alfred R. Wallace, "The Origin of Human Races and the Antiquity of Man Deduced from the Theory of 'Natural Selection,'" p. clxii.

211   "the obligations of enlightened humanity": quoted John C. Greene, "Darwin as a Social Evolutionist," p. 18.

211   "'lower in the scale' of human existence": Ibid.

211   "What a foolish idea seems to prevail": Darwin–Dr. [Carl von] Scherzer, December 26, 1879, quoted *Darwin L.L.*, 3:237.

211   "Have you considered that State Socialism": Huxley–W. Platt Ball, October 27, 1890, *Huxley L.L.*, 2:268.

211   "In all civilised countries": *Descent of Man* (1871), 1:169.

212   "apparently much truth in the belief": Ibid., p. 179.

212   "Darwin, whom I am just now reading": Engels–Marx, December 12, 1859, quoted Conway Zirkle, *Evolution, Marxian Biology, and the Social Scene*, p. 85.

212   "developed in the crude English style": Marx–Engels, December 19, 1860, quoted ibid., p. 86.

PAGE

212 "Darwin's book is very important": Marx–Lassalle, January 16, 1861, quoted ibid.

212 "great work on Capital": Darwin–Marx, October 1, 1873, quoted Erhard Lucas, "Marx und Engels," p. 464.

212 "Part or Volume": Darwin–Marx [Edward Aveling], October 13, 1880, quoted Erhard Lucas, ibid., p. 465.

212 "Moreover though I am a strong advocate": Ibid.

213 "Just as Darwin discovered": Engels on March 17, 1883, at Marx graveside, K. Marx and F. Engels, *Selected Works in One Volume*, p. 429.

213 "You know, all is development": Lady Constance Rawleigh-Tancred in Benjamin Disraeli, *Tancred*, 3 vols.; here 1:225.

213 "Instead of Adam, our ancestry": Monsignore Berwick in Benjamin Disraeli, *Lothair*, 3 vols.; here 1:302.

213 "the impudent lies, and monstrous arithmetic": Guy Raby in Charles Reade, *Put Yourself in His Place*, 3 vols.; here 1:292.

213 "Oh, the new ideas,": Benjamin in Wilkie Collins, *The Law and the Lady*, 3 vols.; here 3:148.

214 "All cells arise from cells": *"Omnis cellula a cellula,"* Rudolf Virchow, *Cellular Pathology*, A, 8 (1855): 23, quoted Erwin H. Ackerknecht, *Rudolf Virchow: Doctor, Statesman, Anthropologist*, p. 83 [afterward referred to as Ackerknecht].

214 "Our experiences give us no reason": Rudolf Virchow, *Vier Reden über Leben und Kranksein*, p. 31.

214 "I have spoken as a friend": K. Sudhoff (ed.), *Rudolf Virchow und die deutschen Naturforscherversammlungen* (Leipzig, 1922), p. 298, quoted Ackerknecht, p. 202.

217 "a hen is only an egg's way": Samuel Butler, *Life and Habit*, p. 134.

217 "To go on investigating": Weismann, "The Significance of Sexual Reproduction in the Theory of Natural Selection," (1886) *Essays upon Heredity*, 2 vols.; here 1:258–342, here p. 305.

217 "Before the excellence of a machine": E. D. Cope, *The Origin of the Fittest*, p. 225.

218 "The hypotheses of Pangenesis": Hugo de Vries, Proposition No. VIII, "De invloed der temperatuur op de levensverschijnselen der planten," ['s-Gravenhage: M. Nijhoff, 1870], "The Influence of Temperature on the Vital Phenomena in Plants," October 6, 1870, quoted Peter W. Van Der Pas, "The Correspondence of Hugo de Vries and Charles Darwin," *JANUS* 57, 2–3 (1970): 173–213; here p. 174.

218 "The fact that cross-fertilisation of plants": Proposition No. IX, ibid.

218 "I have always been especially interested": de Vries–Darwin, October 15, 1881, DAR. 180.

218 "are not chemical molecules": Hugo de Vries, *Intracellular Pangenesis*, p. 70.

218 "Just as physics and chemistry go back": Ibid., p. 13.

219 "The object of the present book": Hugo de Vries, *The Mutation Theory*, 2 vols.; here Preface, 1:viii.

219 "My own conviction": C. Hart Merriam, "Is Mutation a Factor in the Evolution of the Higher Vertebrates?," p. 243.

PAGE

219   "Are we because of the discovery": Ibid., p. 242.

220   "I am reminded by such occurrences": L. C. Dunn, *A Short History of Genetics*, p. 61 [afterward referred to as Dunn].

10 Mathematical Wine for Biological Bottles

221   "Suppose . . . that our common brown owl": Alfred W. Bennett, "The Theory of Natural Selection from a Mathematical Point of View," p. 31.

221   "Let us investigate the value": Ibid.

222   "You have made a convert": Darwin–Galton, December 3 [1869?], Galton, *Memories*, p. 290.

223   "The more bountifully the Parent is gifted": Francis Galton, *Natural Inheritance*, p. 106.

223   "is not a smooth": Francis Galton, *Finger Prints*, p. 20.

224   "With co-operation a big advance might have been made": E. S. Pearson, *Karl Pearson: An Appreciation of Some Aspects of His Life and Work*, p. 35 [afterward referred to as *Pearson Life Work*].

225   "the chief awakening of my life": William Bateson–unknown correspondent, n.d., Beatrice Bateson, *William Bateson, F.R.S., Naturalist*, p. 103 [afterward referred to as *Bateson Life*].

225   "If any man ever set himself to destroy": Bateson–Mrs. Bateson, April 16, 1906, Ibid., p. 102.

225   "Variation and heredity with us": William Bateson's contribution for 1883–84 to "William Keith Brooks: A Sketch of His Life by Some of His Former Pupils and Associates," *The Journal of Experimental Zoölogy* 9, no. 1 (September 1910): 1–52; here pp. 5–8, here p. 7.

226   "ransacked the field": Obituary, "Dr. William Bateson," *The Times*, February 9, 1926.

226   "For there is one obvious consideration": William Bateson and [Miss] Anna Bateson, "On Variations in the Floral Symmetry of Certain Plants Having Irregular Corollas," p. 388.

226   "I see you are inclined to advocate": Huxley–Bateson, February 20, 1894, *Huxley L.L.*, 2:372.

227   "Mathematics were my difficulty": W[illiam] Bateson–Editor of *Nature*, February 17, 1905, *Nature*, vol. 71, no. 1843 (February 23, 1905), p. 390.

227   "attract men of two classes": William Bateson, *Materials for the Study of Variation*, p. 574.

228   "The introduction of a descriptive model": *Pearson Life & Work*, p. 42.

229   "It cannot be too strongly urged": W. F. R. Weldon, "On Certain Correlated Variations in *Carcinus moenas*," p. 329.

229   "The term 'controversial' ": W. Bateson–Major C. C. Hurst, February 2, 1907, Bateson Papers, Coleman D.21a, Cambridge University Library, Cambridge, England.

229   "the view that the method of the Registrar-General": Karl Pearson, "Walter Frank Raphael Weldon, 1860–1906," p. 19 [afterward referred to as Pearson, "Weldon"].

230   "the numerous bodies engaged": Galton–Karl Pearson, July 13, 1906, *Galton L.L.*, 3A:289.

PAGE

230   "Such methods of attempting to penetrate the obscurity": Sir E.
       Ray Lankester–Editor of *Nature*, June 30, 1896, *Nature* 54, no.
       1394 (July 16, 1896): 245–46; here p. 246.

230   "The hypothesis with which I started": Weldon–Editor of *Nature*,
       August 26, 1896, *Nature* 54, no. 1401 (September 3, 1896): 413.

231   "I think that in the study of evolution": W. T. Thiselton-Dyer–
       Editor of *Nature*, May 13, 1895, *Nature* 52, no. 1334 (May 23,
       1895): 78–79; here p. 79.

231   "Weldon's position in writing": Bateson, Notes of Bateson/Wel-
       don meeting, May 21, 1895, Bateson Papers, Coleman B.10.

231   "I can do no more": Weldon–Bateson, May 24, 1895, Bateson
       Papers, Coleman B.10.

231   "The labour involved was excessive": Pearson, "Weldon," p. 27.

232   "The questions raised by the Darwinian hypothesis": Weldon,
       "Remarks on Variation in Animals and Plants," p. 381.

232   "had small desire to assist": *Galton L.L.*, 3A:127.

232   "the Committee you have got together": Pearson–Galton, Febru-
       ary 12, 1897, ibid., p. 128.

232   "It is far too large": Ibid., p. 128.

232   "sadly out of place": Ibid., p. 127.

233   "Mr. [F.D.] Godman then became chairman": Ibid.

233   "To demonstrate that natural selection": Karl Pearson–Editor of
       Nature, September 10, 1896, *Nature* 54, no. 1403 (September 17,
       1896): 460–61; here 460.

234   "We *want* to know the whole truth": William Bateson, "Problems
       of Heredity as a Subject for Horticultural Investigation," p. 54
       [afterward referred to as Bateson, "Problems of Heredity"].

234   "If the work which is now being put": Bateson, "Hybridisation &
       Cross-Breeding," p. 59.

235   "that this scientific obstacle": Rev. Charles Gore, *Buying up the
       Opportunity*, p. 16.

11   First Answers to Inheritance

237   "From these in the next generation": T. H. Morgan, "The Rise
       of Genetics," presidential address at 6th International Congress
       of Genetics, Cornell University, Ithaca, New York, August 25,
       1932, *Science*, 76 (September 23, 1932), pp. 261–267; here p. 262.

237   "among all the numerous experiments": Gregor Mendel, "Ver-
       suche über Pflanzenhybriden" (1865), *Abhandlungen des naturfor-
       schenden Vereines in Brünn*, Bd. IV (1866), pp. 3–47, translated
       " 'Experiments in Plant Hybridisation' by Gregor Mendel with an
       Introductory Note by W. Bateson," in *Journal of the Royal Horticul-
       tural Society* 26 (1901), pt. 1, pp. 1–32; here p. 3.

238   "Artificial fertilisation": ibid., p. 3.

238   "For all that we know to the contrary": Thomas Hunt Morgan,
       "On the Mechanism of Heredity," Croonian Lecture delivered
       June 1, 1922, p. 163 [afterward referred to as Morgan, 1922
       Croonian Lecture].

239   "I know that the results I obtained": Mendel–Karl Wilhelm von
       Nägeli, April 18, 1867, quoted Curt Stern and Eva R. Sherwood
       (eds.), *The Origin of Genetics: A Mendel Source Book*, p. 60 [afterward
       referred to as Stern & Sherwood].

PAGE

239   "External reasons from comparison of floras": Karl Wilhelm von Nägeli, quoted A. G. Morton, *History of Botanical Science*, p. 414.

240   "Lack of time is chiefly to blame": Mendel–Nägeli, November 6, 1867, quoted Stern & Sherwood, p. 71.

241   "The great ideas of the struggle for existence": C. D. Darlington, *Genetics and Man*, p. 97.

241   "From these and numerous other experiments": Hugo de Vries, "Das Spaltungsgesetz der Bastarde" ["The Law of Segregation of Hybrids"] (Preliminary Communication March 14, 1900) in *Berichte der deutschen Botanischen Gesellschaft* 18, (1900), 83–90, here p. 90.

241   Correns's paper: Carl Correns, "G. Mendel's Regel über das Verhalten der Nachkommenschaft der Rassenbastarde" ["G. Mendel's Law Concerning the Behaviour of Progeny of Varietal Hybrids"] (1900), in *Berichte der deutschen Botanischen Gesellschaft* 18 (1900): 158–68.

242   "Our problem is less to explain change": Darlington, *History*, p. 55.

242   "each may get the point of view": Garland E. Allen, *Life Science in the Twentieth Century*, p. 52 [afterward referred to as Allen, *Life Science*].

243   "What we first require is to know": Bateson, "Hybridisation and Cross-Breeding," p. 63.

244   "If the Proceedings of the Brünn Natural History Society": J. B. S. Haldane, "William Bateson," in *Possible Worlds and Other Essays*, pp. 135–38; here p. 135.

244   "had [Mendel's] discovery been delayed": Obituary "Dr. William Bateson," *The Times*, February 9, 1926.

244   "These experiments of Mendel's were carried out": Bateson, "Problems of Heredity," p. 57.

244   "With the views of Darwin": Bateson, "Biographical Notice of Mendel" in W. Bateson, *Mendel's Principles of Heredity* (1909), pp. 309–16; here p. 311 [afterward referred to as Bateson, *Mendel's Principles*].

245   "The starting point of Darwin's theory of evolution": Editorial, *Biometrika* 1, no. 1 (October 1901): 1–6; here p. 1.

245   "a considerable range of recognisably different colours": W. F. R. Weldon, "On the Ambiguity of Mendel's Categories," p. 44 [afterward referred to as Weldon, "Ambiguity"].

246   "In the Study of Evolution": Preface, W. Bateson, *Mendel's Principles of Heredity: A Defence*, p. v [afterward referred to as Bateson, *Defence*].

246   "We have been told of late": Ibid., p. x.

246   "undigested mass of miscellaneous 'facts' ": Bateson, *Defence*, p. 106.

246   "To find a parallel for such treatment": Ibid.,

246   "In this purpose I venture to assist him": Bateson, *Defence*, p. 208.

246   "actually prepared two even stronger statements": William B. Provine, *The Origins of Theoretical Population Genetics*, p. 71.

246   "that [Bateson's] speculations": G. Udny Yule, "Mendel's Laws and Their Probable Relations to Intra-Racial Heredity," p. 194.

PAGE

246   "impossible . . . to believe": William Bateson–C. C. Hurst, March
24, 1903, C. C. Hurst Papers, Add 7955/3/12, Cambridge University Library, Cambridge, England.

247   "acting in good faith": Ibid.

247   "the ugliest means possible": Herbert S. Jennings–Raymond
Pearl, November 15, 1909, quoted Daniel J. Kevles, "Genetics in
the United States and Great Britain, 1890–1930," p. 443.

247   "over the head with a club": Ibid.

247   "It is deeply to be regretted": Weldon, "Ambiguity," p. 54.

247   "the imposing Correlation Table": William Bateson, presidential
address to Zoology Section, August 18, 1904, *Report of the Seventy-fourth Meeting of the British Association for the Advancement of Science,
held at Cambridge in August 1904*, pp. 574–89; here p. 578.

248   "On Pearson resuming his seat": R. C. Punnett, "Early Days of
Genetics," p. 8.

248   "Treasure your exceptions!": W. Bateson, *The Methods and Scope
of Genetics, an Inaugural Lecture Delivered 23 October 1908*, p. 22
[afterward referred to as Bateson, *Inaugural Lecture*].

248   "There was one quality": Francis Darwin, "Rems.," p. 148.

249   He believed that inheritance and variation: William Coleman,
"Bateson and Chromosomes: Conservative Thought in Science,"
p. 256 (afterward referred to as Coleman).

249   "sole effective instruments in heredity": Bateson, *Mendel's Principles*, p. 271.

249   In 1901 Clarence E. McClung postulated: A. H. Sturtevant, *A
History of Genetics*, p. 41 [afterward referred to as Sturtevant, *History*].

249   "I may finally call attention": Walter S. Sutton, "On the Morphology of the Chromosome Group in *Brachystola magna*," p. 39.

249   "But ever in our thoughts": W. Bateson, Presidential address,
"The Progress of Genetic Research," to the Third Conference on
Hybridisation and Plant Breeding, July 31, 1906, in R.H.S., *Report
of the Third International Conference on Genetics, 1906*, pp. 90–97;
here p. 96.

250   "Whoever studies the distinctions": Walter Rothschild and Karl
Jordan, "Lepidoptera Collected by Oscar Neumann in North-east
Africa," p. 492.

250   "The transformation of masses of population": William Bateson,
Problems of Genetics, p. 248.

250   "a nice hard fellow": Ernest Rutherford, quoted E. N. da C.
Andrade, The Rutherford Memorial Lecture, 1957, *Proceedings of
the Royal Society, A.* 244 (1958): 437–55; here p. 439.

251   "As race or family peculiarities descend": Dr. Joseph G. Richardson, reported *The Galaxy* 15, no. 6 (June 1873): 851–52; here p.
852.

251   "At that time nearly all diseases": Archibald E. Garrod, quoted
W. Eugene Knox, "Sir Archibald E. Garrod, 1857–1936," p. 4.

252   "If any one step in the process": Ibid, p. 1.

252   "inborn errors of metabolism": Ibid.

252   "physiological units of as yet unknown nature": W. Bateson and
Miss E. R. Saunders, "Experimental Studies in the Physiology of

PAGE

Heredity" (1902). First report to Evolution Committee of the Royal Society, 1902, pp. 3–160; here p. 159.

253   "No single word in common use": Bateson–Sedgwick, April 18, 1905, *Bateson Life*, p. 93.

253   "Studies in 'Experimental Evolution' ": W. Bateson, review of J. P. Lotsy, *Vorlesungen über Deszendenztheorien mit besonderer Berucksichtigung der Botanischen Seite der Frage gehalten an der Reichsuniversität zu Leiden*, Nature 74, no. 1911 (June 14, 1906): 146–47; here p. 146.

253   "The hypothesis that [some] life": Sir William Thomson, Presidential address to British Association, *Report of the Forty-first Meeting of the British Association for the Advancement of Science; Held at Edinburgh in August 1871*, pp. lxxxiv–cv; here p. cv. [afterward referred to as Thomson, Br. Ass. Pres. address, 1871].

254   "What do you think of Thomson's": Huxley–Hooker, August 11, 1871, *Hooker L.L.*, 2: 126 n.2.

254   "I belong to a school": Karl Pearson, "Darwinism, Medical Progress and Eugenics," p. 175.

254   "I think it is rather the fashion": Ibid.

254   "I often wish he had something to do": Darwin's gardener quoted Lord Avebury, The Linnean Society of London, *The Darwin-Wallace Celebration Held on Thursday, 1st July, 1908, by the Linnean Society of London*, p. 58.

255   "In laying hands upon the sacred ark": John Dewey, *The Influence of Darwin on Philosophy*, p. 1.

255   "a man of strong feelings": E. S. Goodrich, "Sir Edwin Ray Lankester (1847–1929)," *The Dictionary of National Biography, 1922–1930*, pp. 481–83; here p. 483.

255   "The popular view still is": Leader, *The Times*, February 12, 1909.

255   "as usually happens in such cases": Ibid.

255   "in neither of these august evolutionary processions": Ibid.

255   "we seem to be brought once more": Ibid.

255   "have no positive value": Ibid.

256   "It would have seemed strange to Virgil": "Literature and Science," *The Times Literary Supplement*, February 11, 1909, p. 45.

256   "But now for many years": Darwin, Auto., p. 114, quoted ibid.

256   "to take the sudden imaginative leap": "Literature and Science," *The Times Literary Supplement*, February 11, 1909, p. 45.

256   "They have diverged": Ibid., p. 46.

12   The Fly Room

257   "No one can see his experimental garden": Thomas Hunt Morgan, "Darwinism in the Light of Modern Criticism," p. 477.

257   "we are beginning to see the process": T. H. Morgan, "The Origin of Species through Selection Contrasted with Their Origin through the Appearance of Definite Variations," p. 63.

258   "In the modern interpretation of Mendelism": Bateson in 1909 quoted Alfred H. Sturtevant, "Thomas Hunt Morgan, Sept. 25, 1866–Dec. 4, 1945," p. 290, [afterward referred to as Sturtevant, "Morgan Memoir"].

258   "that he felt the Mendelian factors": Ibid.

PAGE

258   "for his discoveries concerning the function": Quoted Göran Liljestrand, "The Prize in Physiology and Medicine," p. 240.

259   "I once heard him say": Sturtevant, "Morgan Memoir," p. 289.

259   "took no stock": H. J. Muller, "Thomas Hunt Morgan, 1866–1945," p. 550 [afterward referred to as Muller, Morgan obit.].

259   "that in an undeveloped subject": Morgan, 1922 Croonian Lecture, p. 164.

260   "accumulated by various more or less unorthodox methods": Sturtevant, "Morgan Memoir," p. 298.

260   "Each carried on his own experiments": Ibid., p. 295.

260   "There's two years' work wasted": Morgan, quoted Professor Ross G, Harrison, "Embryology and Its Relations," p. 370.

261   "Well, how is the white-eyed fly?": H. K. Morgan, "Notes on Thomas Hunt Morgan's Life," p. 4, quoted Garland E. Allen, *Thomas Hunt Morgan: The Man and His Science*, p. 153.

261   "And how is the baby?": Ibid.

261   "follows the same scheme": T. H. Morgan, "The Application of the Conception of Pure Lives to Sex-limited Inheritance and to Sexual Dimonphism," p. 77.

262   "The conception of the gene as an organoid": Wilhelm Johannsen, *Elemente der exakten Erblichkeitslehre*, p. 485

262   "At a glance one sees how far": T. H. Morgan, "Personal Recollections of Calvin B. Bridges," p. 357.

263   "Both linkage and crossing-over are": Thomas Hunt Morgan, *The Scientific Basis of Evolution*, p. 71 [afterward referred to as Morgan, *Scientific Basis*].

263   "However much the story": Muller, Morgan obit., p. 551.

263   "I suddenly realized": A. H. Sturtevant, *History*, p. 47.

264   "A parallel to the maps": Morgan, 1922 Croonian Lecture, p. 188 n.

264   "I may state": T. H. Morgan, "The Theory of the Gene," p. 519.

264   difference in average wing length: J. B. S. Haldane, "Natural Selection" in P. R. Bell (ed.), *Darwin's Biological Work*, pp. 101–49; here p. 110.

265   "dealing with artificial and unnatural conditions": Morgan quoted Allen, *Life Science*, p. 67.

265   "it is inconceivable": W. Bateson, review of T. H. Morgan, A.H. Sturtevant, H. J. Muller and C.B. Bridges, *The Mechanism of Mendelian Heredity*, *Science*, n.s. 44, no. 1137 (October 13, 1916): 536–43; here p. 542.

265   "We are provided with a sketch": Ibid., p. 539.

265   "I am just through a long course": Bateson–C. H. Ostenfeld, July 16, 1916 (B.P.B. 36), quoted Coleman, p. 259.

265   "I get further and further away": Bateson–Ostenfeld, June 15, 1917 (B.P.B. 36), quoted ibid.

266   "It may be that the theory of Natural Selection": D. H. Scott, presidential address to Section K (Botany), "The Present Position of the Theory of Descent, in Relation to the Early History of Plants," *British Association for the Advancement of Science, Report of the Eighty-ninth Meeting, Edinburgh, September 7–14, 1921*, pp. 170–86; here p. 172.

267   "I have recently completed an article": R. A. Fisher–Karl Pearson, n.d., quoted E. S. Pearson, "Studies in the History of Proba-

PAGE

bility and Statistics XX: Some Early Correspondence between W. S. Gosset, R. A. Fisher and Karl Pearson," p. 454 [afterward referred to as "Fisher-Pearson Corr."].

267   "attempted to ascertain the biometrical properties": R. A. Fisher, "The Correlation between Relatives on the Supposition of Mendelian Inheritance," p. 399.

267   "I have not examined in detail": Karl Pearson, "Report on R.A. Fisher's 1916 Paper," n.d., quoted Bernard Norton and E. S. Pearson, "A Note on the Background to, and Refereeing of, R. A. Fisher's 1916 Paper 'On the Correlation between Relatives on the Supposition of Mendelian Inheritance,' " p. 153 [afterward referred to as Norton and Pearson].

268   "I do not think in the present state of affairs": Ibid., p. 154.

268   "I have had another go at this paper": R. C. Punnett, "Report on R. A. Fisher's Paper (1916)," August 8, 1916, quoted Norton and Pearson, p. 154.

268   "However, whatever its value": Ibid., p. 155.

268   "reservations as to its scientific status": Norton and Pearson, p. 153.

269   "demonstrated that the mechanism": Sir Gavin de Beer (ed.), "Darwin's Notebooks on Transmutation of Species. Part I, First Notebook (July 1837–February 1838)," *Bulletin of the British Museum (Natural History)*, Historical Ser., 2, no. 1, (1959): 23–73; here p. 28.

269   "Many thanks for your memoir": Karl Pearson–R. A. Fisher, October 21, 1918, "Fisher-Pearson Corr.," p. 456.

269   "By 1919 De Vries's mutation": Elof Axel Carlson, "The *Drosophila* Group: The Transition from the Mendelian Unit to the Individual Gene," p. 33.

269   "We have turned still another bend": William Bateson, "Evolutionary Faith and Modern Doubts," p. 57 [afterward referred to as Bateson, "Evolutionary Faith"].

13 Toward a New Darwinism: Development and Repercussions

274   "Knowledge of the principles of mutation": Hugo de Vries, *The Mutation Theory*, quoted A. Gustafsson, "Mutations and the Concept of Viability" in *Recent Plant Breeding Research*, New York: John Wiley & Sons, 1963.

275   "was transformed from Shull's magnificent design": Paul C. Mangelsdorf, "Genetics, Agriculture and the World Food Problem," p. 244.

276   "The famine to prevent is the next one": Lenin, quoted Dr. L. C. Dunn, "Science in the U.S.S.R: Soviet Biology," p. 66.

276   "just as rules of sociology are distinct": Theodosius Dobzhansky, *Genetics and the Origin of Species*, p. 15. [afterward referred to as Dobzhansky].

276   "Zinovieff [the Russian leader who had presided over the Third International] . . . speaks in the same breath": W. Bateson, "Science in Russia," p. 681.

277   "But when its whole significance dawns": Bernard Shaw, Preface, *Back to Methuselah*, p. xl.

278   "In dim outline": Bateson, "Evolutionary Faith," p. 58.

278   "The survival of the fittest": Ibid., p. 59.

PAGE

278   "the enemies of science": Ibid., p. 61.

278   "Only a line to say": Bateson–Mrs. Bateson, December 29, 1921, quoted *Bateson Life*, p. 143.

278   "Darwinism Disproved": Bateson–Mrs. Bateson, January 1, 1922, quoted ibid., p. 144.

279   "The variations by which [species] have arisen": W. Bateson, "Progress in Biology," Address on occasion of Centenary of Birkbeck College, London, March 12, 1924, *Nature* 113, no. 2844 (May 3, 1924): 644–46, and no. 2845 (May 10, 1924): 681–82; here p. 646.

279   "seditious, defamatory of the Founding Fathers": Norman F. Furniss, *The Fundamentalist Controversy, 1918–1931*, p. 76 [afterward referred to as Furniss].

279   "must obtain 'certificates of qualification' ": Ibid.

279   "It is better to trust in the Rock of Ages": William Jennings Bryan, *In His Image*, p. 93.

279   "Darwinism, Atheism, Agnosticism": Furniss, p. 81.

279   "a materialistic conception of history": Ibid., p. 83.

280   "the theory that man evolved": Ibid., p. 77.

280   "It shall be unlawful for any teacher": Code of Tennessee, 1932, paragraph 2344, page 290, quoted Samuel H. Thompson, "Tennessee after Eleven Years," p. 121.

280   "The law was the result of cheap politics": Ibid., p. 127.

280   "Why don't I have you arrested": George W. Rappelyea to John Thomas Scopes, quoted Fay-Cooper Cole, "A Witness at the Scopes Trial," p. 121 [afterward referred to as Cole].

281   "Where Will You Spend Eternity?": Furniss, p. 7.

281   "Little cotton apes" and "Absolute Ruler": Ibid.

281   "You can't call my family monkeys": Town barber, quoted ibid.

282   "The law knows no heresy": U.S. Supreme Court decision, quoted Cole, p. 123.

282   "If today you can make teaching": Darrow quoted ibid., p. 123.

282   "Talk about putting Daniel": Bryan quoted ibid., p. 127.

282   "I have never seen greater need": Dudley Field Malone, quoted ibid.

283   "There is the fear!": Malone, quoted ibid.

283   "If a great state has decided by law": Arthur Brisbane quoted Maynard Shipley, *The War on Modern Science*, p. 211.

283   "might reach the jury": Judge John T. Raulston, quoted Cole, p. 128.

283   "You can lock it up": Darrow, quoted ibid.

283   "as a biblical witness": Arthur Garfield Hays, quoted ibid.

283   "What did Scopes teach?": Judge Raulston, quoted ibid.

283   "Your Honor, we are wasting time": Darrow, quoted ibid.

284   "It is less than four years ago": Mr. Bryan's last speech upon "The Tennessee Case," Appendix, William Jennings Bryan and Mary Baird Bryan, *The Memoirs of William Jennings Bryan*, p. 533.

284   "I feel this is the mountain peak": Bryan–Editor of Chattanooga *Daily News*, quoted Furniss, p. 90.

284   "of mental assassination": Furniss, p. 91.

284   "No attempt at repression": Cole, p. 130.

PAGE

284   "The central theme [of the trial]": George M. Marsden, *Fundamentalism and American Culture*, p. 185.

285   "We, the undersigned citizens": Petition to be presented to Forty-sixth General Assembly of the State of Arkansas, January 1, 1927, quoted C. Bush, "The Teaching of Evolution in Arkansas," p. 356.

287   "There is not a shred of conclusive evidence": George H. Bonner, "The Case Against 'Evolution,' " p. 593.

287   "I have always felt that this hypothesis": Thomson, Br. Ass. pres. address, 1871, p. cv.

287   "Of course if the mathematicians are right": The Marquis of Salisbury, presidential address, *Report of the Sixty-fourth Meeting of the British Association for the Advancement of Science, Held at Oxford in August 1894*, pp. 3–15; here p. 13.

288   "Was Darwin right when he said that Man": Sir Arthur Keith, presidential address, "Darwin's Theory of Man's Descent as It Stands Today," *British Association for the Advancement of Science, Report of the Ninety-fifth Meeting (Ninety-seventh Year), Leeds, Aug. 31–Sept. 7, 1927*, pp. 1–15; here p. 15.

288   "Can we accept the idea that man": Ernest William Barnes, Bishop of Birmingham, "The Christian Revelation and Scientific Progress," Sermon in Cardiff Parish Church to Br. Ass. members on August 29, 1920, quoted John Barnes, *Ahead of His Age: Bishop Barnes of Birmingham*, p. 126.

289   "Darwin's assertion that man" and "The stories of the creation": Bishop Barnes, "Walk as children of light," Sermon in Westminster Abbey, September 25 1927, quoted ibid., p. 192.

289   "that on the whole the modern scientific view": Barnes, conclusion of sermon, quoted *The Times*, September 26, 1927.

289   "provoke controversies and raise doubts": Leader, *The Morning Post*, September 26, 1927.

289   "the Over-Bold Dr. Barnes": Leader, *The Church Times*, September 30, 1927, pp. 364–65.

289   "The equality of men is a Christian ideal": The Bishop of Exeter, "Darwinism and What it Implies," p. 670.

289   "lays his finger upon two implications": "Darwinism and Social Ethics," *Nature* 124, no. 3119 (August 10, 1929): 217–18; here p. 217.

14 The New Synthesis Develops

290   "able to penetrate into the interior of living cells": De Vries address in 1904 at dedication of the Station for Experimental Evolution at Cold Spring Harbor, quoted Albert F. Blakeslee, "Twenty-five Years of Genetics (1910–1935)," *Brooklyn Botanic Garden Memoirs* 4 (May 7, 1936): 29–40; here p. 36.

290   "the work [had] been done": Prof. H. J. Muller, "Artificial Transmutation of the Gene," p. 84 [afterward referred to as Muller, "Art. Transmutation"].

291   "Beneath the imposing structure": quoted Dunn, p. 168.

291   "The recognition of this feature of error": E. A. Carlson, "H. J. Muller (1890–1967)," p. 4.

293   "It was the essential pruning": Ibid., p. 9.

PAGE

293 "When the heaviest treatment was given": Muller, "Art. Transmutation," p. 84.

293 "If, as seems likely": Ibid., p. 87.

293 "not philosophical speculation": Bateson, *Inaugural Lecture*, p. 34.

294 "Genetic research will make it possible": William Bateson, presidential address delivered in Sydney, August 20, 1914, *Report of the Eighty-fourth Meeting of the British Association for the Advancement of Science, Australia, July 28–Aug. 31, 1914*, pp. 21–38; here p. 29.

294 "the frequency of the mutations produced": H. J. Muller, "Radiation and Genetics," p. 236.

294 "the Coolidge tube": Elof Axel Carlson, *The Gene: A Critical History*, p. 117.

295 "We have also what are called monstrosities": *Origin* (6th ed., 1872), p. 33.

295 "The majority, no doubt, became extinct": E. Bonavia, *Studies in the Evolution of Animals*, p. 276.

296 "The solution was the existence": Richard B. Goldschmidt, *In and Out of the Ivory Tower*, p. 318.

296 "have played a considerable role": Richard Goldschmidt, *The Material Basis of Evolution*, p. 390.

296 "A monstrosity appearing in a single genetic step": Ibid.

297 "From this one lamb": *Variation*, 1:100.

297 "I am aware, of course": Morgan, *Scientific Basis*, p. 14.

299 *Drosophila melanogaster* . . . sixty-thousandths of a micron in diameter: Morgan, 1922 Croonian Lecture, p. 195.

299 "Most of the earlier Darwinian zoologists": E. B. Ford, "Some Recollections Pertaining to the Evolutionary Synthesis," in Ernst Mayr and William B. Provine (eds.), *The Evolutionary Synthesis: Perspectives on the Unification of Biology*, pp. 334–342; here p. 340 [afterward referred to as *Evolutionary Synthesis*].

300 "Haldane, Wright, and Fisher are the pioneers": Theodosius Dobzhansky, "A Review of Some Fundamental Concepts and Problems of Population Genetics," p. 13.

300 "The permeation of biology by mathematics": Haldane, "Outline of the Mathematical Theory on Natural Selection", Appendix to *The Causes of Evolution*, p. 215.

300 "I will not go so far as to say": A. N. Whitehead, quoted Paul S. Moorhead and Martin M. Kaplan (eds.), *Mathematical Challenges to the Neo-Darwinian Interpretation of Evolution*, p. vii [afterward referred to as Moorhead and Kaplan].

300 "The whole real guts of evolution": C. H. Waddington, quoted ibid., p. 14.

300 Theodosius Dobzhansky, *Genetics and the Origin of Species* (1937); Julian Huxley, *Evolution: The Modern Synthesis* (1942).

301 "a horrible mixture of segregates": Ernst Mayr, "Prologue: Some Thoughts on the History of the Evolutionary Synthesis," in *Evolutionary Synthesis*, pp. 1–48; here p. 21.

301 "had given rise to a false theory": C. D. Darlington, "The Evolution of Genetic Systems: Contributions of Cytology to Evolutionary Theory." in *Evolutionary Synthesis*, pp. 70–80; here p. 76.

302 George Gaylord Simpson, *Tempo and Mode in Evolution* (1944); Julian Huxley (ed), *The New Systematics* (1940).

PAGE

303   "Under the new Stalin régime": C. D. Darlington, "The Retreat from Science in Soviet Russia," p. 159.

303   "Genetics is merely an amusement": Trofim Denisovich Lysenko, Moscow, December 13, 1936, quoted in The New York *Times*, December 14, 1936.

303   "Potato specialists must have gaped": David Joravsky, "The Lysenko Affair," p. 45.

304   "The narrowness of biologists": Muller, quoted Julian Huxley, *Memories*, pp. 201–2.

305   "Work may be condemned by Lysenko": Sir Eric Ashby, *Scientist in Russia*, p. 110.

305   "debased Darwinism and smothered its scientific foundation": Lysenko address to Lenin Academy of Agriculture, July 31, 1948, in *Proceedings of the Lenin Academy of Agricultural Sciences of the U.S.S.R.*, English edition issued by Foreign Language Publishing House of Moscow, 1949, pp. 11–49, here p. 15.

305   "frankly idealistic, essentially mystical concept": Ibid., p.17.

305   "the founders of modern reactionary genetics": Ibid., p. 15.

305   "Comrade Stalin has shown the ways to develop": T. D. Lysenko in *Pravda*, March 8, 1953, quoted Theodosius Dobzhansky, "Crisis of Soviet Biology," p. 332.

306   "in abolishing the Laboratory of Cytogenetics": H. J. Muller–President, Secretary and Membership of the Academy of Sciences of the USSR, September 24, 1948, quoted Conway Zirkle (ed.), *Death of a Science in Russia*, pp. 307–8; here p. 308.

306   "Though Darwin's work is still formally acknowledged": Sir Henry Dale–The President of the Academy of Sciences of the USSR, November 22, 1948, quoted ibid., pp. 313–15; here p. 314.

306   "[Lysenko's] activities on behalf of fantasy": Thomas H. Jukes, *Molecules and Evolution*, p. 262.

15 Molecular Biology Takes Over

307   "the search for explanations": Sydney Brenner, "New Directions in Molecular Biology," p. 785.

308   "the remarkable conclusion that inheritance": Edmund B. Wilson, *An Atlas of the Fertilization and Karyokinesis of the Ovum*, p. 4.

309   "This result startled the researchers": Earl Ubell, "Biological Sciences and Medicine," p. 295.

310   "The evidence presented supports the belief": Oswald T. Avery, Colin M. MacLeod and Maclyn McCarty, "Studies on the Chemical Nature of the Substance Inducing Transformation of Pneumococcal Types," *Journal of Experimental Medicine* 79 (1944): 137–157, here p. 156.

310   "If we are right": Dr. Oswald T. Avery–Roy C. Avery, May 26, 1943, quoted René J. Dubos, *The Professor, the Institute and DNA*, p. 219.

310   "It would have been difficult to say more": Erwin Chargaff, "What Really Is DNA?" p. 305.

311   "One can therefore perform in a test tube": Seymour Benzer, "The Fine Structure of the Gene," p. 70.

PAGE

311   "The great advances in modern genetics": C. H. Waddington, quoted Moorhead and Kaplan, p. 95.

311   "How can the events *in space and time*": Erwin Schrödinger, *What Is Life? The Physical Aspect of the Living Cell*, p. 1.

311   "the number of atoms in [a gene]": Ibid., pp. 61–62.

312   "In the huge molecules of albumen compounds": Johann Friedrich Miescher–Professor Wilhelm His, December 1892, quoted Robert Olby and Erich Posner, "An Early Reference to Genetic Coding," p. 556.

312   "could be thought about in precise terms": Francis Crick–[Robert Olby], June 5, 1969, quoted Robert Olby, "Francis Crick, DNA, and the Central Dogma," p. 943 [afterward referred to as Olby, "Francis Crick"].

312   "to try to show that areas": Ibid.

313   "The particular field which excites my interest": Francis Crick quoted Mrs. Anne Sanderson–[Robert Olby], March 26, 1970, Olby, "Francis Crick," p. 944.

313   James D. Watson, *The Double Helix: A Personal Account of the Discovery of the Structure of DNA* (1968); Robert Olby, *The Path to the Double Helix* (1974).

314   "was quickly drafted and given to Bragg": James D. Watson, *The Double Helix*, p. 146.

314   "shows that Pauling's paper was not delayed": Olby, "Francis Crick," p. 952.

314   "Only those who have experienced the trauma": Robert Olby, *The Path to the Double Helix*, p. 394.

315   "has novel features": J. D. Watson and F. H. Crick, "Molecular Structure of Nucleic Acids: A Structure for Deoxyribose Nucleic Acid," p. 737 [afterward referred to as Watson & Crick, "Molecular Structure"].

315   "The novel feature of the structure": ibid.

315   "one of the most coy statements": Gunther S. Stent, "D.N.A.," p. 920 [afterward referred to as Stent].

315   "that the specific pairing": Watson & Crick, "Molecular Structure," p. 737.

315   "the essential operation required": J. D. Watson and F. H. C. Crick, "Genetical Implications of the Structure of Deoxyribonucleic Acid," p. 965.

315   "The phosphate-sugar backbone of our model": Ibid.

316   "Many of the essential ideas": Stent, p. 924.

318   "This and other examples": Allen, *Life Science*, p. 223.

16 Old Problems, New Challenges

319   "what topic could": Sir Andrew Huxley, "Evidence, Clues and Motive in Science," presidential address at the 139th Annual Meeting of the British Association for the Advancement of Science, Birmingham, August 31, 1937.

321   "Such increases would inevitably have some effect": G. C. Reid, I. S. A. Isaksen, T. E. Holzer and P. J. Crutzen, "Influence of Ancient Solar-Proton Events on the Evolution of Life," p. 179.

321   "low magnetic fields can result": Vlado Valkovic, "A Possible

PAGE

Mechanism for the Influence of Geomagnetic Field on the Evolution of Life," p. 10.

321   "Once primitive life had emerged": R. J. P. Williams, "Natural Selection of the Chemical Elements," Bakerian Lecture for 1981, *Proceedings of the Royal Society*, p. 395.

322   "It is a little surprising": F. H. C. Crick and L. E. Orgel, "Directed Panspermia," p. 344.

322   "we could, if we wished": Ibid., p. 343.

322   "In our view the arrival at the Earth": Fred Hoyle and Chandra Wickramasinghe, *Evolution from Space*, p. 51.

323   "This calculation . . . is nonsense": R. J. Berry, "Happy is the man that findeth wisdom," *Biological Journal of the Linnean Society* 17, no. 1 (February 1982): 1–8; here p. 6. [afterward referred to as Berry].

323   "Thus, for instance, if thousands of rats": Rupert Sheldrake, *A New Science of Life*, p. 14.

324   "Morphic resonance is non-energetic": Ibid., p. 96.

324   "Anyone tempted to take formative causation": Professor D. R. Newth, review of Rupert Sheldrake, *A New Science of Life* in *Nature*, 294, no. 5836 (November 5, 1981): 32–33; here p. 33.

324   "but, rather, put firmly in its place": Leading article, *Nature* 293, no. 5830 (September 24, 1981): 245–46; here p. 246.

324   Julian Huxley . . . wrote an introduction: Pierre Teilhard de Chardin, *The Phenomenon of Man* (1959).

325   "Many of you will have read with incredulous horror": Peter Medawar, quoted Moorhead and Kaplan, p. xii.

325   "From the first dawn of life": *Origin* (1st ed., 1859), p. 411.

325   "The first is that for each species": John Maynard Smith, *Evolution Now*, p. 108.

326   "As the theory of cladistics": *Cladistics*, Colin Patterson, *Biologist* 27 (Nov. 1980) 234–40; here p. 239.

327   "Yes, I cannot see what is wrong in that": Dr. Colin Patterson, quoted L. B. Halstead, "The cladistic revolution—can it make the grade?," p. 760.

327   British Museum (Natural History), *Dinosaurs and their living relatives* (1979); British Museum (Natural History), *Man's Place in Evolution* (1980).

327   "Darwin's Death in South Kensington": *Nature* 289, no. 5800 (February 26, 1981): 735.

328   "Not our direct ancestors": British Museum (Natural History), *Man's Place in Evolution*, p. 74.

328   "This presents the public for the first time": Dr. L. B. Halstead–Editor of *Nature*, n.d., *Nature* 288, no. 5788 (November 20, 1980): 208.

328   "Cladistics is not about evolution": Colin Patterson–Editor of *Nature*, n.d., *Nature* 288, no. 5790 (December 4, 1980): 430.

328   "There are basically two contrasting views": Halstead–Editor of *Nature*, n.d., *Nature* 288, no. 5788 (November 20, 1980): 208.

329   "This has always been a matter of some disquiet": Ibid.

330   It was first outlined: Niles Eldredge and Stephen Jay Gould, "Punctuated Equilibria: An Alternative to Phyletic Gradualism,"

PAGE

in Thomas J. M. Schopf (ed.), *Models in Paleobiology*, pp. 82–115 [afterward referred to as Eldredge & Gould].

330 "it is far more probable": Origin (4th ed., 1866), p. 132.

330 "our profession now wears the glass slipper": Stephen Jay Gould, "The Promise of Paleobiology as a Nomothetic, Evolutionary Discipline," p. 96.

331 "The fate of the more than 400 fossil genera": Thomas J. M. Schopf, "Punctuated Equilibrium and Evolutionary Stasis," p. 162.

331 "So prevalent are missing blocks of time": Ibid., p. 159.

331 "It is considered to range": Ibid., p. 160.

332 "We believe that an inadequate picture": Eldredge & Gould, p. 86.

332 "Paleontologists should recognise that much of their thought": Eldredge & Gould, p. 115.

333 "For example, genetical change": Berry, p. 4.

334 "Our results are consistent": Peter T. Boag and Peter R. Grant, "Intense Natural Selection in a Population of Darwin's Finches (Geospizinae) in the Galápagos," p. 84.

334 "The beneficial effect of widespread acceptance": Luther D. Sunderland, "Prominent British Scientists Abandon Evolution," p. [2] [afterward referred to as Sunderland].

335 "Ah, but you never know": Clark, *Einstein: The Life and Times*, p. 8.

336 " 'antiquated religious traditions' ": H. J. Muller, quoted Dorothy Nelkin, "The Science-Textbook Controversies," p. 33 [afterward referred to as Nelkin].

337 "The Bible is the written Word of God": Creation Research Society, "Statement of Belief," 1972, quoted Thomas H. Jukes, "Two by Two," p. 130.

337 "This will presumably require": "Science and the Citizen—the Monkey War Resumes," *Scientific American* 222, no. 5 (May 1970): 55–56; here p. 55.

337 "Congress shall make no law": First Amendment of the Constitution of the United States of America.

338 "to teach that mankind ascended": Mississippi statute, quoted "Science and the Citizen—Last of the 'Monkey Laws,' " *Scientific American* 224, no. 2 (February 1971): 46.

338 "Many scientists are baffled that such poor science": Laurie R. Godfrey, "The Flood of Antievolutionism," p. 10.

338 "I do not believe that natural scientists": Dr. William Provine, quoted Sunderland, p. 3.

339 "The attempt to legislate the teaching of religious dogma": Editorial, Chicago *Tribune*, March 19, 1980.

339 "How about the Hopi Indians": Therese Klausler–Editor of the Chicago *Tribune*, n.d., Chicago *Tribune*, March 19, 1980.

339 "some good stiff competition": Henry J. Voss–Editor of the Chicago *Tribune*, n.d., ibid., March 29, 1980.

339 "When presented as more than just religious dogma": Joan Beck, "Creationism: That Old-time Religion, or a New Wave?" Chicago *Tribune*, April 11, 1980.

340 "It's a scientific theory": Ronald Reagan at Dallas, August 22, 1980, quoted Leader, Chicago *Tribune*, August 26, 1980.

PAGE

340   "Since [Reagan] is campaigning to be a President": Leader, Chicago *Tribune*, August 26, 1980.

340   "Would Mr. Reagan have teachers stop": ibid., September 6 and 15, 1980.

340   "The verdict leaves evolution": Leader, New York *Times*, March 11, 1981.

341   "slowly, over millions of years": quoted Nelkin, p. 38.

341   "As reptiles evolved from fishlike ancestors": Ibid.

341   In California in 1973: John E. Summers–Editor of *Science*, n.d., *Science* 182, no. 4112 (November 9, 1973): 535.

341   "You're not going to find": Eugene Frank, of Laidlaw Brothers, quoted People for the American Way, Special Report, *The Texas Connection: Countering the Textbook Censorship Crusade* [August 1982], p. 1.

341   "to avoid the publicity": Ibid.

341   "Thus in one sweep": Dr. Wayne A. Moyer, *Young Earth Creationism and Biology Textbooks*, p. 4.

342   "part of the romantic resistence to science": Nelkin, p. 39.

343   "Both the concepts and wording": U.S. District Court Judge William R. Overton, Judgment, Injunction and Memorandum Opinion, January 5, 1982, in McLean *v.* the Arkansas Board of Education, *Science* 215, no. 4535 (February 19, 1982): 934–43; here p. 938.

343   "a theory that is by its own term dogmatic": Ibid., p. 939.

343   "no group, no matter how large or small": Ibid., p. 942.

343   "Some people think": Karl Popper–Editor of *New Scientist*, n.d., *New Scientist* 87, no. 1215 (August 21, 1980): 611.

343   "no longer be approved for listing": Board of Education, New York City–Laidlaw Brothers, June 17, 1982.

343   "the text does not contain": Ibid.

343   "threaded with expressions": Board of Education, New York City–Prentice-Hall, June 17, 1982.

345   "A glance at the current evolutionary literature": Mayr, p. 584.

345   "These are interesting and important questions": Sir Andrew Huxley, "How Far Will Darwin Take Us?," in D. S. Bendall (ed.), *Evolution from Molecules to Men*, pp. 3–19; here p. 8.

Bibliography

THE material recording Darwin's life and work is of exceptional volume, even for a man of his genius and importance. Much of his correspondence is contained in the three volumes of *Life and Letters* edited by his son, Francis, in the two volumes of *More Letters* edited by Francis and by A. C. Seward, and in the two volumes of *Emma Darwin, Wife of Charles Darwin: A Century of Family Letters*, edited by his daughter Henrietta Litchfield. In addition, there is the enormous collection of letters, many unpublished, contained in the Darwin Papers in Cambridge University Library, Cambridge, England, which are numbered from "DAR. 1" onward. Other letters are held by the Library of the Royal Botanic Gardens, Kew; the Gray Herbarium, Harvard University; the American Philosophical Society, Philadelphia; Imperial College, London; and Down House, Downe, Kent.

Various editions of Darwin's *Journal and Researches*, written after he returned to England from the *Beagle* voyage, exist under different titles, and in 1979 there was published a facsimile of the "Journal" written during the voyage and sent back to England in portions as opportunity offered. The original MS of Darwin's "Recollections of the Development of My Mind and Character dated 1876, May 31" is held in the Darwin Papers and numbered "DAR. 26." An expurgated edition was published in the first volume of Francis Darwin's *Life and Letters* of his father, and an unexpurgated version was published by Nora Barlow, Charles Darwin's granddaughter, in 1958, under the title *Autobiography*, a title that is now frequently used for the manuscript even though Darwin himself called it "Recollections."

There are numerous editions of *The Origin of Species*, and *The Descent of Man*, as of many other Darwin titles, and in 1959 Morse Peckham compiled a variorum account of *The Origin* detailing the number and extent of the alterations made in successive editions during Darwin's lifetime.

In addition to this—and to the lives of Darwin's supporters J. D. Hooker, T. H. Huxley, Charles Lyell and Asa Gray—there exists a vast and still growing exegesis on his work, and on the 1842 and 1844 outlines for *The Origin* published by his son Francis in 1909. Much of this is contained in the pages of such specialist publications as the *Journal of the History of Biology* and *ISIS*. Light is thrown on the reception of Darwin's work by reviews in the daily and weekly press and in many of the addresses to the British Association for the Advancement of Science, which are published in the Association's *Reports*.

Post-Darwinian developments are recorded not only in the huge literature of evolutionary research but also in *Nature* and *Science*, and in more specialist journals dealing with biology and its history.

Ackerknecht, Erin H. *Rudolf Virchow, Doctor, Statesman, Anthropologist.* Madison: The University of Wisconsin Press, 1953.

Agassiz, Elizabeth Cary (ed.). *Louis Agassiz: His Life and Correspondence.* 2 vols. London: Macmillan and Company, 1885.

Agassiz, Louis. "Evolution and Permanence of Type," *The Atlantic Monthly* 33 (January 1874): 92–101.

Allan, Mea. *Darwin and His Flowers: The Key to Natural Selection.* London: Faber and Faber, 1977.

Allen, Garland E. "Hugo de Vries and the Reception of the 'Mutation Theory,' " *Journal of the History of Biology* 2 (Spring 1969): 55–87.

———. *Life Science in the Twentieth Century.* New York, London, Sydney and Toronto: John Wiley & Sons, 1975.

———. *Thomas Hunt Morgan: The Man and His Science.* Princeton, New Jersey: Princeton University Press, 1978.

———. "Thomas Hunt Morgan and the Problem of Natural Selection," *Journal of the History of Biology* 1 (Spring 1886): 113–39.

Andrade, E. N. da C. "The Rutherford Memorial Lecture, 1957," *Proceedings of the Royal Society, A.* 244 (1958): 437–55.

Appleman, Philip (ed.). *Darwin.* A Norton Critical Edition. New York: W. W. Norton & Co., 1970.

Argyll, The Dowager Duchess of (ed.). *George Douglas, Eighth Duke of Argyll, K.G., K.T. (1823–1900): Autobiography and Memoirs.* 2 vols. London: John Murray, 1906.

Ashby, Sir Eric. *Scientist in Russia.* Harmondsworth: Penguin Books, 1947.

Ashworth, Professor J. H., F.R.S. "Charles Darwin as a Student in Edinburgh, 1825–27." Address delivered on October 28, 1935. *Proceedings of the Royal Society of Edinburgh* 55 (1934–35): 97–113.

Atkins, Sir Hedley, K.B.E. *Down, the Home of the Darwins: The Story of a House and the People Who Lived There.* London: Published by Phillimore for the Royal College of Surgeons of England, 1974.

Aurelius Antoninus, Marcus. *The Twelve Books of Marcus Aurelius Antoninus, the Emperor.* Translated by George Long. London: George Bell and Sons, 1900.

Bagehot, Walter. *Physics and Politics, or Thoughts on the Application of the Principles of "Natural Selection" and "Inheritance" to Political Society.* London: Henry S. King & Co., 1872.

Bagshaw, Samuel. *History, Gazetteer, and Directory of the County of Kent.* 2 vols. Sheffield: Privately printed, 1847.

Bailey, L. H. "Systematic Work and Evolution," *Science*, n.s. 21 (April 7, 1905): 532–35.

Baker, John Austin (Bishop of Salisbury). "Humanity and Nature," *Biological Journal of the Linnean Society* 17 (February 1982): 69–77.

Barlow, Nora. "The Darwin-Butler Controversy," in Nora Barlow (ed.), *The Autobiography of Charles Darwin, 1809–1882*, App. 2, pp. 167–219.

———. "Robert Fitzroy and Charles Darwin," *The Cornhill Magazine*, n.s. 72 (April 1932): 493–510.

———. (ed.). *The Autobiography of Charles Darwin, 1809–1882. With Original Omissions Restored.* Edited with Appendix and Notes by His Granddaughter. London: Collins, 1958.

Barlow, Nora. *Charles Darwin and the Voyage of the Beagle.* London: Pilot Press Ltd., 1945.

———. *Charles Darwin's Diary of the Voyage of H.M.S. "Beagle,"* edited from the MS. Cambridge: At the University Press, 1933.

———. *Darwin and Henslow, the Growth of an Idea: Letters, 1831–1860.* London: John Murray, 1967, Bentham-Moxon Trust.

———. "Darwin's Ornithological Notes, with an Introduction, Notes and Appendix." *Bulletin of the British Museum (Natural History)*, Historical Ser., 2 (1963): 201–78.

Barnes, John. *Ahead of His Age: Bishop Barnes of Birmingham.* London: Collins, 1979.

Barrett, Paul H. (ed.). *The Collected Papers of Charles Darwin.* 2 vols. Chicago: University of Chicago Press, 1977.

Bartholomew, Michael. "Huxley's Defence of Darwin," *Annals of Science* 32 (1975): 525–35.

Bates, Henry Walter. *The Naturalist on the River Amazons, a Record of Adventures, Habits of Animals, Sketches of Brazilian and Indian Life, and Aspects of Nature under the Equator, during Eleven Years of Travel.* 2 vols. London: John Murray, 1863.

Bateson, Beatrice. *William Bateson, F.R.S., Naturalist: His Essays & Addresses Together with a Short Account of His Life.* Cambridge: At the University Press, 1928.

Bateson, Gregory. *Mind and Nature, A Necessary Unity.* London: Wildwood House; Australia: Bookwise, 1979.

Bateson, William. "Contribution for 1883–84 to 'William Keith Brooks: A Sketch of His Life by Some of His Former Pupils and Associates,'" *The Journal of Experimental Zoölogy* 9 (September 1910): 1–52; here 5–8.

———. "Evolutionary Faith and Modern Doubts," Address to the American Association for the Advancement of Science on December 28, 1921, in Toronto, *Science*, n.s. 55 (January 20, 1922): 55–61.

———. "Hybridisation and Cross-Breeding as a Method of Scientific Investigation" (Read July 11, 1899), *Journal of the Royal Horticultural Society* 24 (1900): 59–66.

———. *Materials for the Study of Variation Treated with Especial Regard to Discontinuity in the Origin of Species.* London and New York: Macmillan and Co., 1894.

———. *Mendel's Principles of Heredity.* Cambridge: At the University Press, 1909.

———. *Mendel's Principles of Heredity: A Defence.* Cambridge: At the University Press, 1902.

———. *The Methods and Scope of Genetics, an Inaugural Lecture Delivered 23 October, 1908.* Cambridge: At the University Press, 1908.

———. *Problems of Genetics.* New Haven: Yale University Press; London: Oxford University Press, 1913.

———. "Problems of Heredity as a Subject for Horticultural Investigation" (Read May 8, 1900), *Journal of the Royal Horticultural Society* 25 (1900–1901): 54–61.

———. "Science in Russia," *Nature* 116 (November 7, 1925): 681–83.

——— and Bateson, Anna. "On Variations in the Floral Symmetry of Certain Plants Having Irregular Corollas" (Read April 2, 1891), *Journal of the Linnean Society: Botany* 28 (1891): 386–424.

Beddall, Barbara G. "Notes for Mr. Darwin: Letters to Charles Darwin from Edward Blyth at Calcutta, A Study in the Process of Discovery," *Journal of the History of Biology* 6 (Spring 1973): 69–95.

———. "Wallace, Darwin and the Theory of Natural Selection: A Study in the Development of Ideas and Attitudes," *Journal of the History of Biology* 1 (Spring 1968): 261–323.

Beecher, Henry Ward. *Evolution and Religion.* 2 vols. London: James Clarke & Co.; New York: Fords, Howard & Hulbert, 1885.

———. *Henry Ward Beecher in England, 1886.* London: James Clarke & Co., 1886.

Bell, P. R. (ed.). *Darwin's Biological Work: Some Aspects Reconsidered by P. R. Bell et al.* Cambridge: At the University Press, 1959.

Bendall, D. S. (ed.). *Evolution from Molecules to Men.* Cambridge, Cambridge University Press, 1983.

Bennett, Alfred W. "The Theory of Natural Selection from a Mathematical Point of View." Paper read to Section D of the British Association, at Liverpool, September 20, 1870. *Nature* 3 (November 10, 1870); 30–33.

Benzer, Seymour. "The Fine Structure of the Gene," *Scientific American* 206 (January 1962), 70–86.

Berry, R. J. "Happy is the man that findeth wisdom," *Biological Journal of the Linnean Society* 17 (February 1982): 1–8.

Bettany, G. T. *Life of Charles Darwin.* London: Walter Scott, 1887.

Blakeslee, Albert F. "Twenty-five Years of Genetics (1910–1935)," *Brooklyn Botanic Garden Memoirs* 4 (May 7, 1936): 29–40.

Blyth, Edward. "An Attempt to Classify the 'Varieties' of Animals . . . ," *The Magazine of Natural History* 8 (1835): 40–53.

———. "Observations on the Various Seasonal and Other External Changes Which Regularly Take Place in Birds," *The Magazine of Natural History* 9 (1836): 399.

———. "On the Psychological Distinctions Between Man and All Other Animals," *The Magazine of Natural History*, n.s. 1 (1837): 1–9, 77–85 and 131–41.

Boag, Peter T., and Grant, Peter R. "Intense Natural Selection in a Population of Darwin's Finches (Geospizinae) in the Galápagos," *Science* 214 (October 2, 1981): 82–85.

Bonavia, E. *Studies in the Evolution of Animals.* Westminster: Archibald Constable and Company, Publishers to the India Office, 1895.

Bonner, George. "The Case Against 'Evolution,' " *The Nineteenth Century and After* 102 (November 1927): 581–96.

Box, Joan Fisher. *R. A. Fisher: The Life of a Scientist.* New York, Chichester, Brisbane and Toronto: John Wiley & Sons, 1978.

Brady, R. H. "Dogma and Doubt," *Biological Journal of the Linnean Society* 17 (February 1982): 79–96.

Brenner, Sydney. "New Directions in Molecular Biology," *Nature* 248 (April 26, 1974): 785–87.

British Museum (Natural History). *Dinosaurs and Their Living Relatives.* London: Cambridge University Press, 1979.

———. *A Handbook on Evolution.* London: Printed by order of the Trustees of the British Museum, 1958.

———. *Man's Place in Evolution.* London: Cambridge University Press, 1980.

———. *Origin of Species.* London: Cambridge University Press, 1981.

Brooks, John Langdon. *Just Before the Origin: Alfred Russel Wallace's Theory of Evolution.* New York: Columbia University Press, 1984.

Bryan, William Jennings. *In His Image.* New York, Chicago, London and Edinburgh: Fleming H. Revell Co., 1922.

———, and Bryan, Mary Baird. *The Memoirs of William Jennings Bryan*, by himself and his wife. Philadelphia: The John C. Winston Co., 1925.

Buffon, Comte Georges Louis Leclerc de. *Histoire Naturelle.* Paris, 1749–89.

Burkhardt, Frederick. "Darwin and the Biological Establishment," *Biological Journal of the Linnean Society* 17 (February 1982): 39–44.

Bush, C. "The Teaching of Evolution in Arkansas," *Science*, n.s. 64 (October 8, 1926): 356.

Butler, Samuel. *Life and Habit.* London: Trübner & Co., 1878.

Butler, Samuel. *Luck, or Cunning, as the Main Means of Organic Modification? An Attempt to Throw Additional Light upon the Late Mr. Charles Darwin's Theory of Natural Selection.* London: Trübner & Co., 1887.

Cannon, Walter F. "The Bases of Darwin's Achievement: A Revaluation," *Victorian Studies* (Indiana University), 5 (1961–62): 109–34.

———. "The Impact of Uniformitarianism: Two Letters from John Herschel to Charles Lyell, 1836–1837." *Proceedings of the American Philosophical Society Held at Philadelphia for Promoting Useful Knowledge* 105 (June 27, 1961): 301–14.

Carlson, Elof Axel. "The *Drosophila* Group: The Transition from the Mendelian Unit to the Individual Gene," *Journal of the History of Biology* 7 (Spring 1974): 31–48.

———. *The Gene: A Critical History.* Philadelphia and London: W. B. Saunders Co., 1966.

———. *Genes, Radiation, and Society.* Ithaca and London: Cornell University Press, 1981.

———. "H. J. Muller (1890–1967)," *Genetics* 70 (January 1972): 1–30.

Carnegie, Andrew. "Wealth," *The North American Review* 148 (June 1889): 653–64.

Carpenter, William B[enjamin]. *Nature and Man: Essays Scientific and Philosophical, with an Introductory Memoir by J. Estlin Carpenter.* London: Kegan Paul, Trench & Co., 1888.

Carroll, P. Thomas (ed.). *An Annotated Calendar of the Letters of Charles Darwin in the Library of the American Philosophical Society.* Wilmington, Delaware: Scholarly Resources Inc., 1976.

[Chambers, Robert.] *Vestiges of the Natural History of Creation.* London: John Churchill, 1844.

Chambers's Encyclopaedia: A Dictionary of Universal Knowledge. New edition, 10 vols. London and Edinburgh: William & Robert Chambers, Ltd.; Philadelphia: J. B. Lippincott Co., 1888–92.

Chargaff, Erwin. "What Really Is DNA? Remarks on the Changing Aspects of a Scientific Concept," *Progress in Nucleic Acid Research and Molecular Biology* 8 (1968): 297–333.

Chil y Naranjo, D. Gregorio. *Estudios Históricos, Climatológicos y Patológicos de las Islas Canarias.* Part I: *Historia.* 3 vols. Las Palmas de Gran-Canaria: D. Isidro Mirando; Madrid: Gaspar y Roig; Paris: Ernest Leroux, 1876.

Churchill, Frederick B. "Darwin and the Historian," *Biological Journal of the Linnean Society* 17 (February 1982): 45–68.

Clark, John Willis, and Hughes, Thomas McKenny. *The Life and Letters of the Reverend Adam Sedgwick.* 2 vols. Cambridge: At the University Press, 1890.

Clark, Ronald W. *Einstein: The Life and Times.* New York and Cleveland: World Publishing, 1971.

Clews, Henry. *Twenty-eight Years in Wall Street.* New York: Irving Publishing Co., 1888.

Cock, A. G. "William Bateson, Mendelism, and Biometry," *Journal of the History of Biology* 6 (Spring 1973): 1–36.

Cole, Fay-Cooper: "A Witness at the Scopes Trail," *Scientific American* 200 (January 1959): 120–30.

Coleman, William. "Bateson and Chromosomes: Conservative Thought in Science," *Centaurus International Magazine of the History of Mathematics, Science & Technology* 15 (1970): 228–314.

Collins, Wilkie. *The Law and the Lady.* 3 vols. London: Chatto and Windus, 1875.

Colvin, Sidney, and Ewing, J. A. (eds.). *Fleeming Jenkin: Papers, Literary, Scientific, etc.* 2 vols. London: Longmans, Green, and Co., 1887.

Cope, E. D. *The Origin of the Fittest: Essays on Evolution.* London and New York; Macmillan and Co., 1887.

Correns, Carl. "G. Mendel's Regel über das Verhalten der Nachkommenschaft der Rassenbastarde" ["G. Mendel's Law Concerning the Behaviour of Progeny of Varietal Hybrids"] *Berichts der deutschen botanischen Gesellschaft* 18 (1900): 158–68.

[Covington, Syms.] "Original Letters of Charles Darwin to an Australian Settler," contributed by Alfred McFarland, *The Sydney Mail* 38 (August 9, 1884): 254–55.

Crick, Francis. *Of Molecules and Men.* Seattle and London: University of Washington Press, 1966.

———, and Orgel, Leslie E. "Directed Panspermia," *Icarus* 19 (1973): 341–46.

Dana, James Dwight. *See* Daniel C. Gilman, *The Life of James Dwight Dana.*

Darden, Lindley. "William Bateson and the Promise of Mendelism," *Journal of the History of Biology* 10 (Spring 1977): 87–106.

Darlington, Cyril D. *Darwin's Place in History.* Oxford: Basil Blackwell, 1959.

———. "The Evolution of Genetic Systems: Contributions of Cytology to Evolutionary Theory," in Ernst Mayr and William B. Provine (eds.), *The Evolutionary Synthesis*, pp. 70–80.

———. *Genetics and Man.* London: George Allen & Unwin, 1964.

———. "Purpose and Particles in the Study of Heredity," in E. Ashworth Underwood (ed), *Science, Medicine and History*, pp. 472–81.

———. "The Retreat from Science in Soviet Russia," *The Nineteenth Century and After* 142 (October 1947): 157–68.

Darrow, Clarence. *The Story of My Life.* New York: Charles Scribner's Sons, 1932.

Darwin, Charles:

AUTOBIOGRAPHY:

Original MS: "Recollections of the Development of My Mind and Character dated 1876, May 31," in The Darwin Papers numbered DAR. 26 at Cambridge University Library, Cambridge, England.

Original publication in Francis Darwin (ed.), *The Life and Letters of Charles Darwin*, 1:26–107.

Unexpurgated version: Nora Barlow (ed.), *The Autobiography of Charles Darwin, 1809–1882. With Original Omissions Restored.*

WORKS AND SELECTED SCIENTIFIC PAPERS:

The Journal of a Voyage in H.M.S. Beagle. Facsimile edition of original MS at Down House, Downe, Kent. Guildford, Surrey, England: Genesis Publications in association with Australia & New Zealand Book Co. Pty. Ltd., 1979.

Vol. III: *Journal and Remarks, 1832–1836,* of Robert Fitz-Roy (ed.), *Narrative of the Surveying Voyages of His Majesty's Ships* Adventure *and* Beagle, *between the Years 1826 and 1836, Describing Their Examination of the Southern Shores of South America, and the* Beagle's *Circumnavigation of the Globe.* 3 vols. London: Henry Colburn, 1839.

Journal of Researches into the Geology and Natural History of the Various Countries Visited by H.M.S. "Beagle," under the Command of Captain Fitzroy, R.N., from 1832 to 1836. London: Henry Colburn, 1839.

Journal of Researches into the Natural History and Geology of the Countries Visited during the Voyage of H.M.S. Beagle *Round the World, under the Command of Capt. Fitz Roy, R.N.* Second edition, corrected, with additions. London: John Murray, 1845.

The Zoology of the Voyage of H.M.S. Beagle, *under the Command of Captain Fitzroy, R.N., during the Years 1832 to 1836.* Edited and superintended by Charles Darwin. 5 parts. Part I: *Fossil Mammalia*, by Richard Owen, with a Geological

Introduction by Charles Darwin (1840); Part II: *Mammalia*, by George R. Waterhouse, with a Notice of Their Habits and Ranges by Charles Darwin (1839); Part III: *Birds*, by John Gould, with Many Descriptions Supplied by Mr. G. R. Gray of the British Museum (1841); Part IV: *Fish*, by Rev. Leonard Jenyns (1842); and Part V: *Reptiles*, by Thomas Bell (1843). London: Smith, Elder & Co., 1839–43.

The Geology of the Voyage of the Beagle, under the Command of Capt. Fitzroy, R.N., during the Years 1832 to 1836, 3 parts. Part I: *The Structure and Distribution of Coral Reefs* (1842); Part II: *Geological Observations on the Volcanic Islands, Visited during the Voyage of H.M.S. Beagle, Together with Some Brief Notices on the Geology of Australia and the Cape of Good Hope* (1844); and Part III: *Geological Observations on South America* (1846). London: Smith, Elder & Co., 1842–46.

A Monograph of the Fossil Lepadidae; or, Pedunculated Cirripedes of Great Britain and *A Monograph of the Fossil Balanidae and Verrucidae of Great Britain*. 2 vols. London: Palaeontographical Society, 1851 and 1854].

A Monograph of the Sub-class Cirripedia, with Figures of All the Species. 2 vols. London: Ray Society, 1851 and 1854.

On the Origin of Species by Means of Natural Selection, or the Preservation of Favoured Races in the Struggle for Life. London: John Murray, 1859.

  [Second edition.] London: John Murray, 1860.

  Third edition, with additions and corrections. London: John Murray, 1861.
  Fourth edition, with additions and corrections. London: John Murray, 1866.
  Fifth edition, with additions and corrections. London: John Murray, 1869.
  Sixth edition, with additions and corrections. London: John Murray, 1872.
    [In the 6th ed. the word "On" is omitted from the title.]

On the Various Contrivances by Which British and Foreign Orchids are Fertilised by Insects, and on the Good Effects of Intercrossing. London: John Murray, 1862.

The Movements and Habits of Climbing Plants. London: John Murray, 1865; 2nd ed., 1875.

The Variation of Animals and Plants under Domestication. 2 vols. London: John Murray, 1868.

The Descent of Man, and Selection in Relation to Sex. 2 vols. London: John Murray, 1871.

  Second edition, revised and augmented. 1 vol. London: John Murray, 1874.

The Expression of the Emotions in Man and Animals. London: John Murray, 1872.

Insectivorous Plants. London: John Murray, 1875.

The Effects of Cross- and Self-Fertilisation in the Vegetable Kingdom. London: John Murray, 1876.

The Different Forms of Flowers on Plants of the Same Species. London: John Murray, 1877.

The Power of Movement in Plants. Assisted by Francis Darwin. London: John Murray, 1880.

The Formation of Vegetable Mould, through the Action of Worms, with Observations on Their Habits. London: John Murray, 1881.

Erasmus Darwin, by Ernst Krause. Translated from the German by W. S. Dallas. With a Preliminary Notice by Charles Darwin. London: John Murray, 1879.

"Observations of Proofs of Recent Elevation on the Coast of Chili, Made during the Survey of H.M.S. 'Beagle,' Commanded by Capt. FitzRoy [1837]," *Proceedings of the Geological Society of London* 2 (1838): 446–49.

"On the Formation of Mould" (Paper read November 1, 1837), *Proceedings of the Geological Society of London* 2 (1837–1838): 574–76.

"Observations on the Parallel Roads of Glen Roy, and of Other Parts of Lochaber in Scotland, with an Attempt to Prove That They Are of Marine Origin," The Royal Society, *Philosophical Transactions* 129 (1839): 39–82.

"Extract from an Unpublished Work on Species, by C. Darwin, Esq., Consisting of a Portion of a Chapter Entitled 'On the Variation of Organic Beings in a State of Nature; on the Natural Means of Selection; on the Comparison of Domestic Races and True Species' " (Read July 1, 1858), *Journal of the Proceedings of the Linnean Society: Zoology* 3 (1859): 46–50.

"On the Movement and Habits of Climbing Plants," *Journal of the Linnean Society: Botany* 9 (1865): 1–118.

"Pangenesis," *Nature* 3 (April 27, 1871): 502.

Questions about the Breeding of Animals [1840]. Facsimile. With an Introduction by Sir Gavin de Beer, F.R.S. London: Society for the Bibliography of Natural History, 1968.

Collected Papers: *See* Barrett, Paul H. (ed.), *The Collected Papers of Charles Darwin.*

LETTERS:

General: Darwin, Francis (ed.), *The Life and Letters of Charles Darwin*; Darwin, Francis, and Seward, A. C. (eds.), *More Letters of Charles Darwin*; Carroll, P. Thomas (ed.), *An Annotated Calendar of the Letters of Charles Darwin in the Library of The American Philosophical Society.*

Family: Barlow, Nora (ed.), *Charles Darwin and the Voyage of the Beagle*; Litchfield, H. E., *Emma Darwin, Wife of Charles Darwin: A Century of Family Letters.*

To Syms Covington, *see* [Covington, Syms] "Original Letters of Charles Darwin to an Australian Settler"; to Francis Galton, *see* Pearson, Karl, *The Life, Letters and Labours of Francis Galton*; to Asa Gray, *see* The Historical Records Survey, *Calendar of the Letters of Charles Robert Darwin to Asa Gray*; to J. S. Henslow, *see* Barlow, Nora (ed.), *Darwin and Henslow, the Growth of an Idea: Letters, 1831–1860*; to Rev. J. Brodie Innes, *see* Stecher, Robert M., "The Darwin-Innes Letters: The Correspondence of an Evolutionist with His Vicar, 1848–1884"; to Hugo de Vries, *see* Van Der Pas, Peter W., "The Correspondence of Hugo de Vries and Charles Darwin"; to Alfred Russel Wallace, *see* Marchant, James, *Alfred Russel Wallace: Letters and Reminiscences.* Vol. I: 127–320.

Unpublished Letters: de Beer, Sir Gavin (ed.), "Some Unpublished Letters of Charles Darwin."

MEMORIAL NOTICES:

Charles Darwin Memorial Notices Reprinted from "Nature." London: Macmillan and Co., 1882.

BIOGRAPHIES:

Among the numerous biographies of Charles Darwin the more reliable and useful include:

Bettany, G. T. *Life of Charles Darwin* (1887).

Poulton, E. B. *Charles Darwin and the Origin of Species* (1909).

Pearson, Karl. *Charles Darwin, 1809–1882* (1923).

West, Geoffrey. *Charles Darwin: The Fragmentary Man* (1937).

Irvine, William. *Apes, Angels and Victorians* (1955).

Keith, Arthur. *Darwin Revalued* (1955).

de Beer, Gavin: *Charles Darwin: Evolution by Natural Selection* (1963).

Huxley, Julian, and Kettlewell, H. B. G. *Charles Darwin and His World* (1965).

Vorzimmer, P. J. *Charles Darwin: The Years of Controversy* (1970).

Allan, Mea. *Darwin and His Flowers: The Key to Natural Selection* (1977).

Darwin, Erasmus [the Elder]. *The Temple of Nature; or, the Origin of Society: a Poem, with Philosophical Notes.* London: J. Johnson, 1803.

——. *Zoonomia, or the Laws of Organic Life.* 2 vols. London: Printed for J. Johnson, 1794 and 1796.

Darwin, Francis. "Reminiscences of My Father's Everyday Life," in Francis Darwin (ed.), *The Life and Letters of Charles Darwin*, 1:108–60.

—— (ed.). *The Foundations of the Origin of Species: Two Essays Written in 1842 and 1844 by Charles Darwin*, edited by his son. Cambridge: At the University Press, 1909.

——. *The Life and Letters of Charles Darwin, Including an Autobiographical Chapter.* 3 vols. Second edition. London: John Murray, 1887.

——, and Seward, A. C. (eds.). *More Letters of Charles Darwin: A Record of His Work in a Series of Hitherto Unpublished Letters.* 2 vols. London: John Murray, 1903.

De Beer, Sir Gavin. *Charles Darwin: Evolution by Natural Selection.* London and New York: Thomas Nelson and Sons Ltd., 1963.

——. "Mendel, Darwin and Fisher," *Notes and Records of the Royal Society of London* 19 (1964): 192–226.

—— (ed.). "Some Unpublished Letters of Charles Darwin," *Notes and Records of the Royal Society of London* 14 (June 1959): 12–66.

——. "Darwin's Journal," *Bulletin of the British Museum (Natural History)*, Historical Series, 2 (1959): 1–21.

——. "Darwin's Notebooks on Transmutation of Species. Part I: First Notebook (July 1837–Feb. 1838); Part II: Second Notebook (February to July 1838); Part III: Third Notebook (July 15, 1838–October 2, 1838); and Part IV: Fourth Notebook (October 1838–July 10, 1839), All with Introduction and Notes," *Bulletin of the British Museum (Natural History)*, Historical Ser., 2 (1959–1960): 23–73; 75–118; 119–50 and 151–83.

——, and Rowlands, M. J. (eds.): "Darwin's Notebooks on Transmutation of Species: Addenda and Corrigenda, with Notes," *Bulletin of the British Museum (Natural History)*, Historical Series, 2 (1961): 185–200.

——, and Skramovsky, B.M. (eds.): "Darwin's Notebooks on Transmutation of Species: Part VI: Pages Excised by Darwin," *Bulletin of the British Museum (Natural History)*, Historical Series, 3 (1967): 129–76.

De Marrais, Robert. "The Double-Edged Effect of Sir Francis Galton: A Search for the Motives in the Biometrician-Mendelian Debate," *Journal of the History of Biology* 7 (1974): 141–74.

Dempster, William J. *Patrick Matthew and Natural Selection: Nineteenth Century Gentleman-Farmer, Naturalist and Writer.* Edinburgh: Paul Harris Publishing, 1983.

Dewey, John. *The Influence of Darwin on Philosophy and Other Essays in Contemporary Thought.* New York: Henry Holt and Co., 1910.

Disraeli, Benjamin. *Lothair.* 3 vols. London: Longmans, Green, and Co., 1870.

——. *Tancred: or, The New Crusade.* 3 vols. London: Henry Colburn, 1847.

Dobzhansky, Theodosius. *Genetics and the Origin of Species.* New York: Columbia University Press, 1937; 3rd ed., rev. 1951.

——. "The Crisis of Soviet Biology." in Ernest J. Simmons (ed.), *Continuity and Change in Russian and Soviet Thought*, pp. 329–46.

——. "A Review of Some Fundamental Concepts and Problems of Population Genetics," *Cold Spring Harbor Symposium on Quantitative Biology* 20 (1955): 1–15.

Dubos, René J. *The Professor, the Institute and DNA.* New York: The Rockefeller University Press, 1976.

Du Chaillu, Paul B[elloni]. *Explorations and Adventures in Equatorial Africa; with Accounts of the Manners and Customs of the People, and of the Chace of the* Gorilla,

Crocodile, Leopard, Elephant, Hippopotamus, and Other Animals. London: John Murray, 1861.

Dunn, L. C. "Mendel, His Work and His Place in History," *Proceedings of the American Philosophical Society* 109 (August 18, 1965): 189–98.

———. "Science in the U.S.S.R.: Soviet Biology," *Science* 99 (January 28, 1944): 65–67.

———. *A Short History of Genetics: The Development of Some of the Main Lines of Thought, 1864–1939.* New York and London: McGraw-Hill Book Co., 1965.

Dupree, A. Hunter. *Asa Gray, 1810–1888.* Cambridge, Mass: The Belknap Press of Harvard University Press, 1959.

Eiseley, Loren C. "Charles Darwin, Edward Blyth, and the Theory of Natural Selection," *Proceedings of the American Philosophical Society* 103 (February 28, 1959): 94–158.

———. *Darwin and the Mysterious Mr. X.* London, Toronto and Melbourne: J. M. Dent & Sons Ltd., 1979.

———. *Darwin's Century: Evolution and the Man Who Discovered It.* London: Victor Gollancz Ltd., 1959

Eldredge, Niles. "The Allopatric Model and Phylogeny in Paleozoic Vertebrates," *Evolution* 25 (1971): 156–67.

———, and Gould, Stephen Jay. "Punctuated Equilibria: An Alternative to Phyletic Gradualism," in T. J. M. Schopf (ed.), *Models in Paleobiology,* pp. 82–115.

Ellegard, Alvar. *"Darwin and the General Reader: The Reception of Darwin's Theory of Evolution in the British Periodical Press, 1859–1872,"* Göteborg: Elanders Boktryckeri Aktiebolag, 1958.

Elwin, Warwick (ed.). *Some XVIII Century Men of Letters: Biographical Essays by the Rev. Whitwell Elwin, Some Time Editor of the "Quarterly Review," with a Mémoir,* edited by his son. 2 vols. London: John Murray, 1902.

Exeter, The Bishop of (The Rt. Rev. Lord William Rupert Ernest Gascoyne Cecil). "Darwinism and Social Ethics," *Nature* 124 (August 10, 1929): 217–18.

———. "Darwinism and What It Implies," *The Hibbert Journal* 27 (July 1929): 666–75.

Fawcett, Henry. "A Popular Exposition of Mr. Darwin on the Origin of Species," *Macmillan's Magazine* 3 (December 1860): 81–92.

Feuer, Lewis S. "Is the 'Darwin-Marx Correspondence' Authentic?" *Annals of Science* 32 (January 1975): 1–12.

Fisher, R. A. "The Correlation between Relatives on the Supposition of Mendelian Inheritance" (Read July 8, 1918), *Transactions of the Royal Society of Edinburgh* 52, pt. 2 (1918–19); published 1921: 399–433.

———. *The Genetical Theory of Natural Selection.* Oxford: The Clarendon Press, 1930.

Fitz-Roy, Robert (ed.). *Narrative of the Surveying Voyages of His Majesty's Ships Adventure and Beagle, between the Years 1826 and 1836, Describing Their Examination of the Southern Shores of South America, and the Beagle's Circumnavigation of the Globe.* 3 vols. and App. to Vol. II. Vol. I: *Proceedings of the First Expedition, 1826–1830, under the Command of Captain P. Parker King, R.N., F.R.S.;* Vol. II: *Proceedings of the Second Expedition, 1831–1836, under the Command of Captain Robert Fitz-Roy, R.N.;* and Vol. III: *Journal and Remarks, 1832–1836.* By Charles Darwin, Esq., M.A., Sec. Geol. Soc. London: Henry Colburn, 1839.

Flourens, [Marie Jean] P[ierre]: *Examen du livre de M. Darwin sur l'Origine des espèces,* Paris: Garnier Frères, 1864.

Ford, E. B. "Some Recollections Pertaining to the Evolutionary Synthesis," in Ernst Mayr and William B. Provine (eds.), *The Evolutionary Synthesis,* pp. 334–42.

Freeman, R. B. "Charles Darwin on the Routes of Male Humble Bees," *The Bulletin of the British Museum (Natural History),* Historical Series, 3 (1968): 179–89.

Freeman, R. B. "The Darwin Family," *Biological Journal of the Linnean Society* 17 (February 1982): 9–21.
———. *The Works of Charles Darwin: An Annotated Bibliographical Handlist.* Folkestone, England, and Hamden, Conn.: Dawson-Archon Books, 1977.
———, and Gautrey, P. J. "Darwin's 'Questions about the Breeding of Animals,' with a Note on 'Queries about Expression,' " *Journal of the Society for the Bibliography of Natural History* 5 (1969): 220–25.
Furniss, Norman F. *The Fundamentalist Controversy, 1918–1931.* New Haven: Yale University Press; London: Oxford University Press, 1954.
Gaissinovitch, A. E. "The Origins of Soviet Genetics and the Struggle with Lamarckism, 1922–1929," *Journal of the History of Biology* 13 (Spring 1980): 1–51.
Galton, Francis. *Finger Prints.* London: Macmillan and Co., 1892.
———. *Hereditary Genius: An Inquiry into Its Laws and Consequences.* London: Macmillan and Co., 1869.
———. *Memories of My Life.* London: Methuen & Co., 1908.
———. *Natural Inheritance.* London and New York: Macmillan and Co., 1889.
———. See Karl Pearson, *The Life, Letters and Labours of Francis Galton.*
Geikie, Sir Archibald. "Charles Darwin: Part II," *Nature* 26 (May 25, 1882): 73–75.
———. *Charles Darwin as Geologist.* The Rede Lecture, given at the Darwin Centennial Commemoration on June 24, 1909. Cambridge: at the University Press, 1909.
———. *A Long Life's Work, an Autobiography.* London: Macmillan and Co., Ltd., 1924.
———. "The Meeting of German Naturalists and Physicians at Innsbruck, Tyrol," *Nature* 1 (November 4, 1869): 22–23.
Geison, Gerald L. "Darwin and Heredity: The Evolution of His Hypothesis of Pangenesis," *Journal of the History of Medicine and Allied Sciences* 24 (1969): 375–411.
George, Wilma. *Biologist Philosopher: A Study of the Life and Writings of Alfred Russel Wallace.* London, Toronto and New York: Abelard-Schuman, 1964.
Gilman, Daniel C. *The Life of James Dwight Dana, Scientific Explorer, Mineralogist, Geologist, Zoologist, Professor in Yale University.* New York and London: Harper & Brothers Publishers, 1899.
Glick, Thomas F. (ed.) *The Comparative Reception of Darwinism.* Austin and London: University of Texas Press, 1972.
Godfrey, Laurie R. "The Flood of Antievolutionism," *Natural History* 90 (June 1981): 4–10.
Goldschmidt, Richard B. *In and Out of the Ivory Tower: The Autobiography of Richard B. Goldschmidt.* Seattle: University of Washington, 1960.
———. *The Material Basis of Evolution.* New Haven: Yale University Press; London: Oxford University Press, 1940.
Goldsmith, Oliver. *An History of the Earth, and Animated Nature.* 8 vols. London: Printed for J. Nourse, 1774.
Gore, Charles. *Buying up the Opportunity: A Sermon Preached before the University of Oxford on the Second Sunday in Advent, 1894.* London: Society for Promoting Christian Knowledge, 1895.
Gosse, Edmund. *Father and Son: A Study of Two Temperaments.* London: William Heinemann, 1907.
———. *The Life of Philip Henry Gosse, F.R.S.,* by his son. London: Kegan Paul, Trench, Trübner & Co. Ltd., 1890.
Gosse, Philip Henry. *Omphalos: An Attempt to Untie the Geological Knot.* London: John Van Voorst, 1857.
Gould, Stephen Jay. "Darwinism and the Expansion of Evolutionary Theory," *Science* 26 (April 23, 1982): 380–87.

Gould, Stephen Jay. *The Panda's Thumb: More Reflections in Natural History*. New York and London: W. W. Norton & Co., 1980.

———. "The Promise of Paleobiology as a Nomothetic, Evolutionary Discipline," *Paleobiology* 6 (1980): 96–118.

Gray, Asa. "Darwin and His Reviewers," *The Atlantic Monthly* 6 (October 1860): 406–25.

———. *Natural Science and Religion: Two Lectures Delivered to the Theological School of Yale College*. New York: Charles Scribner's Sons, 1880.

———. *See* Historical Records Survey, *Calendar of the Letters of Charles Robert Darwin to Asa Gray*.

Gray, Dr. John Edward. "Revision of the Species of Lemuroid Animals, with the Description of Some New Species" (Read April 21, 1863), *Proceedings of the Scientific Meetings of the Zoological Society of London for the Year 1863*, 129–52.

Greene, John C. "Darwin as a Social Evolutionist," *Journal of the History of Biology* 10 (Spring 1977): 1–27.

———. *The Death of Adam*. Ames: Iowa State University Press, 1959.

Gruber, Howard E. "The Eye of Reason: Darwin's Development During the *Beagle* Voyage," *ISIS* 53 (1962): 186–200.

Gruber, Jacob W. *A Conscience in Conflict: The Life of St. George Jackson Mivart*. New York: Published for Temple University Publications, by Columbia University Press, 1960.

Haldane, J.B.S. *The Causes of Evolution*. London: Longmans, Green & Co., 1932.

———. "Natural Selection," in P. R. Bell, (ed.), *Darwin's Biological Work: Some Aspects Reconsidered by P. R. Bell et al.*

———. *Possible Worlds and Other Essays*. London: Chatto and Windus, 1927.

———. "The Theory of Evolution, before and after Bateson," Bateson Lecture Delivered July 18, 1957, at the John Innes Horticultural Institution, *Journal of Genetics* 56 (July 1958): 11–27.

Halstead, L. B. "The Cladistic Revolution—Can It Make the Grade?" *Nature* 276 (December 21/28, 1978): 759–60.

Harrison, Ross G. "Embryology and Its Relations," Address of Retiring Vice-President and Chairman of the Section on Zoological Sciences, American Association for the Advancement of Science, Atlantic City, December 30, 1936, *Science*, n.s. 85 (April 16, 1937): 369–74.

Henkin, Leo J. *Darwinism in the English Novel, 1860–1910: The Impact of Evolution on Victorian Fiction*. New York: Russell & Russell, Inc., 1963.

Hérault de Séchelles, Marie Jean. *Voyage à Montbar, contenant des détails très interessans sur le caractère, la personne et les écrits de Buffon*. Paris, Chez Solvet, 1801.

Herbert, Sandra. "Darwin, Malthus, and Selection," *Journal of the History of Biology* 4 (Spring 1971): 209–17.

——— (ed.). "The Red Notebook of Charles Darwin," *Bulletin of the British Museum (Natural History)*, Historical Series, 7 (1979): 1–64.

Historical Records Survey, Division of Professional and Service Projects. Works Projects Administration. *Calendar of the Letters of Charles Robert Darwin to Asa Gray*. Boston: The Historical Records Survey, 1939.

Hofstadter, Richard. *Social Darwinism in American Thought, 1860–1915*. Philadelphia: University of Pennsylvania Press, 1945.

Holder, Charles Frederick. *Louis Agassiz: His Life and Work*. New York: G. P. Putnam's Sons; London: The Knickerbocker Press, 1893.

Hooker, Sir Joseph Dalton. *The Botany of the Antarctic Voyage of H.M. Discovery Ships "Erebus" and "Terror" in the Years 1839–1843, under the Command of Captain Sir James Clark Ross*. Part I: *Flora Antarctica*. 2 vols. 1844 and 1847. Part II: *Flora*

Novae-Zelandiae. 2 vols. 1853 and 1855. Part III: *Flora Tasmaniae.* 2 vols. 1860. London: Reeve Brothers, 1844–1860.

————. *See* Leonard Huxley (ed.), *Life and Letters of Sir Joseph Dalton Hooker.*

Horner, Leonard. *See* Lyell, Katharine M. (ed.), *Memoir of Leonard Horner, F.R.S., F.G.S.*

Hort, Arthur Fenton. *Life and Letters of Fenton John Anthony Hort*, by his son. 2 vols. London: Macmillan and Co. Ltd., 1896.

Howarth, O. J. R., and Howarth, Eleanor K. *A History of Darwin's Parish, Downe, Kent.* With a Foreword by Sir Arthur Keith. Southampton: Russell & Co. (Southern Counties) Ltd., n.d.

Hoyle, Fred, and Wickramasinghe, Chandra. *Evolution from Space.* London, Toronto and Melbourne: J. M. Dent & Sons, 1981.

Hull, David L. *Darwin and His Critics: The Reception of Darwin's Theory of Evolution by the Scientific Community.* Cambridge, Mass.: Harvard University Press, 1973.

Humboldt, [Friedrich Heinrich] Alexander, Baron von. *Personal Narrative of Travels to the Equinoctial Regions of the New Continent, during the Years 1799–1804, by Alexander de Humboldt and Aimé Bonpland, with Maps, Plans, & Written in French by Alexander de Humboldt, and Translated into English by Helen Maria Williams.* 7 vols. Third edition. London: Printed for Longman, Hurst, Rees, Orme, and Brown, 1822.

Hussey, [Rev.] Arthur. "The Tendency of Species to form Varieties," *The Zoologist: A Popular Miscellany of Natural History* 17 (1859): 6474–75.

Hutchinson, Horace G. *Life of Sir John Lubbock, Lord Avebury.* 2 vols. London: Macmillan and Co., Ltd., 1914.

Huxley, Andrew. "How Far Will Darwin Take Us?" in D. S. Bendall, (ed.), *Evolution from Molecules to Men*, pp. 3–19.

Huxley, Julian S. "Alfred Russel Wallace (1823–1913)," *The Dictionary of National Biography; Supplement 1912–1921*, pp. 546–49.

————. *Evolution: The Modern Synthesis.* London: George Allen & Unwin Ltd., 1942.

————. *Memories.* London: George Allen and Unwin Ltd., 1970.

———— (ed). *The New Systematics.* Oxford: At the Clarendon Press, 1940.

————, *The Stream of Life.* London: Watts and Co., 1926.

————, Hardy, A. C., and Ford, E. B. (eds.). *Evolution as a Process.* London: Allen and Unwin, 1954.

————, with H. G. Wells and G. P. Wells. *The Science of Life.* London: Cassell, 1931.

————, and Kettlewell, H. B. G. *Charles Darwin and His World.* London: Thames & Hudson, 1965.

Huxley, Leonard (ed.). *Life and Letters of Sir Joseph Dalton Hooker, O.M., G.C.S.I., Based on Materials Collected and Arranged by Lady Hooker.* 2 vols. London: John Murray, 1918.

————. *Life and Letters of Thomas Henry Huxley*, by his son. 2 vols. London: Macmillan and Co., Ltd., 1900.

Huxley, Thomas Henry. "The Coming of Age of 'The Origin of Species,' Lecture at Royal Institution, March 19, 1880," *Nature* 22 (May 6, 1880): 1–4.

————. *Evidence as to Man's Place in Nature.* London: Williams and Norgate, 1863.

————. "Mr. Darwin's Critics," *Contemporary Review* 18 (November 1871): 443–76.

————. "On the Reception of 'The Origin of Species,' " in Francis, Darwin (ed.), *The Life and Letters of Charles Darwin*, 2:179–204.

————. "The Struggle for Existence: A Programme" *Nineteenth Century* 23 (February 1888): 161–180.

————. *Twelve Lectures and Essays.* With Introductory Note by Edward Clodd. London: Watts & Co., 1908.

Huxley, Thomas Henry. *See* Leonard Huxley (ed.), *Life and Letters of Thomas Henry Huxley*.

Irvine, William. *Apes, Angels and Victorians*, a joint biography of Darwin and Huxley. London: Weidenfeld & Nicolson, 1955.

Jenkin, Fleeming. *See* Sidney Colvin and J. A. Ewing (eds.), *Fleeming Jenkin: Papers, Literary, Scientific, etc.*

Johannsen, W. *Elemente der exakten Erblichkeitslehre*. Jena: Gustav Fischer, 1909.

Jones, D. F. *Genetics in Plant and Animal Improvement*. New York: John Wiley & Sons, 1925.

Joravsky, David. "The Lysenko Affair," *Scientific American* 207 (November 1962): 41–49.

Judd, J. W. "Darwin and Geology," in A. C. Seward (ed.), *Darwin and Modern Science*, pp. 337–84.

Judson, Horace Freeland. *The Eighth Day of Creation: Makers of the Revolution in Biology*. London: Jonathan Cape, 1979.

Jukes, Thomas H. *Molecules and Evolution*. New York and London: Columbia University Press, 1966.

———. "Two by Two," *Nature* 285 (May 15, 1980): 130.

Keith, Sir Arthur. *The Antiquity of Man*. London: Williams & Norgate, 1915.

———. *Darwin Revalued*. London: Watts & Co., 1955.

Kevles, Daniel J. "Genetics in the United States and Great Britain, 1890–1930: A Review with Speculations," *ISIS* 71 (September 1980): 441–55.

Keynes, Richard Darwin (ed.). *The Beagle Record: Selections from the Original Pictorial Records and Written Accounts of the Voyage of H.M.S. Beagle*. Cambridge, London, New York and Melbourne: Cambridge University Press, 1979.

Kingsley, Charles. *Glaucus; or, The Wonders of the Shore*. Fourth edition. Cambridge: Macmillan and Co., 1859.

Kline, George L. "Darwinism and the Russian Orthodox Church," in Ernest J. Simmons (ed.), *Continuity and Change in Russian and Soviet Thought*, pp. 307–28.

Knox, W. Eugene. "Sir Archibald E. Garrod, 1857–1936," *Genetics: A Periodical Record of Investigations Bearing on Heredity and Variation* 56 (May 1967): 1–6.

Kohn, David; Smith, Sydney; and Stauffer, Robert C. "New Light on 'The Foundations of the Origin of Species': A Reconstruction of the Archival Record," *Journal of the History of Biology* 15 (Fall 1982): 419–42.

Krause, Ernst. "The Scientific Works of Erasmus Darwin," pp. 131–216 in *Erasmus Darwin* translated from the German by W. S. Dallas, with a Preliminary Notice by Charles Darwin. London: John Murray, 1879.

Kropotkin, P. *Memoirs of a Revolutionist*. 2 vols. London: Smith, Elder, & Co., 1899.

———. *Mutual Aid: A Factor of Evoltuion*. London: William Heinemann, 1902.

Lack, David. *Darwin's Finches*. Cambridge: At the University Press, 1947.

Lamarck, J.B.P.A. *Philosophie Zoologique, ou Exposition des Considérations relatives à l'Histoire Naturelle des Animaux . . .* 2 vols. Paris: Chez Dentu, Libraire; Chez L'Auteur, 1809.

Liljestrand, Göran. "The Prize in Physiology and Medicine," in Nobel Foundation (ed.), *Nobel: The Man and His Prizes*, pp. 135–316.

Linnean Society of London. *The Darwin-Wallace Celebration Held on Thursday, 1st July, 1908, by the Linnean Society of London*. London: Printed for the Linnean Society, 1908.

Litchfield, Henrietta E. *Emma Darwin, Wife of Charles Darwin: A Century of Family Letters*, by her daughter. 2 vols. Cambridge: Privately printed at the University Press, 1904.

"Literature and Science," Leader, *The Times Literary Supplement*, February 11, 1909.

Lubbock, Sir John, Lord Avebury. See Horace G. Hutchinson, *Life of Sir John Lubbock, Lord Avebury.*

Lucas, Erhard. "Marx und Engels: Auseinandersetzung mit Darwin zur Differenz zwischen Marx und Engels," *International Review of Social History* 9 (1964): 433–69.

Lucas, J. R. "Wilberforce and Huxley: A Legendary Encounter," *The Historical Journal* 22 (1979): 313–30.

Lurie, Edward. "Louis Agassiz and the Idea of Evolution," *Victorian Studies* (Indiana University), 3 (September 1959): 87–108.

———. *Louis Agassiz: A Life in Science.* Chicago: The University of Chicago Press, 1960.

Lyell, Sir Charles. *Elements of Geology.* London: John Murray, 1838.

———. *The Geological Evidences of the Antiquity of Man, with Remarks on the Origin of Species by Variation.* London: John Murray, 1863.

———. *Principles of Geology, Being an Attempt to Explain the Former Changes of the Earth's Surface, by Reference to Causes Now in Operation.* 3 vols. London: John Murray, 1830–1833.

———. *See:* Mrs. [Katharine Murray] Lyell (ed.), *Life, Letters and Journals of Sir Charles Lyell.*

———. *See* Leonard G. Wilson, *Charles Lyell, the Years to 1841: The Revolution in Geology.*

———. *See* Leonard G. Wilson (ed.), *Sir Charles Lyell's Scientific Journals on the Species Question.*

Lyell, Katharine M. (ed.). *Memoir of Leonard Horner, F.R.S., F.G.S., Consisting of Letters to His Family and from Some of His Friends.* Edited by his daughter. 2 vols. London: Privately printed by Womens Printing Society, Ltd., 1890.

Lyell, Mrs. [Katharine Murray] (ed.). *Life, Letters and Journals of Sir Charles Lyell, Bart.*, edited by his sister-in-law. 2 vols. London: John Murray, 1881.

McCosh, James, D. D., LL.D. *Christianity and Positivism. A Series of Lectures to the Times on Natural Theology and Apologetics.* Delivered in New York, January 16 to March 20, 1871, on the Ely Foundation of the Union Theological Seminary. New York: Robert Carter and Brothers, 1871.

McKinney, H. Lewis. "Alfred Russel Wallace and the Discovery of Natural Selection," *Journal of the History of Medicine and Allied Sciences* (October 1966) 21, 333–57.

Maitland, Frederic William. *The Life and Letters of Leslie Stephen.* London: Duckworth & Co., 1906.

Malthus, Rev. Thomas. *An Essay on the Principle of Population; or, a View of its Past and Present Effects on Human Happiness; with an Inquiry into our Prospects Respecting the Future Removal or Mitigation of the Evils Which it Occasions.* 5th ed. 3 vols. London: John Murray, 1817.

Mangelsdorf, Paul C. "Genetics, Agriculture and the World Food Problem," *Proceedings of the American Philosophical Society* 109 (1965): 242–48.

Marchant, James. *Alfred Russel Wallace: Letters and Reminiscences.* 2 vols. London, New York, Toronto, and Melbourne: Cassell and Company Ltd., 1916.

Marsden, George M. *Fundamentalism and American Culture: The Shaping of Twentieth-Century Evangelicalism: 1870–1925.* New York and Oxford: Oxford University Press, 1980.

Marsh, O. C. "Thomas Henry Huxley," *The American Journal of Science*, 3d ser. 50 (August 1895): 177–83.

Marx, Karl, and Engels, Friedrich. *Selected Works in One Volume*. Moscow and London: Lawrence and Wishart, 1968.

Matthew, Patrick. *On Naval Timber and Arboriculture; with Critical Notes on Authors Who Have Recently Treated the Subject of Planting*. London: Longman, Rees, Orme, Brown, and Green; Edinburgh: Adam Black, 1831.

Mayr, Ernst. "Change of Genetic Environment and Evolution," in J. S. Huxley, A. C. Hardy, and E. B. Ford, (eds.), *Evolution as a Process*, pp. 157–80.

———. "Darwin and Natural Selection," *American Scientist* 65 (May–June 1977): 321–27.

———. "Epilogue," *Biological Journal of the Linnean Society* 17 (February 1982): 115–25.

———. *The Growth of Biological Thought: Diversity, Evolution, and Inheritance*. Cambridge, Mass. and London: The Belknap Press of Harvard University Press, 1982.

———. "Prologue: Some Thoughts on the History of the Evolutionary Synthesis," in Ernst Mayr and William B. Provine (eds.), *The Evolutionary Synthesis*, pp. 1–48.

———. *Systematics and the Origin of Species*. Reprint. Magnolia, Mass.: Peter Smith, 1971.

———, and Provine, William B. (eds.). *The Evolutionary Synthesis: Perspectives on the Unification of Biology*. Cambridge, Mass., and London, England: Harvard University Press, 1980.

Medawar, Peter B. "Darwin's Illness," *New Statesman* 67 (April 3, 1964): 527–28.

Merriam, C. Hart. "Is Mutation a Factor in the Evolution of the Higher Vertebrates?" Address of Vice President and Chairman of Section F—Zoology at the New Orleans Meeting of the American Association for the Advancement of Science (Dec. 29, 1905), *Science*, n.s. 23 (February 16, 1906): 241–57.

Meyer, A. B. "How Was Wallace Led to the Discovery of Natural Selection?" *Nature* 52 (August 29, 1895): 415.

Mivart, St. George Jackson. "Evolution and Its Consequences: A Reply to Professor Huxley," *Contemporary Review* 19 (January 1872): 168–97.

———. "Ape Resemblances to Man," *Nature* 3 (April 20, 1871): 481.

———. "Some Reminiscences of Thomas Henry Huxley," *Nineteenth Century* 42 (December 1897): 985–98.

———. *See* Jacob W. Gruber, *A Conscience in Conflict: The Life of St. George Jackson Mivart*.

Moore, James R. "Charles Darwin Lies in Westminster Abbey," *Biological Journal of the Linnean Society* 17 (February 1982): 97–113.

Moorhead, Paul S., and Kaplan, Martin M. (eds.). *Mathematical Challenges to the Neo-Darwinian Interpretation of Evolution*. A Symposium at the Wistar Institute of Anatomy and Biology, April 25 and 26, 1966. Philadelphia: The Wistar Institute Press, 1967.

Morgan, Thomas Hunt. "The Application of the Conception of Pure Lines to Sex-limited Inheritance and to Sexual Dimorphism," *The American Naturalist* 45 (February 1911): 65–78.

———. "Darwinism in the Light of Modern Criticism," *Harper's Monthly Magazine* 106 (February 1903): 476–79.

———. *Evolution and Adaptation*. New York: The Macmillan Co.; London: Macmillan & Co. Ltd., 1903.

———. "On the Mechanism of Heredity," Croonian Lecture delivered June 1, 1922, *Proceedings of the Royal Society, Series B*. 94 (April 1923): 162–97.

———. "The Origin of Species through Selection Contrasted with Their Origin through the Appearance of Definite Variations," *Popular Science Monthly* 67 (1905): 54–65.

Morgan, Thomas Hunt. "Personal Recollections of Calvin B. Bridges," *The Journal of Heredity* 30 (September 1939): 355–58.
————. *The Scientific Basis of Evolution.* London: Faber and Faber, 1932.
————. "The Theory of the Gene," *The American Naturalist* 51 (September 1917): 513–44.
Morton, A. G. *History of Botanical Science.* London: Academic Press, 1981.
Moyer, Dr. Wayne A. *Young Earth Creationism and Biology Textbooks.* Reston, Va.: National Association of Biology Teachers, August 1982.
Muller, H. J. "Artificial Transmutation of the Gene," *Science* 66 (July 22, 1927): 84–87.
————. "Radiation and Genetics," *The American Naturalist* 64 (May–June 1930): 220–51.
————. "Thomas Hunt Morgan, 1866–1945," Obituary, *Science*, n.s. 103 (May 3, 1946): 550–51.
Nelkin, Dorothy. "The Science-Textbook Controversies," *Scientific American* 234 (April 1976): 33–39.
Nobel Foundation, The, (ed.). *Nobel: The Man and His Prizes.* Stockholm: Sohlmans Förlag, 1950.
Nordau, Max. "Philosophy and Morals of War," *The North American Review* 169 (December 1899): 784–97.
Norton, B. J. "The Biometric Defense of Darwinism," *Journal of the History of Biology* 6 (Fall 1973): 283–316.
————. "Metaphysics and Population Genetics: Karl Pearson and the Background to Fisher's Multi-factorial Theory of Inheritance," *Annals of Science* 32 (1975): 537–53.
————, and Pearson, E. S., F.R.S. "A Note on the Background to, and Refereeing of, R. A. Fisher's 1916 Paper 'On the Correlation between Relatives on the Supposition of Mendelian Inheritance,' " *Notes and Records of the Royal Society of London* 31 (1976–77): 151–62.
Novicow, J[acques]. *La Critique du Darwinisme Social.* Paris: Felix Alcan et Guillaumin, 1910.
Olby, Robert. "Francis Crick, DNA and the Central Dogma," *Daedalus: Journal of the American Academy of Arts and Sciences* 99 (Fall 1970): 938–87.
————. *The Path to the Double Helix.* Seattle: University of Washington Press, 1974.
————, and Posner, Erich. "An Early Reference to Genetic Coding," *Nature* 215 (July 29, 1967): 556.
Overton, Judge William R. "Judgment, Injunction and Memorandum Opinion, Jan. 5, 1982, in McLean *v.* the Arkansas Board of Education," *Science* 215 (February 19, 1982): 934–43.
Owen, Richard. *On the Anatomy of Vertebrates.* 3 vols. London: Longmans, Green and Co., 1866–68.
Paley, William. *Natural Theology: or, Evidences of the Existence and Attributes of the Deity, Collected from the Appearances of Nature.* London: R. Faulder, 1802.
————. *A View of the Evidences of Christianity.* 2 vols. London: R. Faulder, 1794.
Paston, George [Emily Morse Symonds]. *At John Murray's: Records of a Literary Circle, 1843–1892.* London: John Murray, 1932.
Pearson, E. S. *Karl Pearson: An Appreciation of Some Aspects of His Life and Work.* Cambridge: At the University Press, 1938.
————. "Studies in the History of Probability and Statistics XX: Some Early Correspondence between W. S. Gosset, R. A. Fisher and Karl Pearson, with Notes and Comments," *Biometrika* 55 (November 1968): 445–57.
Pearson, Karl. *Charles Darwin, 1809–1882.* London: Cambridge University Press, 1923.

Pearson, Karl. "Darwinism, Medical Progress and Eugenics," The Cavendish Lecture, 1912. *West London Medical Journal* 17 (1912): 165–93.

———. *The Life, Letters and Labours of Francis Galton.* 4 vols. (numbered I, II, IIIA and IIIB). Cambridge: At the University Press, 1914–30.

———. "Walter Frank Raphael Weldon, 1860–1906," *Biometrika: A Journal for the Statistical Study of Biological Problems* 5 (October 1906): 1–52.

Peckham, Morse (ed.). *"The Origin of Species" by Charles Darwin: A Variorum Text.* Philadelphia: University of Pennsylvania Press, 1959.

Perry, Ralph Barton. *The Thought and Character of William James as Revealed in Unpublished Correspondence and Notes, Together with His Published Writings.* 2 vols. Boston: Little, Brown, and Company, 1935.

Phillips, John. *Memoirs of William Smith, LL.D., Author of the "Map of the Strata of England and Wales,"* by his nephew and pupil. London: John Murray, 1844.

Piternick, Leonie K. (ed.). *Richard Goldschmidt: Controversial Geneticist and Creative Biologist.* Basel, Boston and Stuttgart: Birkhauser Verlag, 1980.

Poulton, Edward Bagnall. *Charles Darwin and "The Origin of Species": Addresses, etc., in America and England in the Year of the Two Anniversaries.* London, New York, Bombay and Calcutta: Longmans, Green, and Co., 1909.

Price, George R. "Fisher's 'Fundamental Theorem' Made Clear," *Annals of Human Genetics* 36 (1972): 129–40.

Provine, William B. *The Origins of Theoretical Population Genetics.* Chicago and London: The University of Chicago Press, 1971.

Punnett, R. C. "Early Days of Genetics," *Heredity* 4 (April 1950): 1–10.

Pym, Horace N. (ed.). *Memories of Old Friends, Being Extracts from the Journals and Letters of Caroline Fox of Penjerrick, Cornwall, from 1835 to 1871.* London: Smith, Elder, & Co., 1882.

Rádl, Emanuel. *The History of Biological Theories.* Translated and adapted from the German by E. J. Hatfield. London: Oxford University Press, 1930.

Raverat, Gwen. *Period Piece: A Cambridge Childhood.* London: Faber and Faber Ltd., 1952.

[Ray, John] Raio, Joanne. *Methodus Plantarum nova . . .* London: Henry Faitborne and John Kersey, 1682.

Reade, Charles. *Put Yourself in His Place.* 3 vols. London: Smith, Elder & Co., 1870.

Reed, Edward S. "Darwin's Evolutionary Philosophy: The Laws of Change," *Acta Biotheoretica* 27 (1978): 201–35.

Reid, G. C.; Isaksen, I. S. A.; Holzer, T. E.; and Crutzen, P. J. "Influence of Ancient Solar-Proton Events on the Evolution of Life," *Nature* 259 (January 22, 1976): 177–79.

Rogers, James Allen. "Russia: Social Sciences," in Thomas F. Glick (ed.), *The Comparative Reception of Darwinism*, pp. 256–68.

Rogers, Woodes. *A Cruising Voyage Round the World; First to the South-Seas, Thence to the East Indies, and Homewards by the Cape of Good Hope. Begun in 1708, and Finish'd in 1711 . . .* London: Printed for A. Bell and B. Lintot, 1712.

Romanes, Mrs. George J. (ed.). *The Life and Letters of George John Romanes.* Written and edited by his wife. London, New York and Bombay: Longmans, Green and Co., 1896.

Rothschild, Walter, and Jordan, Karl. "Lepidoptera Collected by Oscar Neumann in North-east Africa," *Novitates Zoologicae* 10 (December 1903): 491–542.

Royer, Mlle. Clémence-Auguste (translator). *De l'Origine des Espèces, ou Des lois du progrès chez les êtres organisés.* Paris: Guillaumin et Cie., 1862.

Ruse, Michael. *Darwinism Defended: A Guide to the Evolution Controversies.* Reading, Mass.: Addison-Wesley Publishing Co., 1982.

Russett, Cynthia Eagle. *Darwin in America: The Intellectual Response, 1865–1912.* San Francisco: W. H. Freeman and Co., 1976.

Sarton, George. "Darwin's Conception of the Theory of Natural Selection (after an Unpublished Letter of 1861)," *ISIS* 26 (March 2, 1937): 336–40.

Schopf, Thomas J. M. "Evolving Paleontological Views on Deterministic and Stochastic Approaches," *Paleobiology* 5 (1979): 337–52.

———. "Punctuated Equilibrium and Evolutionary Stasis," *Paleobiology* 7 (1981): 156–66.

———. (ed.). *Models in Paleobiology.* San Francisco: Freeman, Cooper & Co., 1972.

Schrödinger, Erwin. *What Is Life? The Physical Aspect of the Living Cell.* Cambridge: At the University Press, 1945.

Schuchert, Charles, and LeVene, Clara Mae. *O. C. Marsh, Pioneer in Paleontology.* New Haven: Yale University Press, 1940.

Schweber, Silvan S. "The Origin of the 'Origin' Revisited," *Journal of the History of Biology* 10 (Fall 1977): 229–316.

Sedgwick, Rev. Adam. *See* John Willis Clark and Thomas McKenny Hughes, *The Life and Letters of the Reverend Adam Sedgwick.*

Seward, A. C. (ed.). *Darwin and Modern Science: Essays in Commemoration of the Centenary of the Birth of Charles Darwin and of the Fiftieth Anniversary of the Publication of "The Origin of Species,"* edited for the Cambridge Philosophical Society and the Syndics of the University Press. Cambridge: At the University Press, 1909.

Shaw, [George] Bernard. *Back to Methuselah: A Metabiological Pentateuch.* London: Constable and Company, 1921.

Sheldrake, Rupert. *A New Science of Life: The Hypothesis of Formative Causation.* London: Blond & Briggs, 1981.

Shipley, Maynard. *The War on Modern Science: A Short History of the Fundamentalist Attacks on Evolution and Modernism.* New York and London: Alfred A. Knopf, 1927.

[Sidgwick, Mrs. Isabella.] "A Grandmother's Tales," *Macmillan's Magazine* 78 (October 1898): 425–35.

Simmons, Ernest J. (ed.). *Continuity and Change in Russian and Soviet Thought*, edited with an introduction. Cambridge, Mass.: Harvard University Press, 1955.

Simpson, George Gaylord. *Concession to the Improbable: An Unconventional Autobiography.* New Haven and London: Yale University Press, 1978.

———. *The Major Features of Evolution.* New York: Columbia University Press, 1953.

———. *Tempo and Mode in Evolution.* New York: Columbia University Press, 1944.

Smith, John Maynard (ed.). *Evolution Now: A Century after Darwin.* London: *Nature* in association with the Macmillan Press Ltd., 1982.

Smith, Dr. Sydney. "The Origin of 'The Origin' as Discerned from Charles Darwin's Notebooks and His Annotations in the Books He Read between 1837 and 1842," *The Advancement of Science* 16 (March 1960): 391–401.

Spencer, Herbert. "The Development Hypothesis," *The Leader*, March 20, 1852.

———. *First Principles.* London: Williams and Norgate, 1862, 2nd ed. 1867.

———. *The Principles of Biology.* 2 vols. London and Edinburgh: Williams and Norgate, 1864 and 1867.

———. *Social Statics: or, The Conditions Essential to Human Happiness Specified, and the First of Them Developed.* London: John Chapman, 1851.

Stecher, Robert M. "The Darwin-Innes Letters: The Correspondence of an Evolutionist with His Vicar, 1848–1884," *Annals of Science* 17 (December 1961): 201–58.

Stent, Gunther S. "D.N.A.," *Daedalus* 99 (Fall 1970): 909–37.

Stephen, Leslie. "An Attempted Philosophy of History," *The Fortnightly Review*, n.s. 27 (May 1, 1880): 672–95.

———. *Life of Henry Fawcett.* London: Smith, Elder & Co., 1885.

Stephen, Leslie. *See* Maitland, Frederic William, *The Life and Letters of Leslie Stephen.*
Stern, Curt. "The Continuity of Genetics," *Daedalus* 99 (Fall 1970): 882–908.
Stern, Curt, and Sherwood, Eva R. (eds.). *The Origin of Genetics: A Mendel Source Book.* San Francisco and London: W. H. Freeman and Co., 1966.
Strong, Josiah. *Our Country: Its Possible Future and Its Present Crisis.* New York: The Baker & Taylor Co., rev. ed., 1891.
Sturtevant, Alfred H. "The Early Mendelians," *Proceedings of the American Philosophical Society* 109 (August 18, 1965): 199–204.
———. *A History of Genetics.* New York: Harper & Row, 1965.
———. "Thomas Hunt Morgan, Sept. 25, 1866–Dec. 4, 1945," *Biographical Memoirs, National Academy of Sciences of the United States of America* 33 (1959): 283–325.
Sulloway, Frank J. "Darwin and His Finches: The Evolution of a Legend," *Journal of the History of Biology* 15 (Spring 1982): 1–53.
Sumner, William Graham. *The Challenge of Facts and Other Essays.* New Haven: Yale University Press; London: Oxford University Press, 1914.
Sunderland, Luther D. "Prominent British Scientists Abandon Evolution," *Contrast*, Minneapolis (February 1982): 1–3.
Sutton, Walter S. "On the Morphology of the Chromosome group in *Brachystola magna*," Oct. 17, 1902, *Biological Bulletin* 4 (December 1902): 24–39.
Teilhard de Chardin, Pierre. *The Phenomenon of Man.* With an Introduction by Sir Julian Huxley. London: William Collins Sons; New York: Harper & Row, 1959.
Tennyson, Hallam. *Alfred, Lord Tennyson, a Memoir.* By his son. 2 vols. London: Macmillan and Co., 1897.
Thompson, Samuel H. "Tennessee after Eleven Years," *The Hibbert Journal* 35 (October 1936–July 1937): 121–28.
Thomson, Keith Stewart, and Rachootin, Stan P. "Turning Points in Darwin's Life," *Biological Journal of the Linnean Society* 17 (February 1982): 23–37.
Thomson, William. "Of Geological Dynamics" (paper read April 5, 1869). *Transactions of the Geological Society of Glasgow* 3 (1871): 215–40.
———. "On the Age of the Sun's Heat," *Macmillan's Magazine* 5 (March 1862): 388–93.
Tristram, H. B. "On the Ornithology of Northern Africa," *The IBIS* 1 (October 1859): 415–35.
Tuckwell, Rev. W. *Reminiscences of Oxford.* London: Smith, Elder, 1907.
Ubell, Earl. "Biological Sciences and Medicine in Encyclopaedia Inc. *The Great Ideas, 1962*, pp. 273–313. Chicago, London: William Benton, 1962.
Underwood, E. Ashworth (ed.). *Science, Medicine and History. Essays on the Evolution of Scientific Thought and Medical Practice Written in Honour of Charles Singer.* 2 vols. London, New York and Toronto: Oxford University Press, 1953.
Valkovic, Vlado. "A Possible Mechanism for the Influence of Geomagnetic Field on the Evolution of Life," *Origins of Life* 9 (1977): 7–11.
Van Der Pas, Peter W. "The Correspondence of Hugo de Vries and Charles Darwin," *JANUS: Revue internationale de l'histoire des sciences, de la médecine, de la pharmacie et de la technique* [Leiden] 57 (1970): 173–213.
Virchow, Rudolf. *Vier Reden über Leben und Kranksein.* Berlin: Druck und Verlag von Georg Reimer, 1862.
Vorzimmer, Peter J. "Charles Darwin and Blending Inheritance," *ISIS* 54 pt. 3 (September 1963): 371–90.
———. *Charles Darwin: The Years of Controversy.* Philadelphia: Temple U. Press, 1970; London: University of London Press, 1972.
———. "An Early Darwin Manuscript: The 'Outline and Draft of 1839,' " *Journal of the History of Biology* 8 (Fall 1975): 191–217.
Vries, Hugo de. *Intracellular Pangenesis, Including a Paper on Fertilization and Hybridi-*

zation. Translated from the German by C. Stuart Gager. Chicago: The Open Court Publishing Co., 1910.

Vries, Hugo de. "Das Spaltungsgesetz der Bastarde" (March 14, 1900) ["The Law of Segregation of Hybrids"] (Preliminary Communication)" in *Berichts der deutschen botanischen Gesellschaft* 18 (1900): 83–90.

––––––. *The Mutation Theory: Experiments and Observations on the Origin of Species in the Vegetable Kingdom*. Translated by Prof. J. B. Farmer and A. D. Derbishire. 2 vols. London: Kegan Paul, Trench, Trübner & Co. Ltd., 1910 and 1911.

––––––. *See* Peter W. Van Der Pas. "The Correspondence of Hugo de Vries and Charles Darwin."

Wallace, Alfred Russel. *My Life: A Record of Events and Opinions*. 2 vols. London: Chapman & Hall, Ltd., 1905.

––––––. "On the Law Which Has Regulated the Introduction of New Species," *The Annals and Magazine of Natural History*, 2d ser. 16 (September 1855): 184–96.

––––––. "On the Tendency of Varieties to Depart Indefinitely from the Original Type, Ternate, February 1858" (Read July 1, 1858), *Journal of the Proceedings of the Linnean Society: Zoology* 3 (1859): 53–62.

––––––. "The Origin of Human Races and the Antiquity of Man Deduced from the Theory of 'Natural Selection' " (Read Mar. 1, 1864), *The Anthropological Review, and Journal of the Anthropological Society of London* 2 (May 1864): clvii–clxx.

––––––. *Studies, Scientific and Social*. 2 vols. London: Macmillan and Co. Ltd.; New York: The Macmillan Co., 1900.

––––––. *The Wonderful Century: Its Successes and Failures*. London: Swan Sonnenschein & Co., Ltd.; New York: Dodd, Mead & Co., 1898.

––––––. *See* James Marchant, *Alfred Russel Wallace: Letters and Reminiscences*.

Watson, James D. *The Double Helix: A Personal Account of the Discovery of the Structure of DNA*. London: Weidenfeld and Nicolson, 1968.

––––––, and Crick, Francis H. C. "Molecular Structure of Nucleic Acids: A Structure for Deoxyribose Nucleic Acid," *Nature* 171 (April 25, 1953): 737–38.

––––––. "Genetical Implications of the Structure of Deoxyribonucleic Acid," *Nature* 171 (May 30, 1953): 964–67.

Weinstein, Alexander. "How Unknown Was Mendel's Paper?" *Journal of the History of Biology* 10 (Fall 1977), 241–64.

Weismann, Dr. August. *Essays upon Heredity and Kindred Biological Problems*. Authorised translation. Second edition. 2 vols. Oxford: At the Clarendon Press, 1891 and 1892.

Weldon, W. F. R. "On the Ambiguity of Mendel's Categories," *Biometrika: A Journal for the Statistical Study of Biological Problems* 2 (November 1902): 44–55.

––––––. "On Certain Correlated Variations in *Carcinus moenas*," *Proceedings of the Royal Society* 54 (November 16, 1893): 318–29.

––––––. "Remarks on Variation in Animals and Plants," *Proceedings of the Royal Society* 57 (February 28, 1895): 379–82.

Wells, Kentwood D. "The Historical Context of Natural Selection: The Case of Patrick Matthew," *Journal of the History of Biology* 6 (Spring 1973): 225–58.

West, Geoffrey. *Charles Darwin: The Fragmentary Man*. London: G. Routledge & Sons, 1937.

––––––. *Charles Darwin: A Portrait*. New Haven: Yale University Press, 1938.

Whewell, William. *The Bridgewater Treatise III: On Astronomy and General Physics, Considered with Reference to Natural Theology*. London: William Pickering, 1833.

Willey, Basil. *Darwin and Butler: Two Versions of Evolution*. The Hibbert Lectures, 1959. London: Chatto & Windus, 1960.

Williams, R. J. P. "Natural Selection of the Chemical Elements," Bakerian Lecture, 1981, *Proceedings of the Royal Society*, B 213 (Nov. 24, 1981), 361–97.

Wilson, Edmund B. *An Atlas of the Fertilization and Karyokinesis of the Ovum*, with the cooperation of Edward Leaming. New York and London: Published for the Columbia University Press by Macmillan and Co., 1895.

Wilson, Leonard G. *Charles Lyell. The Years to 1841: The Revolution in Geology*. New Haven and London: Yale University Press, 1972.

————— (ed.). *Sir Charles Lyell's Scientific Journals on the Species Question*. New Haven and London: Yale University Press, 1970.

Wortman, J. L. "Othniel Charles Marsh," *Science*, n.s. 9 (April 21, 1899): 561–65.

Wrangham, Richard W. "Bishop Wilberforce, Natural Selection, and the Descent of Man," *Nature* 287 (September 18, 1980): 192.

Wright, Sewall. "Evolution in Mendelian Populations," *Genetics* 16 (1931): 97–159.

Yates, F., and Mather, K. "Ronald Aylmer Fisher," *Biographical Memoirs of Fellows of the Royal Society* 9 (1963): 91–129.

Yule, G. Udny. "Mendel's Laws and Their Probable Relations to Intra-Racial Heredity," *The New Phytologist* 1 (November 28, 1902): 193–207 and 222–38.

Zirkle, Conway (ed.). *Death of a Science in Russia*. Philadelphia: University of Pennsylvania Press, 1949.

—————. *Evolution, Marxian Biology, and the Social Scene*. Philadelphia: University of Pennsylvania Press, 1959.

Index

About the Author

One of the major biographers of our time, RONALD W. CLARK has taken as his subjects such makers of modern thought as Einstein, Bertrand Russell, Franklin, Freud—and now Darwin. He is, as well, the author of a number of important books on scientific subjects.

Born in London in 1916, Clark was a war correspondent in World War II, landing in France on D-Day, and later covering the Nuremburg and other war-crimes trials in Germany. Clark has traveled extensively in Europe and the United States, and divides his time between homes in London and the West Country of England.